The Great Big Book of Chili

Volume 2

Thomas B. Bailie

AmErica House
Baltimore

First printing

ISBN: 1-4137-2933-9
PUBLISHED BY AMERICA HOUSE BOOK PUBLISHERS
www.publishamerica.com
Baltimore

Printed in the United States of America

Chapter 10
Chili Recipes By Famous People

Background

Many famous people have contributed to the lore of chili. From automobile racing and film to politicians and restaurateurs. Some of the recipes are by restaurants and were favored by actors and actresses. I am not sure why so many politicians seem to have held chili in high esteem; maybe the hot air has a believable explanation. Who knows? The following information about chili and a number of famous people comes from Linda Stradley, author of *"What's Cooking America"* (© Copyright 2000 by Linda Stradley-All rights reserved.) Used with permission.

- Will Rogers (1879-1935), popular actor, cattleman, banker, and journalist, called chili *"bowl of blessedness."*
- It is said that Will Rogers judged a town by the quality of its chili. He sampled chili in hundreds of towns, especially in Texas and Oklahoma and kept a box score. He concluded that the finest chili (in his judgment) was from a small cafe in Coleman, Texas.
- Jesse James (1847-1882), outlaw and desperado of the old American West, refused to rob a bank in McKinney, Texas because that is where his favorite chili parlor was located.
- Some Spanish priests during the 19th century were said to be wary of the passion inspired by chile peppers, assuming they were aphrodisiacs. A few preached a sermon against indulgence in a food that they said was almost as *"hot as hell's brimstone."* *"Soup of the Devil,"* one called it. The priest's warning probably contributed to the dish's popularity.
- Mrs. Lady Bird Johnson had *"chili pangs"* for President Lyndon Johnson's, 36th President of the United States, "Pedernales River Chili" and had cards printed with the LBJ chili recipe. *"It has been almost as popular as the government pamphlet on the care and feeding of children."*
- Eleanor Roosevelt (1894-1962) wife of the 32nd President of the United States, Franklin D. Roosevelt, sought the Chasen's Chili recipe but was refused it (a complimentary order was dispatched to her instead).
- It is said that Chasen's also sent chili to movie actor Clark Gable (1901-1960), when he was in the hospital (he reportedly had it for dinner the night he died).

Enjoy!

A. J. Foyt's 500-Mile Chili
3 Lb. Stew Beef; Cubed
1 Lb. Chorizo Sausage; Mexican Sausage

2 Large Onions; Diced
5 Cloves Garlic; Minced
3 Pods Jalapeño Chiles; Peeled and Diced
3 Tablespoons Olive Oil
½ Teaspoon Cayenne Pepper
3 Tablespoons Chile powder
3 Cans (15 Ounce) Tomato Sauce
1 Teaspoon Salt
1-½ Cup Water
1 Can Mexican Beer

1. Brown Meat, onions, garlic and Jalapeños together in olive oil.
2. While mixture is browning, add cayenne and chile powder. Stir often.
3. Add tomato sauce, salt, water and beer.
4. Cover and cook on low heat for 30 minutes, stirring often.
5. Uncover and simmer for 2 hours.
Serves 6-8.

Al Unser's Indy 500 Chili
2 Tablespoons Oil
2 Teaspoons Salt
½ Cup Onion; Chopped
2 Cloves Garlic; Crushed
1 Lb. Ground Beef
2 Cans (16 Ounce) Kidney Beans; Undrained
1 Can (16 Ounce) Tomatoes; Undrained, Mashed
1 Leaf Bay
½ Cup Green Pepper; Chopped
1 Teaspoon Cumin
3 Dashes Tabasco Sauce
2 Tablespoons Chile powder

1. In 3-quart saucepan, heat oil.
2. Add onions and garlic; sauté, 5 minutes.
3. Add beef; cook, stirring until meat loses redness.
4. Stir in beans, peppers, tomatoes, bay leaf, cumin, chile powder, salt and Tabasco sauce. Heat to boiling.
5. Reduce heat and cover.
6. Simmer for 30 to 45 minutes.

Bert Greene's Peppered Chili

7 Tablespoons Butter
2 Cloves Garlic; Finely Chopped
4 Medium Onions; Finely Chopped
1 Medium Bell Peppers; Finely Chopped
1-¼ Lb. Beef Round; Hamburger Grind
1 Tablespoon Vegetable Oil
1-½ Lb. Beef Shoulder; 2 x ½ inch Strips
3 Tablespoons Red Chili, Mild; Ground
3 Large Tomatoes; Chopped
1 Teaspoon Sugar
1 Leaf Bay
4 Leaves Bay, Fresh, Chopped
1 Teaspoon Thyme; Dried
½ Teaspoon Paprika
½ Teaspoon Cayenne Pepper
½ Teaspoon Allspice
2 Tablespoons Chile Caribe
1 Teaspoon Soy Sauce
½ Teaspoon Hot Pepper Sauce, Liquid
6 Pods Serrano Chiles; Fresh, Chopped (Or more)
½ Cup Dry Red Wine
¾ Cup Beef Broth
1 Teaspoon Salt
½ Teaspoon Black Pepper; Freshly Ground
3 Cups Kidney Beans; Cooked and Drained

1. Melt 3 tablespoons of the butter in a large heavy skillet over medium heat.
2. Add half the garlic, half the onions, and all the green pepper and cook for 5 minutes.
3. Make a large well in the center of the vegetables and place the ground beef in the center.
4. Raise the heat and cook, stirring and scraping the skillet with a metal spatula.
5. Gradually stir in the surrounding vegetables and cook until the meat is evenly browned.
6. Transfer this mixture to a Dutch oven.
7. Heat the vegetable oil and 1 tablespoon of the butter in the skillet.
8. Sauté the beef shoulder, a few strips at a time, over high heat until it is well browned.

9. Transfer the strips to a plate as they are done.
10. Lower the heat, and then wipe out the skillet with paper toweling.
11. Return beef strips to the skillet.
12. Stir in the ground chile and cook 3 minutes over low heat.
13. Transfer to the Dutch oven.
14. Melt the remaining butter in the skillet over medium heat.
15. Add the remaining onions and garlic and cook for 3 minutes.
16. Stir in the tomatoes, sugar, and bay leaf and cook for 10 minutes.
17. Transfer the mixture to the Dutch oven.
18. Stir all the remaining ingredients except the beans into the Dutch oven.
19. Bake, covered, in a 300-degree oven for 3 hours.
20. Stir in the beans; bake ½ hour longer.

Big Boy Chili And Beans
Cooking Live Show

2 Tablespoons Vegetable Oil; Or Bacon Fat
1-½ Lb. Onions; Coarse Chopped
3 Cloves Garlic; Minced or Garlic Press
2 Lb. Beef, Lean, Ground; Sirloin or Chuck
2 Lb. Pork, Lean, Ground
¾ Cup Chile Powder (Pref. a Mix or ½ Ancho and ½ Pasilla) But any will do.
3 Tablespoons Cocoa Powder; Unsweetened
2 Tablespoons Sugar; (2 to 3)
1 Tablespoon Cumin; Ground, Plus 1 Teaspoon
1 Tablespoon Oregano; Crumbled, Plus 1 Teaspoon
2 Teaspoons Fennel Seeds; Optional
2 Teaspoons Salt
½ Teaspoon Cayenne Pepper; Optional
3 Leaves Bay
1 Can (28 Ounce) Tomatoes, Whole; Undrained and Rough Chopped
1 Can (8 Ounce) Tomato Sauce
3 Bottles (12 Ounce) Dark or Medium Beer; Dos Equis, Heineken or Beer

Beans:
6 Slices Hickory-Smoked Bacon; Finely Chopped
1 Lb. Small Pink Beans, Soaked; Still in Their Liquid
1 Large Garlic Cloves; Minced or Garlic Press
2 Teaspoons Salt

1. Spoon the oil into a large, heavy casserole or Dutch oven set over moderate heat.
2. Add the onions and sauté until softened and lightly colored, about 10 minutes.
3. Add the garlic and sauté for 2 minutes. Reserve.
4. Return the pot to moderate heat and crumble in the beef and pork.
5. Increase the heat to high and brown well, without stirring, for 5 minutes.
6. Reduce the heat to moderately high and brown, stirring occasionally, for 15 minutes longer.
7. Return the onions to the pot and stir in ½ cup of the chile powder, 2 tablespoons of the cocoa, 2 tablespoons of the sugar, 1 tablespoon of the cumin, 1 tablespoon of the oregano, fennel seeds, salt, cayenne, and bay leaves.
8. Add the tomatoes and their juices, the tomato sauce, 2 bottles of the beer and 4 cups of water.
9. Bring the mixture to a boil over moderate heat.
10. Reduce the heat to low and simmer, uncovered, for 3 hours.
11. Stir gently every 30 minutes, but do not stir during the last 15 to 20 minutes so all of the fat will rise to the top.
12. Meanwhile, prepare the beans.
13. Put the bacon in a large, heavy saucepan set over moderate heat. Cook, stirring frequently, until crisp and deep golden brown. Spoon off all but 1 tablespoon of the fat.
14. Drain the beans (no matter which soaking technique you have used) and measure the liquid.
15. Add water to make 6 cups.
16. Add the beans and liquid to the bacon in the pan and bring to a boil, stirring frequently, over moderate heat.
17. Reduce the heat to low, partially cover, and simmer for 1 hour.
18. Add the garlic and salt, partially cover, and simmer until the beans are tender, about 1 hour longer. Remove from the heat and set aside.
19. When the chili has cooked for 3 hours, degrease it, skimming off most of the fat.
20. Place a paper towel flat on the surface to soak up any remaining fat repeat, if necessary.
21. Stir in the remaining ¼ cup chile powder, 1 tablespoon cocoa, 1 teaspoon cumin, and 1 teaspoon oregano.
22. Taste for balance of acidity to sweetness and stir in the remaining 1 tablespoon sugar, if needed.
23. Add the beans and their cooking liquid.

24. Set the chili aside to cool to room temperature. If making ahead, cover and refrigerate overnight.
25. Pre-heat the oven to 300 degrees.
26. Stir the remaining 1 bottle of beer into the chili. Bake, uncovered, for 2 hours, stirring once in a while.

Serve hot.

Billy Bob's Texas Chili

10 Lb. Chili Ground Meat; Coarse
1 Cup Chile powder; Hot
1 Cup Chile powder; Mild
¾ Cup Paprika
½ Cup Comino; Cumin
¼ Cup Garlic Powder
¼ Cup Salt
1/8 Cup Red Pepper; Crushed
1 Lb. Suet
3 Quarts Water
¼ Cup Sugar; Twenty Minutes Before Pulling

True Texas chili has no beans and no tomato. None. Billy Bob Barnett's World's Largest Honky-Tonk Texas Style Chili.

1. Add fat first, then meat and seasonings to fat.
2. Add water after it cooks 2 hours. Cook 3 hours total. Stir occasionally.
Now that's Texas Chili! (Although I usually throw in Shiner Bock Beer for part of that water.) This is real good with raw chopped onion on top (plus the ubiquitous saltines).

Bob Evans Farms Sausage Shop Chili

2 Lb. Bob Evans Farms Sausage
1 Can (14 Ounce) Red Kidney Beans
1-½ Cups Tomato Puree
2 Cups Water
1 Can (12 Ounce) Tomato Puree
2 Tablespoons Chile powder
3 Teaspoons Salt
1/4 Cup Sugar
4 Large Onions
1 Cup Water

1. Crumble Bob Evans Farms sausage in a skillet; cook until tender and lightly browned.
2. Cook chopped onions in ½ cup water, until tender.
3. Add onions to tomato puree diluted with 2 cups water.
4. Mix tomato paste, chile powder, salt, sugar and 1 cup of water together.
5. Blend all ingredients in a large pot and bring to a full boil.
6. To enhance the flavor, let cool and refrigerate overnight.
7. Reheat next day.

This chili will keep refrigerated for several days. Or it may be frozen and kept for several months.

Yield: 14 (8 ounce) servings.

Bon Appetit Chili

2 Tablespoons Oil
2 Cloves Garlic; Chopped
3 Medium Onions; Chopped
2 Lb. Chuck; Lean, Coarse Ground
1 Can (28 Ounce) Tomatoes; Whole, Peeled
3 Cups Beef Broth
1 Can (15 Ounce) Red Kidney Beans; Rinsed
1 Can (6 Ounce) Tomato Paste
3 Tablespoons Chile powder
2 Teaspoons Cumin
1 Teaspoon Salt; Up to 2
1 Teaspoon Oregano
To Taste Pepper; Ground

1. Heat oil in large kettle; sauté onions and garlic to soften.
2. Add meat and sauté 10 more minutes.
3. Drain juice from tomatoes into kettle.
4. Chop tomatoes and add along with remaining ingredients.
5. Simmer 1 hour, stirring occasionally.

Carroll Shelby's Chili

½ Lb. Suet; Or
½ Cup Oil
1 Lb. Beef Round; Coarse Ground
1 Lb. Beef Chuck; Coarse Ground
1 Can (8 Ounce) Tomato Sauce
1 Can (12 Ounce) Beer

¼ Cup Red New Mexican Chile; Ground, Hot
1 Clove Garlic; Finely Chopped
1 Small Onion; Finely Chopped
1-¼ Teaspoon Oregano; Dried (Preferably Mexican)
½ Teaspoon Paprika
1-½ Teaspoon Cumin; Ground
1-¼ Teaspoon Salt
To Taste Cayenne Pepper
¾ Lb. Monterey Jack Cheese; Grated

1. Melt the suet or heat the oil in a heavy 3-quart (or larger) pot over medium-high heat.
2. Remove the un-rendered suet and add the meat to the pot.
3. Break up any lumps with a fork and cook, stirring occasionally, until the meat is evenly browned.
4. Add the tomato sauce, beer, ground chile, garlic, onion, oregano, paprika, 1 teaspoon of the cumin, and the salt.
5. Stir to blend.
6. Bring to a boil, and then lower the heat and simmer, uncovered, for 1 hour.
7. Stir occasionally.
8. Taste and adjust seasonings, adding the cayenne pepper.
9. Simmer, uncovered, 1 hour longer.
10. Stir in the cheese and the remaining ½ teaspoon of the cumin.
11. Simmer ½ hour longer, stirring often to keep the cheese from burning.

Chasen's Restaurant Chili-Elizabeth Taylor's Favorite
Dave Chasen-Los Angeles Restaurateur

"Chasen's Restaurant in Hollywood, California probably made the most famous chili. The owner of the restaurant, Dave Chasen, kept the recipe a secret, entrusting it to no one. For years, he came to the restaurant every Sunday to privately cook up a batch, which he would freeze for the week, believing that the chili was best when reheated. *"It is a kind of bastard chili"* was all that Dave Chasen would divulge.

"During the filming of the movie "Cleopatra" in Rome, Italy, famous movie star, Elizabeth Taylor, had Chasen Restaurant in Hollywood, California send 10 quarts of their famous chili to her. She supposedly paid $200 to have it shipped to her in Rome.

"Chauffeurs and studio people, actors and actresses would come to the back door of Chasen's to buy and pick up the chili by the quart. Other famous people craved this chili such as comedian and actor Jack Benny (1894-1974) who ordered it by the quart. J. Edgar Hoover (1895-1972), former Director of the Federal Bureau of Investigation (FBI), who considered it the best chili in the world, and Eleanor Roosevelt (1894-1962) wife of the 32nd President of the United States, Franklin D. Roosevelt, sought the recipe but was refused it (a complimentary order was dispatched to her instead). It is said that Chasen's also sent chili to movie actor Clark Gable (1901-1960), when he was in the hospital (he reportedly had it for dinner the night he died)." © Copyright 2000 by Linda Stradley-All rights reserved. Used with permission.

As a result of the preceding information from Linda Stradley, the following recipe is most likely an approximation by someone who was addicted to Dave Chasen's famous chili.

½ Lb. Pinto Beans; Washed and Soaked Overnight
5 Cups Canned Tomatoes
1 Lb. Green Peppers; Chopped
1-½ Tablespoon Salad Oil
1-½ Lb. Onion; Chopped
2 Cloves Garlic; Crushed
½ Cup Parsley; Chopped
1 Lb. Ground Pork; Lean
2-½ Lb. Beef Chuck; Chili Grind
½ Cup Chile powder
2 Tablespoons Salt
1-½ Teaspoons Black Pepper
1-½ Teaspoons Cumin Seed
1-½ Teaspoons MSG; (Accent)

1. Simmer beans in cooking water until tender.
2. Add tomatoes and simmer for 5 minutes.
3. Sauté the green peppers in oil for 5 minutes.
4. Add onions and cook until tender, stirring often.
5. Add garlic and parsley.
6. Sauté the pork and beef in butter for 15 minutes.
7. Add the meat to the vegetable mixture, stir in the chile powder and cook for 10 minutes.
8. Then put in the beans and spices and simmer, covered, for 1 hour.
9. Uncover the pot and simmer for another 30 minutes.
10. Skim off the grease. That's it.

Cher's Chili
1 Medium Green Pepper
1 Large Onion
1 Lb. Hamburger
1 Can (16 Ounce) Tomato Sauce
1 Can (16 Ounce) Kidney Beans
2 Tablespoons Chile powder
To Taste Salt and Pepper
To Taste Garlic Powder

1. Chop pepper and onion.
2. Sauté in oil then add hamburger.
3. Drain and add seasonings to taste, tomato sauce and kidney beans.
4. Simmer 20 minutes.

Cooks Illustrated Chili Con Carne
To ensure the best chile flavor, I recommend roasting whole dried chiles and grinding them. I use a mini-chopper or spice-dedicated coffee grinder all of which takes only ten (very well-spent) minutes. Select dried chiles that are moist and pliant like dried fruit. Count on trimming one-half to a full pound of waste from your chuck roast, start with a four-pound roast to end up with this to three-and-a-half pounds of beef cubes. For hotter chili, boost the heat with a pinch of cayenne, a dash of hot pepper sauce, or crumbled Pequin chiles near the end of cooking. Serve the chili with any of the following side dishes: warm pinto or kidney beans, corn bread or chips, corn tortillas or tamales, rice, biscuits, or just plain crackers, and top with any of the following garnishes chopped fresh cilantro leaves, minced white onion, diced avocado, shredded cheddar or jack cheese, or sour cream.

3 Tablespoons Ancho Chill Powder or
3 Medium Pods Toasted and Ground, (About ½ Ounce)
3 Tablespoons New Mexico chile powder or
3 Medium Pods Toasted and Ground, (about ¼ Ounce)
2 Tablespoons Cumin Seeds, Toasted In a Dry Skillet Over Medium Heat
    Until Fragrant, About 4 Minutes, and Ground.
2 Teaspoons Dried Oregano, Preferably Mexican
½ Cup Water
1 4-Lb. Beef Chuck Roast, Trimmed of Excess Fat, Cut Into 1-Inch Cubes.
2 Teaspoons Salt Plus Extra For Seasoning
8 Ounces Bacon (7 or 8 slices), Cut into ¼-Inch Pieces

1 Medium Onion, Minced; About 1 Cup
5 Median Garlic Cloves, Minced
4-5 Small Jalapeño Chile Peppers, Cored, Seeded, and Minced
1 Cup Canned Crushed Tomatoes or Plain Tomato Sauce
2 Tablespoons Juice From 1 Medium Lime
5 Tablespoons Masa Harina or;
3 Tablespoons Cornstarch.
To Taste Ground Black Pepper

1. Mix chile powders, cumin, and oregano in small bowl and stir in ½ cup water to form thick paste; set aside.
2. Toss beef cubes with salt; set aside.
3. Fry bacon in large, heavy soup kettle or Dutch oven over medium-low heat until fat renders and bacon crisp, about 10 minutes.
4. Remove bacon with slotted spoon to paper towel-lined plate; pour all but 2 teaspoons fat from pot into small bowl; set aside.
5. Increase heat to medium-high; sauté meat in four batches until well browned on all sides, about 5 minutes per batch, adding additional 2 teaspoons bacon fat to pot as necessary.
6. Reduce heat to medium, add 3 tablespoons bacon fat to now-empty pan.
7. Add onion, sauté until softened, 5 to 6 minutes.
8. Add garlic and Jalapeños, sauté until fragrant, about 1 minute.
9. Add chili paste; sauté until fragrant, 2 to 3 minutes.
10. Add reserved bacon and browned beef, crushed tomatoes or tomato sauce, limejuice, and 7 cups water; bring to simmer.
11. Continue to cook at a steady simmer until meat is tender and juices are dark, rich, and starting to thicken, about 2 hours.
12. Mix masa harina with 2/3-cup water (or cornstarch with 3 tablespoons water) in a small bowl to form smooth paste.
13. Increase heat to medium; stir in paste and simmer until thickened. 5 to 10 minutes.
14. Adjust seasoning generously with salt and ground black pepper.
15. Serve immediately, or preferably, cool slightly, cover, and refrigerate overnight or for up to 5 days.
16. Reheat before serving. Serves 6

Smoky Chipotle Chili Con Carne
Grill-smoking the meat, a technique from food writers John and Matt Lewis Thorne, authors of the Serious Pig (North Point Press, 1996), in combination with Chipotle chiles give this chili a distinct but not overwhelming, smoky

flavor. Make sure you start with a chuck roast that is at least three inches thick. The grilling is meant to flavor the meat by searing the surface and searing it lightly, not to cook it.

To prepare meat:
1. Puree 4 medium garlic cloves with two teaspoons salt.
2. Rub intact chuck roast with puree, and sprinkle evenly with 2 to 3 tablespoons New Mexico chile powder; cover and set aside.
3. Meanwhile, build hot fire.
4. When you can hold your hand 5 inches above grill surface for no more than 3 seconds, spread hot coals to area about the size of roast.
5. Open bottom grill vents, scatter one cup soaked mesquite or hickory wood chips over hot coals, and set grill rack in place.
6. Grill roast over hot coals opening lid vents three-quarters of the way and covering so that vents are opposite bottom vents to draw smoke through and around meat.
7. Sear meat until all sides are dark and richly colored, about 2 minutes per side.
8. Remove roast to bowl; when cool to the touch, trim and cut into 1-inch cubes, reserving juices.

For the chili:
1. Follow recipe for Chili Con Carne, omitting the browning of the beef cubes and substituting 5 minced canned Chipotle peppers in Adobo sauce for Jalapeño.
Serves 6.

Craig Claiborne's No-Salt Chili Con Carne
1 Tablespoon Vegetable Oil
3 Each Onions
1 Each Pepper
1-¼ Lb. Beef; Coarse Ground
2 Cloves Garlic
2 Tablespoons Red Chile, Hot; Ground
1 Tablespoon Red Chile, Mild; Ground
1 Teaspoon Cumin
1 Teaspoon Oregano; Dried (Preferably Mexican)
1 Each Bay Leaves
½ Teaspoon Pepper
4 Cups Tomatoes

1 Tablespoon Red Wine Vinegar
¼ Teaspoon Chile Caribe

1. Heat the oil in a deep skillet over medium heat.
2. Add the onions and green pepper and sauté until the onions are translucent, about 3 minutes.
3. Sprinkle the meat with the garlic, ground chile, cumin, and oregano. Stir.
4. Add the meat to the skillet.
5. Break up any lumps with a fork, stirring occasionally until the meat is evenly browned.
6. Add the bay leaf, pepper, tomatoes, vinegar, and Caribe.
7. Bring to a boil, lower the heat and simmer 1 hour, stirring occasionally.
8. Taste and adjust seasoning.

Crawfish Chili-Justin Wilson
From Justin Wilson's "Gourmet and Gourmand Cookbook"
2 Lb. Ground Beef; Lean
2 Lb. Crawfish Tails
1 Teaspoon Garlic; Chopped, Fine
2 Teaspoons Salt
1 Tablespoon Soy Sauce
1 Teaspoon Cayenne Pepper
1 Teaspoon Mint; Dried
1 Tablespoon Parsley; Dried
3 Tablespoons Chile powder
1 Can (8 Ounce) Tomato Sauce
1 Cup Dry White Wine
As Needed Water
1 Teaspoon Lemon Juice; Or Lime Juice
1 Cup Onion; Chopped
As Needed Bacon Drippings

1. Brown meat in bacon drippings.
2. Combine all other ingredients with meat and bring to a boil.
3. Simmer for a few hours.

Della Reese's Chicken Chili
8 Chicken Thighs
1 Tablespoon Cooking Oil
1 Large Onion; Coarse Chopped

1 Centiliter Garlic; Minced
2 Tablespoons Chile powder
1 Tablespoon Cumin; Ground (Fresh is Better)
1 Tablespoon Oregano
1 Tablespoon Salt
1 Medium Tomato; Chopped
1 Can (15 Ounce) Tomato Soup
2 Cans (15 Ounce) Kidney Beans

1. In a Dutch oven heat oil and add chicken. Turn, browning on all sides. Remove chicken and set aside.
2. Put onions and garlic in remaining oil; sauté until soft.
3. Add spices, tomatoes and soup. Stir well and allow to simmer briefly.
4. Add chicken and cook on low flame for 20 to 25 minutes.
5. Add beans and cook until chicken falls off bone.

From the recipe files of Carole Walberg

Don Henley's Texas Chili

The word "chili" (pronounced "chee-lee") is an Aztec word, but the Spanish version commonly used now is chile (pronounced "chee-lay"). Both words refer to the fruit of the "Capsicum anuum" plant, which was, because of its piquancy, misnamed "pepper" (after the black pepper-corn of the East Indies), by the Spanish explorers. This practice of mislabeling things because they are "like" other things has been going on for centuries and is something that musicians, particularly, have come to know and abhor. The labelers have given us such gems as "country rock," "jazz fusion" (melted jazz?), "Dylanesque," "adult contemporary," "pop-rock," dance music," "punk," "post punk" and my latest favorite, "New Age" music. Who does this stuff? I don't know, but then I don't know who names streets either. At any rate, there are roughly 200 different types of chiles in the world and nobody knows the names of all of them. So, when we refer to a dish as "chili," what we really mean is "chili (or chile), con carne"-chile peppers with meat. Somewhere along the line, the "con carne" was dropped, additional spices were added and the "chili" that we know today evolved. Unfortunately, this evolutionary process also produced several aberrations which cannot be called anything but hog slop. In fact, let's get one thing straight right now: True, authentic "chili" does not-I repeat, not-have beans in it. Beans are a separate dish to be relished and revered in their own right. When you put beans in chili, you insult both the beans and the chili. Now, let's get on with it. Here's what you need to make real chili:

A Case Of beer (Preferably Mexican beer, but American or a light German beer will do). I prefer Corona, Bohemia or Superior.
4 Lb. Lean Beef (I like to use a combination of 2 pounds coarsely ground and 2 pounds cubed)
Medium Onions; Chopped
3 or 4 Tablespoons Vegetable Oil or Olive Oil
2 Cans (8 Ounce) Tomato Sauce (Not Tomato Paste), or 1 Can (15 Ounce) Whole or chopped tomatoes will do if you can't find tomato sauce.
4 Teaspoons Salt
2 Heaping Teaspoons Comino, also known as cumin, seeds or powder (It is best to grind seeds in a molcajete, i.e., a mortar and pestle.)
6 or 8 Cloves Fresh Garlic, Smashed or Chopped
3 Heaping Tablespoons Chile powder (If you live in Europe, call up Gebhardt's Mexican foods Co. in San Antonio, Texas: (512) 227-0157 or the Pecos River Spice Co., PO Box 1600, Corrales, New Mexico. They have a phone number in New York for your convenience: (212) 628-5374, and tell them you need some chile powder. If that fails, go to a Spanish market and see if you can buy some dried, red Ancho or Anaheim chili peppers. Or try out the Online Chili Market.) Take the seeds out (please take the seeds out-- and don't rub your eyes). Then, grind, crush, chop or otherwise mutilate these peppers as best you can.
2 Level Teaspoons Paprika
2 Level Teaspoons Cayenne Pepper
2 Pods Fresh Jalapeño Peppers (Remove seeds and chop--do not rub eyes)
4 Level Teaspoons Oregano
1 Level Teaspoon Ground Coriander or
2 Teaspoons Chopped Fresh Cilantro (Same Thing)
½ Teaspoon Ground Black Pepper
1 Teaspoon Tabasco sauce
2 or 3 Heaping Tablespoons Masa (Corn) Flour. If you can't get corn flour, regular wheat flour or ground yellow cornmeal will do.

Now, have a beer. If you have managed to round up all of the above ingredients, you deserve one. It will also help to give you the correct "attitude" for making chili.

1. In a large skillet, sauté the meat, onions and half the garlic in the oil until the meat is gray in color.
2. Then dump meat, onions and garlic into a large pot with the tomato sauce.
3. Rinse the tomato sauce cans with beer and pour it into the pot.

4. Get yourself another beer.
5. Spread the meat evenly over the bottom of the pot.
6. Add enough water so that the meat is covered by ½ inch.
7. Add the remaining ingredients except the flour.
8. (Note: The cayenne pepper is what more or less determines the fieriness of the chili. If you want hotter chili, use more. If you want milder chili, use less.)
9. Heat all ingredients to a mild boil, turn the flame down immediately and simmer for at least one hour and 15 minutes, stirring occasionally to prevent sticking.
10. Skim off excess grease as it rises to the top.
11. Mix the flour with warm water to make a paste that is thick but pourable.
12. Add this to the pot while stirring and simmer for another 30 minutes-or another three hours-it just gets better.
13. Have another beer.

Consider the above list of ingredients again. Think about what a pain-in-the-ass it is to assemble them. Go to the phone and call:

Caliente Chili, Inc.,
PO Drawer 5340,
Austin, Texas 78763.
Phone (512) 472-6996

And tell Gordon Fowler or any of the other nice folks down there that you are in dire need of some Wick Fowler's 2-Alarm Chili "fixin's" (that's "ingredients" to you). They will in turn send you as many packets as you like of authentic, all natural, pre-measured ingredients to which you only have to add the meat and the tomato sauce (I like to throw in fresh onion and garlic, plus a little beer). This will enable you to make a pot of chili every bit as good (if not better), than the above recipe with a helluva-lot less trouble. And, no, I don't own part of the company, I just like the product. It's good stuff. Have another beer.

Dr. Roy Nakayama's Chili Verde
1 Lb. Beef; Very Lean, Cut in 1 Inch
8 Pods Green New Mexican Chiles; Roast, Peel, Seed and Chop
1 Each Tomato; Chopped Or Mashed Fine
½ Teaspoon Salt
½ Cup Onion; Chopped
½ Cup Tomatoes
½ Cup Water; Hot
½ Teaspoon Salt

1. To make green sauce, combine chopped green chiles, mashed tomato and ½ teaspoon salt.
2. This will keep in refrigerator several days.
3. Sear meat in hot skillet, under low heat, until brown.
4. Then add from 1-¼ to 1-½ cups of the green sauce, ½ tsp. salt, onions tomatoes and hot water.
5. Bring to a boil and simmer until the meat is done and tender.

Emeril's Chili
Emeril Live w/ Emeril Lagasse-TV Food Network-Show
2 Tablespoons Vegetable Oil
2 Cups Onion; Chopped
To Taste Salt
To Taste Cayenne Pepper
2 Lb. Stew Meat
1 Tablespoon Chile powder
2 Teaspoons Cumin; Ground
To Taste Red Pepper; Crushed
2 Teaspoons Oregano; Dried
2 Tablespoons Garlic; Chopped
3 Cups Tomatoes; Crushed
¼ Cup Tomato Paste
2 Cups Beef Stock
1 Cup Dark Red Kidney Beans; Canned
2 Tablespoons Masa Harina Flour
4 Tablespoons Water
1 Bag Tortilla Chips
1-½ Cups Monterey Jack Cheese; Grated
6 Tablespoons Sour Cream
1 Jar (Small) Jalapeño Peppers

1. In a large saucepan, heat the vegetable oil.
2. When the oil is hot, add the onions and sauté for 3 to 5 minutes, or until the vegetables start to wilt.
3. Season with salt and cayenne.
4. Stir in the stew meat, chile powder, cumin, crushed red pepper, and oregano.
5. Brown the meat for 5 to 6 minutes.
6. Stir in the garlic, tomatoes, tomato paste, beef stock, and beans.
7. Bring the liquid up to a boil and reduce to a simmer.

8. Simmer the liquid uncovered for 1 hour, stirring occasionally, or until the beef is tender.
9. Skim off the fat occasionally.
10. Mix the masa and water together.
11. Slowly stir in the masa slurry and continue to cook for 30 minutes.
12. Re season with salt and cayenne.

Place a handful of the chips in each shallow bowl. Spoon the chili over the chips. Garnish with the grated cheese, sour cream and Jalapeños.

This recipe yields 6 to 8 servings.

Eugenia Potter's 27 Ingredient Chili Con Carne
1 Lb. Pinto Beans; Dry, Soak Overnight
½ Cup Butter; Or Margarine
2 Medium Onions; Chopped
7 Ounces Green Chile Peppers; Diced
2 Cloves Garlic; Minced
3 Lb. Chopped Sirloin
1 Lb. Pork Sausage; Browned and Crumbled
2 Tablespoons Flour
1 Can (16 Ounce) Baked Beans
1 Can (4 Ounce) Pimentos
2 Cans (30 Ounce) Tomatoes
¾ Cup Celery; Chopped
½ Lb. Mushroom; Fresh, Sliced
½ Cup Green Pepper; Chopped
½ Cup Red Pepper; Chopped
1 Can (9 Ounce) Ripe Olives; Pitted, Chopped
½ Cup Parsley; Minced
1 Bottle (12 Ounce) Chili Sauce
1 Tablespoon Salt
1 Tablespoon Garlic Salt
2 Teaspoons Black Pepper
1 Tablespoon Cilantro (Fresh); Chopped
1 Tablespoon Oregano
2 Tablespoons Chile powder; 2-4 to Taste
As Needed Orange Peel; Grated
1 Pint Sour Cream

1. Bring pinto beans to a boil in the soaking water and simmer 2-3 hour until tender. Drain.

2. In a large skillet, melt ¼ cup butter and add onions, green and red peppers and garlic. Sauté until soft.
3. Remove to Dutch oven or 8 qt. pot.
4. In remaining butter, cook chopped sirloin, 1-½ Lb. at a time, until meat is brown.
5. Add sausage and sprinkle with flour, stirring to mix. Transfer to pot.
6. Add all remaining ingredients except sour cream.
7. Bring just to boil. Lower heat and simmer about 30 minutes.
8. Skim off fat with a cold spoon as it rises to the top.

Serve with sour cream.

Serves 20. Freezes well.

Glen Campbell's Chili Con Carne
The County Fair Cookbook

3 Lb. Beef Chuck; Coarse Ground
2 Medium Onions
1 Medium Bell Pepper
1 Clove Garlic
½ Teaspoon Oregano
¼ Teaspoon Cumin Seed
2 Cans Tomato Paste
1 Quart Water
To Taste Salt
To Taste Black Pepper; Ground
2 Tablespoons Chile powder; 2 to 3
2 Cans (15 Ounce) Pinto or Kidney Beans

1. Brown the chuck in an iron kettle. (If you don't have an iron kettle, you are not civilized. Go, get one.) Chop the onions and bell pepper and add to the browned meat. Crush or mince the garlic and add to pot. Then add the oregano and cumin seed.
2. Add the tomato paste. If you prefer canned tomatoes or fresh tomatoes, press them through a colander.
3. Add about 1 quart of water.
4. Salt liberally and grind in some black pepper, and for starters, 2 or 3 tablespoons of chile powder. (You may use chile pods, if you wish.)
5. Simmer for 90 minutes or longer, then add the beans.
6. Pinto beans are best; but kidney beans will do. Simmer for 30 minutes more.
7. Throughout the cooking process, taste test from time to time and adjust

seasonings according to individual tastes.
8. When it seems right to you, let it sit for several hours.
9. Heat as much as you require, refrigerating the rest.
Tastes better the 2nd day, much better on the 3rd day and according to Glen, "absolutely superb" on the 4th day. He says you can't imagine the delights awaiting you after 1 week.

From the Maricopa County Fair of Phoenix, AZ. Fair dates: 3rd and 4th weeks in March, for 11 days.

James Beard's Chili
1 Tablespoon Vegetable Oil
1 Tablespoon Butter
6 Medium Onions; Halved and Sliced
3 Lb. Ground Beef; (1.5 Kg.)
¼ Cup Chile powder
2 Teaspoons Oregano; Dried
1 Teaspoon Cumin
2 Cans (28 Ounce) Tomatoes; Undrained
5-½ Ounces Tomato Paste
1 Cup Beer
1 Teaspoon Salt
½ Teaspoon Hot Pepper Sauce, Liquid
2 Cans (12 Ounce) Corn; Drained
To Taste Pepper

1. In large saucepan or Dutch oven heat oil and butter over medium heat; cook onions, stirring occasionally, about 10 minutes until tender, but not brown.
2. Add beef and cook, stirring to break up, until no longer pink. Drain off fat.
3. Stir in chile powder, oregano and cumin; mix well.
4. Add tomatoes, breaking up; tomato paste, beer, salt, and hot pepper sauce.
5. Bring to a boil; reduce heat and simmer, uncovered, 45 minutes.
6. Add corn; simmer 10 minutes longer or until thickened.
7. Taste; adjust seasonings with salt, pepper, and hot pepper sauce.
Makes about 10 servings.

John Wayne's Texas Chili
5 Lb. Beef, Lean; Cubed or Coarse Ground
1 Quart Water

3 Tablespoons Sugar
2-½ Tablespoons Salt
6 Ounces Olive Oil
5 Tablespoons Flour
6 Tablespoons Chile; Ground, Up to 8
5 Cloves Garlic
1 Teaspoon Pepper
2 Teaspoons Oregano
1 Teaspoon Curry Powder

1. In a large pot, combine the water, meat, sugar and salt; bring the mixture to a boil, skim, then reduce heat immediately down to a simmer.
2. Do not let the pot boil again.
3. In a skillet, heat up the oil, add the flour and then stir and cook the mixture for about 2 minutes without browning.
4. Add garlic and spices to oil mixture, cook it briefly and then add the entire mixture to meat.
5. Simmer meat for about 1-½ hours until meat becomes very tender.
Serves 10 to 12.

Johnny Cash's "Old Iron Pot" Family Style Chili
5 Lb. Sirloin Steak
3 Packages McCormick, Lawry's, Schilling's; Or Mexene Chili Powder.
To Taste Spice Island's Chili Con Carne Seasoning
To Taste Cumin
2 Tablespoons Sugar
To Taste Thyme
To Taste Sage Leaves
1 Medium Raw Onion; Chopped
To Taste Chile Peppers; Chopped
3 Cans Red Kidney Beans; 3 or 4
3 Cans Tomatoes; Whole, 3 or 4
1 Can Tomato Paste
To Taste Garlic
To Taste Onion Powder
To Taste Salt

1. Chop steak and cook until medium with a little shortening.
2. Add packages of seasoning mix and cook 5 minutes.
3. Add beans, tomatoes, spices, onions, sugar and chili powder or a cup con

carne mix.

4. Taste, if too hot for children or ladies, add 1 or 2 cans of tomatoes.
5. Add tomato paste.
6. If it gets too thick, add water.
7. Simmer low for twenty minutes.

Serve with soda crackers and Pepsi or Coke. This will serve 12 people, 3 helpings each.

LBJ'S Pedernales River Chili-Post Heart Attack

4 Lb. Venison; Bite Size-Chili Grind Fine
1 Or Chuck beef; Well Trimmed, Ground
1 Large Onion; Chopped
2 Cloves Garlic; Minced
1 Teaspoon Oregano; Preferably Mexican
1 Teaspoon Cumin Seeds
6 Teaspoons Chile powder
1-½ Cups Canned Tomatoes; Whole
1 Dash Liquid Hot Pepper Sauce
To Taste Salt

1. Place meat, onion and garlic in a heavy skillet or Dutch oven.
2. Cook until light colored. Add oregano, cumin, water, chile powder, tomatoes, hot pepper sauce (more or less to taste), and salt.
3. Bring to a boil, lowering heat, and simmer for one hour.
4. Skim off fat during cooking.

Note: Even more fat can be removed if chili is stored in the refrigerator, allowing fat to rise to the top and solidify, when it can be easily removed. LBJ preferred venison in his chili, and so did his doctor, because it is so lean and fat-free. Ground beef heart is leaner still, and has a rich beef flavor with the added value of high vitamin B content. This recipe was tailored to President Johnson after his first heart attack. Not only is it relatively fat-free, it calls for lean venison, when available. The local pronunciation of Pedernales is purr-DIN-Alice, and in this case local extends at least from Texas to Washington, DC, to New York City.

LBJ'S Pedernales River Chili-Pre Heart Attack
Mrs. Zephyr Wright

4 Lb. Chili Meat
1 Large Onion
2 Cloves Garlic

1 Teaspoon Oregano; Dried (Preferably Mexican)
1 Teaspoon Cumin
2 Cups Water; Hot
2 Cans (16 Ounce) Tomatoes; Whole
4 Tablespoons Red Chile, Hot; Ground
2 Tablespoons Red Chile, Mild; Ground

1. Melt the lard or bacon drippings in a large sauté pan over medium heat.
2. Add the meat to the pan.
3. Break up any lumps with a fork and cook, stirring occasionally until the meat is evenly browned.
4. Add the onions and garlic and cook until the onions are translucent.
5. Stir in the salt, oregano, cumin, water, and tomatoes.
6. Gradually stir in the ground chile, testing until you achieve the degree of hotness and flavor the suits your palate.
7. Bring to a boil, then lower heat and simmer, uncovered, for 1 hour.
8. Stir occasionally.
See page 12 in "A Bowl of Red" by Frank X. Tolbert.

Lewis and Clark's White Chili
3 Lb. Great Northern Beans; Canned
2 Lb. Chicken Breast; Skinless and Bone
1 Tablespoon Olive Oil
40 Ml. Garlic; Minced
2 Medium Onions; Chopped
2 Teaspoons Cumin; Ground
1/8 Teaspoon Cloves; Ground
¼ Teaspoon Cayenne Pepper
1 Teaspoon Oregano; Ground
2 Cans (4 Ounce) Mild Green Chiles; Chopped
4 Cups Chicken Stock; Or Broth
20 Ounces Monterey Jack Cheese; Grated
As Desired Sour Cream
As Desired Jalapeño Chile Peppers; Canned, Chopped

1. Place chicken in large saucepan.
2. Add cold water to cover and bring to simmer. Cook until tender, approximately 15 to 20 minutes.
3. Remove from saucepan and dice into ½ in. cubes.
4. Using the same pan discard water and heat oil over medium heat.

5. Add onions until translucent.
6. Stir in garlic, chiles, cumin, cayenne pepper, oregano and cloves. Sauté for 2 to 3 minutes.
7. Add chicken, beans, stock and 12 ounces of cheese; let simmer for 15 minutes.

Ladle into large bowls and top with 1 ounce of cheese. Serve with a side of sour cream and chopped Jalapeño peppers.

Library of Congress Chili

4 Lb. Ground Chuck
2 Cans (15 Ounce) Tomato Sauce; 15 to 17 Ounce Cans
2 Cans (15 Ounce) Dark Red Kidney Beans; 15 to 17 Ounce Cans
1 Can (15 Ounce) Light Red Kidney Beans; 15 to 17 Ounce Cans
1 Can Whole-Kernel Corn
5 Cans Water; 4 to 6
2 Medium Onions; Coarse Chopped
½ Teaspoon Cumin; Ground
½ Tablespoon Cilantro Leaves
¼ Tablespoon Garlic Powder
2 Medium Green Bell Peppers; Chopped
2 Medium Red Peppers; Chopped
3 Tablespoons Mexican Hot Chile powder
1 Teaspoon Red Pepper Flakes
1 Teaspoon Cayenne Pepper
1 Teaspoon Paprika
1 Tablespoon White Vinegar
1 Tablespoon White Sugar
1 Tablespoon Salt
½ Tablespoon Seasoned Salt
½ Tablespoon Seasoned Pepper

1. Brown meat in 2 large skillets.
2. Add onions and peppers with 1 can water. Cook covered for 10 minutes.
3. Add tomato sauce and 2 more cans of water. Cook for 10 minutes.
4. Add all spices and another can of water. Bring to a boil for 10 minutes.
5. Reduce heat and cook for one hour. Keep stirred.
6. Add beans. Cook for another hour, adding 1 - 2 cans of water if too thick.
7. Continue to stir. Simmer for one hour.

Cook time approximately 4 hours.

    Feeds 10 Hungry Librarians Or 20 Book Reviewers.

Linda McCartney's Chili Non Carne
2 Tablespoons Vegetable Oil
1 Medium Onion; Chopped
1-½ Teaspoon (Level) Chile powder; Or More to Taste
4-½ Ounce Packets TVP Chunks; Or
4 Vegetable Burgers; Crumbled
12 Ounces Vegetable Broth; 6 if Using Burgers
1 Can (14 Ounce) Tomatoes; Chopped
1 Can (14 Ounce) Red Kidney Beans
2 Pods Mexican Green Chiles in Brine; Drained and Chopped (Opt)
To Taste Salt and Black Pepper; Fresh Ground

The best chili you'll get this side of Tijuana, according to Linda McCartney. Chili Non Carne was very popular with the road crew on Paul's 1989-90 World Tour-rock and roll's first vegetarian world tour.

1. Heat the oil in a large saucepan and sauté the onion until golden brown.
2. Add the chile powder and TVP chunks and brown for 5 minutes.
3. Add the vegetable stock and tomatoes, together with their juice.
4. Cover and simmer for 20 minutes.
5. Add the kidney beans-and the chiles if you are using them-and simmer for about 15 minutes, adding a little extra stock or water if necessary.
6. Season to taste and serve hot with rice, mashed potatoes or avocado salad.

Lucille's Chili (Slightly Modified)-B.B. King
½ Lb. Sausage
1-½ Lb. Ground Chuck
1 Cup Onion; Chopped
¾ Cup Green Pepper; Chopped
1 Clove Garlic; Minced
1 Can (16 Ounce) Whole Tomatoes; Cut Up
1 Can (16 Ounce) Light Red Kidney Beans; Drained
1 Can (16 Ounce) Red Kidney Beans; Drained
2 Cans (8 Ounce) Tomato Sauce
1 Can (10 Ounce) Tomatoes and Green Chiles; Diced
1 Pod Jalapeño Pepper; Seeded and Chopped
1 Tablespoon Chile powder; Up to 2
1 Tablespoon Oregano Leaves; Fresh Snipped
1 Tablespoon Oregano; Dried and Crushed
2 Teaspoons Cumin; Ground

1-½ Teaspoons Basil; Fresh Snipped
½ Teaspoon Basil; Dried and Crushed
1-½ Teaspoons Salt
¼ Teaspoon Pepper
As Needed Onion; Chopped
As Needed Dairy Sour Cream
As Needed Cheddar Cheese; Shredded

Lucille's Chili-(Modified) Best of Memphis-Beale Street. Please read to the bottom of this recipe.

1. In a four-quart Dutch oven, cook ground chuck, onion, green pepper, and garlic until meat is brown.
2. Drain well.
3. Add undrained tomatoes, drained kidney beans, tomato sauce, undrained tomatoes and green chiles, Jalapeño pepper, chile powder, oregano, cumin, basil, salt, and pepper.
4. Cook over medium heat for 10 minutes.
5. Reduce heat.
6. Cover and simmer for 1 hour.

Serve with additional chopped onion, sour cream, and cheddar cheese for topping.
   Makes 8 main dish servings.

Karis' Hint: Simmer in a crock-pot for an additional 2 hours.
There was a spot on old Beale Street run by Sunbeam Mitchell. Here all of the musicians around, including the notable B.B. King, could eat cheap, and get a bowl of the best chili in town. B.B. remembers: ''If you had 15 cents at that time, you could eat well: a nickel's worth of crackers and a dime's worth of chili!'' "Lucille's Chili," named for B.B.'s famous guitar, is patterned after this memorable feast.

Ma Unser Chili Verde
1 Lb. Pork Shoulder; Cut in ¼ Inch Cubes
2 Tablespoons Lard
2 Tablespoons Flour
½ Cup Onion; Chopped
1 Clove Garlic; Diced
1 Can (16 Ounce) Tomatoes; Coarse Chopped
¼ Teaspoon Oregano

2-½ Teaspoons Salt
2 Cups Water
4 Cans (7 Ounce) Green Chiles

1. Dredge meat in flour.
2. In a deep skillet, brown meat in lard.
3. Add onions and cook until soft.
4. Add remaining ingredients.
5. Simmer, covered for 2 hours.
6. Simmer uncovered 5 to 10 minutes or until the desired consistency.

Mansion Chili-Kentucky Governor Brereton C. Jones
1 Lb. Ground Beef
2 Medium Onions; Chopped (About 1-½ Cups)
½ Medium Green Bell Peppers; (About ½ Cup)
2 Tablespoons Mild Pure Chile Powder; 2 or 3
1 Teaspoon Cumin; Ground
3 Cups Beef Broth; 3 or 4
1 Can (28 Ounce) Tomatoes; Diced or Crushed
1 Can (15.5 Ounce) Red Kidney Beans; Drained
2 Cups Elbow Macaroni; Cooked
6 Ounces Cheddar Cheese; Grated

1. In a heavy chili pot, brown ground beef and drain off fat.
2. Add onions, green peppers, chile powder and cumin and sauté 2 additional minutes.
3. Stir in beef broth, tomatoes and beans and simmer 45 minutes.
4. Serve over cooked macaroni and top with cheese.
Makes 4 servings.

Mrs. Dash Chili
1 Can (15 Ounce) Chili Tomatoes
1 Can (14 Ounce) Red Kidney Beans; Undrained
2 Tablespoons Mrs. Dash Garlic and Herb
1 Tablespoon Sugar
1 Teaspoon Cumin
As Desired Cheese; Grated, Optional
As Desired Onion; Chopped, Optional

1. In medium saucepan, combine all ingredients.
2. Simmer over medium heat for 5-10 minutes.
3. Garnish with grated cheese and onions if desired.

My Chili-Nathalie Dupree
Nathalie Dupree Cooks Show
¼ Cup Vegetable Oil
4 Medium Onions; Chopped
3 Cloves Garlic; Chopped
3 Lb. Ground Chuck; Lean
56 Ounces Tomatoes; Chopped, Reserve Juice
48 Ounces Kidney Beans; Drain and Reserve Juice
½ Cup Red Wine Vinegar
8 Tablespoons Chile powder
1 Tablespoon Cumin Seeds; Ground
1 Tablespoon Oregano; Fresh or Dried, Chopped
2 Teaspoons Cayenne Pepper
1 Can (4 Ounce) Green Chiles; Chopped
To Taste Salt
To Taste Black Pepper; Fresh Ground
To Taste Additional Herbs

1. Heat the oil in a large Dutch oven and in it sauté the onions and garlic until soft.
2. Remove the onions and garlic with a slotted spoon, and set aside.
3. Add the meat to the hot pan and brown over high heat. Drain off excess fat.
4. Reduce heat, return the onions and garlic to the pan, and stir in the tomatoes and their juices, beans, red wine vinegar, chile powder, cumin seed, oregano, cayenne, and chiles.
5. Add bean juices if necessary.
6. Bring to the boil; reduce heat, and simmer, stirring occasionally for 30 minutes.
7. Season to taste with salt, pepper, and additional herbs.
8. Refrigerate and remove fat if time allows.
The chili freezes well. Yield: 12 to 16 servings

Neiman Marcus Chili Blanco
1 Lb. Great Northern Beans; Dried
2 Lb. Chicken Breast

1 Tablespoon Olive Oil
2 Medium Onions; Chopped
4 Cloves Garlic; Chopped
2 Cans (4 Ounce) Green Chiles; Mild
2 Teaspoons Cumin; Ground
1-½ Teaspoon Oregano; Dried and Crumbled
¼ Teaspoon Cayenne Pepper
6 Cups Chicken Broth
3 Cups Monterey Jack Cheese; Grated
1 Cup Sour Cream
1 Cup Salsa
1 Sprig Cilantro; Fresh, Grated

1. Rinse and pick over beans; place in heavy large pot.
2. Add enough cold water to cover by at least 3 inches; soak overnight.
3. Place chicken in large heavy saucepan.
4. If time permits add cut up onions, celery, carrots, salt and pepper for flavor.
5. Add cold water to cover and bring to simmer. Cook until just tender, about 15 minutes. Drain and cool. Remove skin. Cut chicken into cubes.
6. Drain beans.
7. Heat oil in same pot over medium heat.
8. Add onions and sauté until translucent, about 10 minutes.
9. Stir in garlic, then chiles, cumin, oregano, cloves and cayenne and sauté 2 minutes.
10. Add beans and stock and bring to a boil.
11. Reduce heat and simmer until beans are very tender, stirring occasionally, about 2 hours.
12. Beans and chicken can be prepared 1 day ahead.
13. Cover and refrigerate.
14. Bring chili bean mixture to simmer before continuing with recipe.
15. Add chicken and 1 cup cheese to chili and stir until cheese melts.
16. Season to taste with salt and pepper.

Pour cheese into large tureen. Place remaining cheese, sour cream, salsa and cilantro in small bowls around the tureen so that guests can add whatever toppings they want to their chili.

Makes 8 servings.

Original Bowl of Red-Frank (Francis) X. Tolbert
Frank (Francis) X. Tolbert's
One pundit said that if chili were a religion, "A Bowl of Red" would be its Bible and Frank L. Tolbert would be its Moses. Below is the trailblazer's approach to making chili:

12 Pods Dried Ancho Chiles (New Mexico chiles may be substituted)
3 Lb. Lean Beef Chuck, Cut in Thumb sized Pieces (One may substitute "Chili Grind" beef for the chuck)
2 Ounces Beef Suet (May be left out, if you are fat conscious)
1 Tablespoon Cumin, Ground
1 Tablespoon Oregano, Dried
1 Tablespoon Cayenne Pepper
1 Tablespoon Tabasco Sauce
2 Cloves Garlic; Chopped or More
1 Tablespoon Salt
2 Tablespoons Masa Harina (Optional)

1. Break off the stems of the chiles, and remove the seeds.
2. Place the chiles in a small saucepan, and cover them with water.
3. Simmer the chiles for 30 minutes.
4. Puree the chiles in a blender with a bit of their cooking liquid to make a smooth, thin paste.
5. Use as little liquid as possible, unless you want the chili to be soupy.
6. Pour the chile puree into a Dutch oven or large, heavy saucepan.
7. In a heavy skillet, sear the meat in two batches with the beef suet until the meat is gray.
8. Transfer each batch to the chile puree, then pour enough of the chile cooking liquid to cover the meat by about two inches.
9. Bring the chili to a boil, and then reduce the heat to a simmer.
10. Cook the chili 30 minutes.
11. Remove the chili from the heat, and stir in the rest of the ingredients.
12. Return the chili to the heat, and resume simmering for 45 minutes, keeping the lid on except to stir occasionally (too much stirring will tear up the meat).
13. Add more chile and cooking liquid only if you think the mixture will burn otherwise.
14. When 45 minutes are up, add the masa harina if you wish. Not only will it add a subtle, tamale-like taste to the chili, but also it will thicken or "tighten" the chili.

15. Cover the chili again, and simmer it for another 30 minutes, until the meat is done.
16. During this last 30 minutes, do a lot of tasting to see if the seasonings suit you.
17. Adjust the seasonings as you like, although you should go easy on the oregano to avoid ending up with a spaghetti sauce flavor.
18. Take the chili off the heat, and refrigerate it overnight.
19. Skim as much fat as you wish from the chili before reheating it.
20. Serve it hot.

That's it! This chili can be extremely hot so watch out for your tongue! More than once I have made chili too hot for my palate and had to throw the whole mixture out. For more information on Frank Tolbert and the book, "A Bowl of Red," check your local library.

Pedernales River Chili (Lady Bird Johnson's recipe)
4 Lb. Coarsely-Ground Steak; Well Trimmed
1 Large Onion; Chopped
2 Cloves Garlic; Crushed
1 Teaspoon Oregano
1 Teaspoon Cumin Seed; Ground
6 Tablespoons Chile powder
1-½ Cups Canned Whole Tomatoes
2 Dashes Hot Pepper Sauce, Liquid; Generous (2-6)
To Taste Salt
2 Cups Water; Hot

1. Sauté meat, onion, and garlic in a large, heavy pan until meat has lost its color and onions are soft.
2. Add remaining ingredients.
3. Bring to a boil, lower heat, and simmer 1 hour.
4. Skim fat while cooking.
About 8 servings.

Pecos River Bowl Of Chili-Jane Butel
"Chili Madness" by Jane Butel (Queen of Chili)
2 Tablespoons Bacon Drippings; Or Butter, Or Lard
1 Large Onion; Coarse Chopped
3 Lb. Beef; Coarse Ground, Lean
3 Cloves Garlic; Finely Chopped
4 Tablespoons Chili Peppers; Ground, Hot

2 Tablespoons Chile Peppers; Ground, Mild
2 Teaspoons Cumin; Ground
3 Cups Water
1-½ Teaspoons Salt

1. Melt lard, butter, or drippings in a large heavy pot over medium heat.
2. Add the onions and cook until transparent but not browned, about 5 minutes.
3. Combine meat with garlic, ground chiles and cumin.
4. Add this meat-spice mixture with a fork and cook, stirring occasionally, until meat is evenly browned.
5. Stir in water and salt.
6. Bring to a boil, then lower heat and simmer, uncovered, for about 2-½ to 3 hours, stirring occasionally, until meat is very tender and flavors are well blended.
7. Add more water if necessary.
8. Taste and adjust seasonings.

Serves 6.

Polly Bergen's Chili
Files of Carole Walberg
4 Tablespoons Olive Oil
4 Medium Yellow Onions; Chopped
4 Lb. Ground Chuck; Lean
12 Ounces Tomato Paste
1 Teaspoon White Vinegar
1 Tablespoon Salt
3 Cloves Garlic; Whole
2 Large Cloves Garlic; Peeled and Minced
2 Large Green Peppers; Seeded and Minced
3 Lb. Tomatoes; Canned
4 Tablespoons Chile powder
¼ Teaspoon Cayenne Pepper
1 Leaf Bay

1. In an 8-quart Dutch oven, heat the oil; sauté garlic, onions, and peppers until tender.
2. Add chuck, crumbling it loosely.
3. Cook slowly over medium heat for 10 minutes or until chuck loses color.
4. Add tomatoes, cutting large chunks of tomato smaller with two knives;

add tomato paste, chile powder, vinegar, cayenne and salt.

5. Stir in cloves and bay leaf; then cook, uncovered, 1 hour.
6. At end of hour, check liquid content; if there's too much, simmer a bit longer; if too dry, add another can of tomatoes.
7. Refrigerate chili mixture until cool.
8. Turn it into freezer-type plastic bags or containers and freeze up to 1 month.
9. To serve, remove desired amount from freezer.
10. Turn into a Dutch oven and heat over very low heat until hot and bubbly. Serve in bowls.

Red Lobster's Seafood Chili

1 Lb. Medium Shrimp Peeled; Deveined, Tails Removed
½ Lb. Bay Scallops
1 Lb. White Fish; Boneless and Skinless
1 Tablespoon Vegetable Oil
1 Clove Garlic; Chopped
½ Cup Celery; Diced ¼ Inch
½ Cup Red Onion; Diced ¼ Inch
1 Can (Large) Tomato; Whole
1 Can (8 Ounce) Tomato Paste
1 Can Dark Kidney Beans
1 Tablespoon Chile powder
½ Teaspoon Coriander; Ground
2 Leaves Bay; Whole
1 Teaspoon Cayenne Pepper
1 Teaspoon Sugar
1 Tablespoon Salt
1 Teaspoon Black Pepper
¼ Cup Green Pepper; Diced ¼ Inch
½ Cup Red Pepper; Diced ¼ Inch

1. Heat oil in a large saucepan; add onions, garlic, celery and seafood. Sauté until almost cooked.
2. Empty canned whole tomatoes in a shallow bowl and cut into small pieces.
3. This can be done in a blender. Do not puree.
4. Add to the seafood mixture.
5. Reduce heat to medium low and add beans, tomato paste, spices and peppers.

6. Stir together so that the seafood is not stuck on the bottom.
7. Heat until bubbling, then reduce heat, cover and let cook for 30 minutes.
Servings: 6-8

Ronald Reagan's Chili
Executive Chef Henry Haller
½ Cup Bacon Drippings
2 Cups Onion; Chopped
4 Cloves Garlic; Chopped
2 Lb. Ground Beef; Coarse
2 Tablespoons Chile powder
2 Cups Red Wine; Optional
1 Tablespoon Salt
1 Tablespoon Beef Base
4 Cups Tomatoes; Canned, Chopped
1 Leaf Bay
1 Tablespoon Sugar
4 Cups Pinto Beans; Cooked, (up to 6)

President Reagan's favorite homemade chili as prepared by White House Executive Chef Henry Haller will serve about 16 people. Chef Haller has served variations of this chili recipe in the White house since the Johnson administration, and it has proven to be a non-partisan pot of chili.

1. Using a 1-½ gallon heavy pot, melt bacon drippings.
2. When hot, sauté onions and garlic cloves.
3. Add ground beef and chile powder.
4. Stir until meat is well browned.
5. Add red wine (optional).
6. Add salt, beef base, tomatoes, bay leaf and sugar.
7. Simmer chili meat, covered, for 20 minutes, stirring often.
8. Then add pinto beans to the meat.
9. Simmer chili con carne for 1 hour, covered over low flame, stirring gently from time to time.
10. Test for flavor.
Remarks: For a better tasting chili, cook it a day ahead and reheat it in a double boiler.

Rosalyn Carter's Chili Con Carne
From The Files of Carole Walberg
1 Lb. Round Steak; Bite-Size
3 Tablespoons Oil
1 Can (4 Ounce) Green Chiles; Chopped
1 Can (6 Ounce) Tomato Paste
1 Small Onion; Chopped
1-½ Cups Water
1 Clove Garlic; Minced
1-½ Teaspoons Cumin; Ground
½ Teaspoon Oregano; Dried and Crushed
¼ Teaspoon Black Pepper
1-½ Teaspoons Sugar
1-½ Tablespoons Flour
1-½ Teaspoons Salt
2 Tablespoons Chile powder

1. Brown meat in hot oil in heavy pot or large skillet.
2. Add chiles, tomato paste, onion, water, garlic, cumin, oregano, pepper, sugar, flour, salt and chile powder.
3. Simmer about 1 hour or until meat is tender and mixture is thickened.

Senator Barry Goldwater's Expert Chili
1 Lb. Ground Beef; Coarse Ground
1 Lb. Pinto Beans; Dried
1 Can (6 Ounce) Tomato Paste
2 Cups Onions; Chopped
3 Tablespoons Chile powder; Hot, Un-spiced
1 Tablespoon Ground Cumin; salt
To Taste Salt

1. Soak beans in water, covered overnight.
2. In large Dutch oven, cook beef until browned, stirring to keep crumbly; drain off drippings, if needed.
3. Add tomato paste, onions and drained beans.
4. Mix chile powder, cumin and season to taste with salt.
5. Stir into mixture.
6. Bring to boil, reduce heat, cover and simmer until beans are tender, about 5 hours.

Serves 6.

Senator Joseph Montoya's New Mexican Chili
1-½ Lb. Round Steak; Cut in ¼ Inch Cubes
2 Cloves Garlic; Minced
2 Tablespoons Oil
1-½ Teaspoons Flour
3 Tablespoons Chile powder; Un-spiced
2 Cups Water
1 Teaspoon Salt

1. Heat oil in saucepan of Dutch oven, add meat and cook and stir 10 minutes.
2. Add garlic when meat is partially browned.
3. Sprinkle with flour and stir 1 min. longer.
4. Add chile powder, water and salt.
5. Cover and simmer 45 minutes.

Senator John Tower's Texas Chili
3 Lb. Chili Meat
2 Large Onions; Finely Chopped
1 Can (15 Ounce) Tomato Sauce
As Needed Water
1 Teaspoon Tabasco Sauce
4 Tablespoons Chile powder; Heaping
1 Teaspoon Cumin
1 Clove Garlic; Pressed
1 Teaspoon Salt
To Taste Black Pepper
1 Teaspoon Cayenne Pepper
1 Teaspoon Paprika; Level Tsp.
12 Pods Red Peppers; Chopped
4 Pods Serrano Chile Peppers; Seeded and Chopped (4 or 5)

1. Sear meat and onion mixture to meat is gray and add tomato sauce and water.
2. Add remaining ingredients and simmer for one hour and fifteen minutes.
3. Thicken with 2 heaping tablespoons of flour mixed with a little water.
4. Simmer for an additional 30 minutes.

Smith & Wesson Chili
Jerry "Flash" Gordon, Ormond Beach-Florida, circa 1988
3-½ Lb. Flank Steak
2 Medium Onions; Coarse Chopped
2 Cups Tomatoes (Stewed); Chopped
1 Cup Tomato Paste
1 Tablespoon Liquid Smoke
¼ Cup Bullseye Barbecue Sauce
24 Ounces Beer
6 Pods Jalapeño Peppers; Seeded and Chopped
3 Cloves Garlic; Minced
1 Cup Bell Pepper; Diced
3 Tablespoons Chile powder
5 Tablespoons Cumin
3 Tablespoons Masa Harina (Corn Flour)
4 Cups Tomato Sauce
As Needed Salt
2 Teaspoons Black Pepper

1. Cut meat into small cubes approx. 3/8" in size. Brown meat, onions, Bell pepper, and garlic in a heavy skillet.
2. Put the beer into a large pot and bring to a slow boil.
3. Boil for 10 minutes then add the tomato sauce, the stewed tomatoes, the meat and onion/pepper mixture, the Jalapeños, the barbecue sauce, and the Liquid Smoke.
4. Reduce heat to Medium and cook for ½ hour.
5. Stir every few minutes.
6. Add 2 Tablespoons of the cumin, salt, pepper, and Tabasco sauce.
7. Cook for ½ hour more.
8. At this point add the tomato paste, masa harina, and continue cooking for 15 minutes.
9. Add the remaining cumin and cook for 10 minutes more.

U.S. Senate Dining Room Chili
2-½ Lb. Ground Round or Chuck
2 Big Onions; Chopped, 3 Cups
6 Buds Garlic; Mashed or Chopped
3 Cans Luck's October or Pinto Beans
1 Can Kidney Beans
1 Can (Large) Italian Tomatoes

517

1 Can (Large) Libby's Tomato Juice
3 Tablespoons Chile powder; Up to 4
To Taste Salt and Pepper

1. Sauté onions in 3 tablespoons corn oil until slightly browned. Stir often.
2. Add meat and garlic. Stir constantly until meat is lightly browned.
3. Add cut up tomatoes, juice and beans and chile powder. Stir until begins to boil.
4. Turn heat low and let simmer 3 hours.

This is even better the second day. Freezes nicely.

Walt Disney's Own Chili
2 Lb. Ground Beef; Coarse
2 Medium Onions; Sliced
2 Cloves Garlic; Minced
2 Lb. Pink Beans; Dry
½ Cup Celery; Chopped
1 Teaspoon Chile powder
1 Teaspoon Paprika
1 Teaspoon Dry Mustard
1 Can (Large) Solid Pack Tomatoes
To Taste Salt

1. Soak beans overnight in cold water. Drain.
2. Add water to cover 2 inches over beans and simmer with onions until tender (about 4 hours).
3. Meanwhile, prepare sauce by browning meat and minced garlic in oil.
4. Add remaining items and simmer 1 hour.
5. When beans are tender, add sauce and simmer ½ hour.

Serves 6-8.

Walter McIlhenney's Chili
¼ Cup Vegetable Oil
3 Lb. Beef Chuck; Lean, 1-Inch Cubes
1 Cup Onion; Chopped
3 Cloves Garlic; Minced
3 Tablespoons Chile powder
2 Teaspoons Cumin; Ground
2 Teaspoons Salt
2 Teaspoons Tabasco Sauce

3 Cups Water
4 Ounces Green Chiles; Chopped and Drained
As Needed Rice; Cooked
1 Medium Onion; Chopped
As Needed Cheese; Shredded
As Needed Sour Cream

1. In a 5-quart Dutch oven or heavy saucepan, heat the oil over medium-high heat.
2. In three batches, brown the beef well, removing each batch with a slotted spoon.
3. Set aside.
4. Add the onion and garlic to the pot and cook for 5 minutes, or until tender, stirring frequently.
5. Stir in the chile powder, cumin, salt, and Tabasco sauce; cook for 1 minute.
6. Add the water and chiles; bring to a boil.
7. Return the beef to the pot.
8. Reduce the heat and simmer uncovered, 1-½ hours, or until the beef is tender.

Serve the chili over rice with onion, cheese and sour cream, if desired.

Walter Mondale's Chili Con Carne

1 Medium Green Pepper; Chopped
4 Stalks Celery; Chopped
4 Medium Onions; Chopped
As Needed Cooking Oil
2 Slices Bacon; Optional
1 Lb. Ground Beef
1 Teaspoon Salt
1 Tablespoon Sugar
¼ Tablespoon Cloves
¼ Teaspoon Chile powder
1 Leaf Bay
1 Can (16 Ounce) Tomatoes
2 Cans (16 Ounce) Kidney Beans

1. Sauté green pepper, celery and onions in oil. (For more flavor, fry bacon and sauté veggies in drippings.)
2. Add ground beef and brown.

3. Add remaining ingredients and cook over low heat for 1 hour, stirring occasionally.
4. If you like it hotter, add more chile powder.

Mr. Mondale's favorite chili recipe will serve 6 people.

Wednesday Chili (Wendy's)
2 Tablespoons Oil
1-½ Lb. Ground Round
1 Can (10 Ounce) French Onion Soup; Not Creamy
1 Tablespoon Chile powder
2 Teaspoons Cumin; Ground
½ Teaspoon Pepper
1 Dash Tabasco
1 Can (21 Ounce.) Red Kidney Beans; Undrained
1 Can (6 Ounce) Tomato Paste
1 Can (8 Ounce) Tomato Sauce

1. Blend soup and spices in blender then add to browned meat.
2. Heat 20 min. on low.
3. Mash meat to rice size.
4. Add kidney beans, tomato paste and tomato sauce.
5. Heat thoroughly, about 30 minutes.

Steak and Shake Style: Stir in 2 t. Hershey's cocoa powder and 10 oz. Coke.

Wendy's Chili #1
1-½ Lb. Ground Beef
2 Teaspoons Vegetable Oil
1 Can Onion Soup
2 Teaspoons Chile powder
2 Teaspoons Cumin; Ground
½ Teaspoon Pepper
2 Teaspoons Cocoa
2 Cans Kidney Beans; Drained
6 Teaspoons Tomato Paste
15 Teaspoons Tomato Sauce
2 Teaspoons Brown Sugar
1 Teaspoon Vinegar
6 Cups V8 Juice

1. Brown beef in oil. Break meat into tiny rice size pieces.
2. Place onion soup and half of cooked beef into a blender and process on high speed until it resembles cement mortar.
3. Place with unblended beef into 2-½ qt. saucepan.
4. Add remaining ingredients and simmer until flavors are blended.

Servings: 6

Wendy's Chili #2
Top Secret Recipes Version
2 Lb. Ground Beef
1 Can (29 Ounce) Tomato Sauce
1 Can (29 Ounce) Kidney Beans; With Liquid
1 Can (29 Ounce) Pinto Beans; With Liquid
1 Cup Onion; Chopped (1 Medium Onion)
½ Cup Green Chile Peppers; Diced (2 Chiles)
¼ Cup Celery; Diced (1 Stalk)
3 Medium Tomatoes; Chopped
2 Teaspoons Cumin Powder
2 Tablespoons Chile powder
1-½ Teaspoons Black Pepper
2 Teaspoons Salt
2 Cups Water

Here's a favorite recipe for chili that clones the stuff served at the Wendy's chain. Dave Thomas, Wendy's founder, has been serving this chili since 1969; the year the first Wendy's opened its doors. Over the years the recipe has changed a bit, but this version here is an amazing copy of the version of chili served in the early 90's. Try topping it with some chopped onion and cheddar cheese, as you can request in the restaurant.

1. Brown the ground beef in a skillet over medium heat; drain off the fat.
2. Using a fork, crumble the cooked beef into pea-size pieces.
3. In a large pot, combine the beef plus all the remaining ingredients, and bring to a simmer over low heat. Cook, stirring every 15 minutes, for 2 to hours.

Makes about 12 servings.

Tidbits: For spicier chili, add ½ teaspoon more black pepper. For much spicier chili, add 1 teaspoon black pepper and a tablespoon cayenne pepper. And for a real stomach stinger, add 5 or 6 sliced Jalapeño peppers to the pot. Leftovers can be frozen for several months.

Wendy's Chili (Copycat)
2 Lb. Ground Beef
1 Can (29 Ounce) Tomato Sauce
1 Can (29 Ounce) Kidney Beans; With Liquid
1 Can (29 Ounce) Pinto Beans; With Liquid
1 Medium Onion; Diced
2 Pods Green Chiles; Diced
1 Ribs Celery; Diced
3 Medium Tomatoes; Chopped
2 Teaspoons Cumin Powder
3 Tablespoons Chile powder
1-½ Teaspoon Black Pepper
2 Teaspoons Salt
2 Cups Water

1. Brown the beef and drain the fat off.
2. Crumble the cooked beef into pea size pieces.
3. In a large pot, combine the beef plus the remaining ingredients and bring to a simmer over low heat.
4. Cook stirring every 15 minutes for 2-3 hours.

Chapter 11
Chili Recipes by Just Plain Old People

Background

While just about everyone has their own recipe for chili (I don't know a soul who claims to use a recipe to make chili), most haven't shared their recipe with the world. The Internet provides a grand way to tout the excellence of almost anything, and I have found that chili recipes are among the most posted information available. A simple search will produce hundreds of recipes with little effort. I have included a number of them here for posterity. Maybe next time, your recipe will be included. Enjoy!

A Working Woman's Chili
Michelle Bass
As Needed Olive Oil
1 Lb. Ground Round Beef
1 Cup Green Pepper; Diced
½ Cup Celery; Diced
1 Medium Onion; Chopped
1 Clove Garlic; Minced
½ Cup Black Olives; Extra Large
1 Can (15 Ounce) Kidney Beans
1 Can (11 Ounce) Tomatoes (Stewed)
2 Tablespoons Brown Sugar
1 Tablespoon Chile powder
1 Tablespoon Cumin
1 Pod Chile Pepper; Minced
2 Tablespoons Oregano Vinegar
1 Cup Water

1. Sauté ground round in a little olive oil, drain, set aside.
2. Sauté bell peppers, diced celery, onion and garlic until tender.
3. Add the remaining ingredients, except the cup of water.
4. Let simmer for approximately 15 minutes, add water and continue to simmer another 15 minutes. (Can adjust amount of water to whatever consistency desired.)

Notes: The oregano vinegar is made by steeping fresh oregano in white vinegar for at least 10 days, longer is better. Chile pepper; from a can of Chiles Chipotles Adobo plus 1 tablespoon sauce.

Aimee's Chili
Wayne Preston Allen
3-½ Lb. Ground Beef
1 Large Onion
40 Ounces Tomatoes Sauce
1 Large Bell pepper; diced
As Needed Corn Meal
To Taste Salt and Pepper
To Taste Tabasco Sauce
2 Tablespoons Chile powder
As Needed Water

1. Brown meat; add onion and sauté well.
2. Add tomato sauce, seasonings, bell pepper, and chile powder, salt and pepper to taste.
3. Add water until sauce is of desired thickness. Simmer 15-30 minutes.
4. During last 15 minutes of cooking, sprinkle in corn meal and stir.

Alicia's Chili
1 Cup Pinto Beans
1 Cup Kidney Beans
1 Can (Large) Tomatoes; Whole
1 Large Onion; Chopped
2 Cloves Garlic; Crushed
3 Tablespoons Parsley
2-½ Lb. Ground Beef; Coarse Ground
¼ Cup Chile powder; (Up to ½)
2 Tablespoons Salt
1-½ Teaspoons Pepper
1-½ Teaspoons Cumin Seed

1. Wash beans; soak overnight in water (enough to cover beans).
2. Next day, bring beans to a boil in same water and simmer until tender (about 2 to 3 hours).
3. Add tomatoes (I like to cut tomatoes in small chunks or puree them) and simmer a few minutes more.
4. In a large frying pan, fry onions and meat until brown.
5. Add parsley and garlic; stir in chile powder.
6. Add this meat mixture to beans and add spices. Simmer, covered, for at least 30 minutes.

Andrea's First Place Prize Winning Chili
8 Lb. Chili Grind Beef
2 Large Purple Onions; Finely Chopped
2 Medium Yellow Onions; Finely Chopped
2 Medium White Onions; Finely Chopped
1 Stick Butter
1 Bottle Mexene Chile powder
½ Can Gebhardt's Chili Powder
3 Cubes Knorr Beef Bouillon
½ Bottle McCormick's Ground Cumin
1/3 Bottle Garlic Juice

1. Sauté onions in butter a little at time (use about ¼ stick of butter for each batch of onions). Set sautéed onions aside.
2. Brown ground beef. Drain excess grease.
3. Put ground beef and onions together in a large stew pot.
4. Add next 5 ingredients and stir.
5. Add enough water to cover the meat about 1-½ inches. Bring to a boil. Lower heat, cover.
6. Cook over low heat, stirring frequently, for 2 or 3 hours, adding more water when necessary, and add salt to taste.
7. About 30 Minutes before serving, add: 2 teaspoons mustard and 2 teaspoons Heinz 57 Sauce.
8. About 30 minutes before judging, mix together the mustard and 57 Sauce. Stir into chili. Add a sprinkling of cumin. This makes the chili smell delicious. Put the lid back on, and let the chili simmer.

Andy Beal's Chili
Andrew Scott Beal, Lawrence Livermore National Laboratory
1-1/3 Kilograms Beans; Canned, Drained
1-½ Kilograms Stewed Tomatoes
1 Kilogram Beef; Cut in Bite Size Cubes
2 Cloves Garlic; Chopped
3 Medium Jalapeño Peppers; Cut Up
2 Medium Green Bell Peppers; Diced
1 Medium Onion; Diced, 1 to 2
1 Bottle Flavorful Beer
30 Ml. Cumin
10 Ml. Paprika
5 Ml. Cayenne Pepper

1. Sauté the meat and onions. You may do it in the same pan that you are going to put the chili in. The meat should be brown on the outside, but you don't have to cook it much at this time.
2. Drain the fat from the beef. Put everything in a big pot over low heat (a slow cooker is handy) and stir together.
3. Wait half an hour to an hour and check the flavor of the soupy base. Adjust as you see fit. Perhaps add more beer, hot peppers, or spices.
4. Wait as long as you can, stirring occasionally, until the beans and beef are soft. Serve with bread, fresh-baked biscuits or cornbread.

Author's Notes: This is the descendant of the chili that I've been making since 1974. This is best if it has cooked at least overnight. Generally it's ready for consumption after about three hours. If you can't turn your stove down to a very low heat, you're bound to burn the bottom of the chili a little, but as long as you don't scrape it off, it will taste okay. Slow-cookers are great in this regard! At the three hour mark, the chili is somewhat soupy. If you want it to thicken up, turn up the heat a bit and let it boil off the excess water. While doing this, stir every few minutes or you may burn the bottom! I change the proportions of ingredients (double the beef, drop the beans, add lots more cumin) all the time; this recipe is just a general guideline. The amount of garlic given in the recipe is very conservative. Garbanzo beans (chick peas) are nice, but they take a lot longer to cook. With lamb or Italian sausage instead of beef is also interesting. Cherry peppers instead of Jalapeño peppers are very nice also. Do not use wimpy American beer! I have found that Moosehead adds a good flavor, and I bet that Anchor Steam will too.

Andy's Chili
2 Lb. Beef; Ground
1 Cup Water
1 Can Tomato Puree
1 Can (Large) Tomatoes; Break Into Pieces
1 Teaspoon Salt
1 Teaspoon Pepper
½ Teaspoon Garlic Salt
½ Teaspoon Allspice
2 Leaves Bay
1 Package Chile powder
2 Cans Kidney Beans
1 Tablespoon Vinegar

Simmer 2 to 2-½ hours before adding beans. Cook until beans are heated.

Annie Little John's Chili
Annie Little John
5 Lb. Beef Roast
2 Lb. Soup Bones
As Needed Water
3 Lb. Pinto Beans; Cooked
4 Ounces Mexene Powder
½ Teaspoon Cumin Seeds
To Taste Salt
To Taste Cayenne Pepper
To Taste Pepper

1. Cook meat and soup bone separately until tender in enough water to keep covered.
2. Dice roast, strain stock, and add the cooked beans.
3. Stir in the Mexene and cumin seeds.
4. Add salt and pepper (black and red) to taste.
5. Cook very slowly over low flame 1 to 1-½ hours.

Ann's Homemade Chili
1 Lb. Hamburger Meat
2 Tablespoons Shortening
2 Tablespoons Flour
2 Cans Tomato Sauce
2 Tablespoons Mexene Chili powder
To Taste Salt and Pepper
1 Can Ro-tel Diced Tomato and Green Chile; In Blender, Optional
½ Medium Onion; Or
2 Tablespoons Onion Flakes; Optional

1. In 5-quart saucepan melt shortening. Brown hamburger and onions.
2. Add salt and pepper to taste.
3. Add flour and stir until well blended.
4. Add chile powder.
5. Add 2 cans tomato sauce, 4 cans water (using sauce can).
6. Add Ro-Tel tomatoes and simmer 30 minutes.

Ardouss' Chili
5 Cups Pinto Beans
1 Tablespoon Chile powder

1 Can Tomato Sauce; Or
1 Pint Tomato Juice
1 Tablespoon Honey
2 Lb. Hamburger
1 Teaspoon Salt
¼ Teaspoon Pepper
1 Medium Onion
1/8 Medium Green Pepper
1 Tablespoon Catsup

1. Cook beans in crock-pot on high for 5 hours until tender.
2. Fry hamburger until brown with onions and green peppers until tender.
3. Add tomato sauce, honey, salt, pepper, chile powder and beans.
4. Taste and if not spicy enough, add a drop of Tabasco sauce, if not sweet enough, add more honey.
5. If not sloppy enough add more water.

Aunt Linda's Chili
2 Lb. Hamburger &/or Sausage
1 Package Chili-O Seasoning Mix; (1 or 2)
2 Cans (10 Ounce) Tomato Soup
1 Can Water; More If You Like It Less
2 Cans (16 Ounce) Kidney Beans; With Juice
2 Cans Tomatoes (Stewed); With Juice
1 Small Onion; Chopped

1. Brown hamburger and/or sausage and onions. Drain.
2. Add rest of ingredients and simmer for 2 hours.
To double recipe: I use 5 pounds hamburger, 3 packages of Chili-O mix, 5 cans soup and double rest of ingredients.
    This serves 25 to 30 people.

Aunt Nina's Chili
1 Lb. Ground Beef
1 Can Elf Chili Style Beans
1 Medium Onion; Chopped
1 Can (8 Ounce) Tomato Sauce
12 Ounces Water
1-½ Tablespoons Chile powder
½ Teaspoon Salt

¼ Teaspoon Pepper
¼ Teaspoon Garlic; Minced

1. Brown ground beef, onions and garlic in small amount of cooking oil. Drain fat off of meat.
2. Mix in chili beans, tomato sauce, water and seasonings. Simmer for 30 minutes.

Serve with large round Fritos and green salad.

For Frito Chili Pie: Place ½ pint of Fritos in a greased casserole dish. Pour chili over Fritos and top with 1 cup of grated cheese. Bake at 350 degrees for 30 minutes.

Axeclan's Yankee Chili

2 Lb. Ground Beef; Lean
1 Can (Large) Tomatoes; Stewed
1 Large Red Onion
½ Bunch Celery; W/Leaves
1 Can Kidney Beans
2 Medium Bell Peppers; Or 3
3 Pods Jalapeño Peppers; To Taste
½ Bottle A-1 Steak Sauce
2/3 Jar Honey

1. In a large stewpot, brown ground beef and drain.
2. Add chopped onion, tomatoes, chopped celery, beans and chopped bell peppers, let cook for 30 minutes on medium low heat.
3. Chop Jalapeños very fine and add.
4. After 30 more minutes, add A-1 and honey.
5. Cook till everything is roughly the same color (2-½-3 hours).
6. Adjust liquid as needed.

Bear's Goat Gap Chili
James S. "Bear" Brady

2 Lb. Round Steak; Cubed
1 Lb. Pork; Cubed
1 Can (2.4 Ounce) Hot Chile powder
3 Medium Onions; Chopped
4 Cloves Garlic; Minced
3 Tablespoons Fat
1 Can (32 Ounce) Progresso Peeled Whole Tomatoes; Drained

1 Can (7 Ounce) Jalapeño Chile Peppers; Seeded and Chopped, or Less
3 Leaves Bay
1 Tablespoon Oregano
1 Tablespoon Salt
1 Pint Ripe Olives; Pitted, Chopped
1 Tablespoon Masa Harina (Corn Flour); Approximately
2 Tablespoons Brown Sugar
1 Tablespoon Red Wine Vinegar
1 Tablespoon Cumin

1. Brown meat in the fat.
2. Brown the onions, garlic and peppers.
3. Stir all except the flour, in a pot.
4. Cover and cook very slowly for several hours.
5. Add flour at end to bind chili. (Remove bay leaves before serving.)
Serve with grated Cheddar cheese on top.

   Serves 6. (Add "beans" if you wish. Mrs. Brady said "no," but I think it would be okay.)

Big Ed's Chili
1 Lb. Ground Beef
1 Can Kidney Beans
1 Can Tomatoes; Crushed
2 Cans (8 Ounce) Tomato Sauce
1 Medium Onion; Chopped
1 Medium Green Pepper; Diced
2 Tablespoons Chile powder
5 Drops Tabasco Sauce
1 Tablespoon Red Pepper

1. Brown ground beef and drain.
2. Sauté onion and peppers.
3. Combine all ingredients in large pot and simmer for one to several hours, stirring occasionally.

Big Mike's Chili
Mike Crouch
9 Pods New Mexican Red Chili; Dried
9 Pods California Red Peppers; Dried
1 Lb. Bacon; Finely Chopped

4 Medium Onions; Chopped
8 Cloves Garlic; Chopped, Fine
To Taste Louisiana Hot Sauce
To Taste Salt and Pepper
2 Lb. Pork Sausage
5 Lb. Beef; See Note
4 Cups Beef Broth; Fresh is Best
8 Ounces Tomatoes Sauce
2 Tablespoons White Vinegar
6 Tablespoons Cumin; Ground
2 Tablespoons New Mexican Chile Powder
1 Teaspoon Cayenne Pepper
1 Tablespoon Sugar
2 Tablespoons Paprika
2 Tablespoons Chile powder; Regular
1 Tablespoon MSG
1 Can Beer

Note: Use a real good cut like a cross rib roast and have your butcher grind it in "chili grind" dried. Rule #1 in Chili Cookoffs: If you know beans about chili, you know chili ain't got no beans! This recipe is a lot of work, but well worth it!

1. Oregano Tea (bring 2 c water to boil; add 2 tablespoons of dried oregano leaves. Brew like tea; stain, reserving liquid).
2. Remove the stems, seeds, and veins from peppers; add to boiling water 30 minutes. Use a knife and strip meat off peppers, discard skins; put into food processor with enough beer to make the consistency of tomato sauce.
3. Divide the bacon, garlic, onions, sausage and beef into thirds. We are going to fry up the mixture 1/3 at a time.
4. Fry up the bacon (mostly for grease) until just about crisp.
5. Add garlic, and after 30 seconds, add onions, hot sauce to taste, salt and pepper.
6. When the onions are translucent, add the sausage.
7. When about half cooked, add beef.
8. When the mixture is about medium, drain the grease and refry until well done (this sears the meat and keeps the flavor in).
9. When done, put into pot. Repeat for next 1/3 and last 1/3.
10. Stir in the pepper paste (from above), broth, and tomato sauce. Take your time--over low heat.

11. Then add the remaining ingredients, one at a time, slowly.
12. Add enough beer to keep the consistency to your liking.
13. Now adjust the spices like a real expert!
14. Cook over low heat 2+ hours, and you'll have one fine bowl of red! Enjoy!

Big Red's Chili
Don D. 'RED' Caldwell
6 Lb. Chuck; Very Lean, Coarse Grind
6 Cloves Garlic; Crushed
16 Ounces Tomato Sauce
6 Tablespoons Chile powder; Dark Ancho
¼ Teaspoon Habañero Pepper Sauce; Optional
1 Pod Red Chile Pepper
1-½ Teaspoons Salt
1 Teaspoon White Pepper
1-½ Teaspoons Oregano
1 Tablespoon Garlic Powder
2 Large Onions; Minced
6 Pods Jalapeño Chile Peppers; Stemmed
1 Quart Beef Broth
4 Tablespoons Cumin; Ground
6 Tablespoons Light New Mexico Chile powder
2 Tablespoons Paprika
1 Teaspoon Cayenne Pepper
1 Tablespoon MSG

1. Brown meat in skillet, drain and put in large, (7 quart) pot.
2. Add onions, garlic, jalapeños (stemmed and pierced), 1 can tomato sauce, beef broth, dark chile powder, 2 tablespoons cumin and Habañero sauce if desired.
3. Bring to a low boil, cover and cook 45 minutes, adding a little water as necessary.
4. Add light chile powder, 1 can tomato sauce, 2 tablespoons cumin and remaining ingredients.
5. Simmer covered 45 minutes.
6. Adjust salt to taste and serve with cold beer.
Don D. 'Red' Caldwell's favorite recipe for eating chili. San Antonio Express-News Aug 1, 1990.

Bill Klecka's Championship Chili, 1982
2 Tablespoons Shortening; Crisco
½ Cup Onion; Chopped
¼ Cup Green Pepper; Chopped
1 Lb. Ground Beef
16 Ounces Tomato Sauce
1 Can (16 Ounce) Caliente-Style Kidney Beans
1 Teaspoon Salt
2 Teaspoons Chile powder
To Taste Cumin; Optional

1. Brown onion, pepper and beef in a skillet.
2. Add tomato sauce and cook for 5 minutes.
3. Add remaining ingredients and simmer for 15 to 30 minutes to develop the flavor.
4. Adjust seasonings to your personal taste.
5. The flavor improves by making this a day in advance and letting it sit in the refrigerator.

Serves 4 to 6.

Bill's Gallons Of Chili
6 Lb. Ground Beef
2 Large Onions; Chopped
1 Large Green Peppers; Chopped
2 Cans (30 Ounce) Chili Beans
2 Cans (30 Ounce) Tomato Sauce
1 Can (12 Ounce) Tomato Paste
1 Teaspoon Salt and Pepper; To Taste
3 Tablespoons Chile powder; To Taste

1. Brown meat with enough vegetable oil to keep from burning.
2. Add chopped onions and pepper, salt, pepper and chile powder.
3. Add tomato sauce, paste and chili beans, undrained.
4. Add 1-quart water plus rinse cans with water and cook over a medium to low heat for 1-½ hours.
5. Stir occasionally to keep from sticking.
6. Store cooled chili in containers or freezer bags.

This makes good 3-way chili, sauce for chilidogs or a good bowl of hearty chili.

Black Bean Chili From Katherine Smith
San Francisco Chronicle
1 Lb. Black Turtle Beans
1 Tablespoon Cumin Seeds
1 Tablespoon Oregano
2 Cups Onion; Chopped
1 Tablespoon Olive Oil
1 Cup Red Bell Pepper; Chopped
1 Cup Green Bell Pepper; Chopped
4 Pods Jalapeño Chiles; Seeded and Minced
1 Tablespoon Garlic; Minced
2 Leaves Bay
2 Teaspoons Epazote; Crushed-Optional
12 Ounces Beer
1 Can (28 Ounce) Tomatoes; Crushed-With Puree
1 Can (6 Ounce) Tomato Puree
5 Tablespoons Red Chile; Ground
2 Teaspoons Salt
1 Lb. Top Sirloin Steak; Grilled or Broiled and Cubed
¼ Cup Cilantro; Minced

1. Sort through beans and discard any stones. Wash beans in a sieve under cold running water.
2. Put beans in a pot with 6 cups water. Bring to a boil and simmer 3 minutes. Turn off heat, cover and let soak 1 hour.
3. Return to heat and bring to a simmer; cook 1 hour.
4. Meanwhile, toast the cumin seeds in a small pan until they become fragrant, about 2 minutes. Then add the oregano and toast for 1 minute. Be careful not to burn.
5. Pulverize the seeds and oregano in a spice grinder.
6. Sauté the onion in the olive oil for 5 minutes, and then add the bell peppers, Jalapeños and garlic.
7. Sauté 5 minutes longer until the vegetables are quite wilted.
8. Add the spices and half the beer.
9. Simmer until the beer is reduced by a third. Add remaining beer.
10. When the beans are just tender but not falling apart, add the vegetable-beer mixture, the tomato puree and paste, and the chile powder.
11. Simmer 1 hour, then add salt to taste and the sirloin cubes; simmer 15 minutes longer.

Ladle into serving bowls and garnish with minced cilantro.

Blackwelders' Chili Recipe
½ Lb. Pinto Beans; 1 Cup
5 Lb. Tomatoes; Canned
1 Lb. Green Pepper; Chopped
1-½ Tablespoons Salad Oil
1-½ Lb. Onion; Chopped
2 Cloves Garlic; Chopped
½ Cup Parsley; Chopped
½ Cup Butter
2-½ Lb. Ground Chuck
1 Lb. Ground Pork; Lean
1/3 Cup Chile powder
2 Tablespoons Salt
1-½ Teaspoons Pepper
1-½ Teaspoons Cumin Seed
1-½ Teaspoons Monosodium Glutamate; MSG

1. Wash beans and soak overnight in water. Simmer, uncovered, in same water until tender.
2. Add tomatoes and simmer 5 minutes.
3. Sauté green pepper in salad oil 5 minutes.
4. Add onion, cook until tender, stirring often.
5. Add garlic and parsley.
6. Melt butter and sauté meat 15 minutes, stirring and turning until red color is gone.
7. Add to onion mixture.
8. Stir in chile powder and cook 10 minutes.
9. Add this to beans.
10. Add all to beans and add spices.
11. Simmer, covered, for 1 hour.
12. Cook 30 minutes uncovered.
13. Skim excess fat, if any, from top.

Now sit down and eat a bowl of the best damn chili you have ever tasted.

Blake's Favorite Chili
Blake Brown
3 Lb. Ground Beef or Brisket w/Fat Remove; Cubed or Coarse Ground
3 Ounces Sausage
As Needed Fresh Lard From a Good Butcher; Wesson Oil or Kidney Suet
½ Ounce Salt

2 Ounces Gebhardt's Chili Powder
½ Ounce Dark Red Chile powder
½ Teaspoon New Mexican Chile powder; Hot
½ Ounce Cumin; Ground
1 See Note Oregano Tea
To Taste White Pepper
7 Cloves Garlic; Minced, or 8
2 Large White Onions; Chopped Finely
4 Ounces Hunt's Tomatoes Sauce; 4 to 6 Ounces
8 Ounces Beef Broth; Add Water if Necessary
2 Pods Green Chile Peppers (Ortega or Old El Paso; Seeded & Chopped)
¼ Teaspoon Cayenne Pepper
1 Dash Tabasco Sauce
1 Teaspoon Brown Sugar; 1 or 2
Note: Oregano tea, Steep 1-tablespoon oregano leaves in ½ cup hot water.

1. In the large pot the chili will cook in, sauté onions and garlic in lard or other fat until the onions are limp, then add the chile powder, mix well.
2. In a separate pan, brown beef, a pound at a time, pepper (white pepper) while browning, use a little beef broth to keep from sticking.
3. Add browned beef to onions and garlic.
4. Sauté sausage and peeled chopped green chiles for 2-3 minutes, add to pot and cook about 15 minutes.
5. Add remaining spices, Hunt's Tomato Sauce, broth-water, sugar and mix well.
6. Cook about 30 minutes then add oregano tea.
7. Cook about 2 hours or until meat is tender, stirring occasionally.
8. Add salt and cayenne pepper.
9. Simmer for several hours.

Blue-Ribbon Chili (Dottie's Winner)
Dorothy Cross
1-½ Teaspoons Cumin Seeds
5-½ Lb. Beef Brisket; Cut in ¾ Inch Cubes
To Taste Salt and Black Pepper; Fresh Ground
6 Cloves Garlic; Minced
4 Milligrams Jalapeños; Finely Chopped (Or More)
2 Medium Onions; Finely Chopped
½ Cup Commercial Chili Powder; See Note
3 Tablespoons Pure Red Mild Chile Powder; Such As Dark New Mexico

1-½ Teaspoons Coriander; Ground
1 Can (12 Ounce) Beer
6 Cups Beef Stock, Canned Broth; Or Water
1 Can (42 Ounce) Italian Plum Tomatoes, Peeled; Coarsely Chopped, Undrained
1-½ Teaspoons Oregano; Crumbled
½ Lb. Beef Chuck; Coarse Ground
2 Scallions; White and Tender Green Part

1. In a small dry skillet, toast the cumin seeds over moderate heat, stirring constantly, until fragrant, about 2 minutes. Grind the cumin in a spice mill or a mortar.
2. Heat a large enameled cast-iron casserole.
3. Season the brisket with salt and pepper.
4. Working in batches, add the meat to the casserole and cook over moderately high heat until well browned all over, about 8 minutes. Transfer each batch to a large plate.
5. Add the garlic, Jalapeños and onions to the casserole and cook over moderate heat, stirring occasionally, until softened, about 4 minutes.
6. Add the commercial chili powder and pure red chile powder, coriander and half of the ground cumin and cook, stirring, for 2 minutes.
7. Return the cooked brisket to the casserole and add the beef stock, beer, tomatoes and their liquid, and the oregano.
8. Bring to a boil over moderately high heat, then lower the heat and simmer gently, stirring occasionally, for 3 hours.
9. Stir in the ground chuck, season with salt and cook until the brisket is very tender and the sauce is thickened, about 1 hour longer.
10. Stir in the remaining cumin and simmer for 15 minutes.
    Garnish with the scallions and serve.
Note: Rather than the commercial chili, you can use Reno Red Chili Mix, available by mail order from Stewart's Chili Company, P. O. Box 574, San Carlos, CA 94070.

Bo Pilgrims' Chicken Chili
2 Lb. Fryer; Boneless
2 Large Onions; Chopped
3 Cloves Garlic; Chopped
¼ Cup Cooking Oil
1 Can (8 Ounce) Tomato Sauce
3 Cups water

2 Tablespoons Flour
2 Teaspoons Salt
4 Tablespoons Cumin; Ground
1 Teaspoon Sugar
¼ Teaspoon Cayenne Pepper
1 Tablespoon Black Pepper
1 Tablespoon Paprika
5 Tablespoons Chile powder

1. Using a kitchen meat processor, coarsely grind a 2-pound Pilgrim's Pride boneless chicken.
2. In a kettle, sauté onions and garlic in oil until done.
3. Add ground chicken and braise.
4. Add water and tomato sauce.
5. Add remaining ingredients. Mix well.
6. Cover and simmer 4 hours.
Makes 8 servings of 2/3 cup each.

Bob's Chili
1 Lb. Ground Beef; Lean
1 Small Carrot; Diced
½ Stick Celery; Sliced Thin (Garnish)
1 Large Garlic
3 Medium Onions; Sliced
1 Can (46 Ounce) Tomato Juice
1 Can Kidney Beans
1 Can Hot or Chili Beans
2 Teaspoons Chile powder
½ Teaspoon Basil
1 Tablespoon Worcestershire Sauce

1. Brown ground beef in large pot.
2. Add carrot and celery.
3. In separate pan in small amount of bacon grease or oil, sauté, garlic and discard.
4. Add onions and sauté, until glassy.
5. Add to meat mixture in large pot.
6. Add the tomato juice, beans and remaining of ingredients into large pot.
7. Simmer for one hour.

Bob's Chili With Macaroni
1-½ Cups Macaroni
2 Lb. Ground Chuck
1 Large Onion
1 Can Chili Beans
1 Can Tomato Sauce
1 Can Tomatoes With Chiles
4 Tablespoons Chile powder; Or More
To Taste Salt and Pepper
4 Tablespoons Sugar
6 Cups Water
1 Tablespoon Margarine

1. Cook onion in large skillet until half done or cook in microwave oven.
2. Add ground chuck. Cook until done. Drain off grease.
3. Add tomato sauce, tomato chiles, chile powder, salt, and pepper and 1 cup water.
4. Let simmer for 30 minutes in large pot.
5. Add 6 cups water. Bring to boil.
6. Add salt and 1-tablespoon margarine.
7. Add macaroni. Cook until tender.
8. Drain off water.
9. Add all ingredients from skillet.
10. Add beans and sugar. Let simmer for 1 hour.
11. If too thick add water.
12. Season to taste.

Bo's Famous Chili
4 Lb. Chili Meat; Only Yankees Use Hamburger
2 Medium Onions; Chopped
2 Pods Jalapeño Peppers; Sliced
1 Tablespoon Cooking Oil
2 Tablespoons New Mexican Chile Pepper; Fresh Ground
1-½ Teaspoon Salt; Or Substitute
½ Teaspoon Comino; (Cumin)
½ Teaspoon Oregano; Ground
½ Teaspoon Black Pepper; Ground
4 Pods Garlic, Fresh; Smashed, Not Chopped
16 Ounces Tomato Juice
2 Tablespoons Masa Harina (Corn Flour); Or Flour Or Cornstarch

6 Ounces Water
2 Tablespoons Red Chile powder
1-½ Teaspoons Cayenne

1. Brown meat in oil until gray, pour off grease.
2. Add all the seasonings with the water. Simmer for about an hour or until almost dry.
3. Add the tomato juice (purists don't use tomato juice). Simmer another 30 minutes.
4. Add thickener with a little water.
5. Stir well for smoothness.
Serves about 16.

Brother Dave's Chili
3 Lb. Stew Meat; See Note 1
To Taste Black Pepper
1 Tablespoon Salt
2 Large Onions; Chopped
2 Teaspoons Paprika
2 Teaspoons Oregano
1 Can (12 Ounce) Tomato Sauce
½ Cup Masa Harina (Corn Flour)
1 Tablespoon Red Pepper; Dried, See Note 2
1 Dash Pehchaud's Bitters
1 Tablespoon Corn Oil; If Needed
½ Cup Chile powder
3 Medium Bell Peppers; Chopped
2 Teaspoons Ground Comino and Seeds
2 Teaspoons Cayenne Pepper
2 Cups Chicken Stock; Or Your Choice
6 Whole Tomatoes; Sliced Up
1 Can (48 Ounce) V-8 Juice
To Taste Japanese Chile Peppers
1 Pinch Nutmeg
3 Cloves Garlic; Large, Chopped, Up to 6
2 Leaves Magnolia; Minced, Up to 3

Note 1: Or chuck roast coarse chopped.
Note 2: Santa Fe variety works here.

1. Brown the meat; work in the spices, onions, and peppers.
2. Simmer about 30 minutes or until it looks good.
3. Add tomato sauce, tomatoes, and broth and simmer several hours until it looks good.
4. Add the Masa to thicken the mix and when it's ready, add the Peychaud's and nutmeg to set it off.
5. You'll know it's ready when you can't identify anything in the pot. (Get rid of those bay leaf stems.)

This really goes good with cornbread, but what doesn't?

Bud's Sunday Afternoon Football Chili
Bud Cloyd

1 Lb. Beef; (Tip Steak) Cubed
1 Lb. Beef; Ground
2 Medium Onions; Coarse Chopped
2 Small Green Peppers; Chopped Medium
½ Cup Burgundy
6 Tablespoons Chile Powder; Mexene
4 Tablespoons Cumin
3 Centiliters Garlic; Small
1 Teaspoon Oregano
1 Tablespoon Cilantro Leaves
2 Tablespoons Hot Sauce; LaPreferida
1 Teaspoon Sugar
2 Dashes Salt
1 Can Tomatoes; Peeled, With Juice
1 Can (16 Ounce) Tomatoes (Stewed)
1 Can (8 Ounce) Tomato Sauce
1 Can (15.5 Ounce) Chili Hot Beans

1. Brown meat with 1 of the chopped onions. Drain grease.
2. Place meat onions, remainder of onions, green peppers, and the rest of the ingredients into stockpot. Bring to boil.
3. Reduce heat and simmer 1 or 2 hrs, covered.
4. Cool 1 hour.
5. Reheat before serving.

Concocted by Bud Cloyd (who had nothing better to do on a particular Sunday afternoon).

Butch's Camp Chili
3 Lb. Ground Chuck
2 Cans (Large) Kidney Beans; Or 3
2 Cans (Large) Tomatoes
1 Large Green Pepper
2 Medium Onions
6 Slices Bacon; Or 7
1 Tablespoon Chile powder; Or 2
2 Tablespoons Vinegar
4 Tablespoons Sugar
To Taste Salt and Pepper

1. Cut bacon into small pieces and fry.
2. Chop the green pepper and onion and add to the bacon.
3. Add the ground meat to this mixture and brown.
4. Then add kidney beans, tomatoes, chile powder, vinegar and sugar. Simmer for at least 1 hour.
5. Stir often to prevent sticking.
Chili may be served alone or on a bed of rice.
    Variation: Diced potatoes or elbow macaroni may be added to chili. This is a good budget stretcher.

C.W. Gregg's Chili
1 Lb. Hamburger Meat
As Needed Chile Pods; Dried
½ Cup Water; Warm
1 Tablespoon Oregano
1 Teaspoon Cumin
1 Clove Garlic; Chopped
4 Tablespoons Flour
1 Can (Large) Tomato Sauce
¼ Cup Red Wine Vinegar

1. Hint: to test chile pod's heat, take a small nibble of dry chile in your mouth, when cooked, it will about double in strength.
2. Brown hamburger meat in large skillet.
3. While browning, make chile paste.
4. Take 6-8 dried chile pods, remove some seeds, and leave some in for flavor. Remove stems.
5. Put in blender with about ½ cup warm water or so just enough to make a

paste. Too wet will be difficult.

6. When hamburger meat is browned, drain fat.
7. Add chile paste, oregano, cumin and garlic cloves.
8. Add salt to taste.
9. Brown mixture well, Don't burn!
10. Add 4 tablespoons of flour. Brown this, immediately remove from heat.
11. In another large saucepan, add tomato sauce and red wine.
12. Add browned mixture.
13. Simmer, simmer, simmer (3 hours or more) you can do this in slow cooker.
14. Thin if necessary, salt to taste, adjust cumin and oregano as needed, these flavors strengthen with cooking (cumin tends to add a sweet hint of taste). Salt enhances all flavors.

Hint: Buy more tomato sauce than you need, if chili is too hot when done, add more tomato sauce.

Serve with sour cream, grated mild cheddar cheese or whatever you like.
Hint: Drink iced tea with chili; it's the best beverage for hot mouth!

Carlota Robinson's Weird Chili
The County Fair Cookbook

1-½ Lb. Chuck; Ground
1-½ Lb. Pork Sausage; Lean, Casing Removed
2 Large Onions; Chopped
6 Centiliters Garlic; Minced
2 Tablespoons Sugar
1 Tablespoon Cocoa Powder; Unsweetened
¼ Cup Chile powder; Hot, Use Less
1 Tablespoon Cumin; Ground
1 Tablespoon Paprika
To Taste Black Pepper; Fresh Ground
2 Cans Kidney Beans
2 Cans Tomato Sauce
2 Cans Tomatoes; Crushed
1 Can Tomato Paste; Diluted With
1 Can Water
1 Can Beer

1. In large stewpot, cook the meat and onions over moderate heat until the meat loses its red color.
2. Drain off the fat and return the pot to the stove.

3. Stir in the remaining ingredients.
4. Cover the pot and simmer 4 hours, or all day long.
5. Check often and lower the heat if the chili boils; if the liquid is cooking away too fast, add a little water.

Serve with garlic cheese toast.

Recipe provided in the section from Dade County Youth Fair and Exposition, Miami, Florida. Fair is held mid-March for 18 days.

Carol's Favorite Vegetarian Chili
Carol Verge
1 Large Onion; Chopped
3 Cloves Garlic; Crushed and Pressed
2 Tablespoons Oil
1 Ribs Celery; Diced
1-½ Teaspoons Chile powder
1 Teaspoon Cumin
½ Teaspoon Cayenne Pepper
1 Cup Tomato; Chopped
2 Tablespoons Tomato Paste
4 Cups Beans (Kidney, Black, Pinto); Cooked
½ Lb. Tofu; Crumbled-Optional
1-½ Teaspoons Salt
1 Teaspoon Oregano

1. Sauté onion and garlic in oil until onion is soft.
2. Add celery and spices. Sauté another 2-3 minutes.
3. Add tomato and paste.
4. Mash 2 cups of the beans and add beans and tofu to the pot along with the salt and oregano. Simmer 30 minutes.

To cook raw beans:
1. Soak beans in water overnight, or boil for 2 minutes and let sit, covered, for 1 hour.
2. Bring to a boil in same water, simmer about 1 hour or until tender. (Beans approximately double in volume, i.e., two cups raw = 4 cups cooked.)

Notes: I like cooking my own beans rather than buying canned beans. I use as many different beans as I have at home. Usually at least 3 of the 4 mentioned, and one of the 3 must be black beans because they are my absolute favorite. Add or subtract cayenne pepper for hotness level. A bit more cumin may be good too; I have yet to determine this, though.

Casa Gonzales' Chili Beans
2 Lb. Pinto Beans
1 Can (Large) Tomatoes; Whole
1 Lb. Ground Beef; Extra Lean
1 Lb. Pork Sausage; Ground
1 Large Bell Pepper
1 Large Onion
½ Jar (3 Ounce) Gebhardt's Chili Powder
2 Tablespoons Cumin Seeds; Ground
2 Teaspoons Garlic Powder
2 Teaspoons Salt
¼ Cup Oil

1. Pick beans and wash in cold water. Use large pot to cook beans in 8 cups of water; add salt.
2. Beans should cook about 2-½ hours. If beans need more water, use boiling water.
3. Brown ground beef; drain all grease.
4. Add chopped onion.
5. Cook pork sausage and drain all grease.
6. Add finely chopped pepper when beans have cooked an hour.
7. Add oil, tomatoes and meats.
8. Make paste from chili powder with juice from beans.
9. Add to beans and stir well.
10. Add ground cumin seed; continue to cook for ½ hour.
Serve with crusty bread and a tossed green salad. What a meal. Enjoy!
    Serves 6.

Chapians Chili
1 Lb. Sausage
1 Lb. Pinto Beans; Dried
2 Cans (16 Ounce) Tomatoes
1 Lb. Green Peppers; Seeded and Coarsely Chopped
1-½ Lb. Onions; Chopped
1-½ Tablespoons Salad Oil
2 Cloves Garlic; Crushed
½ Cup Parsley; Finely Chopped
½ Cup Butter
2-½ Lb. Ground Chuck
1 Lb. Ground Pork; Or

1 Lb. Jimmy Dean Sausage
½ Cup Chile powder
2 Tablespoons Salt
1-½ Teaspoons Pepper
1-½ Teaspoons Cumin; Ground

1. Wash beans. Place in pan. Add water 2-inches above beans and soak overnight. Simmer covered in same water until tender.
2. Add tomatoes and simmer 5 minutes.
3. Sauté peppers slowly in salad oil 5 minutes.
4. Add onions and cook until tender.
5. Add garlic and parsley.
6. In large skillet, melt butter and sauté beef and pork for 15 minutes.
7. Add meat to onion mixture.
8. Stir in chile powder and cook 10 minutes.
9. Add this mixture to beans and season with salt, pepper and cumin. Simmer covered 1 hour.
10. Remove cover and cook 30 minutes longer.
11. Skim fat off top.

Charlie's Chili
2 Medium Green peppers
2 Cans (Large) Tomatoes
4 Cans Brook's Hot & Spicy Chili Beans; 4 or 5
5 Stalks Celery; 5 or 6
1-½ Teaspoons Chile powder; Up to 3
2 Medium Onions
1 Lb. Hamburger
5 Pods Hot Peppers-Cubanella or Habañero; 5 or 6

1. Brown hamburger.
2. In large pot combine hamburger, onions, celery, peppers and tomatoes.
3. Cook on top of stove about 45 to 60 minutes.
4. Add beans and put in oven for about 30 minutes at very low temperature, about 325 degrees.

Charlie's Chuck Wagon Chili
1/2 Lb. Bacon
1-½ Lb. Ground Chuck
4 Medium Onions; Chopped

1 Medium Green Pepper; Chopped, Optional
4 Cloves Garlic; Cut Up
4 Tablespoons Chile powder
To Taste Salt
2 Tablespoons Brown Sugar
2 Quarts Tomatoes; Stewed
1 Can (Large) Tomato Juice
1 Can Red Kidney Beans

1. Cut up bacon in small pieces and brown in large skillet.
2. Drain off fat except 2 tablespoons brown onions and beef in bacon drippings.
3. Add garlic.
4. In large kettle, put tomatoes, juice and meat mixture.
5. Add chile powder, sugar and salt to taste; simmer for 1-½ hours.
6. Add kidney beans last ½ hour.

Charm's Chili
2 Lb. Ground Beef
1 Medium Onion; Chopped Fine
1 Cup Celery; Chopped
1 Cup Green Pepper; Chopped
1 Tablespoon Chile powder
1 Can (Large) Tomato Juice
To Taste Salt and Pepper
1 Teaspoon Sugar
1 Tablespoon Flour
1 Can Chili Beans; Optional

1. Brown ground beef (drain fat).
2. Sauté onions with beef.
3. Add tomato juice, salt and pepper, chile powder, sugar and flour. Simmer for about one hour.
4. Add celery and green pepper. Simmer another 15 minutes.
5. If you desire add chili beans. Cook until heated.
Serve with shredded cheese and chopped onions.

Chester's Choice Chili
1 Medium Onions; Diced, Up to 2
1 Clove Garlic; Diced

1 Medium Green Pepper; Diced
2 Cans Kidney Beans
1 Lb. Ground Beef; Or Diced Stew Beef
2 Cans (6 Ounce) Tomato Paste
1 Can (16 Ounce) Tomatoes; Optional
To Taste Chile powder
To Taste Salt and Pepper
The following seasonings are optional: Bay leaf, celery salt, basil, hot sauce, sugar, rosemary, cayenne pepper, garlic salt, oregano, onion salt or vinegar.

1. In a 12-inch skillet sauté the onion, green pepper and garlic in a little fat or oil until cooked to the degree desired.
2. Add the ground beef and cook, mashing and mixing it well with a large fork.
3. Drain off most of the fat, after the meat is done.
4. Add the spices (but no sugar or vinegar). Mix well and set aside.
5. Into a 4-quart saucepan pour the beans, tomato paste and tomatoes.
6. Add 1 to 2 bean cans full of water, depending upon how thick or thin you want your chili.
7. Add the meat mixture and mix thoroughly. Bring to a boil and then simmer, stirring frequently.
8. Taste test from time to time; if the tomato flavoring is too strong, add a little sugar; if it tastes too sweet, pour in some vinegar (be very sparing with the sugar and vinegar).
9. Have a good time adding any or all of the spices and seasonings to taste. This makes a delicious meal or snack in itself with crackers or toast.

Chili A La Franey
1 Tablespoon Olive Oil
1 Lb. Beef; Very Lean, Coarse Grind
1 Lb. Pork; Very Lean, Coarse Grind
3 Large Onions; Chopped Finely
1 Single Bell Pepper
2 Stalks Celery; Chopped Finely
1 Tablespoon Garlic; Chopped Finely
1 Tablespoon Oregano, Dried; Preferably Mexican
2 Leaves Bay
2 Teaspoons Cumin; Ground
3 Cups Tomatoes; With Tomato Paste
1 Cup Beef Broth

1 Cup Water
To Taste Salt
To Taste Pepper; Freshly Ground
½ Teaspoon Chile Caribe
2 Tablespoons Red Chile; Ground (Mild-Hot)
2 Cups Kidney Beans; Cooked and Drained

1. If possible, have the beef and pork ground together, or else mix meats together in a bowl.
2. Heat the oil in a large heavy pot over medium heat. Add the meat to the pot.
3. Break up any lumps with a fork and cook, stirring occasionally, until the meat is evenly browned.
4. Add the onions, green pepper, celery, garlic, oregano, bay leaves, and cumin. Mix well.
5. Add the tomatoes, broth, water, salt, pepper, Caribe, and ground chile.
6. Bring to a boil, then lower heat and simmer, uncovered, for about 20 minutes. Stir often.
7. Add the beans and simmer for 10 minutes longer.
8. Taste and adjust seasonings.

Chili Carol Sharp
1 Lb. Ground Beef; Browned and Drained
1 Medium Onion; Diced
1 Small Green Pepper; Diced
1 Can (No. 1) Tomatoes; Diced
1 Can (No. 1) Chili Beans
1 Can (Small) Tomato Paste
½ Cup Red Wine
1 Package Chili Seasoning Mix
1 Tablespoon Chile powder

Mix everything together in the crockpot and cook on low 6 or more hours. This is really good with some cheese stirred in just before serving and a dab of sour cream on top.

Chili Created By Mr. B.
3 Lb. Ground Beef
1 Medium Onion; Diced
¼ Cup Green Bell Peppers

¼ Cup Red Bell Peppers
2 Cans (16 Ounce) Red Kidney Beans
1 Cup Tomatoes (Stewed)
1 Cup Tomato Sauce; 6 Ounces.
1 Package Chili-O Seasoning Mix
1 Teaspoon Chile powder
½ Teaspoon Garlic Powder
1 Teaspoon Cumin
1 Pinch Cinnamon; No More
To Taste Salt and Pepper
½ Teaspoon Sweetener
2 Cups Water

1. Fry ground beef, diced onion, green and red bell peppers until meat is well done.
2. Drain thoroughly. Be sure to stir while frying.
3. Combine all the remaining ingredients with the fried beef and cook for about 1 hour on simmering flame, stirring occasionally.

Now, the secret ingredient, I use small, dried chile peppers to give it a "kick"; 1 pepper for a mild lady's chili, 2 peppers for a man's chili and 3 peppers for a "hot Mexican chili!" Ole!

Chili Florence Style
3 Lb. Hamburger
1 Medium Onion; Diced
1 Clove Garlic
1 Teaspoon Tabasco
2 Tablespoons Chile powder
1 Tablespoon Oregano
1 Tablespoon Cumin Powder
1 Teaspoon Salt
1 Teaspoon Cayenne
2 Cans Red Kidney Beans
1 Teaspoon Paprika
2 Small Chile Peppers
2 Cans Tomato Juice

1. Brown hamburger.
2. Add onion and garlic.
3. Add other ingredients and simmer.

Chili John's Hot Chili
2 Lb. Hamburger
1 Teaspoon Cumin Seed
3 Tablespoons Flour
½ Teaspoon Pepper
¼ Cup Chile powder
1 Teaspoon Salt
4 Cups Water
½ Teaspoon Red Pepper
1 Teaspoon Garlic Salt

1. Fry hamburger and garlic salt for 15 minutes.
2. Mix in spices, flour and water. Cover and cook 15 minutes more.
3. Cook spaghetti and beans separately.
4. First put spaghetti then beans in bowl.
5. Top with meat mixture.
I use Brooks red-hot beans.

Chili Krieghauser
2 Lb. Ground Beef
½ Teaspoon Salt
1 Can Onion Soup; Condensed
1 Tablespoon Chile powder; Or More To Taste
2 Teaspoons Cumin
½ Teaspoon Black Pepper; Ground
2 Cans (8 Ounce) Tomato Sauce
1 Can (21 Ounce) Kidney Beans
2 Teaspoons Cocoa
8 Ounces Coke

1. Brown ground beef for 20 minutes, or until dark and crumbly. Pour off excess fat.
2. Add salt, onion soup, chile powder, cumin, pepper and tomato sauce.
3. Simmer for a while, and then add undrained kidney beans, cocoa and Coke. Simmer until ready.

Chili Mike Van Pelt
1 Leaf Bay
2 Cups Black Or Red Bans; Soaked, Up to 3
4 Teaspoons Cumin

4 Teaspoons Oregano
4 Teaspoons Paprika
½ Teaspoon Cayenne Pepper
To Taste Ground New Mexico Chile powder; However Much Looks Good
To Taste Gebhardt's Chili Powder; However Much Looks Good
To Taste Chile Negro or Chile Ancho
As Needed Peanut Oil
2 Large Onions; Chopped
4 Cloves Garlic; Minced, Up to 6
To Taste Salt
4 Cups Tomatoes; Chopped, Fresh, Peeled or
1 Teaspoon Chipotle Peppers; Chopped, Up to 2
¼ Cup Red Wine
1 Tablespoon Vinegar; Wine, Cider, Rice, Up to

1. Cover beans and bay leaf with 2 inches of fresh water, bring to boil. Lower heat and simmer.
2. Toast cumin and oregano over med. heat, stirring so they don't burn.
3. When they're fragrant, add paprika, cayenne, and chile powders toast a few seconds. Remove from heat.
4. Then grind with mortar and pestle.
5. Dry the chile Negro or Ancho in a hot oven (400) for a few minutes. Cool and remove stem, seeds, and veins.
6. Shred it and then grind in food processor, blender, etc.
7. Sauté onion in oil till soft, add garlic, salt, ground herbs and chile, and cook 5 min.
8. Add tomato, juice, 1-teaspoon chipotle, and some red wine, cook about 20 min.
9. Add to the beans and add more water to cover beans by 1 inch.
10. Cook till beans are soft (1 hr.) Taste chili, add vinegar to taste.
11. Adjust seasoning (cumin, oregano, salt, chile powder, chipotle, vinegar).

If you can wait, it's best to serve it a day later. Very good with cornbread.

Chili My Family's Own
2 Lb. Ground Beef; Or Chicken
1 Can (8 Ounce) Tomato Sauce
2 Cans (8 Ounce) Water
6 Tablespoons Chile powder
2 Teaspoons Salt
2 Teaspoons Cayenne Pepper; Optional

2 Teaspoons Paprika
1 Tablespoon Cumin
1 Teaspoon Oregano
1 Medium Onion
1 Clove Garlic; Large
2 Tablespoons Masa Harina (Corn Flour)

1. Cook meat until gray in color (not brown).
2. Add all other ingredients, mix and simmer 1 hour and 15 minutes.
3. Then mix 2 pounds masa meal with enough warm water to make thin paste mixture; add to chili.
4. Simmer 15 to 20 minutes more.

Adding less chile powder and cayenne may make a milder chili. Freezes well. Beans may be added when serving. All in all, it's good chili.

Note: My mother used chicken a lot and that is a special treat.

Chili Pat's Recipe
1 Lb. Hamburger
1 Medium Onion; Chopped
1 Tablespoon Fat
1 Can Kidney Beans
1 Can Tomato Soup
2/3 Cup Water
1 Teaspoon Salt
2 Teaspoons Vinegar
½ Teaspoon Chiles; Or
1 Teaspoon Chiles; To Taste

1. Heat fat in fry pan, add onion and hamburger and brown.
2. Add rest of ingredients and simmer till thick.

Very Good.

Chili Primero-Jim Vorheis
Crème de Colorado Cookbook (1987)
1 Lb. Smoked Bacon; Cut in ¼ Inch Pieces
4 Lb. Round Steak; Cut in ¼ Inch Cubes
56 Ounces Tomatoes; Canned
1 Can (15 Ounce) Tomato Sauce
1 Can (6 Ounce) Tomato Paste
1 Can (7 Ounce) Green Chiles; Diced

2 Tablespoons Jalapeño Chile Peppers; Optional
1 Can (4 Ounce) Pickled Cactus; Drained and Diced
2 Cups Onion; Chopped
2 Cups Green Bell Pepper; Chopped
1 Cup Parsley (Fresh); Minced
2 Teaspoons Coriander; Ground
3 Cloves Garlic; Minced
8 Teaspoons Cumin; Ground
1 Teaspoon Cayenne Pepper
¼ Teaspoon Oregano, Dried
¼ Teaspoon Paprika
2 Teaspoons Salt
1 Teaspoon Black Pepper; Freshly Ground
1 Tablespoon Lemon Juice (Fresh)
2 Tablespoons Chile powder; Mild
½ Teaspoon Chile powder; Medium
½ Cup Masa Harina (Corn Flour)
As Needed Sour Cream
As Needed Cheddar Cheese; Shredded
As Needed Monterey Jack Cheese; Shredded

1. In large skillet, brown bacon, drain and set aside, reserving grease.
2. In same skillet, brown round steak.
3. Put browned round steak and bacon pieces in large stockpot.
4. Stir in tomatoes with liquid, tomato sauce, tomato paste, green chiles, Jalapeños and cactus. Heat to simmering.
5. In same skillet, sauté onions in ½ reserved bacon grease until transparent. Add to stockpot.
6. Repeat with green peppers.
7. Stir in parsley, coriander, garlic, cumin, cayenne pepper, oregano, paprika, salt, pepper, lemon juice and chile powders.
8. Cook over low heat for 1 hour, stirring occasionally to prevent sticking.
9. Sprinkle masa harina over soup and stir. Simmer covered for 4 hours.
Garnish each serving with sour cream and shredded cheese.

Chili Stephanie Da Silva
3 Cups Dried Beans; ½ Pinto, ½ Black Bean
1 Can S & W Salsa
1 Bulb Garlic; 6-8 Cloves of Garlic
1/3 Cup Chile powder; I Used ½ Cup, It Was Mild

1 Tablespoon Cumin
1.5 Lb. Ground beef; Chili Grind, or Braising
¼ Teaspoon Oregano
3 Chipotle Peppers, Or 4 or 5...
1 Large Onion

1. Soak the beans overnight.
2. Brown the ground beef, and drain off the fat.
3. If the chipotles are dried, soak them for 5 minutes in hot water, then pulverize them with the onion and garlic in a blender.
4. Add onion, oregano, chile powder, cumin, beef, garlic, and beans to crock pot, with "enough" water. Let simmer for about 12 hours.
5. About an hour before it's done, add the can of salsa.

The "chile powder" is bulk powdered "chile powder" chiles, New Mexico chiles, I think. Not the mixture with all kinds of other spices in it that is more common in grocery stores. I like my chili heavier on the chile powder, lighter on the tomatoes.

Chili Van Pelt
1-½ Cups Pinto Beans; Dried
1-½ Cups Red Beans; Dried
1 Can S & W Salsa
6 Cloves Garlic
1/3 Cup Chile powder
1 Tablespoon Cumin
1-½ Lb. Ground Beef; Chili Grind
¼ Teaspoon Oregano
3 Pods Chipotle Chile Pepper
1 Large Onion

1. Soak the beans overnight.
2. Brown the ground beef, and drain off the fat.
3. If the chipotles are dried, soak them for 5 minutes in hot water, then pulverize them with the onion and garlic in a blender.
4. Add onion, oregano, chile powder, cumin, beef, garlic, and beans to crock pot, with "enough" water. Let simmer for about 12 hours.
5. About an hour before it's done, add the can of salsa.

The "chile powder" is bulk powdered "chile powder" chiles, New Mexico chiles, not the mixture with all kinds of other spices in it.

Chili Vion
¼ Cup Corn Oil
3 Lb. Chuck; Lean, Cubed
5 Lb. Ground Round
3 Lb. Italian Sausage
4 Large White Onions
1 Bunch Celery; Diced
4 Cloves Garlic; Mashed
3 Large Green Bell Peppers; Seeded and Chopped
¼ Lb. Hot Banana Peppers; Seeded and Chopped
1 Can (3.5 Ounce) Jalapeño Peppers; Seeded and Chopped
5 Leaves Bay
1 Tablespoon MSG
1 Tablespoon Salt; To Taste
2 Teaspoons Pepper; To Taste
1 Tablespoon Basil; Dry
3 Tablespoons Cumin; Ground
5 Ounces Chile powder
3 Cubes Beef Bouillon
1 Package (1.375 Ounce) Onion Soup Mix
6 Cans (28 Ounce) Tomatoes; Mashed
45 Ounces Tomato Sauce
12 Ounces Tomato Paste
And last but not least 1 fifth white wine Gallo French Colombard is recommended.

1. In large skillet or Dutch oven, heat oil, add meats, brown and transfer with slotted spoon to large cooking pot.
2. In oil remaining in skillet, add onions celery, garlic, and the peppers, cook till soft, 7 to 10 minutes.
3. Mix onion mix with meat in the big pot and add the rest of the fixin's in order of listing.
4. Bring to boil, reduce heat and simmer, un-covered about 3 hours stirring often.

Chili Willie's Chili
1 Lb. Pinto Beans; Dried
1-½ Lb. Ground Beef
2 Quarts Water
1 Large Onion; Chopped

556

2 Cloves Garlic; Minced
1 Medium Green Pepper; Seeded and Chopped
1 Can (12 Ounce) Whole Tomatoes
1 Can (6 Ounce) Tomato Paste
1 Can Condensed Beef Broth
3 Tablespoons Chile powder; Or
2 Tablespoons Chile Pepper; Ground
2 Tablespoons Oregano Leaves; Crumbled
1 Tablespoon Cumin; Ground
1 Tablespoon Salt

1. Wash and sort beans, soak. Cook beans.
2. Brown meat slowly in its own fat in a large kettle or Dutch oven.
3. Add onion, garlic and green pepper.
4. Drain fat from kettle and add tomatoes with their liquid, tomato paste, broth, chile powder, oregano, cumin and salt. Stir.
5. Cut up tomatoes; bring to boil.
6. Cover and simmer 1 hour. If using beans, add and cook 2 to 3 hours.
Note: Add 1 to 2 Jalapeño peppers at the end of cooking time.

Chill Lee's Two Time Texas State Championship Recipe
Ed Paetzel-1974 and 1979 Texas Men's State Champion
5 Lb. Chili Meat; Coarse Ground
1 Package Chill Lee's Championship Texas Home Style Chili Makings
1 Can (15 Ounce) Tomato Sauce
1 Can Beer
16 Ounces Water
2 Tablespoons New Mexico Ground Red Chiles
1 Teaspoon Paprika
1 Teaspoon Black Pepper; Ground
1 Teaspoon MSG
1 Teaspoon Salt
4 Cloves Garlic; Finely Chopped
1 Large Onion; Finely Chopped
2 Pods Jalapeño Chile Peppers; W/Seeds, Fresh or Canned

1. Brown meat.
2. Brown onions, garlic and Jalapeños together.
3. Before adding beer and water, mix all the ingredients with meat and stir well.

557

4. Add beer, and let marinate for 1 hour.
5. After marinating, add water.
6. Cook for approximately 2 hours on medium heat, or until meat is tender.
7. If necessary add more water during cooking.

Do not add more beer. I've lost more Cookoffs that way!

Serves 8.

Chili Con Carne-By Jose Kahan And Many Friends V2.0

150 Grams Grounded Beef Meat; Up to 200
1 Can Kidney Beans; (AKA Red Beans)
2 Fresh Tomatoes
1 Large Onions
3 Cloves Garlic
As Desired Chile Peppers; Dried
As Desired Chile Peppers; Fresh
As Desired Tomato Sauce
As Desired Lemons
As Desired Assorted Spices; (Herbs, Cumin, ...)
As Needed Oil
As Needed Water
As Needed Water Bottles

1. Quantities? It depends on how much you want to eat and also on how spicy! Calculate your usual meat doses; if a can of beans seems too much for you, and then use ¾ of it. It's very intuitive, sorry about it. If you cook too much, keep it for next day (but make sure to cook enough for next day also).
2. Separate the meat into little pieces; add some spices to it and a little juice to season it.
3. Mix up a little and wait some minutes so that the meat absorbs your seasoning.
4. Put very little oil in a frying pan and place the pan over the fire.
5. When it's hot add the meat; turn with a wooden spoon.
6. Remove meat when it's about half done.
7. Don't add too much oil as the meat is naturally greasy.
8. Cut onions, garlic, and tomatoes into exotic patterns, such as lines, squares, etc.
9. Make thin little pieces (you're going to eat them, not frame them).
10. Put a little oil in a cooking pot. It must at least cover the bottom.
11. Cook at medium heat.

12. When it's hot, then add the following, making a little pause each time: onions, garlic, tomatoes, and peppers.
13. At the same time add the spices: lemon juice, chili sauce, tomato sauce, etc.
14. Make sure that the onions and garlic don't get overcooked; remove the pot if necessary from the fire from time to time.
15. When you appreciate they are almost cooked add some water and stir. Ease the fire a bit.
16. Wait around 5 minutes.
17. Open the bean cans; add the beans and the meat to the pot.
18. If you think it's quite dry, add more water, but not too much: you're trying to make a chili, not a soup.
19. Stir to mix the ingredients.
20. Try squashing some of the beans against the inside walls of the pot using the spoon; this gives a good texture and taste to the dish.
21. Let the experiment rest around 25-30 minutes, stirring it (and squashing it if you feel like it) from time to time.
22. If you find it's becoming too gooey and dry, don't hesitate to add a little water.
23. Taste it occasionally to verify it's not overcooking.
24. When you think it's almost done, taste it; if you find it's not enough spiced, it's the right moment to add more hot chili sauce.
25. Stir a bit and let it simmer over the fire for ten more minutes.
26. Take the pot out of the fire.
27. Place in dishes, and if you think you spiced it too much, place the water bottles near to you.

Chilly's Chili
1 Lb. Ground Beef
1 Large Yellow Onion; Chopped
16 Ounces Kidney Beans; Optional-I Don't Like Beans
16 Ounces Tomatoes (Stewed)
6 Ounces Tomato Paste; (Or 12 Ounces. Tomato Sauce)
12 Ounces Beer; (Or More)
2 Cloves Garlic; (Or More to Taste)
1 Tablespoon Chile powder; (Or More to Taste)
½ Tablespoon Chill's Cajun Spice, (Careful it's Hot)
1 Tablespoon Italian Seasonings
2 Dashes Louisiana Brand Hot Sauce; (Or More to Taste)

1. Brown the meat and onions, separately if desired.
2. In a large, heavy pot, combine all ingredients.
3. Bring to a boil.
4. Lower temperature and simmer at least one hour. Six or more hours are better.

Notes: Can make hotter or milder by regulating the amount for Cajun Spice added. Exact measurements are not necessary. The flavor is best if the chili sits for a day before being served.

Time: 15 minutes preparation, 1 to 6 hours cooking.

Christine's Hot Chili
1 Lb. Ground Beef
1 Large Onion; Chopped
2 Cloves Garlic; Crushed
1 Tablespoon Chile powder
½ Teaspoon Salt
1 Teaspoon Cumin; Ground
1 Teaspoon Oregano; Dried
1 Teaspoon Cocoa
½ Teaspoon Red Pepper Sauce
1 Can (16 Ounce) Tomatoes; Crushed
1 Can (15.5 Ounce) Red Kidney Beans; Optional

This is the best recipe I've tried. Spices are for a milder chili. I happen to like mine very hot, so I double the spices.

1. Cook beef, onion and garlic in 3 qt. saucepan and drain.
2. Stir in remaining ingredients except beans. Heat to boiling.
3. Reduce heat. Cover and simmer 1 hour.
4. Stir in beans. Heat to boiling. Simmer uncovered 20 minutes.

To serve, top with shredded cheddar cheese and enjoy. Hope you like it as much as we do.

Clyde's Chili
3 Tablespoons Cooking Oil
2 Medium Onions
3 Lb. Beef; Coarse Ground
2 Tablespoons Worcestershire Sauce
3 Cloves Garlic
4 Tablespoons Hot Red Chile; Ground

4 Tablespoons Mild Red Chile; Ground
2 Teaspoons Cumin
1 Teaspoon Oregano; Preferably Mexican
2 Teaspoons Salt
16 Ounces Kidney Beans
15 Ounces Chili Sauce

1. Heat the oil in a Dutch oven or heavy 5-quart saucepan over medium heat.
2. Add the onions and cook until they are translucent.
3. Add the beef to the pot with the onions.
4. Break up any lumps with a fork and cook, stirring occasionally, until the meat is evenly browned.
5. Add the Worcestershire sauce and garlic and cook for 3 minutes.
6. Stir in the ground chile, cumin, oregano, and salt and cook, uncovered, for 5 minutes.
7. Add the beans and chili sauce and simmer, uncovered, for 1 hour.
8. Taste and adjust seasonings.

Craig Lefebvre's Pawtucket Chili
1 Can (40 Ounce) Kidney Beans; Or
2 Cans (16 Ounce) Kidney Beans
1 Can (15 Ounce) Chick Peas
2 Cloves Garlic; Minced
1 Medium Onion; Chopped
1 Tablespoon Olive Oil
1 Can (8 Ounce) Tomato Sauce
1 Can (14-½ Ounce) Tomatoes; Whole
1 Tablespoon Oregano
½ Teaspoon Thyme
1 Teaspoon Cumin
½ Teaspoon Basil
3 Tablespoons Chile powder

1. Rinse kidney beans and chickpeas to remove salt. Set aside.
2. Sauté garlic and onion in olive oil.
3. Add beans, chickpeas, and remaining ingredients and bring to a boil.
4. Simmer for 20 minutes (or longer) until thick.

D. J. Spicy Chili
1 Lb. Ground Chuck
½ Cup Onion; chopped
½ Cup Green Bell Pepper; Chopped
2 Cans (10.5 Ounce) Tomatoes
3 Cans Red Chili Beans
To Taste Salt and Pepper
3 Tablespoons Chile powder
½ Teaspoon Garlic Powder
2 Tablespoons Vinegar
1 Can (8 Ounce) Tomato Sauce

1. Cook ground beef with onions and bell pepper until meat is done.
2. Drain off excess fat, add 2 (10 ounce) cans of tomatoes, chili beans, salt, pepper, chile powder, garlic powder, vinegar and tomato sauce.
3. Cook over a medium heat for 1 hour.
Makes 8 to 10 servings.

Daddy Mike's Chili
½ Lb. Ground Beef; Suet
3 Lb. Ground Beef; Coarse
4 Buds Garlic
1-½ Tablespoons Paprika
3 Tablespoons Chile powder
1 Tablespoon Cumin Seed
1 Tablespoon Salt
1 Teaspoon Pepper
3 Large Dried Sweet Red Chile Pods; Ground
3 Cups Water; Boiling

1. Heat beef suet until tallow is thoroughly rendered.
2. Add ground beef, finely chopped garlic and seasonings. Cover and simmer slowly 3 to 4 hours.
3. Add boiling water; continue simmering until slightly thickened, about 1 hour.
Serves 6 real chili heads!
   Daddy Mike was a chili purist who believed any ingredient other than those given here was sacrilegious and it is a criminal offense to add anything but boiling hot water to chili!

Daddy's Chili
1 Field Chili Roll
1 Lb. Ground Beef
1 Can Tomato Soup
1 Can Red Chili Beans
1 Cup Spaghetti; Bite-Size
1 Tablespoon Chile powder

1. In large soup pot put: 1-½ quart of water, chili-roll, 1 can of tomato soup, 1 can of red chili beans, 1 cup of bite-size spaghetti and 1 tablespoon chile powder.
2. While all these are cooking, fry ground beef in skillet, drain grease away and add to soup when spaghetti is soft.
3. Add water if needed.

Dad's Chile Con Carne
2 Cans (Large) Tomatoes; Whole
1 Lb. Bulk Whole Hog Sausage
3 Large Onions; Chopped
3 Tablespoons Garlic; Fresh Minced
2 Cans Beef or Chicken Broth; Bullion May Be Used
1 Lb. Kidney Beans; (Or 2 Large Cans)
2 Lb. Round Steak; Lean
4 Tablespoons Chile powder
2 Tablespoons Cumin Seeds; Ground
5 Pods Jalapeño Peppers; Fresh, Rinsed and Sliced-6
1 Bottle Beer
To Taste Salt
To Taste Cayenne Pepper

1. Liquefy tomatoes with a blender, food mill, or a potato masher.
2. Brown sausage and drain fat.
3. Put tomatoes, onions, sausage, broth and chile powder in a large pot or Dutch oven.
4. Fill to top with beer. Bring to a boil. Reduce heat until barely simmering.
5. Cook down to about half volume, stirring and adjusting heat occasionally to maintain a slow simmer.
6. Meanwhile, cook the beans and cut the round steak into ½ inch cubes, eliminating fat.
7. When the liquid is cooked down, add the beans, beef, garlic, and jalapeño

peppers. Cook slowly until beef is tender.
8. Add salt, cayenne, and more chile powder, if desired, to taste.
Serve hot with raw chopped onions sprinkled on top and crackers or flour tortillas.

Dad's Chili # 1
3 Cans Beans; Precooked Kidney or Chili
1 Lb. Ground beef
½ Cup Onion; Chopped
½ Cup Celery; Chopped
1 Large Green Pepper; Chopped
1 Bud Garlic; Chopped
1 Can (Small) Tomato Paste
1 Can (15 Ounce) Tomatoes
1 Can (15 Ounce) Tomato Sauce
1-½ Teaspoons Chile powder; Up to 3
To Taste Salt and Pepper

1. Brown ground beef, onions, celery, garlic and green pepper.
2. Add all tomato ingredients and 1 can (15 ounce) water.
3. Add chile powder, salt, pepper and beans. Simmer 1-½ to 2 hours.
4. Taste for flavor.
5. Add chile powder if necessary. (If you like it hot, add Tabasco sauce!)

Dad's Chili # 2
3 Lb. Chop Meat
5 Cloves Garlic; Smashed or Diced Fine
1 Bottle Chili Sauce
1 Bottle (Small) Ketchup
½ Can Chile powder
To Taste Tabasco Sauce
2 Cans Kidney Beans; Optional

1. Brown beef and garlic; drain thoroughly.
2. Add chili sauce, ketchup, chile powder, Tabasco for hot chili and cook on low flame for 40 minutes.
3. Add kidney beans.
Serve with rice or alone.

Dad's Chili # 3
½ Cup Onion; Chopped
1 Lb. Ground beef
1 Can (15 Ounce) Tomatoes
1 Can (8 Ounce) Tomato Sauce
1 Teaspoon Salt
½ Leaf Bay
2 Teaspoons Chile powder
1/8 Teaspoon Cayenne Pepper
1/8 Teaspoon Paprika
1/8 Teaspoon Oregano; Ground
1 Can (15 Ounce) Kidney Beans

1. Sauté onion with ground beef while browning. Pour off excess fat.
2. Add all other ingredients, mixing as you go. Cover and simmer on low at least 2 hours, stirring occasionally.
3. This works in crock-pot too, browning ground beef first.
4. Simmer all day.

Dad's Chili Con Carne
1 Lb. Ground beef
½ Cup Onion; Chopped
½ Cup Green Pepper; Chopped
1 Clove Garlic; Minced, (Up to 2)
3 Teaspoons Chile powder
1 Teaspoon Salt
1 Can (15.5 Ounce) Kidney Beans; Undrained
¼ Teaspoon Pepper
¼ Teaspoon Hot Pepper Sauce, Liquid
¾ Cup Water
1 Can (28 Ounce) Tomatoes; Whole, Cut Up
1 Can (10.75 Ounce) Condensed Tomato Soup
1 Can (6 Ounce) Tomato Paste
1 Can (4 Ounce) Green Chile Peppers; Chopped, Undrained

1. In medium skillet brown ground beef with onions; drain.
2. In large saucepan combine ground beef mixture and remaining ingredients except kidney beans. Cover; simmer over low heat for 2 hours.
3. Add kidney beans; heat thoroughly.
Makes 5 (1-½ cup) servings.

Dale's Chili
2 Cans (28 Ounce) Tomatoes; Diced
3 Medium Onions
3 Lb. Loin Tip Steak
1 Lb. Anaheim Chile Peppers
¼ Cup Chile powder
1 Teaspoon Cayenne Pepper
1 Dash Habañero Pepper; If You Dare To

1. Cube steak and lightly brown in large pan with a little oil.
2. Chop the onions.
3. Remove seeds from the Anaheim peppers and chop into pieces about the same size as the meat.
4. In a large pot or crockpot add the browned meat, onions and peppers.
5. Add the rest of the ingredients and cook slowly.

May be served when the onions and peppers are tender. Serve with crackers or cornbread.

Dan's True, Honest To God, One And Only Chili
½ Medium Onion; Chopped
1 Clove Garlic; Chopped Fine
1 Pod Jalapeño Pepper; Deseed, Rinsed and Chopped
2 Tablespoons Chile powder
1 Tablespoon Paprika
½ Teaspoon Cumin
½ Teaspoon Oregano
To Taste Salt; I Use None
½ Tablespoon Masa Harina (Corn Flour)
½ Teaspoon Tabasco Sauce; Up to 1

Beans are a side dish!
Ingredients are stated in amounts to be used per pound of meat. This chili is best made on day 1, refrigerate overnight and reheat for consumption next day.

1. Trim away fat from beef and cube into ½ inch cubes. Any lean cut of beef is acceptable. I use chuck roast, round steak, stew meat or sirloin tip. Use whatever is on sale.
2. Sear meat in Teflon lined fry pan.
3. Place the meat in a large pot.

4. Add onion, garlic, pepper, chile powder, paprika, cumin and oregano and enough water or beer to cover. Bring to boil, reduce heat and simmer two hours.
5. Add Masa Harina or cornmeal and simmer 30 minutes.
6. Fine tune taste by adding as needed salt and Tabasco sauce.

Dave Brum's Prize Winning Chili
4 Lb. Round Steak; Chili Grind
4 Teaspoons Garlic Powder
1 Large Onion; Chopped Fine
4 Teaspoons Cocoa
2 Teaspoons Coriander; Ground
3 Tablespoons Kraft Beef Base.
24 Ounces V-8 Juice; (Straight or Picante)
1 Teaspoon Cayenne Pepper
8 Tablespoons Chile powder
4 Teaspoons Cumin
1 Can Green Peppers; Old El Paso or La Perfidia
1 Cup Strong Coffee; Optional
½ Teaspoon Brown Sugar; Optional

1. Use a 12-inch cast iron Dutch oven.
2. Toss 4 pounds of chili-grind round steak into the pot, start browning it.
3. Add 1 teaspoon of garlic powder per pound of meat.
4. While meat is browning chop a large onion reasonably fine.
5. When ground round no longer shows pink add the diced onion and 1 teaspoon cocoa (Hershey's or Nestle) per pound of meat.
6. Toss in 2 teaspoons ground coriander.
7. Stir in 3 tablespoons of Kraft Beef Base. (Note: This is pretty salty-watch it.)
8. Add about half of a 48 ounce can of V8 (straight or Picante) juice and 1 teaspoon of cayenne pepper.
9. Continue to simmer and stir.
10. When onions are clear toss in 2 tablespoons per pound of meat of chile powder, (I use Chili Man, Mexene, or Gebhardt's) and 1 teaspoon per pound cumin.
11. Add a 4 ounce can of Old El Paso or La Preferida green chiles (chop and seed if you grabbed the whole peppers by mistake).
12. Continue to simmer and stir until onions are tender and completely transparent adding V8 juice as necessary.

13. If you run out of V8 use either unsalted 'mater juice or strong coffee to add liquid.
14. Total cooking time about 90 minutes.
15. If you're cooking at home you can serve this batch at this point. See below for longer schedules and the "kicker."
16. If you're on a 3 hour schedule-most cook offs are-turn off stove and let your pot marinate for about an hour.
17. About 30 minutes before turn-in time relight the stove and bring the chili back to a simmer.
18. Taste carefully and critically. This is final adjustment time.
19. If it's too salty try adding about ½ teaspoon of brown sugar.
20. If the chili has died or gone flat, add 1 teaspoon chile powder and ½ teaspoon cumin per pound of meat and simmer right up to time to put in judging cups.

Something's Cooking in Uncle Dirty Dave's Kitchen.

David's Durango, Texas Chili
3 Lb. Hamburger; Browned
2 Cans (28 Ounce) Tomatoes; Whole, Peeled
1 Can (46 Ounce) Tomato Juice
3 Medium Onions; Diced
2 Medium Green Bell Peppers; Diced
45 Ounces Caliente Style Chili Sauce; Approximately
2 Packs Franks Buena Vida Chili Powder
1 Pinch Salt
1 Pinch Pepper
1 Pinch Seasoned Salt
5 Shakes Red Hot Sauce

1. Brown hamburger.
2. Cut up tomatoes into chunks.
3. Mix burger and cut tomatoes, beans, juice, onions, peppers, powder, seasoning and sauce, simmer for 1 hour. (Maybe 15 minutes more until peppers and onions are soft.)

Serve. Enjoy!

Dawn's Chili
2 Lb. Chuck; Ground
2 Cups Onion; Chopped
4 Cloves Garlic; Crushed

4 Stalks Celery; Chopped
1 Cup Green Pepper; Chopped (Optional)
1 Tablespoon Chile powder; Regular
3 Cans (28 Ounce) Tomatoes; Whole
1 Can Tomatoes; Crushed
To Taste Salt and Pepper
1 Can (15 Ounce) Kidney Beans
1 Can (15 Ounce) White Beans; (Great Northern)

1. Sauté ground chuck. Drain off all grease.
2. Add onions and garlic and cook gently until vegetables are tender.
3. Add celery and green pepper and cook gently 15 minutes more.
4. Add 3 cans tomatoes. Break up tomatoes with spoon.
5. Turn up heat, as soon as it starts to boil, turn down to medium and simmer for at least 30 minutes.
6. Add red and white beans.
7. Heat through over medium heat, then turn low and remove lid.
8. Simmer for at least another 30 minutes, longer is better.

Yields 8 servings.

We enjoy this with crisp carrot sticks and crusty round rolls.

Del's Chili
2 Tablespoons Olive Oil; Virgin
1 Medium Onion; Chopped
2 Lb. Stew Meat; Cubed
1 Can Black Beans
1 Can (Small) Tomato Sauce
1 Can Refried Beans
1 Can (16 Ounce) Tomatoes
2 Cans Beef Broth
To Taste Salt
1 Can (Small) Mushrooms
2 Packages Old El Paso Chili Seasoning Mix

1. Cube the meat into ¼ inch cubes. Brown in skillet with olive oil. Drain off grease.
2. Combine all ingredients into a large cooker. Cover and cook on low heat for 1-½ hours, stirring occasionally.
3. As residue forms on top of chili, remove with a spoon and discard.
4. Add water to make consistency you desire. Enjoy.

Denton's Dilly Of A Chili
2 Lb. Ham Steak; Cubed
2 Lb. Venison; Diced
2 Lb. Sirloin; Coarse Ground
2 Lb. Ground Pork; Lean
4 Large Red Onions; Chopped
2 Cloves Garlic; Crushed
2 Jars (15 Ounce) Salsa Sauce; Mild
2 Pods Chile Peppers; Chopped
6 Tablespoons Chile powder
4 Tablespoons Cumin; Ground
1 Tablespoon Paprika
2 Ounces Worcestershire Sauce
2 Medium Green Peppers; Chopped
1 Jar Red Pimentos; Chopped
1 Cup Bacon; Crumbled
1 Can (15 Ounce) Plum Tomatoes
2 Cans (15 Ounce) New Orleans Style Red Kidney Beans
½ Cup Celery; Chopped
½ Cup Beef Bouillon
½ Cup Fatback Grease
1 Tablespoon Black Pepper; Cracked
½ Teaspoon Cayenne Red Pepper
To Taste Salt and Pepper

1. Brown all meats well in fatback grease. Drain.
2. Then sauté onions, garlic, green peppers, celery, pimento, and chile peppers for 5 minutes.
3. Add chile powder, ground cumin, paprika, red pepper and black pepper. Stir well.
4. In a very large stockpot, place browned meats, seasonings that have been sautéed, then add salsa sauce, Worcestershire sauce, bacon, tomatoes, beef bouillon.
5. Taste for salt, pepper. Stir through.
6. Cook, covered on medium heat for 2-½ hours. Stir often.
7. Add beans and continue to cook on low heat for 30 minutes.
8. Spoon grease off of top.
9. If needed thicken with flour or cornstarch.

Dick's Chili
2 Lb. Hamburger; Cooked
1/3 Cup Onion; Cut Small
½ Cup Celery; Cut Small
1 Teaspoon Salt
4 Teaspoons Chile powder
½ Teaspoon Red Pepper; Crushed
1 Dash Garlic Salt
1 Can (Medium) Tomatoes (Stewed); Or Whole
1 Quart Can Tomato Juice
¼ Cup Green Pepper; Cut Small
1 Teaspoon Black Pepper
1 Can Chili Beans
1 Teaspoon Hot Chile powder
1 Dash Oregano
1 Can (Small) Tomato Soup
1 Can (Small) Tomato Sauce
1/3 Can Beer

1. Let simmer for 2 hours.
2. Use approximately ½ pound spaghetti noodles. Cook noodles 8 minutes.
3. Rinse and add to soup.
Eat at your own risk.

Dixon's Chili
2 Lb. Ground Beef
1 Teaspoon Chile powder
5 Teaspoons Cumin
1 Teaspoon Oregano
To Taste Salt and Pepper
To Taste Garlic Powder

1. Add spices to meat.
2. Cover with water and cook on medium heat until water evaporates.
3. Drain excess liquid.

Doc's Diner Chili
10 Lb. Ground Meat
3 Lb. Suet
10 Tablespoons Chile powder

5 Tablespoons Chile Pepper; Not Red Pepper
6 Tablespoons Comino Seeds
¼ Lb. Peanut Butter
1 Large Box Corn Flakes
Do not use water in cooking!

1. Cook ground meat until done. Salt suet to taste.
2. As soon as meat is done, add chile powder and chile peppers. Mix well.
3. If you don't have chile peppers, add 5 more tablespoons of chile powder.
4. Can use crushed red pepper, but not much. It will be too hot.
5. Add comino seed, peanut butter and crushed corn flakes. Mix all together well.
6. If you cannot find the seed, use ground cumin.
7. Put mixture into containers.
8. Let it get hard.
9. Use what you want when you need it.
10. Refrigerate or freeze the rest.
11. Take what you want out of containers. Add water.
12. Can also add onions, garlic and tomatoes as desired.
You can also make half of batch.

Dom's Nuclear Chili
6 Pods New Mexican Chiles; Dried (Or 8)
4 Pods Ancho Chile Peppers; Dried
4 Pods Pasilla Chile Peppers; Dried
2 Pods Cascabel Chile Peppers; Dried
2 Pods Chipotle Peppers; Dried
1 Pod Habañero Pepper
2 Cloves Garlic
2 Teaspoons Cumin
1 Bottle Beer
To Taste Salt
To Taste Oregano
2 Lb. Meat (Chili Meat); Ground or Cut up
1 Medium Green Pepper; Chopped
1 Medium Red Pepper; Chopped
1 Medium Onion; Chopped
3 Cloves Garlic; Chopped
1 Can (16 Ounce) Beans; Or Corn

Prepare sauce.
1. Add 8 cups boiling water to New Mexico, Ancho, Pasilla, Anaheim, and Cascabel Chiles. Let soak 30 minutes.
2. Place in blender with ½ of soaking water plus fresh water and beer.
3. Add 2 cloves of garlic and blend for 3 minutes. Strain the resulting puree into a pot.
4. Add cumin, salt, oregano, and Chipotle and Habañero chiles. Simmer.

Prepare rest of chili.
1. Add garlic, peppers, and onion to bacon fat and cook 2 minutes.
2. Add meat, and brown.
3. Add chili sauce. Simmer for a few hours.
4. Add corn or beans about 1 hour before serving.
5. Skim fat before serving.
Notes: You may use a different variety of chiles. Be creative and experiment. The Habañero Chili is very hot. If you want a milder chili, do not add.

Donaldo's Prize Winning Chili Por Gringos (Olé)
1 Lb. Ground Beef
To Taste Salt and Pepper
1 Medium Onion; Chopped
3 Tablespoons Chile powder; Divided
1 Tablespoon Shortening
2 Cups Tomato Juice; Or Water
2 Stalks Celery; Diced
1 Can (Medium) Tomatoes
1 Can Hot Chili Beans
1 Package William's Chili Seasoning

1. Season ground beef with salt and pepper and brown with onion mixed with 1-tablespoon chile powder, William's chili seasoning in the shortening.
2. Add tomato juice and remaining chile powder and simmer slowly for 45 minutes.
3. Add tomatoes or (for extra spice) Ro-Tel and simmer 15 minutes longer.
4. Add kidney beans, pinto beans and celery.
5. Simmer 15 minutes longer.
Yield: 8 servings.

Donna Gee's Chili

5 Lb. Chili Meat
1 Large Onion; Diced
2 Cans (Small) Tomato Paste
2-½ Teaspoons Comino Seeds
5 Tablespoons Chile powder
1 Teaspoon Black Pepper
5 Teaspoons Salt
2/3 Cup Flour
¾ Teaspoon Garlic Powder

1. Brown meat, onion and comino seed with salt, pepper and garlic powder.
2. Add chile powder and mix.
3. Add tomato paste and fill pan with water. Simmer 3 to 4 hours.
4. About 2 minutes before done, mix flour in glass of water. Stir into chili to thicken.
5. Add more salt if needed.

Donna's Award-Winning Fire Extinguisher Chili

2 Cans (30 Ounce) Tomatoes; Whole
2 Cans (30 Ounce) Kidney Beans
2 Lb. Ground Beef; Extra Lean
1 Large White Whole Onion
1 Large Green Pepper
2 Handfuls Chile Peppers; Whole
¼ Cup Lea and Perrins BBQ Sauce
¼ Cup Worcestershire Sauce
1 Teaspoon Red Pepper; Crushed, To Taste
1 Teaspoon Black Pepper; To Taste
1 Teaspoon Celery Salt; To Taste
1 Teaspoon Lemon Pepper; To Taste
1 Teaspoon Cayenne Pepper; To Taste
1 Teaspoon Garlic Powder; To Taste
1 Large Cooking Pot
1 Cast Iron Frying Pan
1 Electric Crockpot With Thermostat

My friend Donna won the 1994 San Diego regional Chili Cookoff with this recipe. She does it from memory, but I wrote it down for her once when she made it for me. Note the simmering time before you try this!

1. Empty beans and tomatoes into large pot, crushing tomatoes by hand.
2. Add chile peppers and red pepper. Allow to soak.
3. Dice green pepper to fingernail size.
4. Chop onion finely.
5. Sauté peppers and onions in ungreased frying pan until onions are lightly browned. Empty into pot.
6. In same pan, sauté ground beef slowly in onion/pepper residue.
7. Slowly add Worcestershire sauce.
8. Add remaining spices and L&P sauce.
9. When meat is half-cooked, begin heating pot with low heat.
10. As meat reduces, pile meat in center of pan.
11. Use slotted spoon to scoop dry meat off the top and into pot, do not stir.
12. Make sure to minimize fat transferred to pot.
13. Continue until all meat is a layer on top of other ingredients in pot. Stir.
14. Cover pot; raise heat to medium high until boiling. Stir often.
15. Reduce heat. Simmer 2 hours, stirring occasionally.
16. Set crockpot to low, transfer contents of cooking pot to crockpot. Simmer 12-15 hours.
17. As serving time approaches, if chili is still too watery, stir in 1 tablespoon white flour once per hour.
18. Serve forth--supply fire extinguishers.

Dowd Family Chili
1 Lb. Ground Beef
1 Medium Onion; Chopped
1 Can Brooks Chili Hot Beans
1 Can Tomato Soup
2 Tablespoons Sugar
2 Tablespoons Chile powder
2 Tablespoons Butter
To Taste Salt and Pepper

1. One can of water for each can of ingredients (except for can of chili beans).
2. Brown and drain hamburger.
3. Add each of the ingredients.
4. Mix well and simmer over low heat for an hour.
Note: John usually adds more chile powder.

Dr. Shipp's Chili From Lorena, Texas
4 Lb. Round Steak; Lean
½ Lb. Beef Tallow
1 Slice Bacon
16 Tablespoons Chile powder
1 Tablespoon Cumin or Comino Seasoning
6 Pods Chile Peppers; Dry, See Note
½ Dozen Hot Green Chile Peppers; See Note
2 Teaspoons Black Pepper
1 Button Garlic
1 Large Onion; Chopped Fine
2 Quarts Water

Suggestion: Cut back on chile peppers and hot green peppers, unless you like it hot. Buy lean round steak and have it chopped coarsely. Buy beef tallow.

1. Cook slice of bacon in a deep iron pot and let it melt.
2. Sear the meat in the pot and add chile powder, cumin or comino seasoning, chile peppers, hot green peppers and black pepper.
3. The last additions are garlic button and onion, chopped fine.
4. Add water and let the chili cook about 5 hours and you will have something good to eat.
5. The chili must cook slowly, just above a simmer.
6. It should be covered and stirred occasionally.
7. More water may be needed as it cooks.

Dr. W. F. Shipp practiced medicine in Lorena, Texas (near Waco) beginning around the turn of the century as a young man. He died in 1962 or 1963 at age 93 and he had practiced medicine in Lorena for most of those years. He has a grandson, who is now a doctor in Waco. My sister-in-law in Stephenville, Texas sent me a cookbook from there, and someone had entered this recipe. She said she had clipped this recipe from the Waco paper about 40 years ago. Grandmother and Grandpa Cupp (Martin and Molly) lived in Lorena many years and are buried in the cemetery there along with Stephen T. Cupp. My Mother and Dad met and married there and Dr. Shipp brought my brother, Charles, into the world. Maybe some of the other Cupps knew him, too.

E. Degolyer's Chili
1 Large Onion; Chopped
6 Cloves Garlic; Chopped

2 Cups Rendered Beef Kidney Suet
2-½ Lb. Chuck Beef; Extra Lean, Cubed
1 Lb. Ham; Cubed
2 Cups Water
1 Teaspoon Cumin; Ground
2 Teaspoons Oregano
1 Cup Red Chile Pulp; Or
6 Tablespoons Chile powder
1 Tablespoon Salt; To Taste

1. Cook onion and garlic in rendered beef suet until onion is limp and yellow.
2. Add beef and ham and cook, stirring often, until it is a uniform gray color.
3. Add water, mix well, and simmer one to one and a half hours.
4. Add cumin, oregano, chile pulp or powder, and salt to meat mixture.
5. Stirring frequently to prevent sticking, simmer for an additional hour.

Earl's Chili
2 Lb. Chili Meat
1-½ Tablespoons Paprika
1 Tablespoon Cumin Seed
1 Tablespoon Salt
1-½ Tablespoons Sweet Pepper; Diced
3 Cloves Garlic
3 Tablespoons Chile powder; Or
3 Diced Chile Peppers
1 Teaspoon White Pepper
3 Cups Water

1. Sauté meat.
2. Add garlic and other seasoning. Cook slowly for 4 hours.
3. Stir occasionally.
4. Add a little water if needed and cook another hour.

Editor's Choice Chili
2 Lb. Ground Beef; Lean
1 Teaspoon Salt
2 Medium Onions
1 Medium Bell Pepper
2 Cans (15 Ounce) Tomatoes

2 Cans (4 Ounce) Tomato Sauce
2 Cans Tomato Paste
4 Cups Water
3 Teaspoons Chile powder
2 Teaspoons Oregano
1 Teaspoon Cumin
1 Teaspoon Red Pepper; Crushed
¼ Teaspoon Allspice; Optional
2 Cans (Large) Red Kidney Beans; Optional
[Hey, put away that noose. I said the beans were optional]

"We need a chili recipe for this PR," they said. "We promised a different chili recipe in each issue." "Ahem, well, I do have chili recipes," I replied. "I can put one of mine in." They looked at me askance. I grew up in Oklahoma, you see, and only recently became a Texan by marriage. Texans seem to have a hard time believing that anyone not born a native can cook chili. "Well, okay," they replied, not having a better offer at the moment, and wanting to get the PR published and into the hands of eagerly awaiting fans. However you serve it, enjoy, and don't be afraid to experiment! I looked through my recipes. One listed half a dozen different kinds of fresh and dried peppers, instead of premixed chile powder and included chocolate and beer. Another listed rattlesnake meat, but I have never had the nerve or the rattlesnake to make it. So I dug out my basic chili recipe that has been with me since college and this is what I found. I turned over the card-nothing. All I had written down was a list of ingredients. It was then that I realized I had probably not made my chili the same way twice in over 20 years. After all, a recipe is just a guideline and can be adjusted to accommodate the taste of those to whom it will be served as well as the whim of the cook. Making the recipe and watching how I made it seemed the best way to write down the instructions. I went to the grocery to buy my ingredients, and right off the bat "the whim of the cook" sabotaged my recipe. Instead of ground beef, I came home with 2 pounds of lovely lean stew meat cut in 1-inch chunks. (I usually use ground round so I don't have to skim any fat.) In a large Dutch oven I heated a tablespoon or so of olive oil (I prefer olive oil, but any good cooking oil will do). and browned two finely chopped cloves of garlic before adding the meat. Uh-oh, it's not in the recipe. I've put the garlic in for years and never bothered to write it down. The chunks of meat browned nicely and gave the added bonus of a rich brown stock that I don't get with the ground beef. After the meat was browned on all sides, I added the tomato paste, tomato sauce, tomatoes (quartered), water and spices. While this mixture was coming to a boil, I chopped the onions and green pepper (I like the pieces about ¼ to ½ inch) and sautéed them in another tablespoon or so of olive oil. After the onions turn transparent, I usually let them sit undisturbed for a while until the sugar in them just starts to caramelize. This adds a nice dimension to the flavor without adding the sugar, which I have found listed in other recipes. Stir the onions and peppers into the meat mixture and all that's left is the waiting. (Oh, darn. I left out the salt again. I haven't added extra salt to anything in years if I could help it. If you want to use the salt, it's best to sprinkle it over the meat as it is browning.) Now, at this point there is a significant difference between using ground beef and using the chunks of stew meat. If you use the stew meat, the chili needs to simmer gently for at least 2 to 3 hours or until the chunks of meat separate easily into fibers when mashed against the side of the pan with a spoon. Mash all the chunks. At this point the sauce should be reduced to a thick, rich consistency. If not, let it cook a little longer until it is where you want it, but keep an eye on it so that it doesn't burn. Oh yes, If your audience doesn't threaten to string you up, you can add the beans to the ground beef version after the chili has cooked for about an hour and continue cooking just until they are heated through before serving. If you are cooking for a Texas crowd, I suggest cooking the beans of your choice separately and serving them on the side so each person can add them at their own risk. This is the best way to serve beans with the stew meat version. However you serve it, enjoy, and don't be afraid to experiment!

Erskine Bufano's Prize Winning Chili
S. L. Kinsey
2 Lb. Beef Sirloin; Lean, ½ Inch Cubes
¾ Lb. Country Pork Sausage
4 Tablespoons Mild Chile powder
2 Tablespoons Hot New Mexico Style Chile powder
2/3 Teaspoon Garlic Powder
2/3 Teaspoon Red Cayenne Pepper
1 Can (12 Ounce) Tomato Sauce
1 Cup Onion; Finely Chopped
2 Tablespoons Cumin; Ground
¼ Teaspoon Oregano; Dried
1 Can (10 Ounce) Beef Stock; Or 2, See Note
Note: Or make Bouillon with beer.

This is a recipe for chili that an old college friend of my mother's won a chili contest "Down by The Border" with. It is quite a bit easier to manage than 5 gallons, and I have found it worthy of its prize.

1. Brown beef and sausage and drain well.
2. Combine chile powder, garlic powder and cayenne.
3. Sprinkle ¾ of this over browned meat.
4. Add tomato sauce, onions, cumin and oregano.
5. Simmer 2 hours covered, adding bouillon to keep the meat barely covered.
6. Add rest of spice mix and simmer covered ½ hour more until thick.
7. Season chili with salt and pepper.

Serve with pinto beans and cornbread-add beans to your portion of chili until it reaches the desired "hotness."

Never, never cook chili with the beans already in it.

Esther's Homemade Chili Soup

2 Lb. Hamburger
1 Can (Large) Tomato Paste
1 Lb. Pinto Beans
2 Medium Onions
5 Slices Bacon
¼ Cup Sugar
3 Cups Water; 3 or 4
½ Teaspoon Salt
¼ Teaspoon Pepper
½ Package Chile powder

1. Cook 2 pounds of hamburger, saving enough grease to brown the onions.
2. Add hamburger and onions to the cooked beans and bacon.
3. Then add tomato paste and 3 or 4 cups of water.
4. Add sugar, salt and pepper and stir well, then add the chile powder.

Felipe's Chili Con Carne
Philip T. Willis
2-½ Lb. Fresh Kidney Suet From Choice Beef
10 Lb. Choice Beef Round; Coarse Ground
1 Pint Water
1 Cup Fresh Garlic Buttons
2 Large Onions
2 Cans El Chico Green Chiles

10 Tablespoons Paprika
2 Tablespoons Oregano
3 Tablespoons Comino
4 Tablespoons Salt
To Taste Cayenne Pepper
24 Ounces Tomato Juice
12 Ounces Carrot Juice
4 Large Chile Pods; Dried
1-½ Cups Oyster Crackers; Pulverized to a Fine Powder
1 Cup Water

1. Grind suet, slowly melt in a large heavy cooking pot until liquefied. Add meat and water. Stir often to brown evenly.
2. Combine garlic, onions, and green chiles in blender and blend into juice.
3. Add dry seasonings and tomato and carrot juices.
4. Stir often and simmer until meat is tender.
5. Float dried chile pods on top. Cook about 3 hours.
6. Near end of cooking time, prepare cracker meal by adding pulverized crackers to a cup of water, stirring into a liquid and add to chili. Stir well.
7. Remove chile pods before serving.
8. If possible, leave chili in pot and allow to marinate overnight-it develops the flavor.

Source: Prize-Winning Recipes from the State Fair of Texas, 1976.

First Time Chili (Brenda's)
2 Lb. Stew Meat; Boneless, Ground Once
2 Medium Onions
1 Stalks Celery
¼ Medium Bell Pepper
2 Tablespoons Cooking Oil
1 Package Lipton Onion Soup
1 Can (14-½ Ounce) Tomatoes (Stewed)
1 Can (14-½ Ounce) Tomatoes; Whole
1 Can (8 Ounce) Tomato Sauce
1 Jar (32 Ounce) Ragu Sauce (Chunky Style)
2 Leaves Bay
To Taste Chile powder
To Taste Crab Boil Oil; Creole
To Taste Garlic Powder
Note: the crab boil oil is liquid crab boil.

1. Brown ground beef in large pot.
2. Then add chile powder, Creole seasoning, and garlic powder.
3. In a skillet sauté chopped onions, celery and bell pepper.
4. Add sautéed seasoning to ground beef.
5. Add tomatoes, tomato sauce, and onion soup.
6. Add remaining ingredients, let simmer for 20 minutes or until done, do not over cook.

Source is Brenda (last name unknown), a co-worker. This is her award winning chili.

Fred Winston's Chili-Almost (Chili Cook Off 1987)

2 Lb. Ground Round
1 Large Onion
1 Medium Green Pepper
2 Pods Jalapeño Peppers
1 Clove Garlic
2 Tablespoons Chile powder
1 Tablespoon Paprika
½ Teaspoon Oregano
½ Teaspoon Cumin
½ Teaspoon Red Pepper; Crushed
1 Dash Hot pepper sauce
1 Pinch Sugar
1 Can (32 Ounce) Tomatoes
1 Can (8 Ounce) Tomato Sauce
½ Cup Beef Broth
½ Cup Beer; Flat

1. Brown meat, drain and set aside.
2. Chop onions, green pepper, Jalapeños, and garlic. Sauté, stir in spices.
3. Add tomatoes, tomato sauce, broth, beer and meat.
4. Simmer, covered, one hour, uncovered for two more, stirring frequently.
5. Refrigerate overnight, Reheat and serve.

Fred's Almost Award Winning Texas Red Chili

¼ Lb. Suet; Finely Chopped
6 Lb. Lean Beef
1 Cup Chile powder; About 4-½ Ounces
2 Tablespoons Cumin; Ground
2 Tablespoons Oregano; Ground

2 Tablespoons Salt
1 Tablespoon Cayenne Pepper
4 Cloves Garlic; Minced
2 Quarts Beef Stock
½ Cup Corn Meal
½ Cup Cold Water

1. Fry suet until crisp. Then add beef and brown, stirring as it cooks. Brown beef 1 pound at a time.
2. When all beef is browned, return to pot and add seasoning and beef stock. Cover and simmer 1-½ to 2 hours. Skim off fat.
3. Combine cornmeal and cold water and stir in chili. Simmer 30 minutes. Makes about 3-¾ quarts.

If venison is available, use 3 pounds venison and 3 pounds beef.

Freida's Chili
3 Tablespoons Cooking Oil
1 Lb. Round Steak; Lean, cut into Bite Size
1 Cup Onion; Chopped
1 Cup Red and/or Green Bell Pepper; Chopped
2 Cloves Garlic; Minced
1 Can (16 Ounce) Kidney Beans; With Liquid
2 Cups Tomatoes; Chopped
1 Can (16 Ounce) Tomato Sauce; Low Sodium
1 Cup Beef Broth
1 Package (16 Ounce) Freida's Black-eyed Peas
1 Package or 2 Freida's Dried Habañero Chiles; Reconstituted, Seeded, Chopped
2 Tablespoons Freida's Fresh Cilantro; Chopped
1 Tablespoon Freida's Fresh Basil; Chopped
1 Tablespoon Brown Sugar; Packed
1 Teaspoon Worcestershire Sauce
1 Each Freida's Bay Leaf
1 Cup Niblet Corn; Low Sodium
To Taste Salt

This is a commercial chili recipe.
Use just one of the dried Habañero chiles if you like chili with a bearable kick; add more if your diners are eager to sweat!
To serve: Warmed tortillas, shredded sharp cheddar cheese.

1. In a large Dutch oven or stockpot, heat half of the oil.
2. Brown meat in hot oil on all sides; remove from pan with a slotted spoon.
3. Drain off fat.
4. Add remaining oil to pan; sauté onion, bell pepper, and garlic for 3 minutes.
5. Stir in cooked beef, kidney beans and liquid, chopped tomatoes, tomato sauce, broth, black-eyed peas, Habañero chiles, cilantro, basil, brown sugar, Worcestershire and bay leaf.
6. Bring mixture to boiling; reduce heat.
7. Simmer, partially covered for 35 to 45 minutes, or until vegetables are tender.
8. Stir in corn and salt to taste; cook 5 minutes more.
9. Remove bay leaf.

Serve in bowls topped with shredded cheese; pass warm tortillas.

Makes 8 cups chili.

Gene Bartz World Famous Chili

2 Lb. Hamburger
2 Cans Red Kidney Beans; Medium Cans
2 Cans Tomato Soup
2 Teaspoons Chile powder
1 Can Ketchup; Bean Size Can

Mix all ingredients and cook in crockpot on low for 8-10 hours.

Glen's "Green Floater" Chili

3 Lb. Ground Beef; Lean
2 Lb. Steak; Lean, cut into 1/4 to 1/2
2 Tablespoons Garlic; Minced
2 Large Yellow Onions; Coarse Chopped
3 Large Bell Peppers; Coarse Chopped
4 Large Tomatoes; Coarse Chopped
1 Lb. Mushroom; Fresh or Canned, Sliced Thin
50 Pods Serrano Chile Peppers; Whole, Stems Removed
25 Pods Jalapeño Chile Peppers; Whole, Stems Removed
2 Cans (28 Ounce) Tomatoes; Whole, Chopped
12 Tablespoons Chile powder; About 1 4.5-Ounce Jar
2 Tablespoons Cumin; Ground
2 Tablespoons Oregano; Ground
1 Tablespoon Paprika; Ground

1 Tablespoon Red Pepper; Ground
½ Tablespoon Marjoram; Ground
1 Tablespoon Salt
3 Cans (23 Ounce) Ranch Style Beans; these are Pinto Beans
3 Cans (15 Ounce) Dark Red Kidney Beans; Drained
3 Cans (15 Ounce) Light Red Kidney Beans; Drained

1. Start browning the meat in a large pot.
2. Add the garlic.
3. Start chopping the vegetables in the order listed and then add to the pot as you chop them. Stir after each addition.
4. Add the peppers whole. Do not cut up! If you do, the chili will be brutally hot!
5. Add in the juice from the canned tomatoes, and add the chopped canned tomatoes. Simmer all this for 2-3 hours.
6. Add in the beans.
7. Simmer another 30 minutes to heat the beans and serve.

This is best made the day before, refrigerated, and then reheated before serving.

Serve the chile and add a "floater" or two for those who like their food hot.

Note: If you get to some point in adding ingredients that your pan starts to overflow, divide what you have into two pans, then split the remaining ingredients between the pots.

Hint: Adjust seasonings to your liking. Adding more ground red pepper will make it hotter. Adding more whole chiles will not make the chili itself any more hotter, but you sure will have more "green floaters!"

Beware: You can use other chiles than what I listed, but be very careful that the ones you use do not have thin skins or they will break apart during cooking and cause the chile to be very hot! The large green chiles are not well suited for this, as their skins are too tough! Besides they are mild!

Yield: 30 servings.

Graeme's 'Last Resort' Chili
Graeme Caselton BSc

500 Grams Frozen Minced Meat; Beef, Lamb, Chicken or Turkey
1 Tablespoon Oil
12 Pods Habañero or Scotch Bonnet Chile Pepper; Frozen
1 Handful Green Bell/Sweet Peppers; Dried, Chopped

2 Handfuls Onions; Dried, Chopped
1 Pinch Garlic; Dried, Chopped
2 Teaspoons Cumin; Ground
1 Teaspoon Coriander; Ground
1 Pinch Salt
2 Teaspoons Black Pepper; Fresh Ground
2 Cans (14 Ounce) Tomatoes
2 Handfuls Black Beans; Dried, See Note
Note: Use a can of Baked Beans if dried black beans unavailable.

1. 24 hours before starting to cook the chili, place the dried black beans in a bowl and cover with cold water.
2. 12 hours before starting to cook the chili, take the meat and chile peppers out of the freezer and let them defrost.
3. Drain the water from the black beans and recover with fresh cold water.
4. When ready to cook, drain the black beans.
5. Place into a saucepan, cover with fresh cold water, bring to the boil and cook vigorously for 20 minutes. Drain and put to one side.
6. Cover the dried onions in boiling water and let stand for 10 minutes.
7. In a casserole, crockpot or suitable stove top cooking container, brown the meat in the oil.
8. Add the sweet peppers.
9. De-stem the chile peppers and place in a food processor.
10. Chop up finely. Do not remove seeds or veins from the chile peppers. Add to the cooking pot.
11. Add the onions, garlic, cumin, coriander, salt and pepper to the cooking pot.
12. Add the tomatoes, breaking them up into small chunks in the pot.
13. Add the beans.
14. Stir well and reduce to a simmer once bubbling. Cook for 1-2 hours.
Serve with rice or crusty bread. Add Hot-Pepper Sauce as required.

Designed to use the dried items of 'last resort' stored in the back of the kitchen cupboard or frozen and forgotten in the freezer. Yield: 5 servings.

Grandma Dillon's Famous Chili
1 Cup Tiny Elbow Spaghetti
½ Lb. Hamburger; Up to 1
1 Large Onion; Or
2 Small Onions
2 Tablespoons Chile powder; Level

2 Teaspoons Salt
1 Teaspoon Black Pepper
2 Cans Tomato Soup
1 Can Chili Hot Beans
1 Chunk Butter

1. Cook hamburger in greased skillet.
2. Cook spaghetti and drain.
3. Cut up onions into hamburger and add salt, pepper and chile powder.
4. Put spaghetti in a 5 or 6-quart kettle; dump in soup, beans, meat and small chunk of butter.
5. Simmer for 10 minutes.

Grandma Wyatt's Chili
10 Lb. Chili Meat
3 Large Onions; Chopped
To Taste Salt and Pepper
1 Tablespoon Garlic Powder
2/3 Cup Chile powder
4 Tablespoons Cumin
1 Can (30 Ounce) Las Palmas Chili Sauce

1. In large kettle combine meat, onions, salt, pepper and garlic powder. Simmer on medium-low heat about 3 hours.
2. Add rest of ingredients and simmer about 1 hour longer.
3. Put into freezer containers and freeze.
4. When ready to use, use as is or add beans as desired.

Grandma's Texas Chili
2 Lb. Chili Meat; Lean
1 Medium Onion; Chopped
1 Clove Garlic; Chopped
To Taste Salt and Pepper
1 Tablespoon Oregano
1 Tablespoon Flour
To Taste Chile Pepper or Powder
1 Can (Small) Tomato Paste

1. Brown the meat with the onion and garlic.
2. Add the chili seasonings, salt and pepper, oregano during the browning.

3. Add enough chili seasoning until you think it's spicy enough.
4. Add flour to thicken after the meat is brown.
5. Add tomato paste to meat after it's brown.
6. Add enough water to make it soupy.
7. Let simmer on the stove over low to medium heat to let the flavor become enhanced.

Real Texas chili does not have beans but if you like beans you may add them when the water is added.

Grandma's Ohio Farm Chili
Tom and Gail Heffner
3 Cans Tomato Soup
4 Cans Water
1 Lb. Hamburger
1 Lb. Hot Sausage
1 Large Onion; Minced
3 Cans Kidney or Chili Beans
2 Tablespoons Cumin
3 Leaves Bay
3 Teaspoons Tabasco
1 Teaspoon Salt

Brown hamburger and sausage, drain off grease, then dump it all in a big pot, bring it to a boil, then simmer for 45 minutes.
Serve over a scoop of mashed potatoes in a large bowl.

Grandmother's Chili
2 Lb. Ground Beef
1 Lb. Roll Chili Without Beans
2 Large Onions
1 Medium Green Pepper
1 Can (Large) Tomato Juice
5 Bulbs Garlic
1 Cup Tomato Ketchup
1 Tablespoon Chile powder
To Taste Black Pepper and Salt
3 Cans Kidney Beans; (2 Cans Mashed, 1 Can Whole)
½ Cup Sweet Pickle Vinegar; Approximately
1 Quart Water

1. Mix ground beef (slightly browned), onions and green pepper to quart water and cook until chopped onions are tender.
2. Then add tomato juice, ketchup and chile powder and vinegar mixture.
3. In separate pot, heat slowly the chili roll and mashed beans. Stir several times.
4. Then add this mixture back to the other mixture, along with the whole can of kidney beans, and let cook slowly 30 minutes.

Makes 2 gallons.

Granny's Country Chili
Waycross (Georgia) Journal-Herald 17th Annual Cookbook

8 Ounces Black-eyed Peas; Dried
1 Lb. Sausage
3 Cans Tomatoes
2 Cups Water
1 Tablespoon Black Pepper
2 Tablespoons Garlic Salt
2 Tablespoons Chile powder

1. Cover the black-eyed peas in water and soak overnight. Drain peas.
2. Sauté sausage meat until done.
3. Add tomatoes, water, and spices. Simmer one hour.

Note: This recipe appeared in the Waycross (Georgia) Journal-Herald 17th Annual Cookbook, November 16, 1990 and was submitted by Ms. Edith King of Blackshear, Georgia.

Greg's Chili

2 Cans Brooks Chili Hot Beans
2 Lb. Hamburger
1 Medium Green Bell Pepper
1 Package Chili-O Seasoning Mix
1 Can (8 Ounce) Hunt's Tomato Sauce
1 Can (6 Ounce) Hunt's Tomato Paste
1 Medium Onion
100 Sticks Spaghetti
1 Teaspoon Black Pepper
2 Teaspoons Chile powder
2 Cups Water
1 Teaspoon Salt

1. Brown hamburger; drain excess meat juices.
2. Add onion (cut up), green pepper (cut up), chili mix, tomato sauce, tomato paste, salt, pepper, chile powder and beans.
3. Blend well over medium heat.
4. Add water and spaghetti. Cook on low for 30 minutes. Stir occasionally.
5. Then cook on warm for another 30 minutes.

Harold's Chili

3 Lb. Chili Meat
1 Large Onion
1 Clove Garlic
1 Can (16 Ounce) Tomatoes
2 Cans (8 Ounce) Tomato Sauce
1 Teaspoon Oil
2 Teaspoons Chile powder
3 Tablespoons Morton's Chili Blend; To Taste
As Needed Water
½ Teaspoon Salt

1. Lightly brown meat in oil; then drain.
2. Add chopped onion and garlic; cover and cook for a few minutes.
3. Add tomatoes, tomato sauce and chile powder.
4. Add water enough to cover meat and ½ teaspoon salt.
5. Then as it cooks, add Morton's Chili Blend to suit your taste.
6. Cook approximately 3 hours over medium burner.

Harriet's Chili Recipe

1 Can (46 Ounce) Tomato Juice
2 Lb. Ground Beef; Or Ground Chuck
3 Cans (16 Ounce) Dark Red Kidney Beans
1 Large Onion; Finely Chopped
2 Large Green Peppers; Or 3 Small
2 Package French's Chili-O Season Mix
As Needed Margarine; For Sautéing
As Desired Tomatoes; Optional

1. Use crock-pot for this because it's easier, but it works fine in any large pot, it just requires more stirring.
2. In skillet heat margarine, sauté onion and green peppers, drain off excess oil, put vegetables in chili pot.

3. Use skillet without washing it to brown ground beef, drain and add to pot.
4. Add tomatoes if desired.
5. Drain and rinse kidney beans and add to pot.
6. Add tomato juice and stir.
7. Add seasoning mix and cook over medium heat about 1 hour until it cooks down.
8. The longer it cooks, the better!

Howie's Favorite Chili
2 Tablespoons Butter
4 Lb. Beef Sirloin; Coarse Ground
6 Ounces Tomato Paste
4 Cups Water
3 Medium Onions
1 Medium Bell Peppers
4 Cloves Garlic
3 Tablespoons Red Chile; Hot, Ground
1 Tablespoon Oregano, Dried; Preferably Mexican
½ Teaspoon Basil
1 Tablespoon Cumin
To Taste Salt
To Taste Pepper

1. Heat the oil or butter (or a blend of the two) in a heavy 4-quart pot over medium heat.
2. Add the meat to the pot.
3. Break up any lumps with a fork and cook, stirring occasionally, until the meat is evenly browned.
4. Stir in the remaining ingredients. Bring to a boil, then lower heat and simmer, uncovered, for 2 to 3 hours.
5. Stir occasionally and add more water if necessary.
6. Taste and adjust seasoning.

J. I.'s Chili
2 Lb. Chili Ground Meat
1 Can Enchilada Sauce
¼ Teaspoon Cumin
¼ Lb. Suet
1 Can Water
1 Dash Salt

591

1 Medium Onion; To Large
1 Teaspoon Chile powder
As Desired Pepper
2 Cloves Garlic
1 Teaspoon Oregano

1. Put suet in skillet or pan large enough to cook chili and let it melt.
2. While it is melting, chop onion and garlic. (If suet is not available, use bacon drippings, oil, butter, etc.)
3. Add onion and garlic to melted grease; sauté, until softened.
4. Add meat, a little salt, pepper and a little chile powder (red, preferably).
5. Stir and cook until meat is pretty well done.
6. Add enchilada sauce, water, chile powder, cumin and oregano.
7. Continue cooking until well done.
Makes about 6 cups.

Jack And Dick's Chili
1 Large Onion; Chopped
3 Lb. Chili Meat
3 Tablespoons Chile powder
1 Tablespoon Salt
3 Teaspoons Paprika
2 Teaspoons Garlic Powder
1 Teaspoon Cumin
½ Teaspoon Red Pepper
2 Cups Water; (Beer is Better)
3 Tablespoons Oatmeal
¼ Lb. Tallow

1. Melt tallow in large skillet.
2. Add chopped onion and brown.
3. Then add chili meat and brown.
4. Add remaining ingredients in order given: chile powder, salt, paprika, garlic powder, cumin, red pepper, water or beer and oatmeal. Cook slowly 3 to 4 hours.

Jack's Outpost Chili
2 Lb. Kidney Beans; Dried
3 Lb. Hamburger; 3 or 4
1 Can No. 10 Tomatoes (Stewed)

3 Large Onions; 3 or 4
2 Large Green Peppers; 2 or 3
2 Cans Tomato Sauce; 2 or 3
To Taste Chile powder
To Taste Salt and Pepper

1. Pick over and wash beans. Soak overnight in a large pan (I use one about 10 quarts). Be sure beans are fully covered with water.
2. Next morning after breakfast, build up campfire in good shape and let flames die back a bit. Cover and simmer beans for several hours. Check once in a while to be sure they don't go dry (also make sure fire doesn't go completely out). Stir occasionally; add salt and pepper and taste once in a while to determine when beans are tender. By now it's lunchtime.
3. After lunch, put pot on the back of fire to barely simmer and go swimming for a couple of hours.
4. When you return, build the fire back up and fry hamburger in a large frying pan. Drain hamburger and add to the pot of beans.
5. Save enough of the fat to sauté the onions and peppers (after you have sliced them).
6. As soon as they are tender, add them to the pot.
7. Now, add tomatoes and tomato sauce. See now why you need a large pot?
8. Season to taste with chile powder.
9. Heat gently and stir often to prevent sticking.
10. Simmer as long as you can or until supper time, whichever comes first. Serve 15 hungry kids and adults and there may still be some left for tomorrow's lunch.

Serve with plenty of biscuits or saltine crackers. I've used variations of this recipe for the past 8 years and haven't lost anyone yet. A favorite recipe at Sentinel Baptist Camp, Tuftonboro, New Hampshire.

Jay's Chili
2 Medium Onions; Finely Chopped
1 Medium Green Bell Pepper; Finely Chopped
1 Stalks Celery; Finely Chopped
2 Cloves Garlic; Minced
2 Teaspoons Oil
4 Lb. Ground Beef; Lean
2 Cans (14-½ Ounce) Tomatoes (Stewed)
1 Can (15 Ounce) Tomato Sauce
1 Can (6 Ounce) Tomato Paste

¼ Cup Green Chile Salsa
1 Pod Jalapeño; Finely Chopped
¾ Cup Chile powder
1 Can (4 Ounce) Green Chiles; Diced
½ Cup Water
1 Teaspoon Salt

1. In Dutch oven, sauté first four ingredients in hot oil until tender.
2. Add meat, 1 pound at a time, stirring until meat loses redness. Drain; add water.
3. Add remaining ingredients, stirring after each addition. Simmer 2-½ to 3 hours, stirring frequently.
4. Season to taste with garlic salt and pepper, if desired.

Jean Ashcraft's Prize Winning Chili-First Place 1980 and 81
2 Cups Onion; Chopped
4 Cloves Garlic; Crushed
1 Large Green Pepper; Chopped
1 Lb. Ground Round or Sirloin
4 Tablespoons Chile powder; See Note
1 Teaspoon Salt
¼ Teaspoon Black Pepper; Coarse
1 Teaspoon Cumin
1 Can (31 Ounce) Brook's Hot and Spicy Chili Beans
1 Cup Water
1 Can (15 Ounce) Tomato Sauce
1 The Secret Ingredient
(Better Than Ed Flesch's)

1. Put onions, garlic and green pepper in a large kettle. Spread ground meat on top.
2. Cook on medium until meat is to the pink stage. Remove from heat and add spices.
3. Blend well and let mix rest for 20 minutes.
4. Add tomato sauce and cup of water. Simmer for 20 minutes.
5. Add beans and simmer additional 20 minutes.
6. Cool completely, refrigerate until ready to serve.
7. Add the secret ingredient, heat and serve.
Note: Since chile powders vary in hotness, it is best to start out with less. If you use less chile powder, increase the amount of cumin.

Jeanne Owen's Chili Con Carne
1/3 Cup Olive Oil
3 Lb. Beef Round; Lean, 1-inch cubes
2 Medium Onions; Finely Chopped
3 Cloves Garlic; Finely Chopped
To Taste Salt
4 Cups Water; Boiling
1 Teaspoon Caraway Seeds
2 Teaspoons Sesame Seeds
½ Teaspoon Oregano; Preferably Mexican
3 Tablespoons Red Chile, Hot; Ground
1 Cup Green Olives; Pitted
2 Cans (16 Ounce) Kidney Beans

1. Heat the oil in a large sauté pan or 6-quart braising pan over medium heat.
2. Add the beef cubes a few at a time, stirring to brown evenly.
3. As they are browned, remove cubes to a plate and set aside, add more cubes to the pan.
4. Continue the process, adding more oil if necessary, until all the meat is browned.
5. Add the onions to the pan and cook, stirring, for a few minutes, and then add the garlic.
6. Cook until the onions are translucent.
7. Return the beef cubes to the pan, season with salt to taste, then add the boiling water, caraway and sesame seeds, and oregano.
8. Bring to a boil, and then lower the heat and simmer, covered, for 1 hour.
9. Gradually stir in the ground chile, tasting until you achieve the degree of hotness and flavor that suits you palate.
10. Add the olives and simmer, covered, 1 hour longer.
11. Taste and adjust seasonings, the mix in the kidney beans and heat through.

Jenny's Chili
2 Lb. Ground Beef
1 Large Onion; Chopped
2 Cans (15 Ounce) Kidney Beans in Chili Gravy
2 Cans (16 Ounce) Whole Tomatoes; Peeled
2 Teaspoons Salt
¼ Cup Brown Sugar
1 Tablespoon Chile powder; Or More To Taste

1. Combine onion and hamburger in skillet, cook, stirring frequently, until meat is brown and crumbly. Pour off excess fat.
2. Transfer to large pot; add kidney beans, canned tomatoes, salt, brown sugar and chile powder. Cook slowly-the longer you can allow the chili to simmer the better it is.
3. Add more chile powder to taste.

Jenny's Infamous Chili
1 Can Beer; Any Brand, Lite if on a Diet
1 Can (Large) Chili Beans; Optional
2 Lb. Ground Beef; 2 or 3
1 Large Onion; Chopped
1 Package Chili Mix; Name Brand
1 Teaspoon Cumin; For Stomach
To Taste Louisiana Hot Sauce; Optional
To Taste Chile powder; Optional
To Taste Mrs. Dash; Optional
2 Packages Field Chili Bloc
1 Can Tomato Juice; Generic
1 Quart Home Canned Tomatoes
1 Large Green Pepper; Chopped
1 Package (Large) Cheese; Shredded
1 Package Elbow Macaroni; Or Noodles, Drained
1 Teaspoon Curry Powder; Optional
To Taste Garlic Powder; Optional
1 Can Beer(s); Extra For The Cook

Begin early. Takes at least 2 to 3 hours of slow simmering.
1. Brown ground beef, onions and green pepper. Drain.
2. Mix in spices, juice, tomatoes, chili blocks, beans and mix; add cumin. Let simmer stirring frequently.
3. Add more of spices to taste.
4. Gradually stir in beer.
5. Add by small amounts stirring as adding. Let simmer.
6. Add a little more as beer brings out flavor and spices.
Top each bowl with cheese. (Feeds small army.)

Jer's Famous Brown Chili
2 Lb. Top Sirloin
2 Tablespoons Corn Oil

5 Medium White Onions
4 Cans (10 Ounce) Bush's Best Chili Hot Beans
6 Stalks Celery
1 Cup Lea & Perrins Worcestershire Sauce
2 Tablespoons Celery Salt
3 Tablespoons Chile powder
1 Tablespoon Black Pepper; Ground
2 Tablespoons Blackstrap Molasses
4 Each Fennel Seeds
1 Tablespoon Cayenne Pepper; Crushed
2 Teaspoons Louisiana Hot Sauce
1 Lb. Wisconsin Aged Sharp Cheddar Cheese
8 Ounces Wisconsin Cultured Sour Cream
1 Gallon Gallo Burgundy Wine
14 Inch Frying Pan
8 Quart Pot

1. Cut sirloin into cubes 3/8-inch on a side (5/16 is okay, too).
2. Add oil to pan, add heat under pan, and add sirloin to oil. Stir.
3. Chop 4 of the onions, keeping the other one for later. Stir meat.
4. Chop celery.
5. Stir meat.
6. When meat is semi (sort of) browned or gray, add onions and celery.
7. You'll get lots of moisture for a while, and then as the onions go translucent, the moisture will reduce.
8. Pour 8 ounces of wine in large wine glass. Have a couple of gulps.
9. Add celery salt, chile powder, and black pepper. To the pot, not the wine glass.
10. Stir until well mixed.
11. Add four fennel seeds.
12. Stir until fennel has disappeared.
13. Add Lea & Perrins.
14. Cook in frying pan, constantly stirring, until moisture has reduced to maybe a half a cup puddle in the pan. See if there's any more Lea & Perrins in the bottle. If there is, add another three ounces or so, and stir it in. Whether there is or not, have another couple of gulps of wine.
15. Transfer frying pan contents to pot.
16. Pour a splash of wine in the frying pan, loosen all the scrapings and run-away seasonings by stirring, and add to the pot.
17. Add beans to the pot. If you're a chili purist, skip the beans and double

the meat.
18. Have a gulp of wine.
19. Add the molasses, crushed pepper, and hot sauce.
20. Stir, but do not taste. Have another gulp of wine, instead.
21. Cover the pot, gulp some wine, and simmer (the chili) on low for an hour and a half.
22. Turn off the heat, and let it sit for an hour with the cover on. Gulp some wine.
23. With your palette appropriately cleared and sharpened, taste the chili.
24. Don't inhale with the spoonful of chili near your open mouth.
25. Take another spoonful.
26. Adjust seasoning until chewing, swallowing, and inhaling partially paralyzes the trachea at the bronchial juncture.

Serving: Mince the last onion. Reheat chili until just barely bubbling. Ladle into bowls. Sprinkle minced onion over surface of chili. Grate cheddar cheese on top of the onion. Add a generous tablespoon of sour cream on top of the cheese. Pour another glass of wine. Why wine instead of beer? For some reason, beer makes you sweat while you're eating Jer's Famous Brown Chili.

Jess Poling's Chili
3 Medium Onions; Chopped Fine
2 Medium Bell Peppers; Chopped Fine
3 Stalks Celery; Chopped Fine
8 Lb. Sirloin Beef; Coarse Ground
2 Cans (No. 2) Tomatoes (Stewed)
3 Cloves Garlic; Chopped Fine
1 Bottle (3 Ounce) Gebhardt's Chili Powder
2 Ounces Green Chile Salsa
1 Sprinkling Oregano
3 Tablespoons Salt
1 Pod Hot Green Chile, Canned
To Taste Garlic Salt
To Taste Black Pepper
4 Cans Vista Pinto Beans

1. Heat 1 tbsp oil, add onions, bell peppers and celery and cook until transparent.
2. Add beef and brown thoroughly, stirring often. Drain off excess grease.
3. Add tomato sauce, stewed tomatoes, tomato paste (to thicken), and two

tomato sauce cans water.

4. Add chili powder, and stir thoroughly.
5. Add salt, pepper, garlic, oregano, and stir.
6. Add chili sauce and hot green chile and stir. Simmer on low heat for 5 to 6 hours.
7. If chili begins to stick, add water, stir often.

You may cut down cooking time, but the longer you let it simmer, the better the chili will be. Some people will tell you if you cook with beans it is not chili. For those people I say, "You cook chili your way and I'll cook mine my way." If you want to add beans to this recipe, do so, I prefer the Sun Vista Pinto Beans. Served with homemade bread or French bread and salad makes for a complete meal. This recipe will serve approximately 20 persons.

Jim And Susan Alcorn's Nearly Famous Chili

8 Lb. Sirloin Roast; Whole
¼ Cup Oil; Or Enough to Brown Meat
4 Medium Yellow Onions; Chopped
2 Large Green Peppers; Chopped
120 Ounces Tomato Sauce
1 Tablespoon Salt
¼ Cup Worcestershire Sauce
1 Tablespoon Garlic Powder
¼ Cup Brown Sugar
¼ Box (53 Gram) Paprika
To Taste Cayenne Pepper
1 Box (4 Ounce) Chile powder; See Note
1 Can (16 Ounce) Applesauce
1 Can Jalapeño Relish
1 Ounce Mexican Pepper Sauce
2 Cans (12 Ounce) Beer; At Least
2 Tablespoons Masa Harina Flour; Instant
Note: (That may or may not contain cumin and oregano.) "Secret Stock" (Containing 8 whole cloves and 2 bay leaves.)

1. Trim meat of all fat. Cut into 1-inch cubes. Process with steel knife in food processor or shred and dice by hand.
2. Brown in hot oil. Drain.
3. Add rest of ingredients, except masa harina. Simmer uncovered about three hours, stirring every 15 minutes.
4. About 30 minutes before serving, mix masa harina with some of the chili

liquid in a small jar, shake well and add back to chili, stirring well. Simmer 30 minutes more.

Makes 2 gallons or serves 16 to 20.

Jim Carson's Chili

3 Tablespoon Olive Oil

1 Large Onion; Chopped

1 Medium Yellow Bell Pepper; Chopped

1 Medium Red Bell Pepper; Chopped

6 Cloves Garlic: Crushed and Minced

Heat oil, then sauté the above items in a large pot for 10-20 minutes, basically until the onion's kind of pale. While you're waiting for this to happen, prepare the other ingredients:

1 Medium Carrot; Grated into Near Subatomic Units (e.g., Small Bits).

1 Small Nub Ginger Root, Grated (See Note)

3 Large Fresh Tomatoes; Coarsely Chopped

2 Cans Mild Green Chiles; Chopped, Gooey "Juice" and all

1 Bunch Cilantro, Coarsely Chopped

Reduce heat, and then stir in the above items. Gradually add:

½ Lb. Beef Chorizo Sausage

1-½ Lb. Ground Chuck

1 Can (6 Ounce) Salsa Jalapeño (Essentially a Mix of Tomatoes, Onion,
    Jalapeño, and some other stuff-Good to Keep Around the House for a
Quick Meal)

1 Cup Vegetable Base (or Bullion)

5 Tablespoon Chile Powder

1 Tablespoon Paprika

1 Leaf Bay (Be Sure to Remove Before Serving)

2 Pods Anaheim Peppers; Seeded and Chopped

2 Pods Jalapeño Peppers; Seeded and Chopped

1 Pod Ancho Pepper; Seeded and Chopped

2 Tablespoons Cumin Seeds

½ Cup Sour Mash Whiskey

½ Bottle "Ole Nick" beer (from Whole Foods, the Other Half of the Bottle Mysteriously Disappeared)

Cook about an hour, or long enough for the excess liquids to boil off (one error I made)

Notes:

1. Except for the beer and whiskey, all of the ingredients are available from Fiesta on 38-½ and I-35.
2. There's a little porcelain doodad called a ginger grater that's great for this (and probably not much else).
3. If were I more adventurous, I would have tried chipotles instead of plain Jalapeños?

Jim's Chili

2 Lb. Beef; Diced
2 Lb. Jimmy Dean Sausage
As Needed Cooking Oil;
½ Lb. Suet, Fried In Oil
1 Jar (Small) Chile powder
4 Leaves Bay
4 Teaspoons Oregano
½ Teaspoon Cayenne Pepper
4 Cloves Garlic; Minced
4 Cans (Large) Italian Tomatoes
2 Cans (Large) Tomato Sauce
4 Tablespoons Red Wine Vinegar
1 Can (Small) Mushrooms
1 Can (Small) Olives
1 Jar Bacon Bits
2 Large Onions; Chopped
2 Large Bell Peppers
3 Teaspoons Liquid Brown Sugar

1. Add Beef, sausage, onions and bell peppers to pot.
2. Sauté onions and bells while browning meat.
3. Add remaining ingredients. Simmer 1 hour or more.
Optional-add drained, canned beans-kidney, black, etc.

Jim's Favorite Chili

3 Links Manda's Mild Sausage; Sliced Thin (Garnish)
2 Large Onions; Diced
3 Ribs Celery; Finely Diced
1 Medium Bell Pepper; Chopped
4 Lb. Ground Meat; Lean
2 Tablespoons Cumin; To Taste

601

2 Tablespoons Chile powder; To Taste
2 Tablespoons Masa Harina (Corn Flour)
1 Can (Large) Tomatoes; Chopped
2 Cans (Large) Tomato Sauce
3 Cans New Orleans Style Red Kidney Beans
To Taste Salt

1. Sauté, sausage in large soup pot (5 or 6 quarts).
2. Add onions, celery and bell pepper. Sauté, until translucent.
3. Add ground meat and brown.
4. Add cumin, chile powder and masa, mixing well.
5. Add tomatoes, tomato sauce and beans.
6. Add salt to taste. (If you like a thinner chili, water may be added.)
7. Simmer for about 2 hours. (The taste intensifies after slow simmering.)
Serve in large bowls.

   Top with shredded cheese, chopped green onion tops and 1 teaspoon of
sour cream or serve plain.

Joe Cooper's Chili
3 Lb. Beef; Ground or Cubed
¼ Cup Olive Oil
1 Quart Water
2 Leaves Bay
8 Pods Chile Pepper; Dried Or
6 Tablespoons Chile powder
3 Teaspoons Salt
10 Cloves Garlic; Chopped
1 Teaspoon Cumin
1 Teaspoon Oregano
1 Teaspoon Cayenne Pepper
½ Teaspoon Black Pepper; Freshly Ground
1 Tablespoon Sugar
3 Tablespoons Paprika
¼ Teaspoon Cocoa; Optional
3 Tablespoons Flour
6 Tablespoons Corn Meal

1. In a six-quart pot, sear meat in hot olive oil, stirring constantly over high
   heat until gray, but not brown.
2. Add water and mix well.

3. Add bay leaves now, but remove and discard after 15 minutes of cooking. Simmer covered 1-½ to 2 hours, stirring occasionally.
4. Add remaining ingredients, except for flour and cornmeal.
5. Cocoa should be added now. Simmer, stirring frequently, for 30 minutes.
6. Skim off any excess fat.
7. Adjust seasonings and add flour and cornmeal blended with a little cold water to make a paste.
8. Cook, stirring constantly to prevent sticking, until chili is the desired consistency.

Joel's Chili
1 Tablespoon Vegetable Oil
1-½ Cup Onion; Chopped
1 Cup Green Pepper; Chopped
1-¼ Lb. Ground Veal, Beef or Pork
1-½ Tablespoons Garlic; Finely Minced
3 Tablespoons Chile powder
1 Teaspoon Cumin; Ground
1 Teaspoon Oregano
1 Leaf Bay
½ Teaspoon Black Pepper
4 Cups Tomatoes; Canned
1 Tablespoon Red Wine Vinegar
¼ Teaspoon Red Hot Pepper Flakes

1. Heat the oil in a skillet.
2. Add the onion and green pepper. Cook until wilted.
3. Add the meat.
4. Use the edge of a heavy kitchen spoon to stir and chop the meat to break up any lumps.
5. Sprinkle the meat with garlic, chile powder, cumin and oregano. Stir to blend.
6. Add the bay leaf, pepper, tomatoes, vinegar and crushed hot pepper.
7. Bring to a boil and cook for 1 hour, stirring occasionally.

Joe's "Hot" Chili
4 Pods Jalapeño Peppers
1 Medium Green Pepper
1 Large Onion
1 Bottle Old Mexico Hot Sauce

2 Teaspoons Peanut Butter
2 Teaspoons Chile powder
2 Cans Chili Beans
1 Can Kidney Beans
1 Can Chili Mix
1 Lb. Hamburger

1. Cut onions and peppers into fourths and put in blender, then liquefy.
2. Mix in pot with sauce, powder, beans and chili mix.
3. Cook hamburger.
4. Bring to boil.
5. Put in hamburger and peanut butter and simmer.
6. Add spices to your taste (optional).

Joe's Indian Chili
5 Lb. Ground Beef
3 Lb. Ground Pork; Fresh
2 Cans Green Chiles; Whole
1 Can (Small) Hot Tomato Sauce
5 Cloves Garlic; Chopped
2 Tablespoons Prepared Mustard
2 Tablespoons Vinegar
2 Large Onions; Chopped
2 Medium Bell Peppers; Chopped
1 Tablespoon Cumin Powder
1 Dash Oregano
6 Tablespoons Lard
2 Tablespoons Flour
2 Cans (Medium) Beef Broth
4 Tablespoons Tabasco Sauce
2 Tablespoons Salt
1 Tablespoon Pepper
2 Tablespoons Worcestershire Sauce
As Desired Pinto Beans; Cooked

1. Brown meat in two tablespoons lard in large skillet. Pour into chili pot.
2. Sauté garlic, onions, bell pepper and chiles in two tablespoons lard. Add to chili pot.
3. Heat two tablespoons lard in skillet. Add flour and brown.
4. Pour in chili sauce.

5. Stir until smooth, and then pour into chili pot. Bring to a boil.
6. Then add other ingredients, cook slowly for 2-½ hours, stirring often.

Johnny's Chile Verde
John Fraga "Recipes To Kill For"
6 Tablespoons Chile powder
1 Can Tomatillos; Or 8-10 Fresh, Chopped
1 Medium Onion; Chopped
1 Medium Tomato; Chopped
3 Each Serrano Chile Peppers; Chopped
½ Teaspoon Cumin
½ Teaspoon Mexican Oregano
½ Teaspoon Salt
½ Teaspoon Black Pepper; Fresh Ground
¼ Cup Chicken Broth
4 Cloves Garlic; Split
2 Lb. Pork Shoulder; Lean, Cubed
1 Tablespoon Cooking Oil
1 Teaspoon Cornstarch; Optional
2 Teaspoons Water; Optional

1. Place ingredients 1 thru 11 (using only 3 cloves of garlic) in a food processor and process until well mixed.
2. Add oil to a large hot fry pan and brown pork a few minutes.
3. Sprinkle chile powder over pork in pan and continue to cook for 5 more minutes.
4. Place pork in a medium size pot.
5. Add tomatillos mixture to pot. Stir to combine with pork. Simmer for 1-2 hours until pork is very tender.
6. Crush and mince last clove of garlic, and add to pot during last 5 min. of cooking.
7. If mixture needs thickening, combine cornstarch and water, mix well and slowly stir into pot a little at a time until desired consistency.

Johnny's Chili
John Fraga "Recipes To Kill For"
2 Tablespoons Olive Oil
2 Lb. Beef; Lean, Cubed
2 Cans Pinto Beans; Drained
6 Ounces Water

1 Large Onion; Chopped
½ Large Red Bell Pepper; Chopped
3 Cloves Garlic; Diced
7 Tablespoons Chile powder
1 Tablespoon Cumin; Crushed
1 Tablespoon Mexican Oregano; Crushed
2 Cans Tomatoes; Stewed
2 Pods Pasilla Chile Peppers; Roasted and Chopped
2 Pods California (Anaheim) Chiles; Roasted and Chopped
3 Pods Habañero Peppers; Minced
3 Pods Serrano Chile Peppers; Diced
1 Tablespoon Balsamic Vinegar
1 Teaspoon Black Pepper; Fresh Ground

1. Roast pasilla, California and bell pepper under broiler till blackened all over. Place chiles in a paper bag and close tightly to steam (15-20 min.). Remove blackened skin, stem, and most of the seeds.
2. Add olive oil to a "hot" large fry pan.
3. Add meat and sear quickly for a few minutes.
4. Distribute chile powder over meat and continue to cook over medium heat.
5. Add cumin and Mexican oregano.
6. Add onion and garlic and cook 4-5 min.
7. Add meat mixture to a large pot.
8. Add tomatoes, water, roasted chiles, Serranos, and ground pepper.
9. Add Habañeros "Warning" Habañero peppers are the hottest pepper on the face of the earth. Use extreme caution when handling these little buggers.
10. Simmer chili mixture 2-4 hours, stirring occasionally till meat is very tender and flavors are well blended. 15-20 minutes before chili is done add beans until they are heated through.
11. Add salt to taste.
12. Just before serving, add balsamic vinegar (don't overdo it or the whole pot will have a vinegar taste). Add a little at a time then taste.
"Enjoy."

Judy's Redeye Chili
2 Tablespoons Oil
2 Medium Onions; Chopped
1-½ Lb. Ground Chuck or Round

¼ Lb. Ground Breakfast Sausage
3 Cloves Garlic; Minced
1 Can (15 Ounce) Tomatoes; Drained and Chopped
1 Can (6 Ounce) Tomato Paste
1 Can Beer
½ Cup Strong Black Coffee
1 Can Beef Bouillon
3 Tablespoons Chile powder; (3-4)
1 Tablespoon Cumin Seed; Toasted
1 Tablespoon Cocoa Powder
1 Teaspoon Oregano
1 Teaspoon Red Pepper; To Taste
1 Teaspoon Coriander
To Taste Salt
3 Cans Kidney or Pinto Beans
To Taste Jalapeño Chile Peppers; Chopped
As Desired Accompaniments

Here is a great chili recipe that I concocted. It gets its name from the "secret ingredient," coffee, which is a key ingredient in Redeye Gravy. Placed 2nd in local chili cookoff! I use home grown powdered chiles, Ancho, NM, etc.

1. In a small skillet, brown sausage. Drain and reserve.
2. Pour oil into a large stockpot and sauté onion, ground beef and garlic.
3. Cook until meat is lightly browned. Drain grease.
4. Add rest of ingredients except Jalapeños.
5. Cook for 1-½ hr. and then add beans and salt to taste. Simmer for 30 minutes more.
6. Thicken with masa harina mixed with a little water if necessary.

Serve with chopped onions, shredded Monterey Jack cheese, chopped Jalapeño peppers, and Cowpoke Cornbread.

Judy's Austerlitz Chili
3 Lb. Kidney Beans; (Goya or Progresso)
3 Lb. Ground Meat; Lean
1 Jar Chile powder; (Use a Whole Jar--Yes!)
1 Bacon End; (Or 2 Strips Bacon)
2 Medium Onions; Chopped Up
2 Cans Progresso Peeled Whole Tomatoes
As Needed Monterey Jack Cheese

To Taste Scallions
2 Cloves Garlic

1. In a heavy iron kettle brown the bacon end in olive oil (just enough to cover the bottom of the pan).
2. Add the chopped up onion. When onion is yellow, brown the meat.
3. As you brown the meat, add chile powder and paprika. (If you use bacon, don't add any salt.)
4. After meat is brown, add 2 big cloves of garlic, chopped up.
5. Then add the tomatoes, then beans.
6. Stir all together, and then add more chile powder. (You should be almost through with the jar by now.)
7. Set oven to 125 degrees and bake 4 to 5 hours (or longer; doesn't matter).
8. An hour or so before you eat, slice the Monterey Jack cheese thin and cover the surface with the slices. It will melt down.

Chop scallions and serve in a bowl to be sprinkled by diners on their chili.

Optional: You can also add Tabasco sauce, Worcestershire, etc. while chili is cooking.

You can add a little more chile powder each time you stir.

Karen's Chili

1 Can (14-½ Ounce) Tomatoes; Whole
1 Can (14-½ Ounce) Tomatoes; Crushed
1 Can (14-½ Ounce) Tomato Sauce
2 Cans (14-½ Ounce) Dark Red Kidney Beans
1 Small Onion; Chopped
1/3 Cup Green and/or Red Peppers; Chopped
1 Lb. Ground Chuck; Browned and Well Drained
3 Centiliters Garlic; Minced
3 Tablespoons Chile powder
1-½ Teaspoons Cumin

1. Brown ground chuck in a Dutch oven. Drain thoroughly.
2. Add onion, garlic, and pepper and cook until vegetables are softened.
3. Add remaining ingredients and cook over low heat for 2 hours.
4. Stir occasionally and check every so often to correct the seasoning.
5. This can also be done in a crock-pot by browning the ground chuck in a skillet, draining, and then adding this and all the other ingredients to the crock-pot.
6. Cook on high for the first hour, then turn to low and cook all day.

Serve in a pasta bowl over corn bread (recipe follows) with a dab of sour cream (low fat) and a sprinkle of cheddar or jack cheese.

Cornbread: It's just as easy to prepare cornbread from scratch as from a mix, and you won't believe how much better it is! This is essentially right off the bag:

2 Cups Cornmeal Mix
1-¼ to 1-½ Cups Milk
¼ Cup Vegetable Oil (I use Olive)
1 Egg
1 to 2 Tablespoons Sugar

1. Preheat a well-greased 8 - 10 inch cast iron skillet in a 425-degree oven.
2. Blend all ingredients and pour into the pan.
3. Bake for 20-25 minutes.
Cut into 8 servings. Yield: 8 servings

Kasvi's Nuclear Chili!
1 Kilogram Cheap Cow
800 Grams Tomatoes; Crushed
1 Bottle Beer
1/2 Dl. Extra hot chile powder; or
1 Dl. Regular Chile powder
15 Ml. Cumin; (Jeera)
10 Ml. Cayenne Pepper
30 Ml. Brown Sugar
1 Big Red Onion; Coarse Chopped
2 Big Garlic Cloves
8 Pods Preferably Different Kinds Chiles
5 Pods Chiles; Dried
3 Medium Bell Peppers
2 Cubes Meat Stock
30 Grams Corn Flour
200 Grams Various Kinds of Beans
1 Can Whole Champignons; Very Optional
As Needed Food Oil
As Needed Water

1. Chop the onion coarse, peel garlic gloves, seed and chop bell peppers into small cubes, seed fresh chiles and cut them into rings and cut the meat into 1 cm cubes.
2. Put the crushed tomatoes and the beer into a big pot and the pot to the fire.
3. Brown the meat cubes in oil.
4. When the pot boils, put the browned meat cubes into it, add chile powder, chopped onion, fresh and dried chiles, bell peppers, meat stock cubes, sugar and cayenne pepper.
5. Crush about half of the garlic cloves to the pot, too.
6. Add some oil, if the meat had no fat in it.
7. Put the lid on the pot and let the chili simmer slowly for some four hours and stir it every now and then.
8. Add the champignons, cut the garlic gloves into half and add them too.
9. Wait for another hour.
10. Add the beans.
11. Mix the corn flour into about a deciliter of water and pour the water into the pot.
12. Simmer for another half hour, stirring regularly.
13. The chili burns easily to the pot bottom at this stage.

Enjoy with rice, green salad, lots of beer and handkerchiefs.

Kathy Pitts' New Mexico Chili

I don't have a real recipe for New Mexico-style chile, although I do make it occasionally when I manage to drag home more fresh Anaheim or Poblano chiles than I can dispose of otherwise. (Kroger's sometimes has big bags of them for 99 cents a bag.)

1. What I do is first roast the chiles (either in the broiler or -- better -- over charcoal). The number of chiles I use depends on the size/heat of the chiles, and can range from 2-3 to 10 or more. If the chiles are really hot (it happens sometimes, even with Anaheims), I'll also add 3-4 roasted green bell peppers to give the dish the required pepper taste without rendering it inedible by anyone without an asbestos esophagus.
2. After the chiles have cooled a bit, I peel and seed them, and cut them into coarse dice.
3. I sometimes (not always) will also roast/peel 5-6 tomatoes to place in the chiles, but tomatoes are optional in this dish, and I usually don't use 'em.
4. Next, cut up 3-4 pounds of lean boneless pork (beef is sometimes used, but isn't as good in this dish, and I would imagine lamb would be very

good here indeed).

5. Coat the meat in seasoned flour, and brown it in hot lard.
6. Remove from the pan and set aside.
7. Toss a couple of chopped onions into the pot, along with a clove or two of garlic.
8. When the onions are golden, I add enough flour to make a roux, and cook until the roux is light brown.
9. I then add chicken broth to make a fairly thin gravy, the pork, chiles, tomatoes (if used), and season the dish with cumin and Mexican oregano.
10. Simmer for a couple of hours, until the pork is tender and the flavors have blended.

The end dish should have a pronounced green chile/pepper flavor and be the consistency of a thick stew. It's very good by itself, or as a filling for burritos/soft tacos, and is wonderful reheated the next morning and served as a side dish with scrambled eggs for breakfast. Wes, for some bizarre reason, likes it over rice.

Sorry for the inexact recipe/directions. I learned to make this dish from an ex-neighbor who was of mixed Hispanic/Native American ancestry, and never quite got around to rendering her directions into a real recipe. (She served the dish with fry bread, and a pot of white beans on the side -- have no idea whether this was traditional or simply the way she liked it.)

Ken Haycook's Award Winning Chili

3 Lb. Beef Brisket; Diced
2 Centiliters Garlic; Minced
1 Teaspoon Black Pepper
2 Tablespoons Cumin
1 Teaspoon Ginger
1 Tablespoon Red Pepper
1 Can (Small) Tomato Paste
1-½ Cups Boiling Water
1 Medium Tomato; Finely Chopped
1 Can (4 Ounce) V-8 Juice
¾ Cup Onion; Diced
1 Tablespoon Salt
3 Tablespoons Chile powder
1 Tablespoon Paprika
1 Tablespoon Dry Mustard
1 Teaspoon Oregano
1 Can (Large) Tomato Sauce

½ Can Cheap American Beer
1 Pod Jalapeño; Finely Chopped
Only use Brisket. Do not use ground beef. The best chili is made from slow simmered brisket.

1. Brown the brisket with a little oil.
2. Drain and remove meat.
3. Sauté onion and garlic in the left over oil.
4. Add all the spices and let pan roast.
5. Add the beef back to the pot and add the tomato paste, tomato sauce, water, V8 juice, tomato, Jalapeño, and beer.
6. Cover and simmer for 3 hr.
7. Add more beer if chili gets too dry.

Ken's Chili
2-½ Lb. Ground Chuck; Coarse
2 Cans (8 Ounce) Tomato Sauce
24 Ounces Water
2 Cans Pinto Beans; With Liquid
2 Large Onions
2 Cloves Garlic; Minced
2 Teaspoons Red Pepper
½ Cup Chile powder
1 Teaspoon Paprika
1-½ Teaspoons Cumin
2 Teaspoons Masa Harina Flour

1. Sauté onions and garlic in light oil till brown.
2. Sear meat in large skillet.
3. Add tomato sauce and water.
4. Stir in all ingredients, except flour and beans*. Cover skillet and simmer 1 hour. Stir occasionally.
5. Stir in flour into ¼ cup warm water to make a thick, but flow able mixture.
6. Add flour mixture to chili; simmer another 15 to 20 min.
7. Add beans and juice and cook another 15 min.*
8. Best when allowed to refrigerate for 24 hour but who can wait?
*Optional

Kevin and Linda Nealon's Delicious and Simple Chili
The Compassionate Cook-by Ingrid Newkirk
1 Tablespoon Olive Oil
1 Large Onion; Diced
½ Medium Green Bell Pepper; Chopped
3 Cans (28 Ounce) Tomatoes; Crushed
2 Cans (40 Ounce) Dark Red Kidney Beans
3 Tablespoons Chile powder; Or To Taste
1 Teaspoon Salt
1 Tablespoon Sugar; Optional

1. Heat the olive oil in a very large frying pan or Dutch oven over medium heat.
2. Sauté the onions and pepper until tender, about 5 to 7 minutes.
3. Add the remaining ingredients and bring the mixture to a boil.
4. Lower the heat and simmer, covered, for 1 hour.
Preparation time: 10 minutes Cooking time: 1 hour.

L.J's Chili Con Carne Y Judia
4 Lb. Stew Beef
2 Lb. Pork
3 Cans (14 Ounce) Red Kidney Beans
1 Can (14 Ounce) Pinto Beans
2 Cans (14 Ounce) White Kidney Beans
3 Cans (14 Ounce) Brown Beans
1 Can Hunt's Tomato Paste; Large
1 Cup Ketchup
2 Large Green Peppers
2 Large Red Peppers
1 Tablespoon Black Pepper
1 Tablespoon Salt; To Taste
½ Cup Chile powder
1 Cup Potatoes; Mashed (See Note)
¼ Single Banana; Mashed (See Note)
1 Tablespoon Lemon Juice
1 Quart Tomatoes; Canned, Peeled
1 Tablespoon Red Chile Flakes; Or More To Taste
2 Tablespoons Blackstrap Molasses
2 Teaspoons Cumin Seeds; Ground
1 Teaspoon Coriander

1 Teaspoon Paprika; Hungarian
1 Teaspoon Oregano
1 Teaspoon Cayenne Pepper
3 Large Spanish Onions
3 Cans (8 Ounce) Mushroom; Button
*If plantains are available, don't use the potato or banana, slice the plantain into ¼ inch pieces.

1. Cut meat into 1 inch chunks or thereabouts.
2. Let meat soak in a bowl with the tomatoes and juice, lemon juice, mushrooms, black pepper, crushed chiles, diced peppers and onions over night.
3. Remove the meat and brown in a skillet. It takes a while but worth it.
4. In large pot place all the ingredients except the beans including the above marinade and slow cook for three hours.
5. Next stir in your beans and cook slowly for one more hour.
6. Do not cook with the lid on the pot, as the chili will not "thicken."
7. If chili is not thick enough you can add flour (corn) mixed with water.
8. With the thick "soupy" ring around the pot; stir back into the simmering chili.
9. You might like the chili hotter or maybe milder, depends on your taste.
10. What ever you do, don't ruin the chili by making it hotter with hot sauces, this has a tendency to make the chili into "superficial" body heat not a deep solid heat.

Landureth's Chili
Jim Landureth
4 Lb. Meat (Chili Meat)
4 Cloves Garlic
6 Tablespoons Flour
2 Tablespoons Caminos
4 Tablespoons Paprika
1 Tablespoon Salt
4 Tablespoons Chile powder
As Needed Water

1. The meat may be browned or placed in a crock-pot without browning.
2. Cubes or beef or hamburger meat may be used, but the hamburger tends to become very mushy and may also contain too much fat.
3. Add all ingredients. Cover with water. Stir until flour, paprika, salt, and

chili are dissolved.
4. Cook several hours over low heat.
5. The cloves of garlic may be removed before serving.
Notes: The topic of chili is often discussed, and the bean controversy comes up again and again. In Texas, *serious* chili gourmets consider cooking chili with beans an abomination! Uncouth! Pinto or ranch beans may be a side dish. My family ate chili with side dishes of pinto beans and Spanish rice. My chili recipe, passed down from grandma Vilchez, has no tomatoes.

Lee Daniel's Chili
2 Lb. Beef; (Pork or Rabbit can be used)
¼ Cup Chile powder
¼ Cup Cumin
3 Tablespoons Cayenne Pepper; Ground
3 Tablespoons Oregano
2 Tablespoons Black Pepper
2 Tablespoons Paprika
2 Medium Jalapeño Peppers; Minced
1 Pod Habañero Pepper; Minced
3 Cloves Garlic; Minced
2 Pods Chipotle Chile Pepper; Chopped
1 Tablespoon Red Pepper Flakes
1 Medium Onion; Minced
5 Tablespoons Bacon Fat
2 Cans Pabst Blue Ribbon Beer
8 Ounces Tomato Paste
12 Ounces Tomatoes; Crushed
1 Small Can Mild Green Chiles; Roasted
1 Each Bay Leaf
1 Can (16 Ounce) Kidney Beans; Or Pinto Beans
As Needed Water
As Needed Corn Flour; Optional

1. Sear the meat in an iron skillet on both sides with hot bacon fat, garlic, onion, and Jalapeño. Empty all of it into a pot.
2. Add rest of ingredients, bring to a boil, turn down heat and simmer for 1-½ to 2 hrs. (until meat is tender) stir regularly.
3. If it gets too thick add some more beer (from the one you're sippin' on).
4. If it gets too watery stir in some corn flour (or fine ground corn meal) or cook it down till it thickens up add 16 oz of kidney or pinto or black

beans the last 15 minutes (hey it's not Texas).

Serving Ideas: Diced green onions, cornbread, and cracklins.

Notes: For the obligatory "weenie" batch I leave out the chipotles, Habañero, cut the Jalapeño, cayenne and black pepper amounts in ½ and add a little more chopped tomatoes and beans, and add 1 small green pepper seeded and minced.

Be sure and have plenty of beer.

We do this every Super Bowl; usually have around 25-30 folks over. Its always fun to watch the first timers be brave; then we start watchen 'em sweat a little under their forehead, then they begin to sniffle, then they turn red, and finally break out in a full capsicum rash and then, if they don't run for more sour cream and cheese, they can only grunt" umm-ahhh-man!-Whoaa." Lots a fun!

Leeman's Chili

1 Lb. Ground Beef
1 Can Manwich
1 Medium Onion
To Taste Salt
½ Package William's Chili Seasoning
2 Cans Bush's Chili Beans
1 Quart Tomato Juice
2 Tablespoons Brown Sugar
To Taste Chile powder

1. Brown ground beef and onion (diced) together; drain and mix with beans, Manwich, sugar and juice.
2. Add salt and chile powder to taste. Cook over medium heat for 10 to 15 minutes.

Serve hot.

Lee's Chili Surprise

2 Lb. Chili Ground Beef
2 Lb. Lean Beef; Cut in ½ Inch Cubes
2 Lb. Smoked Sausage; Cubed
3 Cans (4 Ounce) Chile Peppers; Chopped
2 Cups Onion; Chopped
2 Cans (28 Ounce) Tomatoes (Stewed); Chopped
2 Cloves Garlic; Crushed
2 Cans (15 Ounce) Chili Sauce

2 Teaspoons MSG
2 Teaspoons Pepper; Coarse Ground
2 Tablespoons Cumin
1 Tablespoon Sugar; Optional
1-½ Teaspoons Sweet Basil
3 Teaspoons Salt
2 Teaspoons Paprika
2 Teaspoons Oregano
4 Leaves Bay
4 Tablespoons Chile powder
5 Cans (15 Ounce) Red Kidney Beans
To Taste Cayenne Pepper; Ground
Note: Venison may be substituted for beef.

1. Brown the beef and sausage in large pot over medium heat.
2. Add chili peppers and onion.
3. Continue to cook until onions are translucent.
4. Add MSG, garlic, pepper, salt, cumin, oregano and sweet basil and continue to simmer over medium heat.
5. Add tomatoes in juice, tomato sauce, paprika, and chile powder and continue to simmer on low for 30 minutes.
6. Add kidney beans and bay leaves and simmer 4 to 8 hours over low heat.
7. Maintain liquid level by adding water or beer as necessary.
8. If you like your chili thick, add cornstarch to thicken.

Note: This is a relatively mild chili. To increase the hotness, add cayenne pepper or Jalapeño peppers to taste, but be careful, it's easy to add more but tough to take away. Also be aware that different chile powders offer different heats.

Little John's Chili
5 Lb. Beef Roast
2 Lb. Soup Bones
As Needed Water
3 Lb. Pinto Beans; Cooked
4 Ounces Mexene Chili Powder
½ Teaspoon Cumin Seed
To Taste Salt
To Taste Cayenne
To Taste Black Pepper

1. Cook meat and soup bone separately until tender in enough water to keep covered.
2. Dice roast, strain stock, and add the cooked beans.
3. Stir in the Mexene and cumin seeds.
4. Add salt and pepper (black and red) to taste.
5. Cook very slowly over low flame 1 to 1-½ hours.

Author's Note: Leftover roast beef will do a good job too, as will canned pintos.

Longie's Chili

1 Lb. Hamburger
2 Cans Kidney Beans
1 Medium Onion
1 Medium Green Pepper
1 Teaspoon Chile powder
As Needed Ketchup; until as red as You Want

Brown hamburger, onions and peppers, add other ingredients. Cook about 20 minutes on medium heat.

Mac's Irish Chili

2 Lb. Ground Beef; Lean
1 Medium Onion; Sliced and Diced
1 Can Black Olives (Ripe); Pitted and Sliced
2 Cans (Large) Chili Beans
2 Cans (Medium) Chili Con Carne
½ Cup Brown Sugar

1. Brown and crumble ground beef in iron skillet and break up until large pieces are small pieces.
2. Cover and keep hot while preparing rest of chili.
3. In a large crock or pot, add chili beans, chili con carne, tomatoes and let simmer (low heat) for ½ hour or until bubbles begin to pop on surface.
4. Stir quite often so nothing sticks or scorches on bottom.
5. Now sprinkle in the chile powder and brown sugar and mix thoroughly.
6. Add the browned and crumbled ground beef. Mix thoroughly.
7. Add the diced onion. Mix thoroughly.
8. Now simmer (low heat) for 15 minutes.

Serve while hot with crackers of choice (saltines, Ritz, Wheat Thins, etc.).
   Serves 6 to 8.

Keep lid on pot to keep hot. Turn off cooking heat. Sprinkle diced olives over top of each bowl. Remainder, if any, can be frozen.

Mama's Chili
1-½ Lb. Hamburger
4 Medium Onions; Chopped
4 Sticks Celery; Chopped
1 Medium Bell Pepper; Chopped
3 Cloves Garlic; Diced
1 Can Tomatoes; Pureed
To Taste Garlic Powder
2 Leaves Bay
1 Can (Small) Tomato Sauce
1 Can Chili Beans
To Taste Chile powder

1. Brown hamburger meat; drain off fat.
2. Add onions, celery, bell pepper, garlic and garlic powder and sauté.
3. Put sautéed ingredients in a large pot; add tomatoes and tomato sauce.
4. Add water to cover ingredients.
5. Add chile powder to taste. Cook on low to medium heat, stirring regularly until ingredients are tender.
6. Add chili beans and simmer for 45 minutes.

Mana's Lake O' Pines Chili
2 Lb. Ground Meat; Typically Coarse Ground
½ Medium Sweet Onion; Chopped
1/3 Cup All Purpose Flour
½ Teaspoon White Sugar
2 Tablespoons Olive Oil; For Browning Ground Meat
6 Tablespoon Mana's Chili Spice; Hold Back 1 Tsp. to add later

Hint: Meat texture is better when not finely ground. To make your own is actually the best way. You can cut sirloin into ¼" cubes or put pieces of trimmed meat into food processor and process until chopped, but not too fine.

1. Work flour into ground meat.
2. Add dash of salt and pepper if you wish for browning.
3. Don't add too much, but instead add later during cooking.
4. Brown meat in small quantities in a hot skillet with oil. (A hint to prevent

sticking is to have pan hot before adding cold oil and begin browning immediately.)

5. Add onion to last of browning meat mixture and brown with meat until onions are sweated clear.
6. Remove browned meat and onions into 6-quart saucepan.
7. With some of the water or tomato juice, deglaze the skillet you browned the meat in, and put glaze in saucepan with all remaining ingredients.
8. Bring to high simmer, but do not boil.
9. Cook uncovered 1-½ to 2 hours, stirring occasionally.
10. Hints to correctly taste test chili as it cooks. To taste test your chili, use a piece of white bread or unsalted soda cracker, never taste off the end of a spoon, the spices will fool you.
11. Add remaining tablespoon of Mana's Chili Spice if you like real hot chili.
12. Remember this point: the ingredients in your chili will absorb flavors as it cooks and then after it cools, spicy flavors may intensify.
13. Go easy on spices. They can always be added a little at a time later. Go with your first impression of the taste.
14. Consistently tasting chili will allow the 'heat' of the chile powders to overcome your sense for the other spices and will not give you a good indication of how it tastes. You might find later that chili that was over sampled will end up being too hot, or will exhibit a taste you couldn't detect earlier.
15. Your chili is done when the meat stays suspended in the 'gravy' after stirring.
16. Always skim all fat from your chili as it cooks, it will mask the flavors of the spices as you sample and provide an unwanted taste texture.

Enjoy.

Manuelita Lopez's New Mexico Chili

2 Lb. Chopped Meat; Cubed Pork or Beef
1-½ Cups Water
1 Teaspoon Oregano
1 Teaspoon Garlic Powder
7 Pods Chile Peppers; (up to 8), Or
¼ Cup Chile Powder
1 Cup Water
1/8 Cup Flour
As Desired Salt

1. Brown meat thoroughly. Drain off fat.
2. Blend 1-½ cups water, oregano, garlic powder and chile peppers (or powder) in a blender. (If using chile peppers, be sure they are ground well.)
3. Over medium heat, stir chili mixture slowly into meat.
4. Add 1-cup water to meat chili mixture. Stir well.
5. Slowly stir in 1/8-cup flour. Cook until mixture boils.
6. Add salt to taste and stir well. Lower heat and simmer for 20 to 30 minutes or until chili thickens.

Note: This recipe does not call for refried beans. In New Mexico, they are served as a side dish.

Margaret's Chili

4 Large Onions; Chopped
6 Cloves Garlic; Crushed
3 Large Green peppers
¼ Cup Vegetable Oil
1 Teaspoon Oregano
2 Teaspoons Cumin; Ground
2 Leaves Bay
2 Lb. Ground Beef
1/8 Cup Chile powder
1 Quart Tomatoes
4 Cans (16 Ounce) Kidney or Pinto Beans
2 Teaspoons Salt
3 Tablespoons Cider Vinegar or Red Wine Vinegar
1 Bottle (6 Ounce) Chili Sauce

1. In a large 6 quart or 8 quart Dutch oven or large pot, sauté, onions, peppers and garlic in oil for 10 minutes, stirring occasionally.
2. Add oregano, cumin, bay leaf and beef. Cook stirring for about 10 minutes or until meat is browned.
3. Add chile powder, tomatoes and 2 cans of beans.
4. Heat mixture to boiling; reduce heat and simmer uncovered, stirring occasionally, 1-½ hours.
5. Add chili sauce, remaining beans, salt and vinegar. Heat to boiling.
6. Reduce heat and simmer covered 15 minutes.
7. Add more chile powder if desired.

Serve with garlic bread.

Marie's Dad's Chili (From Harvard Chili Cook Off 1987)
1 Lb. Hamburger
1 Can No. 2 Dark Kidney Beans
1 Can No. 2 Tomatoes
1 Small Green Pepper
1 Tablespoon Chile powder
1 Medium Onion
1 Clove Garlic; Large
1 Lb. Mushrooms
1-½ Teaspoons Caraway Seeds
1-½ Teaspoons Flour
1-½ Teaspoons Black Pepper
1-½ Teaspoons Salt
2 Tablespoons Butter

1. Melt 1-tablespoon butter in fry pan. When hot, add meat, spread and brown.
2. Add mushrooms.
3. Place meat and mushrooms in greased pot over moderate fire.
4. Add beans, tomatoes, chile powder, salt and pepper.
5. Mince onion, crush garlic; sauté, in remaining tablespoon of butter to rich brown. Add to pot.
6. Crush caraway seed with mortar and carefully brown with flour in small skillet. Add to pot; simmer over low heat 1 hour or more.

Great doubled and tripled. Easy to freeze. Number of servings: 6. Preparation time: 1-½ hours.

Marisa's Yummy Chili
2 Lb. Ground beef; Or Turkey
1 Clove Garlic
1 Tablespoon Vegetable Oil
1 Medium Onion
¼ Cup Chile powder
1 Pod Jalapeño Pepper; Chopped into Cubes
1 Teaspoon Salt
1 Teaspoon Pepper
1 Can Pinto Beans; Drained
2 Cans (8 Ounce) Tomato Sauce

1. Add oil to pan and sauté garlic and onion for 5 minutes or until onion is soft.
2. Add beef or ground turkey and brown. Drain the fat.
3. Add tomato sauce, pinto beans, Jalapeño pepper cubes, salt, pepper, and chile powder. Mix well.
4. Cover and simmer for 30 minutes.

Serve hot with sprinkled Cheddar cheese shreds. Serves 4 hearty bowls of chili.

Mark's Chili Recipe:
Mark Muller
1 Lb. Chuck Roast; Lean, Diced Finely
1 Large Yellow Onion; Diced
6 Cloves Garlic; Minced
1 Can (15 Ounce) Tomatoes; Diced
2 Cans (15 Ounce) Small Red Beans; Rinsed and Drained
4 Pods Pasilla Chile; Dried
3 Pods Ancho Chile Peppers; Dried
3 Pods Chipotle Peppers
1 Tablespoon Oregano; Dried
1 Tablespoon Cumin; Ground
To Taste Black Pepper; Fresh Ground
20 Ounces Hot Water
As Needed Vegetable Oil

1. Seed and deveined dried chiles, tear into small pieces, and soak in hot water for 30 min.
2. Put water and chile mixture in blender or food processor and puree till smooth.
3. Brown beef in bottom of stockpot with vegetable oil.
4. Add onion to pot and cook till somewhat soft.
5. Add the rest of the ingredients (including the chile puree) to the pot, and simmer for 1-2 hours, depending upon your patience.

Mark's Cookoff Winner Chili!
¼ Cup Olive Oil
2 Lb. Hot Pork Sausage
2 Lb. Stew Beef; Cubed
1 Can Ro-tel Diced Tomato and Green Chile
8 Cloves Garlic; Minced

1/3 Cup Chile powder
4 Tablespoons Cumin
¼ Cup Jalapeño Chile Peppers; Sliced
1 Teaspoon Tabasco Sauce
2 Cans (Large) Tomatoes; Crushed
4 Large Onions; 2 White-2 Red
2 Lb. Ground Chuck
1 Bottle V8 Juice; Hot
2 Cans Beef Broth
2 Cans (Large) Chili Beans; Hot
2 Teaspoons Paprika
1 Tablespoon Red Pepper; Dried
2 Teaspoons Coriander
1 Can Tomato Sauce
6 Tablespoons Red Wine Vinegar

This recipe will feed a whole troop.
1. In a large skillet, sauté onions in olive oil, set to the side.
2. In a #14 Dutch oven, brown pork sausage and chuck, then add stew meat.
3. Season with salt and pepper to taste. Cook for about 20 minutes.
4. Add onion mixture.
5. Stir in spices and cook 5 minutes.
6. Add V8, tomatoes, tomato sauce and beef broth. Bring to boil, lower heat and simmer 1 hour.
7. Stir in garlic, Tabasco, peppers and hot chili beans. Simmer another 10 minutes.
8. You can dissolve some cornstarch in about a ¼ cup of warm water and then add to the chili until thick.
Sprinkle with cheese, popcorn, Frito chips or fixin's of your choice. We will sometimes cook the meats two days ahead of time, place in gallon freezer bags and keep in the cooler. Also to save time chop the onions and garlic and assemble in a gallon freezer bag ahead of time to cut down on prep time.

Mark's Killer Chili
2 Lb. Ground Beef; Fresh
1 Can (28 Ounce) Tomatoes; Peeled
1 Can Ro-tel Diced Tomato and Green Chile; Diced
2 Cans (Large) Chili Beans
1 Medium Onion
1 Package Barzi Chili Powder Red Pepper

½ Teaspoon Paprika
1 Clove Garlic; Small
1 Dash Salt
As Needed Wheat Flour
3 Cups Water

1. Brown ground beef.
2. Put tomatoes, onion, Ro-Tel and garlic in blender and chop.
3. Add mixture to ground beef and stir, add beans.
4. Add water, salt, chile powder and paprika while stirring. Simmer on low heat, stirring often.
5. Use wheat flour to thicken chili as needed.
6. Season to taste with red pepper. I personally prefer 2 tablespoons red pepper! Folks, that's hot!

This chili can be served as main course or used as anti-freeze, whichever you prefer.

Martha's Chilly Day Chili
2 Lb. Hamburger; Lean
1 Medium Green Pepper; Chopped
2 Medium Onions; Chopped
1 Can Tomatoes
½ Cup Ketchup
1 Can (15 Ounce) Tomato Sauce
2-½ Tablespoons Chile powder
2 Teaspoons Salt
¼ Teaspoon Pepper

1. Sauté onions and green pepper in a small amount of vegetable oil.
2. Add ground beef, stirring to break up. Cover and simmer 30 minutes.
3. Add tomatoes and next 5 ingredients. Simmer, uncovered, for 30 minutes.
4. Stir occasionally.
5. Add kidney beans and simmer 15 minutes more.

Martta's Chili
1 Lb. Chopped Meat; Lean
1 Can Tomatoes; Whole
1 Can (16 Ounce) Red Beans
4 Stalks Celery; Chopped, Up to 5
2 Cloves Garlic; Crushed

¼ Cup Green Pepper; Chopped
2 Pods Hot Peppers; Fresh, Chopped Up to 3
1 Tablespoon Vegetable Oil
To Taste Chile powder
As Needed Rice

1. In large saucepan, heat oil until very hot.
2. Stir-fry celery, onion, peppers and garlic until onions are soft.
3. Gradually add in pieces of meat and cook until brown.
4. Add drained red beans; stir.
5. Add can of tomatoes and bring to a boil for 5 minutes.
6. Reduce heat to simmer and cook for 45 minutes, adding about a teaspoon of chile powder to taste.
7. Do not cover but stir occasionally.

Serve over rice. Serves 5.

Mary Jo's Chili
4 Lb. Hamburger
1 Large Onion
2 Cloves Garlic
1 Teaspoon Oregano
1 Teaspoon Cumin; Or Curry
6 Teaspoons Chile powder
1-½ Cups Tomatoes; Or
1 Quart Home Canned Tomatoes
2 Cans Kidney Beans; Or
2 Cups Chili Hot Beans; (Number of Cans Can Vary)
2 Dashes Tabasco Sauce; Up to 6
2 Cups Hot Water

1. Brown meat and onions.
2. Add other ingredients and simmer.
3. I like to serve with chopped onions, grated cheese and oyster crackers as toppings.

Maw Maw's Chili
2 Lb. Ground Beef
2 Cans (8 Ounce) Tomato Sauce
2 Cans Ranch Style Beans
2 Cans Tomatoes (Stewed); Chopped

4 Cloves Garlic; Chopped
1 Medium Onion; Chopped
1 Package 2 Alarm Chili Ingredients (See Note)
2 Cans Water
Note: Use only ¾ chile powder, ¼ red pepper, and dash of oregano, all of onion and garlic mix.

1. Brown meat.
2. Sauté, onions and garlic.
3. Add remaining ingredients and simmer for two hours.
Real tasty!

Meg's Chili
1 Lb. Ground Chuck; Or Ground Turkey
1 Medium Onion
1 Can (Large) Tomatoes
1 Can (Medium) Tomatoes
1 Can (Large) Kidney Beans
1 Can (Medium) Kidney Beans
1 Can (6 Ounce) Tomato Paste
2 Tablespoons Worcestershire Sauce
1 Tablespoon Chile powder; Up to 2
As Needed Water

1. Brown ground meat (but not onions).
2. Cut up onions and tomatoes.
3. Combine everything in a big pot, including juice from tomatoes. Bring to a boil, reduce heat and simmer for 1 hour.
4. Add water to desired consistency. Stir occasionally.

Michael Cron's Chili Seven Ingredients
"Eatin' Chili Red, Hot, And You" September 1993 Volume 1,
1-½ Lb. Lean Beef; Cut in 1/8-Inch Cubes
6 Tablespoons Chile powder
1 Bottle Dos Equis Beer; Or Any Other Mexican Beer
1 Tablespoon Salt
1 Large Onion; Minced
2 Tablespoons Garlic; Minced
4 Cups Brown Stock

1. Combine the chile powder and salt in a bowl, pour beer over mix, and set aside.
2. Heat ¼ cup of olive oil in a sufficiently sized sauté pan until it smokes.
3. Add beef, using a fork to break up any pieces that stick together.
4. Cook, stirring occasionally, over high heat until meat is well seared (but not burnt).
5. Add onions and garlic, reduce heat, and cook until onions are translucent.
6. If meat has been seared in small batches, add all meat, onions and garlic to a stockpot.
7. Add beer/spice mixture to pot. Cook until liquid is well reduced (be careful not to scorch).
8. After liquid has reduced, add 2 cups of stock. Bring to a boil, reduce heat, and simmer uncovered for 2 hours.
9. Use remaining stock to adjust consistency during cooking.

Mike's Chili
4 Lb. Ground Chuck
6 Lb. Brook's Hot and Spicy Chili Beans
2 Large Onions; Chopped
3 Cans (16 Ounce) Hunt's Tomatoes and Herb Sauce
3 Cans (16 Ounce) Water
2 Package French's Chili-O Season Mix
1 Cup Mauls Barbecue Sauce
2 Tablespoons Sugar
½ Teaspoon Garlic; Minced
2 Tablespoons Chile powder
2 Tablespoons Lawry's Seasoned Salt
1 Tablespoon Black Pepper
2 Tablespoons Salt
1 Cup Catsup
1 Cup Oats
½ Tablespoon Red Pepper

Mix all the ingredients in a very large kettle; cook for 6 to 7 hours on a very low heat.

Mike's Three Meat Texas Red Chili Southern
2 Lb. Pork; Cut in ½ Inch Cubes
2 Lb. Beef; Cut in ½ Inch Cubes
2 Lb. Veal; Cut in ½ Inch Cubes

½ Cup Chile powder; Mix
2 Tablespoons Cumin
2 Tablespoons Garlic; Chopped
1 Cup Onion; Chopped
½ Cup Green Pepper; Chopped
2 Tablespoons Oregano
1 Cup Corn Meal; Fine
4 Cups Water
1 Teaspoon Salt
¼ Cup Sugar

1. Brown meat, pork first then beef and veal. Remove from pan and drain.
2. Place meat into a large pot.
3. Pour off most of the oil used to brown meat.
4. Sauté onions and green peppers, add to the meat.
5. Add remaining ingredients except corn meal and water. Simmer for 3 hours.
6. Mix corn meal with water and add to pot for thickening. Cook until desired consistency.

Note: This can be cooked in a crockpot on low for 8 to 10 hours. If you use a pressure cooker, cook at 15 lbs. pressure for 45 minutes to 1 hour. Serve with grated cheddar cheese and chopped raw onions on top, or sour cream. Last served on Memorial Day, 1993.

Mitch Murdock's Now That's Chili...
3 Lb. Center Cut Chuck Roast; Coarse Ground
2 Lb. Center Cut Chuck Roast; Cubed
1 Cup Vegetable Oil
2 Large White Onions; Diced
¼ Medium Green Bell Pepper; Diced
1 Can (4 Ounce) Green Chiles; Diced Or
2 Pods Fresh Jalapeño Peppers; Diced
2 Cloves Garlic; Finely Minced
4 Cups Water; Preferably Bottled
½ Can (6 Ounce) Beer; Warm
1 Can (8 Ounce) Tomato Sauce
1 Can (6 Ounce) Tomato Paste
7 Tablespoons Chile powder
2 Leaves Bay
3 Tablespoons Cumin; Ground

1 Teaspoon Oregano; Ground
¼ Teaspoon Coriander; Ground
½ Teaspoon Beau Monde Spice Mixture
½ Teaspoon Hot Pepper Sauce, Liquid
1 Teaspoon Cayenne Pepper
1 Tablespoon Honey
1 Teaspoon MSG
½ Teaspoon Mole Paste
1 Teaspoon Beef Bouillon Granules
1 Teaspoon Paprika
¼ Teaspoon White Pepper
1 Teaspoon Salt
½ Teaspoon Black Pepper; Coarse Ground
2 Teaspoons Masa Harina (Corn Flour)

1. Heat ½ cup of oil in a large pot.
2. Add the onions, green pepper, Jalapeños and green chiles and garlic and sauté until soft.
3. Remove from pot and reserve.
4. Heat the remaining ½ cup oil. When very hot, add the meat, cooking it in batches to prevent crowding, and brown toughly. Drain off the Oil and fat and add the vegetables to the meat.
5. Add 3 cups of water, beer, tomato sauce, tomato paste and chile powder.
6. Stir well as liquid comes to a boil, then lower heat and simmer for 20 min.
7. Add remaining ingredients except for masa harina.
8. Mix masa with remaining cup of water while bringing liquid to a boil again.
9. Slowly stir masa mixture into liquid.
10. Lower heat, partly cover pot and allow chili to simmer for 2 hours, stirring often.
Serves 10 to 12

Molly's Mojac Chili
2 Lb. Honeysuckle White Turkey; Chopped
1 Tablespoon Cooking Oil
1 Large Onion; Chopped
4 Cloves Garlic; Pressed
3 Tablespoons Chile powder; (Up to 4)
2 Teaspoons Salt
2 Teaspoons Oregano

1 Teaspoon Cumin
4 Cubes Beef Bouillon; (4 Tsp. of The Powder)
4 Cups Water
½ Cup Corn Meal; + Water to Make 1 Cup
1 Can Pinto Beans; Drained (Up to 2)
As Desired Cheddar Cheese; Grated
As Desired Onion; Chopped

1. Brown turkey in oil.
2. Add chopped onions and garlic and cook until limp.
3. Add seasonings, bouillon cubes, and four cups of water. Cook for 30 minutes.
4. Just before serving, add water to cornmeal.
5. Pour mixture slowly into chili while stirring, being careful to stir out any lumps that form. Cook for about 10 minutes more or until chili is thickened.
6. Add drained beans and serve chili topped with cheddar cheese and onion.

Mom's Best Chili
2 Lb. Chili Meat
2 Leaves Bay; 2 or 3
4 Buttons Garlic; About 2 Teaspoons
1 Small Amount Onion; Chopped
1 Can (Small) Tomato Sauce

1. Cover chili meat with water, with 2 or 3 bay leaves in kettle.
2. Cook on medium heat about 1-½ hours or until meat is tender, but not mushy.
3. May need to add more water.
4. Turn heat to simmer and add 4 level teaspoons chili powder. I use Morton's Chili Blend. (Four Level teaspoons or to taste).
5. Salt to taste, also black pepper and crushed pepper if you have it.
6. Add 1 level teaspoon cumin and dash of nutmeg. Let simmer 2 or 3 minutes.
7. You may use venison ground chili and will be just as good, if you follow these simple directions.
8. Put meat on low heat, covered with water. Let heat but do not boil.
9. Drain this water off.
10. Add more water then proceed the same as if you were using beef.

Mom's Chili
1 Lb. Ground Chuck
To Taste Onion Powder
To Taste Garlic Powder
24 Ounces Tomato Sauce
3 Cups Water
1 Teaspoon Chile powder
½ Teaspoon Paprika
1 Can (16 Ounce) Hunt's Chili Beans

1. Brown the hamburger in a pan; add salt, pepper, onion powder and garlic powder to taste.
2. Add the tomato sauce, water, chile powder and paprika. Stir well.
3. Put all ingredients except chili beans together in the pot. Let cook about 7-8 hours.
4. Add the chili beans in the last 2 hours or so.
5. If you don't have time for that, you can cook it all in the pot, then transfer it to a stockpot before adding the chili beans.
6. Heat that on the stove for a few minutes.

Makes enough for 4 people with lots of leftovers. (It tastes even better reheated the next day!)

Serve with crackers or biscuits.

Mom's Fast Chili
365 Easy One-Dish Meals, Harper and Row
1 Lb. Ground Beef
1 Medium Onion; Chopped
½ Teaspoon Garlic Powder
1 Tablespoon Chile powder
2-½ Teaspoons Cumin; Ground
28 Ounces Tomatoes With Added Puree; Crushed
15 Ounces Kidney Beans; Canned
6 Ounces Tomato Paste

1. In a large 4-quart Dutch oven or large saucepan, cook beef and onion over medium-high heat, stirring often to break up meat, until lightly browned, 5 to 10 minutes. Drain off any excess fat.
2. Stir in all remaining ingredients. Heat to boiling.
3. Reduce heat to medium low and simmer, uncovered for 10-15 minutes.

Mom's Old Fashioned Chili
1-½ Lb. Ground Beef
1 Can (6 Ounce) Tomato Sauce
16 Ounces Chili Beans
1 Package Chili Seasoning Mix
16 Ounces Kidney Beans
1 Can water
To Taste Chile powder
1 Onion, Diced

1. Brown ground beef; drain.
2. Add seasoning mix, tomato sauce, chili beans (undrained), kidney beans (drained) and 1 can of water; simmer.
3. Add chile powder to taste.

Mom's Slow Cook Chili
Pat Stockett
1 Lb. Ground Chuck
3 Cans (8 Ounce) Tomato Sauce
1 Teaspoon Chile powder
1 Can (Large) Hunt's Chili Beans
To Taste Onion Powder
To Taste Garlic
3 Cups Water
½ Teaspoon Paprika

1. Brown the hamburger in a pan or at the bottom of the pressure cooker.
2. Add salt, pepper, onion powder and garlic powder to taste.
3. Add the tomato sauce, water, chile powder and paprika. Stir well.
4. Mount the lid on the pressure cooker and bring to full pressure.
5. Let the gauge rock for 10 minutes slowly.
6. Bring pressure down immediately by immersing in water or letting water run over the top of the cooker.
7. Remove lid and add entire can of chili beans.
8. Place on stove at low-medium heat until mixture heats thoroughly.
Makes enough for 4 people with lots of leftovers. (It tastes even better reheated the next day, we think!) Serve with crackers or biscuits.

If you use a crock-pot instead:
1. Follow basic directions, putting all ingredients except chili beans together

in the pot.
2. Let cook about 7-8 hours.
3. Add the chili beans in the last 2 hours or so.
4. If you don't have time for that, you can cook it all in the pot, then transfer it to a stockpot before adding the chili beans.
5. Heat that on the stove for a few minutes.

Mother Weber's Quick Chili (Not Hot Or Spicy)
1 Lb. Ground Beef
1 Large Onion; Diced
1 Can (7 Ounce) Tomato Puree
1 Can (15-½ Ounce) Joan of Arc Kidney Beans
1 Can (15-½ Ounce) Franco-American Spaghetti
1 Tablespoon Chile powder; To Taste
½ Teaspoon Salt
½ Teaspoon Pepper

1. Brown ground beef in skillet; add onions, salt, pepper and chile powder. Cook until onions are tender.
2. Put in large pan. Add rest of ingredients.
3. As you empty each can, fill it with water and add to mixture.
4. Don't drain any of the cans; add the whole thing. Cook down and serve. It's delicious.

Moveta's Chili Soup
1 Lb. Hamburger Meat
1 Can (32 Ounce) Tomato Juice
1 Teaspoon Chile powder
1 Teaspoon Salt
½ Cup Water
1 Large Onion
1 Cup Macaroni; Cooked
½ Teaspoon Black Pepper
1 Can Bush's Best Chili Hot Beans

1. Brown hamburger and onion. Do not drain the grease.
2. Add 1 teaspoon chile powder, ½ teaspoon black pepper, 1 teaspoon salt, 1 can Bush's chili hot beans, 1 cup tomato juice and ½ cup water.
3. Stir together with hamburger and cook until it boils.
4. Drain the macaroni.

5. Add the meat mixture to the macaroni.
6. Add the rest of the 32-ounce can tomato juice and 2 cups of water. Bring to a boil and simmer for 15 minutes.
7. Refrigerate and let it set overnight.

Mr. Carle's Chili
¼ Ounce Chili Peppers; Caliente
1 Lb. Hot Italian Sausage
3 Cans Tomatoes; Whole
1 Can Tomato Paste
1 Lb. Ground Beef
3 Cloves Garlic; Diced and Crushed
3 Ounces Red Wine
1 Can Chili Beans; Optional
2 Medium Onions; Diced
3 Medium Green Peppers; Diced
As Needed Extra Virgin Olive Oil
¼ Cup Olives; Diced
¼ Cup Pimentos
1 Teaspoon Cayenne Pepper

1. Stir-fry diced vegetables in olive oil.
2. Brown sausage and ground beef.
3. Mash whole tomatoes with paste.
4. Thicken to desired consistency.
5. Add red wine and chili beans, if desired.
6. Add ¼ ounce chile peppers to tomato sauce.
7. Sprinkle liberally with cayenne pepper.
8. Drain meat and dump in chili.
9. Drain vegetables.
10. Mix it up and let it cook for many hours.

Mrs. Garber's Chili Recipe With Texas Noodles
5 Lb. Chili Meat
To Taste Salt and Pepper
To Taste Onion Flakes
2 Quarts Tomatoes
1 Teaspoons Red Pepper
1 Teaspoon Chile Pepper
1 Teaspoon Comino

1 Teaspoon Oregano
2 Cans (Large) Ranch Style Beans
As Needed Cornstarch
As Needed Corn Chips
As Needed Cheese
As Needed Salad
As Needed Texas Noodles

1. Brown, drain and rinse chili meat, seasoned with salt, pepper and onion flakes.
2. In a large crock-pot, add meat to 2 quarts tomatoes and the following seasonings: red pepper, chile pepper, comino and oregano.
3. Add more to taste, if desired.
4. Cook in crock-pot approximately 12 hours; add Ranch Style beans last 2 hours.
5. Thicken with small mix of cornstarch, if necessary.
6. Serve with corn chips, cheese, salad and Texas noodles for fun!

Murray's Fabulous Chili
3 Lb. Ground Chuck
2 Cubes Beef Bouillon
1 Tablespoon Paprika
1 Teaspoon Cumin
1 Tablespoon Salt
3 Tablespoons Chile powder
1/8 Teaspoon Oregano
½ Teaspoon Cayenne
1 Teaspoon Sugar
¼ Teaspoon MSG
½ Teaspoon Marjoram
¼ Teaspoon Garlic Powder
½ Teaspoon Red Pepper; Crushed
1 Teaspoon Black Pepper
1 Tablespoon White Vinegar
4 Dashes Worcestershire Sauce
4 Dashes Tabasco Sauce
3 Pods Jalapeño Peppers; Chopped Fine
1 Medium Onion; Coarsely Chopped
1 Medium Bell Pepper; Coarsely Chopped

1. In a large pot or skillet, brown meat evenly.
2. Dissolve bouillon cubes in ½ cup hot water. Add to beef.
3. Premix all dry spices in a bowl; stir to blend. Add to beef and mix well.
4. Add vinegar, Worcestershire sauce, Tabasco sauce, Jalapeños and 3 cups water. Stir and bring to a boil.
5. Reduce heat and simmer, uncovered, 2 hours, stirring occasionally.
6. Thirty minutes before chili is done, add chopped onions and green peppers.

Pat says it is great chili.

My Easy Chili
5 Lb. Ground Beef; Lean
5 Large Onions; Chopped
40 Ounces Tomato Puree; Canned
15 Ounces Tomato Paste; Canned
30 Ounces Kidney Beans; Rinsed and Drained
2-½ Quarts Water; Or More
10 Tablespoons Chile powder
2-½ Cloves Garlic; To Taste
To Taste Oregano

1. Sauté the onion in a non-stick pan, or in a little butter until tender.
2. If you want the chili hot, sauté with the chile powder.
3. When the onions are limp, add the beef, and brown, breaking up with a spoon. (Drain if you like.)
4. Add puree, paste, and chile powder if you didn't brown it, beans, and 16 oz. water. And salt and pepper if you like it.
5. Cover and simmer over low heat for 2 hrs. stirring occasionally.
6. Add more water if it gets too thick.

Good served over mashed potatoes. You may need more water, depending on the cooking temperature. And you can adjust the amount of chile powder to taste. And you can add spices of your choice. This is an easy dish for camping.

My Favorite Chili
Adapted from Cooking for Good Health by Gloria Rose
1 Stalks Celery; Cut in 4 or 5 Pieces
1 Large Onion; Quartered
2 Large Carrots; Cut in Pieces
2 Centiliters Garlic

1 Can (16 Ounce) Chicken or Veggie Stock; No-Salt Added
1 Medium Tomato
1 Can (6 Ounce) Tomato Paste; No-Salt Added
1 Medium Red Bell Pepper; Diced
1 Can (4 Ounce) Green Chiles; Chopped
1 Cup Mushrooms; Fresh, Quartered
2 Cups Tomato Juice; No-Salt Added
2 Tablespoons Salsa
1 Tablespoon Chile powder
1 Teaspoon Cumin; Ground
1 Teaspoon Bay Leaf; Dried
1 Tablespoon Parsley (Fresh); Minced
2 Cans (16 Ounce) Kidney Beans; Rinsed and Drained
1 Lb. Flank Steak; Lean, Ground Or
1 Lb. Ground Beef; Very Lean

1. Coarsely chop vegetables and cook in broth until soft; add tomatoes, tomato paste and bell pepper. Cook 5 minutes.
2. Add chiles, mushrooms, salsa and tomato juice and simmer 5 minutes.
3. Add remaining ingredients and cook another hour.
Serve hot. Makes 6 servings. Variation: Add 1-tablespoon red pepper flakes for a spicier dish.

My Favorite Chili Soup
2 Lb. Hamburger; Browned
1 Can (Tall) Tomato Juice
1 Package Chili Mix
To Taste Salt
To Taste Garlic Salt
1 Small Onion; Or
1 Teaspoon Onion Flakes
1 Can (Large) Chili Beans
To Taste Chile powder
To Taste Pepper
To Taste Oregano

1. Brown hamburger; drain and mix rest of ingredients.
2. Sprinkle seasonings to taste.
3. May use a crock-pot.
4. Put on low for the day if used for evening meal.

My Grandkid's Favorite Chili
1-½ Lb. Ground Chuck
1/3 Cup Onion; Chopped
3 Tablespoons Peppers; Chopped
1 Quart Tomato Juice
6 Ounces Tomato Paste
2 Cans (16 Ounce) Kidney Beans
1-¼ Teaspoon Salt
¼ Package Chili Mix

1. In skillet, brown ground chuck, onion and green peppers for about 30 minutes. Drain off grease.
2. Stir in chili seasoning mix and salt. Simmer about 15 minutes.
3. In crock-pot mix tomato juice, paste and beans.
4. Add ground chuck mix and cook on medium/high 1-½ hours.

If desired, top each bowl of chili with Cheddar cheese. Serves 6 to 8.

Myra's Chili
10 Lb. Beef Chuck Roast
4 Lb. Boston Butt Pork Roast
6 Medium Onions
4 Cans (16 Ounce) Chili Hot Beans
2 Cans (4 Ounce) Green Chiles; Chopped
2 Cans (28 Ounce) Tomatoes; Crushed
1 Package (2 Ounce) Mild New Mexico Chile powder
As Needed Masa Harina (Corn Flour)
12 Cloves Garlic
2 Ounces Chile powder
2 Ounces Cumin
4 Teaspoons Paprika
2 Teaspoons Salt

1. Salt and pepper Beef chuck roast, dredge in Masa Harina.
2. Brown on all sides in a heavy skillet.
3. Add 4 cups water to pan, bake slowly in 350 degree oven until tender.
4. Salt and pepper Boston Butt Pork Roast, brown on all sides in heavy skillet.
5. Add 1-cup water, bake slowly in 350-degree oven until tender.
6. If your pan is large enough, you may bake beef and pork together.
7. Break off stems and crack the mild dried New Mexico Chile pods,

shaking outmost of the seeds.
8. Rinse pods and towel or drain dry.
9. Cover and soak the cleaned pods with 2 cups boiling water.
10. Allow at least 30 minutes for pods to soften or they will be fine if left to soak overnight.
11. Peel the garlic cloves (A quick way to peel garlic, is to take the wide side of a chef's knife and smash the pod on a cutting board. The skin will slip right off.)
12. Puree the garlic cloves and reconstituted chile pods and water the pods were soaked in.
13. Pick the bones and as much fat as you can manage from the beef and pork roasts.
14. Place meat and liquid from the roasting pans in a large cooker.
15. Add tomatoes, onions, green chiles, crushed tomatoes, chili hot beans and the puree of chile and garlic. Add chile powder, cumin, paprika, and salt to taste.
16. Add water as needed to maintain a chili consistency. Simmer for hours.
Serve hot with crackers.

Nancy's Chili
½ Lb. Ground Beef; Up to 1 Lb.
1-¼ Teaspoons Chile powder
1 Teaspoon Salt
1 Small Onion; Diced
2 Pints Tomatoes; With Juice
1 Can Kidney Beans
1 Can (Small) Tomato Sauce; Or
1 Can (Small) Tomato Paste
1 Can (Small) Water
To Suit Macaroni

Preparation time: About 1 hour.

1. Brown ground beef and onion. Drain grease.
2. Add chile powder and salt; stir in.
3. Add rest of ingredients; bring to boil. Cover and cook on simmer for 15 minutes.
Makes 4 servings.

Nick And Nancy's Prize Winning Chili, 1984
1 Medium Onion; Chopped
½ Teaspoon Salad Oil
1 Lb. Ground Beef; Up to 2
1 Teaspoon Chile powder; Up to 2
¼ Teaspoon Oregano
½ Teaspoon Salt
1 Can (Large) Tomatoes
1 Cup Water
1/ Can Beer; Up to 1
Toppings For Chili
2 Medium Onions; Chopped
1 Cup Raisins
12 Ounces Cheddar Cheese; Coarsely Grated

1. Sauté onions in oil.
2. Add meat, stirring until brown.
3. Add remaining ingredients. Stir, cover and simmer 1 hour.
4. Adjust seasoning to taste.
5. May need to add a dash or two of Tabasco.
To assemble: Put chili in a large serving dish. Line the outer edges with the onions. Then line the inner edge of onions with cheese. Sprinkle center of the dish with raisins.

Pam's Homemade Chili
1-½ Lb. Hamburger
2 Cans (Small) Tomato Sauce
1 Can Pork and Beans
1 Can Tomatoes; Diced
3 Teaspoons Chile powder

1. Brown meat.
2. Add the remaining ingredients. Simmer for 30 minutes.
3. Serve over hot dogs.
For chili in a bowl, add an extra can of tomato sauce. This is a mild tasting chili. Add more chile powder for spicier chili.

Pappy's Chili
2 Lb. Ground Beef
As Needed Olive Oil

2 Cloves Garlic
1 Tablespoon Paprika
2 Teaspoons Oregano
2 Tablespoons Chile powder; Or More
To Taste Salt and Pepper
1 Teaspoon Comino Seeds
1 Pinch Sugar
1 Cup Onion; Minced
1 Can (Small) Tomatoes
1 Cup Hot Water or Consume; Up to 2
2 Cans Red Kidney Beans

1. Brown ground beef in olive oil.
2. Add garlic, oregano, salt and pepper, chile powder, comino seed and sugar.
3. Cook for a few minutes, then add onion, tomatoes, consume and kidney beans. Simmer an hour or two.

Pat's Special Diet Chili
3 Lb. Ground Meat
1 Medium Red Onion; Chopped
2 Medium Bell Peppers; Chopped
1 Can (46 Ounce) Tomato Juice
2 Cans French Cut Green Beans
¾ Jar (3.5 Ounce) Chile powder
1 Teaspoon Cumin
To Taste Garlic Powder
To Taste Salt and Pepper
2 Packages Artificial Sweetener

1. Brown meat and drain fat.
2. Combine meat with other ingredients into large pot and cook to chili consistency.
Serves 6.

Paw Paw's Chili
3 Lb. Chili Meat Taller
3 Chile Pods
3 Garlic Pods
1 Tablespoon Chile powder

1 Teaspoon Italian Seasonings
½ Teaspoon Cumin Seed; Up to ¾
1 Teaspoon Black Pepper
1 Teaspoon Red Pepper
1 Sprinkle Pepper Flakes; Use Coarse Black Pepper

1. Cook until meat is done (tender).
2. You may add water and/or canned tomatoes.
3. Use more chile pods and chile powder, if you prefer your chili hotter.

Perry's Chili
1-½ Lb. Ground Chuck
1 Cup Onion; Chopped
1 Chili Roll
1 Can (Large) Brooks Chili Hot Beans
½ Cup Green Pepper; Chopped
1 Can (Large) V-8 Juice
2 Cups Water; Or 3
½ Cup Macaroni
To Taste Chile powder
To Taste Salt and Pepper

1. Sauté onion.
2. Add ground chuck; cook until pink is gone.
3. Add all ingredients except macaroni. Bring to boil, stirring frequently.
4. Add macaroni. Simmer 1 hour, stirring frequently.

Peter's Red Hot Chili
Best of the Best from New England
3 Tablespoons Oil
2 Lb. Stew Meat; Beef
5 Cups Water
1 Medium Green Pepper; Diced
1 Medium Onion; Diced
1 Medium Tomato; Diced
1-½ Tablespoons Salt
2 Teaspoons Cayenne Pepper
1 Tablespoon Garlic; Granulated
¼ Cup Chile powder
2 Tablespoons Cumin

1-½ Cups Water
1/3 Cup Corn Meal
1 Can (6 Ounce) Tomato Paste
As Desired Monterey Jack Cheese; Grated

1. Brown beef in oil.
2. Add next 9 ingredients and simmer for 2 hours.
3. In a small bowl mix the water, cornmeal, and tomato paste.
4. Stir cornmeal mixture into chili to thicken. Simmer another 20 minutes.
5. Garnish with sliced raw onions and grated Monterey Jack cheese.

Perfect Black Bean Chili
4 Cups Black Beans; Dried
2 Each Green Pepper; Chopped
4 Tablespoons Olive Oil
4 Tablespoons Cumin; Ground
2/3 Teaspoons Cinnamon; Ground
8 Cloves Garlic; Minced
2 Teaspoons Fresh Ginger; Grated
2 Tablespoon Smoke Flavoring
2 Can (16 Ounce) Tomatoes; Crushed
To Taste Cayenne Pepper
3 Lb. Ground Chuck; Lean
4 Each Onions; Chopped
8 Tablespoons Paprika
½ Teaspoon Nutmeg; Ground
2 Teaspoons Oregano
6 Tablespoons Molasses
4 Tablespoons Cocoa Powder
3 Cans (8 Ounce) Tomato Sauce
As Needed Chicken Stock

1. In a large stock pot, brown the ground chuck, draining off as much fat as possible when it has finished browning.
2. While the chuck is browning, sauté the chopped onions, garlic and green pepper in the oil in a separate pan.
3. Add the sautéed onion, garlic, and green pepper to the browned meat, along with all the other ingredients.
4. Thin it to the desired thickness with the chicken stock, beef stock, or beer.
5. Simmer for one to two hours covered. Uncover for the last half-hour or

so if it has thinned out more than you want.
Refrigerate overnight, skim any grease off and reheat over a very low heat..
Much better the second day.

An Easy Way For Black Beans
This chili recipe calls for starting with two cups of dried black beans.
Prepare the beans as you will, as there are plenty of cookbooks with
instructions for soaking overnight, but an easier way to do it is to pressure
cook them for forty-five minutes after the steam releases the first time.
1. Rinse two cups of dried black beans well, and put them in the pressure
   cooker with at least four cups of water.
2. Seal the pressure cooker and heat until the steam release hisses the first
   time then, turn down the heat to medium-low, and start a timer for forty-
   five minutes.
3. Steam release will hiss every few minutes or so.
4. When they're done, drain them, and they're ready to put in the chili pot.

Pierre's Chili
1 Tablespoon Olive Oil
1 Lb. Lean Beef; Ground
1 Lb. Lean Pork; Ground
2 Cups Onion; Chopped
1 Cup Green Pepper; Chopped
1 Cup Celery; Chopped
1 Tablespoon Garlic; Minced
1 Tablespoon Oregano; Dried
2 Leaves Bay
2 Teaspoons Cumin
3 Tablespoons Chile powder
3 Cups Tomatoes; Crushed
1 Cup Beef Stock
1 Cup Water
To Taste Red Pepper Flakes
To Taste Salt
To Taste Pepper; Fresh Ground
2 Cups Kidney Beans; Cooked
As Desired Monterey Jack Cheese; Shredded
As Desired Lettuce; Shredded
As Desired Red Onion; Chopped
As Desired Coriander; Chopped

As Desired Sour Cream
As Desired Lime Wedges

1. Heat oil in heavy Dutch oven.
2. Add beef and pork cooking and breaking up until lightly browned.
3. Add onions, green pepper and celery; sweat two minutes.
4. Add other ingredients except beans, mixing well. Bring to a boil, reduce heat, cover and simmer 20 minutes.
5. Discard bay leaves, add beans, mix well and simmer another 10 minutes. Ladle into warm soup bowls and serve with warm tortillas, tortilla chips or crackers. Pass garnishes separately.
   Yield: 8 to 10 servings.

Piers Thompson's Very Tasty Chili
3 Pods New Mexican Red Chiles; Dried
2 Pods Chipotle Peppers
1 Pod Habañero Chiles
4 Cloves Garlic; Minced
1 Teaspoon Ground Cumin
1 Teaspoon Oregano; Dried
1 Tablespoon Vegetable Oil
1 Large Onion; Chopped
½ Lb. Minced Beef
1 Can (15 Ounce) Tomatoes
1 Can (15 Ounce) Kidney Beans

1. Cut the tops off the dried chiles.
2. Toast them in a hot frying pan for a few minutes until fragrant and then soak them in hot water for 20 minutes.
3. Liquidize them with some of the soaking water.
4. Roughly chop the Habañero and the garlic and add them to the liquidizer along with the cumin and oregano.
5. Puree some more.
6. Heat the oil in a saucepan and fry the onion until softened.
7. Add the meat and cook until browned.
8. Add the chile puree, tomatoes and beans. Cover and simmer for at least half an hour.
9. Uncover, raise the heat a little and allow the excess liquid to evaporate (about 10 minutes).
Serve it any way you fancy!

Powter Chili

1-½ Cups Pinto Beans; Dried, Or
3 Cups Pinto Beans; Canned, Rinsed
1 Medium Onion; Chopped
1 Leaf Bay
1 Teaspoon Salt
4 Cups Water
1 Tablespoon Olive Oil
1-¾ Cups Onion; Chopped
2 Tablespoons Garlic; Minced
1 Large Green Pepper; Cut into Cubes
2 Pods Jalapeño Peppers; Chopped
2 Teaspoons Oregano
1 Tablespoon Cumin
¼ Teaspoon Cayenne
2 Teaspoons Salt
2 Leaves Bay
4 Tablespoons Chile powder; To 5 Tbs.
1 Can (20 Ounces) Tomatoes; Chopped

1. Soak dried beans overnight in water to cover. Drain beans and put in pot. Reserve liquid.
2. Add onion, bay leaf, salt, and water.
3. Cook over med high heat for 45 minutes, or until beans are tender but not mushy. Drain beans and save liquid.
4. In a large skillet over med high heat, sauté onion, garlic, and peppers in oil for 10 minutes.
5. Add the spices and sauté 5 minutes more.
6. Add tomatoes and beans, cook 45 minutes, or until all flavors are blended.
7. If chili is too dry, add 1 or more cups of the liquid from the beans and bring to a boil.

Randy Robinson's Chili
Betty Crocker International Chili Society 1991

3 Lb. Beef Round, Boneless; Cut Up or Coarse Ground
1 Tablespoon All-Purpose Flour
1 Tablespoon Cooking Oil
½ Lb. Ground Pork
½ Cup Onion; Chopped
1-½ Teaspoon Garlic; Granulated

1 Can (14.5 Ounce) Beef Broth
2 Cans (14.5 Ounce) Chicken Broth
1 Can (8 Ounce) Tomato Sauce
1-½ Teaspoons Cumin; Ground
1 Can (4 Ounce) Mild Green Chiles; Chopped and Drained
1 Pod Jalapeño Chile; Chopped
1 Teaspoon Black Pepper
3 Tablespoons Chile powder
1 Can (8 Ounce) Tomato Sauce
4 Tablespoons Chile powder
2 Tablespoons Mild New Mexico Chile powder
2 Tablespoons Cumin; Ground
1 Teaspoon Garlic; Granulated
1 Teaspoon Tabasco Sauce
1-½ Teaspoons Brown Sugar

1. Coat beef with flour, heat oil in Dutch oven over medium heat.
2. Cook beef and ground pork in oil, stirring occasionally, until beef is brown; drain.
3. Stir in remaining ingredients down to tomato sauce. Heat to boiling; reduce heat. Cover and simmer 1-½ hours.
4. Uncover; stir in remaining ingredients. Simmer uncovered about 45 minutes or until beef is tender.

Rebelette Chili
1 Package Lowry's Texas-Style Chili Seasoning
2 Lb. Hamburger Meat
1 Can (8 Ounce) Tomato Sauce
1 Can (16 Ounce) Tomatoes (Stewed)
1 Can (16 Ounce) Kidney Beans
1 Cup Water

1. Cook chili as directed on package, adding the stewed tomatoes and kidney beans and changing the 2 cups of water to only 1 cup of water.
2. A reminder to drain grease.
Great with "Rebelette Cornbread."

Red Gomer's Chili Recipe
2 Quarts Boiling Water
5 Lb. Ground Beef; Brown, Seasoned and Drained

2 Cups Onion; Minced
1-½ Cups Bell Pepper; Diced Or
¾ Cup Bell Pepper; Dried
2 Tablespoons Oregano
2 Tablespoons Cumin
1 Teaspoon Garlic Powder
6 Leaves Bay; Up to 8
2 Teaspoons Celery Leaves; Up to 3
3 Cans (16 Ounce) Tomatoes
1 Can (16 Ounce) Tomato Sauce
2 Cubes Beef Bouillon
1-½ Tablespoons Chile powder; Per Pound of Meat

First Place, 1986 Chili Contest, Third Place 1987.

1. To water, add the following, browned meat (salt and pepper to taste while browning), canned tomatoes, tomato sauce, bouillon cubes, minced onions, green peppers, celery leaves, oregano, cumin, garlic powder and bay leaves. (Do not add chile powder yet.)
2. Bring mixture to boil. Cook briskly 1 to 1-½ hours.
3. Add 1-½ to 3 tablespoons chile powder per pound of meat.
4. You may need to add water if mixture is too thick. Boil briskly and stir for 5 minutes.
5. Turn heat to simmer for 1 to 3 hours, stirring occasionally. The longer cooking time is preferred.

If you like beans with your chili, cook dark red kidney beans separately in water and salt. If you plan to freeze chili, freeze beans separately.

Rhonda's Chili

3 Lb. Ground Meat
1 Medium Onion; Chopped
1 Medium Green Pepper
1 Can (Large) Tomatoes; Crushed
2 Cans Tomato Sauce
4 Cans Tomato Soup
1 Can Mushroom Soup
4 Cans Red Kidney Beans; Up to 5
To Taste Salt and Pepper
To Taste Chile powder

1. Fry ground meat, onion and pepper, and then drain all grease.
2. Then add in a large pot tomatoes, tomato sauce, tomato soup, mushroom soup, beans and mix the ground meat mixture all together.
3. Add two or three teaspoons of black pepper, 3 teaspoons of chile powder and salt.

Makes enough for 6 people.

Richard's Chili
2 Tablespoons Olive Oil
4 Cloves Garlic; Minced
1-½ Teaspoons Salt
To Taste Cumin
1-½ Tablespoons Chile Pepper
16 Ounces Dry Beans; (Pinto or Kidney)
1 Large Green Peppers; Minced
1 Lb. Hamburger
½ Teaspoon Pepper
To Taste Oregano
1-½ Lb. Tomatoes; (Canned/Fresh/Frozen)

1. Cover dry beans with 3 times their volume of water. Let stand about 12 hours.
2. In a pan combine oil, green pepper, onion and garlic. Cook about 5 minutes.
3. Brown hamburger in a pan.
4. In a pot combine all ingredients and bring to a boil. Reduce heat and simmer about 3 hours.

Rick Poston's Chili
The County Fair Cookbook
1 Tablespoon Crisco
2-½ Lb. Chuck, Tender; Cut in 1/8-Inch Cubes-

Dump1
2 Cans (14-½ Ounce) Swanson's Beef Broth
1 Teaspoon Beef Bouillon Granules
1 Tablespoon Chicken Bouillon Granules
1 Teaspoon Pendery's El Rey Chili Pepper
4 Teaspoons Pendery's High Color Paprika
5-¾ Teaspoons Onion Powder

½ Teaspoon Garlic Powder
1 Can Tomato Sauce
3 Pods Serrano Chile Peppers; Pierced

Dump 2
½ Teaspoon Pendery's 40K Cayenne Pepper
½ Teaspoon Sazon Goya
¼ Teaspoon White Pepper; Ground
¼ Teaspoon Black Pepper; Ground
2 Teaspoons Cumin; Ground
1 Teaspoon Garlic Powder
1 Tablespoon Pendery's Original Chili Powder
Gebhardt's Chili Powder

Dump 3
½ Teaspoon Sazon Goya
½ Teaspoon Onion Powder
1 Tablespoon Pendery's Original Chili Power
2 Teaspoons Cumin; Ground
3/8 Teaspoon Pendery's 60K Cayenne Pepper
Gebhardt's Chili Powder Kicker
3/8 Teaspoon Salt
1-½ Teaspoon Cumin; Ground
1-½ Teaspoons Gebhardt's Chili Powder

The ingredient list and instructions are "specific." Rick notes that you should cook this by the "Dumps." Makes just over 2 quarts.

1. In a large heavy Dutch oven or kettle, heat the Crisco until sizzling.
2. Brown the meat cubes, stirring often.
3. Pour off accumulated juices, and add the first Dump.
4. Cook the chili covered through all stages and Dumps, and stir it frequently.
5. If additional liquid is needed during cooking, add more beef broth.
6. Cook Dump 1 for 1 hour.
7. Squeeze the chile pod juices into the pot.
8. Discard the pods.
9. Add ingredients in Dump 2 and cook for 1 hour 25 minutes, then add Dump 3 ingredients.
10. Five to ten minutes before presentation to judges or guests, add the Kicker

ingredients.

11.Stir well, dish up. It is very, very rich.

Note: Pendery's does an extensive mail order business. Write Pendery's Inc., at 1221 Manufacturing, Dallas, Texas 75207-6505, or call 1-800-533-1870. This prizewinner comes from Red River Valley Fair of Paris Texas. Fair Dates: Week before Labor Day, 6 days.

Rick's Chili

2 Lb. Ground Beef
2 Lb. Chili Meat
2 Package Tio Sanchez Chili Mix
1 Can (15 Ounce) Hunt's Spicy Tomato Sauce
1 Can (Large) V-8 Juice
1 Can Ro-tel Diced Tomato and Green Chile
1 Bottle Del Monte Chili Sauce
½ Clove Garlic; Diced
1 Tablespoon Chile powder; Heaping
1 Large Onion; Chopped

1. Brown meat in large pot with onion and garlic.
2. When brown, stir in chili mix and powder.
3. Add Ro-Tel, tomato sauce and chili sauce.
4. Add large can V-8 juice and salt to taste.
5. Cook over low heat 2 hours or until you can't stand it any more.
6. Add tomato juice while cooking to desired consistency.

Rob Young's Rot-Gut Chili

1-1/3 Lb. Ground Beef; Lean
2 Cans (16 Ounce) Light Red Kidney Beans
1 Can (16 Ounce) Pinto Beans
1 Package Chili Mix
1 Can (14 Ounce) Tomato Juice
1 Box (7 Ounce) Spaghetti; Thin
2 Medium Onions
1 Medium Green Pepper

1. Brown ground beef in skillet, adding chopped onions and green pepper.
2. Boil spaghetti in pan of water.
3. When beef is browned, dump contents of skillet into Dutch oven along with the cooked spaghetti.

4. Add the tomato juice, beans and package of chili mix.
5. Heat to boiling, stirring frequently, to prevent scorching.
6. Serve hot and be sure to keep the Rolaids handy.

Rod's Chili
Barry Weinstein
1-¾ Lb. Chili Grind Meat
3 Slices Bacon
1 Tablespoon Cumin Seeds; Roasted and Ground
1 Tablespoon New Mexican Chile Powder; Plain
1 Tablespoon Ancho Chile Powder; Plain
1 Tablespoon California Chile Powder; Plain
1 Teaspoon Oregano; Mexican, Crushed
¼ Teaspoon Thyme
¼ Teaspoon Allspice
¼ Teaspoon Cilantro; Dried
1 Large Onion; Chopped Fine
2 Stalks Celery; Chopped Fine
1 Can El Paso Green Chiles; Mild
3 Pods Jalapeño Chiles; Seeded and Chopped Fine
1 Pod Habañero Chiles; Seeded and Chopped Fine
1 Clove Garlic
2 Cans (15 Ounce) Tomatoes (Stewed); Pureed in Blender
1 Can (12 Ounce) Beer
1 Teaspoon Beef Base
3 Teaspoons Paprika; Sweet
1 Teaspoon Coriander Powder
¼ Teaspoon Cayenne Pepper
1 Shot Jim Beam Bourbon Whisky
2 Tablespoons Olive Oil
As Needed Masa Harina (Corn Flour)

1. Cook bacon and reserve grease for sautéing onions and garlic.
2. In a large chili pot, sauté onion and garlic.
3. Remove onions and garlic and set aside.
4. Add olive oil and cook meat until gray in color, but not browned.
5. Add onion and garlic back to chili pot.
6. Add dry spices and cook while stirring for 3 or 4 minutes.
7. Add stewed tomatoes, bacon bits, chiles, beer, celery, and whiskey, beef base. Bring to a boil and then simmer until done. 3 to 4 hours.

Roger Hebebrand's Chili
1 Lb. Hamburger; Up to 2
2 Medium Green Peppers; Chopped
2 Small Onions
To Taste Garlic Salt
To Taste Onion Salt
To Taste Hickory Salt
To Taste Lemon Pepper
2 Cans Mushrooms; Whole
3 Cans Chili; No Beans
2 Cans Green Beans; Cut Up
2 Cans Tomato Sauce
2 Tablespoons Brown Sugar
2 Tablespoons Soy Sauce
2 Tablespoons Tabasco Sauce
1 Package Chili Seasoning Mix
2 Tablespoons Chile powder
3 Cups Kidney Beans

1. Brown hamburger, peppers, onions, garlic salt, onion salt, hickory salt and lemon pepper in skillet. Drain grease.
2. Add rest of ingredients and simmer at least an hour.

Ron's Ranchero Chili
8 Lb. Chuck; Coarsely Ground Once
16 Tablespoons Chile powder
2 Tablespoons Cumin
2 Tablespoons Beef Bouillon Crystals
1 Tablespoon Paprika
1 Tablespoon Salt
1 Tablespoon Oregano
1 Teaspoon Hershey's Instant Cocoa
1 Teaspoon Dijon Mustard
1 Teaspoon Thyme
½ Teaspoon Black Pepper
32 Ounces Tomatoes; Canned
32 Ounces Tomato Sauce
4 Ounces Green Chiles
16 Ounces Onion; Chopped
8 Ounces Green Pepper; Chopped

4 Cloves Garlic; Mashed
2 Carrots; Shredded
2 Ribs Celery; Chopped Small
2 Ounces Tequila
12 Ounces Beer

1. Brown half of the meat.
2. Put in half of the chile powder and cook 10 to 15 minutes.
3. Repeat with the remaining meat and chile powder.
4. When done, combine with first batch of browned meat.
5. Add all of the other ingredients. Cook four hours. It has to be four hours.
6. Taste. Depending on how it tastes, you may have to add salt or something.
Makes 12 Servings.

Rosemary's Chili
2 Lb. Ground Beef
3 Onions; Chopped
2 Cans Tomatoes
1 Can Water
1 Tablespoon Cumin Seed; Crushed
To Taste Garlic
4 Ounces Chile powder
To Taste Salt
1 Can Green Chiles; Chopped
2 Tablespoons Red Pepper; Dried
½ Cup Pace Picante Sauce

1. Brown ground beef; drain fat. Simmer all ingredients together for 2 hours.
2. Add 3 to 4 cans pinto beans.

Rosie's Chili
2 Lb. Hamburger Meat
1 Small Onion
To Taste Salt and Pepper
1 Can (46 Ounce) Ranch-Style Beans With Peppers
1 Can Tomatoes; Whole
1 Can Tomato Soup
1 Package Chili Seasoning Mix; Small
4 Cups Water

1. Brown hamburger and onions in skillet.
2. Salt and pepper to taste.
3. In large pot, combine beans, tomatoes, soup, chili seasoning mix, water.
4. When hot, combine browned meat with bean mixture. Simmer 30 minutes.

Rudy's Hot Dog Chili
Rudy's Hot Dog Restaurants
3 Lb. Hamburger
3 Large Onions; Diced
3 Cloves Garlic; Minced
3 Tablespoons Chile powder; To Taste, Up to 4
3 Tablespoons Cumin Powder; To Taste, Up to 4
2 Tablespoons Paprika; To Taste, Up to 3
½ Teaspoon Salt; To Taste, Up to 1
½ Teaspoon Pepper; To Taste, Up to 1

1. Sauté and drain hamburger, onions and garlic.
2. Mix all ingredients and simmer on low about 1-½ hours.
3. Chili should be thick.
4. Spoon over hot dogs on warm buns.
Chili served in Rudy's Hot Dog Restaurants.

Rusty's Chili Soup
3 Lb. Hamburger
½ Cup Onion
1 Teaspoon Salt
1 Teaspoon Sugar
1 Dash Pepper
½ Teaspoon Oregano
1 Teaspoon Cumin
½ Teaspoon Chile powder
1 Can (Large) V-8 Juice
1 Can Tomato Sauce; Regular Size
1 Can Tomatoes (Stewed); Regular Size
1 Can Kidney Beans; Regular Size
1 Handful Macaroni

1. Brown hamburger; add everything else except uncooked macaroni. Simmer 2 hours.

2. Ten minutes before serving, throw in your handful of macaroni.

So simple, so good. Regular chili and I don't get along so this has been a delicious substitute.

Rutherford's Homemade Chili
Clarence Rutherford

1 Lb. Hamburger Meat
1 Package Chili-O Seasoning Mix
1 Can (8 Ounce) Tomato Sauce
4 Tablespoons Shortening; Or Suet
1 Teaspoon Hot Chile Powder; Heaping

1. Pat meat into 1 big patty in skillet.
2. Cut meat into strips in pan, and then cut strips into chunks.
3. Fry until meat is done, not hard cooked.
4. When done, sprinkle in Chili-O mix.
5. Put 2 tomato sauce cans full of water. Cook until the chili soup is at desired level.

This is my Father's recipe "Clarence Rutherford."

Ryan's Revenge Chili
Midwest Living Magazine's All-Time Best Recipes

3-½ Lb. Beef Chuck, Boneless
2 Lb. Pork Sirloin
3 Cans (12 Ounce) Beer
½ Cup Chile powder; Plus 3 Tablespoons
¼ Cup Cumin; Ground
2 Tablespoons Paprika
4 Teaspoons Beef Bouillon Granules
1 Tablespoon Oregano; Mexican, Dried and Crushed
4 Lb. Chuck Beef; Coarse Ground
1 Tablespoon Cooking Oil
4 Medium Onions; Chopped
3 Pods Anaheim Chile Peppers; Seeded and Chopped
10 Cloves Garlic; Minced
1 Can (8 Ounce) Tomato Sauce
2 Tablespoons Coriander; Ground
2 Tablespoons Green Chile Sauce
1 Tablespoon Mole Poblano
1 Tablespoon Sugar

2 Tablespoons Lime Juice
As Needed Monterey Jack Cheese; Shredded

1. Cut boneless beef chuck and pork sirloin into ½ inch cubes.
2. In a Dutch oven, combine 2-½ cups water, beer, chile powder, cumin, paprika, bouillon granules and oregano. Bring to boiling.
3. Meanwhile, in skillet, brown meats in small batches. Drain off fat.
4. Add meats to liquid in Dutch oven.
5. Add ½ tsp. salt and ½ tsp. pepper.
6. In the skillet, heat cooking oil.
7. Add onions, chile peppers and garlic. Cook till tender.
8. Add to mixture in Dutch oven.
9. To chili mixture, stir in tomato sauce, coriander, chili sauce, and mole Poblano (found in Mexican-food section of large supermarkets) and sugar. Return to boiling. Reduce heat. Cover and simmer for 2 hours.
10. Stir in limejuice.
Top with Monterey Jack cheese.
Makes 8 to 10 servings.
Note: The volatile oils in chile peppers can burn your skin and eyes, so avoid touching the peppers unless you're wearing plastic or rubber gloves. If your skin touches the peppers, wash well with some soap and water.
From Murphysboro, Ill., John Ryan's spicy prizewinner goes well with crusty bread. If you can't find Mexican oregano, substitute regular dried oregano.

Sally's West Coast Chili
Sally Grisham "Prize-Winning Beef" Recipe booklet.
1 Lb. Bacon; Diced
2 Lb. Beef Stew Meat; Cut into Cubes
2 Medium Onions; Chopped
4 Cloves Garlic; Minced
1 Cup Barbecue Sauce
1 Cup Chili Sauce
½ Cup Honey
3 Cans (16 Ounce) Tomatoes; Chopped
4 Cubes Beef Bouillon
1 Leaf Bay
1 Tablespoon Chile powder
1 Tablespoon Unsweetened Baking Cocoa
1 Tablespoon Worcestershire Sauce
1 Tablespoon Dijon Mustard

1-½ Teaspoons Cumin; Ground
¼ Teaspoon Cayenne Pepper; Optional
3 Cans (16 Ounce) Red Kidney Beans
As Needed Cheddar Cheese; Shredded

1. In a large kettle or Dutch oven, cook bacon until crisp; remove to paper towel to drain.
2. Drain all but 3 Tablespoons of drippings.
3. Brown stew meat in the drippings.
4. Add onions and garlic; cook until onions are soft.
5. Return bacon to kettle.
6. Add all the remaining ingredients except kidney beans and cheese. Bring to a boil; reduce heat.
7. Cover and simmer until beef is tender, about 3-4 hours.
8. Add beans and heat through.

Top each serving with cheese. Yields: 4 quarts

"We often have chili cook-offs at our church, so we trade lots of different recipes. I was always mixing and matching ingredients and experimenting, trying to come up with an original recipe that would be a little different. That's how I developed this one, and I never fail to get compliments on it!"

Sam Huddleston's Chili

2 Tablespoons Cumin; Whole
2 Medium Onions; Diced
3 Cloves Garlic
As Needed Vegetable Oil
3-½ Lb. Lean Beef; Cut in ½ Inch Cubes
2 Tablespoons Paprika
6 Tablespoons Chile powder
As Needed Water
To Taste Salt
As Needed Cracker Crumbs
As Needed Browned Flour; For Tightener

1. In a skillet, slightly toast the whole cumin. To wake up the flavors crush them with a rolling pin. Powdered cumin may be substituted, but do not toast.
2. Sauté, onion and garlic in a little oil until transparent.
3. In same skillet, add a little more oil and sear meat until it has a grayish color.

4. Put cumin, onion, garlic and meat in a large vessel.
5. Add paprika and chile powder, stirring to mix all ingredients, as you add enough water to cover.
6. Simmer for about 1-½ hours, adding salt to taste after the chili has cooked somewhat.
7. Make a paste of the cracker meal or browned flour by mixing with a little water.
8. About 10 minutes before chili is ready, stir in this tightener, and cook until chili is thick.

Sam's Chili
3-½ Lb. Lean Beef; Cut in ½ Inch Cubes
2 Medium Onions; Chopped Coarse
3 Cloves Garlic; Finely Minced
2 Tablespoons Paprika
6 Tablespoons Chile powder
To Taste Salt
2 Tablespoons Cumin; Whole

1. Toast cumin's in skillet, crushing with wooden spoon.
2. Add onions, garlic and a little oil and sauté, till tender.
3. Sear the meat in the same skillet until grayish in color, adding a little more oil if needed.
4. Turn all into chili pot, add water to cover. Let simmer over low heat.
5. Salt after it's cooked awhile. Simmer about 2 hours.
6. Thicken with a little paste made form flour and water. Simmer another 15 minutes.

Sandi's Chili
Sandi Cutright
3 Lb. Hamburger; Browned and Drained
2 Medium Onions; Chopped
1 Can (Large) Tomato Paste
1 Teaspoon Pepper
20 Whole Cloves
1 Leaf Bay
3 Tablespoons Chile powder
2 Cans (Large) Tomato Juice
3 Cans (Large) Chili Beans; With Juice
¼ Cup Sugar

1. Brown and drain hamburger and onions.
2. Add drained meat and onion to a large pot along with the following.
3. Add tomato paste, chile powder, and cloves. Mix well.
4. Slowly mix in tomato juice.
5. Add bay leaf and pepper; stir. Bring to a boil; reduce heat to a slow simmer.
6. Cook, stirring occasionally, 1 to 1-½ hours.
7. Add chili beans and sugar. Heat through, stirring often to keep beans from sticking.

Note: This is also Excellent served over spaghetti, and sprinkled with Parmesan. This is my own secret recipe, which has been in my family for decades. Enjoy!

Sandy's Chili
1/3 Cup Oil
3 Medium Onions; Chopped
2 Stalks Celery; Chopped
4 Cloves Garlic; Minced
1 Medium Bell Pepper; Chopped
1 Pod Jalapeño Peppers; Minced
2 Lb. Tofu; Chunks
2 Tablespoons Red Chile; Ground
2 Tablespoons Oregano; Ground
2 Tablespoons Cumin; Ground
1 Leaf Bay
2 Cups Water
2 Cans (28 Ounces) Tomatoes
1 Can (6 Ounces) Tomato Paste
2 Cans Kidney Beans
To Taste Salt

1. Sauté, the first five ingredients in oil until limp.
2. Add tofu and sauté, until browned.
3. Mix the spices together in a bowl and sprinkle into the pot. Mix thoroughly.
4. Add water, tomatoes and tomato paste. Stir. Bring to a boil.
5. Reduce heat and simmer for 2 hours, stirring occasionally.
6. If desired, at this point, add the kidney beans.
7. Taste and correct seasoning.

The addition of 1 teaspoon to 1 Tablespoon of cayenne pepper can make this gradually spicier.

As the recipe reads, it's fairly tame.

Note: The ground chiles are not chili powder. Most chili powder is made up of a combination of chiles, oregano, cumin, salt and garlic. If chili powder is all you can find, you will have to readjust the cumin and oregano amounts.

Scheele's Super Chili

1-½ Lb. Ground Beef; Lean
1-½ Cups Onion; Thinly Sliced
1 Cup Celery; Finely Diced
1 Clove Garlic; Peeled and Cut Fine
½ Green Pepper; Diced
3 Cups Tomatoes; Canned
1 Tablespoon Chile powder; Up to 2, To Taste
2 Teaspoons Salt
1 Teaspoon Sugar
1 Teaspoon Worcestershire Sauce
3 Cups Red Kidney Beans; Cooked or Canned, To Taste
1 Cup Bean Liquid
1 Can (10 ½ Ounce) Tomato Soup
½ Can Water

1. Brown meat and spoon off excess grease.
2. Add onions, celery, garlic and green pepper.
3. Continue stirring and frying until onions are golden (about 10 minutes).
4. Add tomatoes, chile powder which has been mixed with the salt, sugar and Worcestershire sauce.
5. When boiling, cover and simmer about 1 hour.
6. Add beans and bean liquid, tomato soup and water. Cook, uncovered, until well heated and chili is desired thickness. (For thinner chili, add more tomatoes or water.)

Cayenne pepper may be substituted for chile powder, for very hot chili. This is really excellent on the second day.

Scott Robinson's $25,000.00 World Chili Champ

Ingredients/Phase 1
3 Lb. Beef
½ Lb. Ground Pork
1 Tablespoon Flour
1 Tablespoon Vegetable Oil

1/3 Cup Onion; Chopped
½ Tablespoon Garlic; Granulated
1 Can Beef Stock
2 Cans Chicken Stock
1 Can (8 Ounce) Tomato Sauce
½ Tablespoon Cumin; Ground
1 Can (4 Ounce) Green Chiles; Chopped
1 Pod Jalapeño Chiles; Chopped
1 Teaspoon Black Pepper
3 Tablespoons Chile Powder

Ingredients/Phase 2
1 Can (4 oz) Tomato Sauce
4 Tablespoons Chile powder
2 Tablespoons Mild New Mexico Chile Powder
2 Tablespoons Cumin; Ground
1 Teaspoon Garlic; Granulated
1 Teaspoon Tabasco
½ Tablespoon Brown Sugar

Makin' It/Phase 1:
1. Sauté the meat in oil, drain and add to a 4-quart pot.
2. Add all the rest of the Phase 1 ingredients and simmer, covered for 1-½ hours.
Note: Meat should be cut into ½ inch cubes.

Makin' It/Phase 2:
1. Uncover; add the ingredients from Phase 2 and simmer, uncovered for 45 minutes.
Please notice that there are no beans involved in Scott's recipe. Per ICS rules, the use of beans or any other filler in competition chili is prohibited. But if ya gotta have 'em, add 3 or 4 cans of drained pintos just at the end, in time to warm 'em up before serving. But try it without the beans first so you can taste a $25,000 bowl of red.

Shelby's Chili
½ Cup Vegetable Oil
1 Small Onion; Finely Chopped
1 Lb. Beef Round; Coarse Ground
1-¼ Teaspoon Oregano

1 Lb. Beef Chuck; Coarse Ground
½ Tablespoon Paprika
8 Ounces Tomato Sauce
1-½ Tablespoon Cumin; Ground
12 Ounces Beer
1-¼ Tablespoon Salt
¼ Cup Red Hot Chile
To Taste Cayenne Pepper
2 Cloves Garlic; Finely Chopped
¾ Lb. Monterey Jack Cheese; Shredded

1. Melt the suet or heat the oil in a heavy 3-quart (or larger) pot over medium-high heat.
2. Remove the unrendered suet and add the meat to the pot.
3. Break up any lumps with a fork and cook, stirring occasionally, until the meat is evenly browned.
4. Add the tomato sauce, beer, ground chile, garlic, onion, oregano, paprika, 1 teaspoon of the cumin, and the salt. Stir to blend.
5. Bring to a boil, and then lower the heat and simmer, uncovered, for 1 hour. Stir occasionally.
6. Taste and adjust seasonings, adding the cayenne pepper. Simmer, uncovered, 1 hour longer.
7. Stir in the cheese and the remaining ½ teaspoon of the cumin. Simmer ½ hour longer, stirring often to keep the cheese from burning.

Sheldon's Chili Muey Bueno
2 Lb. Beef Chuck; Cut in ½ Inch Cubes
2 Lb. Beef Chuck; Ground
2 Lb. Pork Butt; Ground, I always Grind My Own
¼ Cup Lard; Or Corn Oil
3 Cups Yellow Onion; Chopped
1 Head Fresh Garlic; Crushed and Chopped
1 Cup Celery Tops; Chopped
3 Large Celery; Chopped
1 Large Green Bell Pepper; Chopped
1 Large Red Bell Pepper; Chopped
2 Cans (28 Ounce) Tomatoes; Crushed
6 Leaves Bay; Large
¼ Cup Mild Chile powder; Unsalted
½ Cup Fresh Flat Leaf Parsley; Chopped

3 Tablespoons Oregano; Dried
3 Tablespoons Thyme; Dried
1 Teaspoon Cumin Seeds; Hand Rubbed
2 Pods Chipotle Peppers; Rough Chopped, See Note.
1 Tablespoon Adobo; Unsalted
2 Teaspoons Fresh Black Pepper; Coarse Ground
4 Tablespoons White Vinegar
1 Square Baker's Chocolate; Unsweetened
2 Cans (16 Ounce) Red Kidney Beans; Drain and Reserve Liquid
2 Cans (16 Ounce) Black Beans; Drain and Reserve Liquid
Note: Morita (Red Jalapeño-Smoked)

1. In heavy stainless steel, 10-quart pot, heat lard, or corn oil, and brown meat, a small amount at a time, on high heat.
2. Remove meat to bowl with slotted spoon.
3. When all meat is browned, return to pot, and add onions. Cook until translucent, not brown.
4. Add garlic, and cook briefly.
5. Add celery, and bell peppers, and cook briefly.
6. Add tomatoes, and reserved bean liquid, lower heat, bring to low simmer.
7. Add bay leaves, chile powder, parsley, oregano, thyme, cumin, chipotle peppers, vinegar, adobo, black pepper, and chocolate. Simmer slowly, partially covered for 2 hours.
8. Stir frequently, and add water if necessary.
9. Add beans, and heat through.
10. Salt to taste with kosher salt.
11. If hotter chili is to your taste, add red pepper flakes, not Louisiana hot sauce.
12. Do not forget to remove bay leaves.

Serve over rice, with warmed corn tortillas. Garnish with shredded white cheddar, or Latin type cheese if available, chopped raw yellow onion, sour cream, avocado, fresh diced tomatillo, or tomato, and lime wedges. Mucho cold cervesa, or margaritas to be offered as accompaniment. Comer!

Sherrie's Hot Chili
3 Lb. Hamburger Meat
1 Large Onion
3 Cans Kidney or Hot Chili Beans
6 Tablespoons Mexican Chile powder
3 Cans Tomatoes; Mash up Fine

3 Cans Tomato Sauce
20 Pods Jalapeño Peppers; Chopped Up

1. In a skillet, brown hamburger meat. When brown, drain off grease and put in a large pot.
2. Mix all ingredients together and cook for about 5 hours or until your taste.
3. The longer peppers cook, the hotter it gets.

Shirl's Hot Chili

2 Lb. Ground Meat; Lean
1 Large Onion; Diced
1 Large Green Pepper; Diced
2 Sticks Celery; Diced
2 Cans Tomato Soup
1 Can Tomato Sauce
2-½ Cups Water
3 Cans Kidney Beans
1 Tablespoon Garlic Salt
2 Tablespoons Red Pepper
2 Tablespoons Chile powder
1 Package (8 oz) Cheddar Cheese; Shredded

1. Brown ground meat; add onion, green pepper and celery.
2. Add garlic salt, red pepper and chile powder. Mix well. Simmer 10 to 15 minutes.
3. Add tomato soup, tomato sauce and water. Simmer for 1-½ hours.
4. Add drained kidney beans. Cook for another 15 to 20 minutes.
Serve hot topped with grated Cheddar.
   Note: You can substitute crushed tomatoes, if desired. Just put 2 cups of water in instead of 2-½ cups.

Sponge's Mom's Chili

1 Lb. Hamburger; Up to 1.5
1 Can Dark Kidney Beans
1 Can Stewed Tomatoes
2 Cans (Small) Tomato Sauce
1 Small Onion
2 Tablespoons Chile powder
1 Dash Red Pepper Flakes; Approximately ¼ Tsp.
1 Dash Cayenne Pepper

1 Dash Black Pepper
1/2 Teaspoon Salt

1. Brown Meat with onions.
2. Drain grease, place mixture in a large pot.
3. Coat the mixture with all dry ingredients and brown until meat is well coated.
4. Add two (2) cans tomato sauce.
5. Rinse each can out and two full cans of water.
6. Pour entire can of stewed tomatoes.
7. Rinse out can, adding a full can of water.
8. Add entire can of beans.
9. Bring to a rolling boil, and then reduce to simmer. Simmer until desired consistency (usually about an hour).

Serve with shredded cheese and onions.

Stanley Synar's Famous Chili Recipe

8 Large Onions; Finely Chopped
8 Medium Bell Peppers; Finely Chopped
14 Stalks Celery; Finely Chopped, Use Fresh
20 Lb. Ground Beef; Coarse Ground
½ Lb. Beef Fat
3 Cans (8 Ounce) Tomato Paste
6 Cans No. 2 Stewed Tomatoes
2 Cans No. 2 Water
9 Cloves Garlic; Finely Chopped
8 Boxes (3 Ounce) Gebhardt's Eagle Brand Chili Powder; Must be Gebhardt's
7 Tablespoons Salt; Or To Taste
3 Sprinkles Oregano
7-½ Ounces Hotter-Than-Hot Chili Salsa
2-½ Medium Green Chile Peppers; Finely Chopped
To Taste Pepper; Coarse Ground
1-½ Can Jalapeño Peppers; Finely Chopped, 20 to 24
½ Teaspoon Cayenne Pepper Powder
1 Dash This and a Dash of That...

1. Rub a 10-gallon pot with cooking oil or beef fat.
2. Add onions, peppers and celery. Cook gently, stirring often, for about 12 minutes.

3. Brown meat in a separate pan. When browned, add to pot.
4. Add remaining ingredients and bring to a boil.
5. Then reduce heat and simmer about 5 hours, stirring occasionally.
6. Let chili age overnight.
7. Reheat and serve.

Makes 30 to 40 servings.

Stan's Chili

2 Lb. Ground Beef
1 Lb. Sirloin
2 Teaspoons Mustard Seeds
4 Ounces Green Chile Peppers; Chopped
24 Ounces Tomato Juice
To Taste Salt and Pepper
1 Medium Onion
1 Package Old Hired Hand Chili Mix
1 Can Jalapeño Chili Beans

1. Cut sirloin into ½ inch cubes.
2. Chop onion, brown ground beef and sirloin cubes.
3. Drain, and then add onion, chiles and chili mix.
4. Stir while cooking on medium heat for 5 minutes.
5. Add mustard seed, chili beans and tomato juice and simmer for 1 hour.
6. Stir occasionally and add salt and pepper to taste.
7. Add water or tomato juice to obtain consistency wanted.

Stark's Chili

1-½ Lb. Ground Sirloin; Very Lean
½ Lb. Loose Sausage Whatever You Have; (Good Chorizo Can't Be Beat)
3 Medium Onions; Peeled and Chopped Fine
2 Medium Green Bell Peppers; Minced
5 Pods Jalapeño (Red or Green) Chile Pepper; Chipotles Are Good Too.
1 Head Garlic; Peeled and Minced
3 Cans (Medium) Pinto Beans; Drained
2 Cans (Medium) Red Kidney Beans; Drained
3 Medium Italian Plum Tomatoes; Cubed
2 Tablespoons Extra Virgin Olive Oil
3 Tablespoons Cumin; Ground (Rounded)
2 Tablespoons Cilantro; Heaping (Coriander Leaf)
1-½ Tablespoons Marjoram; Dried

1-½ Tablespoons Sage; Dried
1 Teaspoon Salt

This is a chili based on the assumption that classic, Mexican chili con carne is made, literally, from chiles and meat, with little or none of that other stuff. Having never been to Mexico, I recognize that this may or may not be correct, but there you have it and there you go.

The recipe is based on the further assumption that I like beans, and that my chili should, therefore, contain a bunch of 'em, whether the Mexicans do it that way or not.

The last assumption I'll mention is that I'm a purist, who insists on using only dry beans. This assumption is entirely incorrect: I want my chili fast, so I use only canned, pre-cooked beans. Here's what's in it:

1. Heat olive oil in a large, cast-iron vessel (stock pot or Dutch oven).
2. Sauté, onions, bell peppers, Jalapeños and Habañero, until onions are clear.
3. Add sausage. Sauté, until brown, then cook, covered, for 15 minutes.
4. Add ground sirloin. Sauté, until brown, then add garlic.
5. Cook for five minutes, turning and chopping constantly.
6. Be sure not to let the garlic turn brown.
7. Add tomatoes, cumin, cilantro, marjoram, sage and salt.
8. Cook, stirring constantly, for five minutes.
9. Add canned beans.
10. Mix thoroughly, then cook, covered, stirring every five minutes, until beans have disintegrated to a paste (about 1-2 hours).
11. Correct seasoning, by adding liberal quantities of garlic, cumin, salt and whatever hot sauce (except Tabasco) you may have. Tabasco sauce tastes more like vinegar than peppers, and shouldn't ever be used in my chili, let alone any Mexican food: use a good Salsa Chipotles instead. You can get one from Mo-Hotta, Mo-Betta.

Serve in bowls over rice, or with Premium Oyster Crackers.

Stephanie's Chilly Day Chili
Stephanie Needham
2 Medium Onions; Chopped
1 Medium Green Pepper; Chopped
2 Tablespoons Vegetable Oil
2 Lb. Ground Beef
1 Can (16 Ounce) Tomatoes

1 Can (15 Ounce) Tomato Sauce
½ Cup Ketchup
2 Tablespoons Chile powder
¼ Teaspoon Pepper
2 Cans (15-½ Ounce) Kidney Beans

1. Sauté the onions and peppers in oil. Add ground beef.
2. Cook until lightly browned, stirring occasionally. Drain fat and set aside.
3. Partially drain kidney beans.
4. Stir in tomatoes, sauce, ketchup, chile powder, salt and pepper to meat mixture. Simmer, uncovered, for 30 minutes.
5. Stir in kidney beans, and simmer 15 minutes longer.

Serve with hot cornbread and honey butter.

Stephndon's Chili
2 Lb. Ground beef; Or Turkey
2 Cans (15.5 Ounce) Kidney Beans; With Liquid
2 Cans (15.5 Ounce) Chili Beans; With Sauce
1 Can (29 Ounce) Tomato Sauce
1 Can (15 Ounce) Tomatoes; Chopped
1 Medium Onion; Diced
1 Can (4 Ounce) Green Chiles
2-½ Tablespoons Chile powder
1-½ Teaspoons Cumin Powder
1-½ Teaspoons Salt
1 Teaspoon Pepper
1-½ Cups Water
As Needed Onion; Diced
As Needed Cheddar Cheese; Shredded, Optional Topping
Note: To make it even hotter, add 1 Tablespoon of cayenne pepper, or for something burning, add some sliced Jalapeño peppers!

1. Brown the ground beef in a large pot over medium heat; drain.
2. Using a pastry blender or fork, crumble the beef into very small pieces.
3. Return beef to pot and add remaining ingredients except diced onions and cheese.
4. Stir to combine well, bring to a boil over medium-high heat.
5. Reduce heat; cook, stirring occasionally, for 2 to 3 hours.

Garnish with onions and cheese, if desired. Yield: 12 servings.

Steve Strattman's Winning Chili

3 Lb. Beef Chuck; Tender
2 Tablespoons Onion Powder
2 Tablespoons Paprika
1-½ Teaspoons Cayenne Pepper
2 Cubes Beef Bouillon
½ Cup Beef Broth; Canned
3 Ounces Tomato Sauce
1 Tablespoon Juice From Cooked Jalapeño; See Note
1 Quart Water
6-½ Tablespoons Chile powder
1 Tablespoon Cumin
1-½ Teaspoons Garlic Powder
½ Teaspoon White Pepper
3/8 Teaspoon Salt

Note: To make Jalapeño juice, chop pepper coarsely and boil in small amounts of water, reduce slightly, then strain out pepper and seeds.

1. Cut meat in cubes, brown in a large, heavy Dutch oven.
2. Add onion powder, paprika, cayenne, bouillon, broth, tomato sauce, Jalapeño juice and water.
3. Cook over low heat for about 2 hours, adding more water as needed, until meat is tender.
4. Add chile powder, cumin, garlic powder and pepper, cook for 20-30 minutes more.
5. Add salt just before serving

Steve's Chili

2 Lb. Ground Beef
1 Medium Onion; Chopped
2 Cloves Garlic; Minced
½ Teaspoon Salt
60 Ounces Tomato Sauce
8 Ounces Green Chiles; Diced, (2 Standard Cans)
3 Medium Tomatoes; Sliced
¼ Cup Chile powder
½ Teaspoon Allspice; Ground
2 Teaspoons Red Pepper; Crushed
½ Teaspoon Black Pepper; Ground

1 Dash White Pepper; Ground
1 Dash MSG
1 Dash Oregano
1 Dash Cloves; Ground
1 Teaspoon Sugar
To Taste Seasoned Salt
1 Lb. Red Kidney Beans
8 Ounces Pepperoni; Sliced

1. Fry together the ground beef, onion, garlic, and salt until beef is browned.
2. Meanwhile in a large kettle, mix together the tomato sauce, green chiles, and tomatoes and heat over low heat.
3. When the hamburger is done, mix in with tomato sauce mixture.
4. Add the spices, salt, and sugar, stir well, and adjust ingredients to taste.
5. It will taste hotter later than it does now.
6. Simmer for about 1-1/2 hours, and then add beans and pepperoni. Simmer for 30 minutes longer.

Serve over rice, topped with shredded cheddar cheese.

Susan's Quick And Easy Chili
1 Lb. Ground Beef
1 Can Ranch Style Jalapeño Pinto Beans
1 Can Ranch Style Beans
1 Can Tomatoes (Stewed)
To Taste Salt and Pepper
1 Tablespoon Hot Mexican Style Chile powder; Up to 2

1. Brown meat and drain off grease.
2. Add rest of ingredients and simmer 20 to 30 minutes.

Serve over rice with crackers. Yum, Yum.

Note: If you don't like super hot chili, spoon out the Jalapeño before cooking. The beans will still have the flavor but not all the heat.

Sylvia's Halltown Cafe Chili and Beans
3 Tablespoons Onion; Chopped
2 Tablespoons Green Pepper; Chopped
3 Cloves Garlic; Minced
2 Tablespoons Vegetable Oil
1 Lb. Ground Beef; Coarse Ground
2 Tablespoons Chile powder

1 Can (16 Ounce) Tomatoes
1 Can (16 Ounce) Pinto Beans

1. Sauté onions, green pepper, and garlic in vegetable oil until tender.
2. Add ground beef and brown thoroughly.
3. Add chile powder, tomatoes, and beans. Heat thoroughly, adding water it needed.

Makes 4 to 5 servings.

Tom Skipper's 1983 Terlingua Championship Chili
3 Lb. Meat; Cubed
1 Can Tomato Sauce
1 Medium Onion; Chopped
4 Tablespoons Chile powder
1 Teaspoon Garlic Powder
1 Teaspoon Paprika
2 Teaspoons Salt; Plain Salt Preferred
2 Tablespoons Cumin
½ Teaspoon Cayenne Pepper
½ Teaspoon Oregano; Ground
1 Teaspoon MSG
1 Teaspoon Black Pepper
1 Teaspoon Brown Sugar

1. Put meat, tomato sauce and onion in a large pot.
2. Add enough water to cover the meat by about an inch.
3. Bring to a boil, cover, reduce heat, and cook until meat is tender, this should take about 2 hours.
4. Keep adding water as need to prevent the liquid from cooking away.
5. Liquid should cook down to the level of the meat.
6. When the meat is tender, stir in the all the spices and the brown sugar, cover and cook for 30 more minutes.

Tom Threepersons Chili
6 Pods Habañero Peppers; Dried
3 Lb. Chuck; Boneless, Dice ¼ Inch.
6 Tablespoons Olive Oil
4 Medium Onions; Chopped
4 Cloves Garlic; Minced
1-½ Teaspoons Cumin

1 Can (Large) Tomatoes; Swished
1 Can (Large) Chili Hot Beans
1 Tablespoon Cocoa
2 Leaves Bay; Crushed
1 Teaspoon Oregano

1. Heat a skillet over mod-high heat and toast peppers, turning often, for 1-2 min. Let cool, and crush.
2. Combine with 1-cup water in a small pot and bring to boil. Simmer 5 minutes.
3. Sauté meat in a Dutch oven with olive oil until lightly browned.
4. Add onions and garlic and cook until onions are softened.
5. Add cumin and cook 1 minute.
6. Add rest of ingredients.
7. Add enough water to cover barely, bring to boil, cover, simmer 2 hours.
Serve with lots of cold drinks.

Tom Wayman Chili
½ Cup Butter; Or Margarine
2 Lb. Top Sirloin Steak; Coarse Ground
3 Medium Green Peppers; Chopped
3 Large Onions; Chopped
3 Tablespoons Garlic; Minced (I Use More)
½ Cup Parsley; Snipped
3 Cans (16 Ounce) Tomatoes (Including Liquid); I Use The Cut-up Tomatoes
¼ Cup Chile powder; I Use New Mexican Hotter
2 Tablespoons Salt; I Use Less
1-½ Teaspoons Cumin
1-½ Teaspoons Black Pepper; I Never Measure
1 Ounce Tabasco Sauce

1. In a large cooking pot, brown meat in the butter or margarine.
2. Pour off 1/3 cup liquid from meat and sauté, green pepper, onion, garlic and parsley in separate skillet until tender.
3. Add to meat mixture and stir in chile powder, salt, pepper and cumin.
4. Add Tabasco and tomatoes.
5. Simmer entire mixture 1 hour covered, remove lid and simmer at least 30 min. longer. Stir occasionally.
Makes 10 servings.

Tom Wopat's Chili
Denise Dutton
1 Teaspoon Oil
2 Lb. Ground Beef; (the leaner the better)
2 Cups Onion; Chopped
2 Cups Green Pepper; Chopped
3/4 Cup Red Wine; I Use Sweet Wine
1 Can (12 Ounce) Kidney Beans
1 Can (16 Ounce) Tomatoes; I Use a Can of Rotels.
1 Can (8 Ounce) Tomato Sauce
To Taste Cayenne Pepper; I Think 2 Teaspoons Are not too much.
To Taste Salt and Pepper
1 Teaspoon Worcestershire Sauce
To Taste Hot Sauce

1. Cook beef with oil and cayenne until browned.
2. Drain fat (add to crock pot, or cook beef in large Dutch oven).
3. Add everything else.
4. Cook all day (if in crock pot) or for at least one hour (if in Dutch oven).
Note: I add 2 teaspoons of cumin to this, but what is above is as close to Tom's recipe as I could get from snatching it from the tube. It's great. Serve with the rest of that wine you used to cook it-sweet wine and hot chili goes great. Enjoy!

Tommie Arenas' Chili Beans
The County Fair Cookbook
4 Cups Pinto Beans; Rinsed and Sorted
2-½ Quarts Water
½ Lb. Round Steak; Ground
¾ Teaspoon Cumin Seed
2 Cloves Garlic; Peeled
1 Medium Carrot; Cut Up
3 Tablespoons Gebhardt's Chili Powder
1 Can Tomato Sauce
2 Slices Bacon; Cut Small
1 Tablespoon Salt; To Taste

1. In heavy skillet, bring the beans and water to boil.
2. Lower heat, cover and cook gently for 2 hrs, checking frequently to see that beans are just covered with water. If necessary, add a little boiling

water. Stir from time to time.

3. Cook the ground round in a skillet until well browned. Drain off any fat.
4. In a blender or processor, grind together the cumin seed, garlic and carrot.
5. Stir the meat, cumin mixture and chili powder into the beans.
6. Stir in the tomato sauce and bacon and add the salt.
7. Cook 1-½ hours longer, or until the beans are tender. Keep them moist.

From The Big Fresno Fair of Fresno, CA. Fair Dates: Early October, for 17 days.

Tom's Famous Chili

¼ Cup Vegetable Oil
1 Medium Bell Pepper; Diced
1 Tablespoon Garlic; Chopped
½ Cup Chile powder; Or To Taste
2 Cans (16 Ounce) Bush's Best Chili Hot Beans
6 Ounces Tomato Juice
1 Teaspoon Salt
1 Teaspoon Black Pepper
1 Large Yellow Onion; Diced
4 Stalks Celery; Chopped
2 Lb. Ground Chili Meat
1 Can (28 Ounce) Whole Tomatoes; Crushed
2 Cans (15 Ounce) Dark Red Kidney Beans
1 Quart Water
1 Teaspoon White Pepper
1 Teaspoon Onion Powder

1. Heat oil in 8 quart stew pot.
2. Add onion, bell pepper, celery and garlic. Sauté 2 to 3 minutes.
3. Add chili meat. Cook over medium heat, stirring often, until meat no longer is pink, about 10 minutes. Drain off excess fat.
4. Add chile powder; stir to mix.
5. Add remaining ingredients. Simmer uncovered about 2 hours, stirring several times while cooking.

Best if prepared the day before serving. Freeze leftover chili.

Trish's Southern Vegetable Chili Soup

1 Lb. Ground Beef
1 Tablespoon Salt
1 Teaspoon Worcestershire Sauce

½ Package Chili-O Seasoning Mix
1 Can (6 Ounce) Tomato Paste
1 Can (16 Ounce) Tomatoes
1 Package (16 Ounce) Vegetable Gumbo Mix; Frozen
½ Cup Barley
4 Ounces Egg Noodles; Or More if Desired
4 Cups Water; Up to 5

1. Brown beef; add salt, Worcestershire sauce and Chili-O mix. Stir over low heat until well blended. Drain.
2. Stir in tomato paste, add tomatoes and 4 cups water.
3. Bring mixture to boil and add frozen vegetable mix and barley, return to boil, cover and simmer for 45 minutes, checking occasionally.
4. Add noodles and more water if needed. Cook another 10 minutes or until noodles are tender.

Uncle Bob's Chili
2 Tablespoons Mexene Chili Powder
2 Lb. Ground Meat
1 Large Onion; Chopped
3 Cloves Garlic; Minced
1 Teaspoon Salt
2 Tablespoons Flour; (Up to 3)
1 Tablespoon Cumin Seeds

1. Method: combine all ingredients in Dutch oven and brown meat.
2. Cover well with water and bring to a boil; lower heat, cover and simmer about 2 hours or until done.

Uncle Ted's Cincinnati Chili
1 Quart Water
2 Lb. Beef; Ground
1 Clove Garlic
2 Medium Onions; Chopped
1-½ Tablespoons Vinegar
1 Can (6 Ounce) Tomato Paste
1 Teaspoon Cinnamon
1 Teaspoon Cumin
1 Teaspoon Red Pepper; Ground
1 Teaspoon Chile powder

2 Teaspoons Salt
3 Whole Allspice; up to 5*
4 Leaves Bay; Up to 5*
2 Small Chile Peppers; Up to 3 if Desired*
* Remove these ingredients before serving.

1. Bring water to a boil.
2. Add ground beef and stir to separate.
3. Add remaining ingredients. Simmer 2 to 3 hours, uncovered.
Serve over hot cooked spaghetti. Add the following, as desired: red kidney beans, fresh chopped onion and freshly grated Cheddar cheese.

Vaughn's "That's Purty Near Chili"
¼ Lb. Suet; Finely Chopped
5 Lb. Sirloin Tip; Cubed
1 Lb. Pork Loin; Cubed
4 Onions; Chopped
4 Green Peppers; Chopped
1 Can (4 Ounce) Green Chiles; Chopped
1 Can (10 Ounce) Tomatoes and Green Chiles
2 Tablespoons Cumin; Ground
2 Tablespoons Oregano; Ground
1 Tablespoon Paprika
2 Tablespoons Salt
1 Tablespoon Cayenne Pepper
1 Can (12 Ounce) Contadina Tomato Paste
4 Cloves Garlic; Minced
¼ Cup Sugar
1 Tablespoon Chile Pod Pulp
1 Quart Stock
1 Quart Tomatoes; Chopped
½ Cup Masa Harina (Corn Flour)
½ Cup Cold Water

1. Fry suet in skillet until crisp.
2. Add beef about 1 pound at a time, brown, stirring as it cooks.
3. Remove each pound after browning.
4. When all meat is browned, return it to the kettle.
5. Add seasonings and beef stock or broth. Cover and simmer 1-½ to 2 hours; skim off fat.

6. Combine masa harina or cornmeal with cold water and stir thoroughly into chili. Simmer 30 minutes.

Vern's Chili
2 Lb. Ground Chuck
1 Bag (12 Ounce) Onions
1 Can (16 Ounce) Tomatoes
1 Can (32 Ounce) V-8 Juice
1 Jar (8 Ounce) El Paso Taco Sauce
1 Tablespoon Garlic Powder
To Taste Salt
1 Can (32 Ounce) Kidney Beans
To Taste Chile powder

1. Put ground chuck and onions in pan and cook until done.
2. Then pour in 8-quart pan; add the rest of the ingredients.
3. Cook and season to your taste with chile powder and salt. Let it simmer for 20 minutes and serve.

Vince's Chili
2 Lb. Ground Beef
15 Ounces Tomato Paste
15 Ounces Kidney Beans
15 Ounces Tomato Sauce
28 Ounces Taco Dip; Mild

1. Cook and drain the meat.
2. Combine meat, tomato sauce and paste, and taco dip in large pot and simmer for at least 45 minutes.
3. Additional spices are not needed!

Walton Burrage's Chili
1 Package William's Chili Mix
2 Lb. Chili Meat
3 Pods Garlic; Crushed, Up to 4
2 Teaspoons Comino Seeds
To Taste Black Pepper
To Taste Red Pepper; Crushed
To Taste Salt

1. Bring chili meat and ½ cup water to boil in heavy saucepan.
2. Reduce heat and simmer until meat is almost done (about 45-60 minutes).
3. Add all other ingredients.
4. Continue to simmer until flavors are blended and meat is done. Simmer this on lowest heat possible and the longer it cooks, the better.
5. Add a little water, as needed.

Hot! I sampled this chili at Walton's house. It was delicious and he gave me the recipe.

Waylan's Texas Chili

2 Lb. Coarse Ground Meat; Beef, Deer, Etc.
1 Can (8 Ounce) Tomato Sauce
¾ Teaspoon Cumin
½ Teaspoon Oregano
1-¼ Teaspoons Salt
2 Cloves Garlic; Minced
1 Small Onion; Minced
1 Tablespoon Paprika
½ Cup Chile powder
1 Pod Red Pepper; Optional, Hot About 1 Tsp
2 Cups Water; Up to 3
2 Tablespoons Masa Harina (Corn Flour)

1. Cook meat in a heavy skillet until light gray colored; pour off grease.
2. Add all the other ingredients except the masa (corn meal). Simmer on low for 1 hour.
3. Make up a thin, soupy mixture of meal and water (about ¼ cup of warm water) and stir into the chili and simmer 15 to 30 minutes more, stirring often. Serves about 4.

For Texas style chili, serve pinto beans on the side, not in the chili. Serve with crackers, tortillas, corn bread and a cool beverage.

Wild Parson's Chili

3 Lb. Ground Beef
6 Cans (15-½ Ounce) Mexican Style Chili Bean
1 Can (29 Ounce) Hunt's Tomato Sauce
1 Package Mickey Gilley's Wild Bull Chili Mix

1. Pour chili beans in a four-quart pot.
2. Add the can of tomato sauce and the Wild Bull chili seasoning. Bring to

a slow boil, seasoning with the red chili seasoning (be careful partner!).

3. Add 3 pounds of fried ground beef (drain first), to the chili beans and simmer together for about 45 minutes, stirring occasionally.

William Richhart's Chili

4 Cans (Regular) Tomato Soup
3 Cans Brook's Chili Hot Beans
2 Lb. Ground Beef
1 Large Onion
3 Cups Macaroni
¼ Cup Milk
3 Teaspoons Sugar
To Taste Salt and Pepper
To Taste Garlic Powder
To Taste Cumin

1. Brown hamburger and onion in large skillet; drain.
2. Add seasonings.
3. In a very large pot combine soup, beans, 4 cups water, milk and sugar.
4. In a separate pot, cook macaroni until tender.
5. Combine hamburger to large pot, then while soup is cooking, add macaroni. Bring to boil, then reduce heat and add chile powder to taste.

Enjoy!

Willie's Chili

1 Lb. Ground Beef
1 Large Onion; Diced
½ Medium Green Pepper; (Or Hot Peppers) Diced
1 Can (Small) Mushrooms
1 Can (Medium) Corn
1 Can (15 Ounce) Chili Beans
1 Can (15 Ounce) Tomatoes, Whole; Cut into Bit Size Pieces
8 Ounces Tomato Sauce; Or Spaghetti Sauce
½ Lb. Sharp Cheddar Cheese; Shredded
1 Tablespoon Chile powder; (Up to 2)
1 Teaspoon Garlic Powder
1 Teaspoon Black Pepper; Red Pepper, Whatever
To Taste Hot Sauce; Optional
1 Tablespoon Soy Sauce; Optional

1. Lightly sauté the onions and brown the meat.
2. Then just dump in the rest of the ingredients except the cheese.
3. When everything is blended and hot, add the cheese and stir until it's melted in. Simmer for a few minutes until done.

This makes about 3 quarts of chili.

If you follow the recipe it will not come out too hot. Adjust spice to your taste. I find it's best if you stick it in the fridge and let it sit overnight so the flavors blend.

Woodie's Homestyle Chili
2 Tablespoons Cooking Oil
5 Medium Onions
4 Lb. Beef Chuck; Coarse Ground
5 Cloves Garlic
4 Tablespoons Oregano; Preferably Mexican, Dried
2 Teaspoons Woodruff
1 Tablespoon Red Chile, Hot; Ground
1 Teaspoon Cayenne Pepper
2 Tablespoons Paprika
3 Tablespoons Cumin
2 Teaspoons Chipenos (Pequin Chiles)
4 Dashes Hot Pepper Sauce, Liquid
30 Ounces Tomato Sauce
6 Ounces Tomato Paste
As Needed Water
4 Tablespoons Masa Harina (Corn Flour)

1. Heat the oil in a large heavy skillet over medium heat.
2. Add the onions.
3. Season with salt and pepper and cook, stirring, until the onions are translucent. Remove to a large heavy pot.
4. Add the meat to the skillet, pouring in more oil if necessary.
5. Add garlic and 1 tablespoon of the oregano.
6. Break up any lumps with a fork and cook over medium-high heat, stirring occasionally, until meat is evenly browned. Add this mixture to the pot.
7. In a small plastic or paper bag, shake together the remaining 3 tablespoons of oregano, the woodruff, ground chile, cayenne pepper, paprika, cumin, and the Chipenos.
8. Add the blended spices to the pot as well as the liquid hot pepper sauce, tomato sauce, and tomato paste.

9. Add enough water to cover.
10. Bring to a boil, then lower the heat and simmer, uncovered, for at least 2 hours.
11. Taste and adjust seasonings.
12. Cool the chili and refrigerate it overnight.
13. The next day, skim off the excess fat.
14. Reheat the chili to the boiling point and stir in a paste made of the masa harina and a little water.
15. Stir constantly to prevent sticking and scorching, adding water as necessary for the desired texture.

Woody Chili
5 Medium Onion; Chopped
As Needed Oil
To Taste Salt and Pepper
4 Lb. Beef Chuck; Chili Grind
5 Cloves Garlic; Minced
4 Tablespoons Oregano
2 Tablespoons Woodruff; An Herb
1 Teaspoon Cayenne Pepper
1 Tablespoon Paprika
1 Tablespoon New Mexico Chile powder
3 Tablespoons Ground Cumin
1 Teaspoon Chipenos; Chili Petines Pepper
4 Dashes Tabasco Sauce
3 Cans (10 Ounce) Tomato Paste
4 Tablespoons Masa Harina (Corn Flour)

1. Brown onion in oil, season with salt and pepper then transfer to chili pot.
2. Brown beef in skillet, adding more oil if necessary.
3. Add garlic and 1 tablespoon oregano.
4. In paper sack, shake together rest of oregano with next 6 ingredients.
5. Add this mixture, meat and all other ingredients except Masa and enough water to cover meat. Simmer at least 2 hours or till meat is tender.
6. Cool and refrigerate overnight.
7. Warm and thicken with a paste of Masa and water. Heat through.

Working Mother's Chili (Chili Cook Off 1987)
1-½ Lb. Ground Beef
1 Small Onion; Chopped

1 Teaspoon Black Pepper
2 Cans (15 Ounce) Hunt's Tomato Sauce; With Tomato Bits
1 Can (22 Ounce) Brook's Chili Hot Beans
1 Can (30 Ounce) Dark Red Kidney Beans
1 Can (6 Ounce) V-8 Juice
1 Cup Celery; Chopped
To Taste Cumin
To Taste Chile powder

1. Brown the beef with onions and pepper. Drain off excess grease.
2. Add the next four ingredients and simmer slowly for 30 minutes.
3. Microwave the celery for 2 minutes and add with the rest of ingredients.
4. Simmer again for a few minutes before serving. Actually, the amount of cooking time can depend upon your family schedule.

Also good if made ahead and heated in single bowl. Number of servings: 10 to 12.

World's Best (Mom's) Chili
1 Tablespoon Olive Oil
2 Large Yellow Onions; Coarse Chopped
1 Large Green Pepper; Coarse Chopped
6 Stalks Celery With Leaves; Sliced
1 Any Any Leftover Vegetables; Cooked (Corn, Green Beans)
1 Can (16 Ounce) Tomatoes; Squished
1 Can (28 Ounce) Tomatoes; Diced
1 Can (16 Ounce) Beef Stock; Or Homemade
1 Tablespoon Tomato Paste; 1 or 2 to Thicken to Taste
1 Can (28 Ounce) Dark Red Kidney Beans; Pinto or Other Beans
1 Can (15 Ounce) Kidney, Black, Pinto or Other Beans
½ Teaspoon Paprika
1 Tablespoon Garlic; Fresh, Crushed
1 Tablespoon Worcestershire Sauce; Or More To Taste
1 Tablespoon Chile powder; Adding More to Taste
2 Tablespoons Steak Sauce
To Taste Tabasco Sauce; Several Dashes
To Taste Salt and Black Pepper; Fresh Ground
1 Lb. Cooked Lean Ground Beef, (Very Optional)

1. Heat large pot over medium heat.
2. Add oil immediately, followed by the onions, green pepper and celery

with leaves; cook 5 minutes.

3. Add any additional cooked leftover vegetables, peeled and squished tomatoes, diced tomatoes and all remaining ingredients. Bring chili to a boil, reduce heat and simmer for at least 1 hour.
4. Adjust seasoning to taste.

Serve hot with any number of condiments or alone. Cooked spaghetti noodles or rice, cheddar cheese, sour cream, Jalapeño peppers, etc. I think a heavy moist cornbread is a must! 8 servings.

Zesty Chili

In the food processor, chop:

1 Lb. Carrots
1 Lb. Zucchini
1 Lb. Onions

1. Heat ¼ Cup Vegetable Oil in a 6-quart pot.
2. Add vegetables.
3. Cook over medium-high heat 15-20 minutes, stirring 3 or 4 times until almost tender.
4. Put 3 Lbs. ground turkey (or beef) and 1 tablespoon Minced Garlic in an 8-quart pot.
5. Cook, breaking up meat, until it is no longer pink.
6. Stir in the vegetables, four 28-ounce cans crushed tomatoes in puree (drain some of the juice or it might be too watery), a 15 ounce can of tomato sauce and 2 teaspoons salt.
7. Bring to a boil; reduce heat to medium-low. Simmer 15 to 20 minutes for flavors to develop.
8. You will have about 22 cups of meat sauce.
9. You can use the sauce as is for spaghetti sauce or freeze some for future chili. (Or you can decrease proportions and make less to begin with.)
10. With 7 cups of the meat sauce, add 38-ounce can of kidney beans and 2 or more tablespoons chile powder.

Top with shredded cheese and onions.

Refrigerate up to 5 days. Freeze up to 4 months.

Chapter 12
Chili Recipes From Firehouses, Jails and Taverns

Background

Firemen are famous for their cooking and a frequent pot on the stove sends the delicious smell of chili wafting through the firehouse. I have included several recipes that come from firehouses from across the country. Prisons and jails are equally lauded for their chili recipes. Some say it is good for hiding saltpeter however, I suspect it is more for the low cost of the meals than anything else. Taverns as well have been touted as having great chili and it is as good a way as any to increase the consumption of beer. I suspect that more money is made on the beer than on the chili. Enjoy!

Firehouses

Arizona Forest Fire Chili
Chef Keith W. Cochran

2 Cans Red Beans
2 Cans Kidney Beans
2 Cans Tomatoes; Crushed
2 Medium Tomatoes; Diced
1-½ Cups Celery; Sliced
2 Cups Onion; Medium Dice
1 Cup Green Pepper; Diced
2-½ Lb. Beef; Ground
½ Cup Green Chiles; Diced
¼ Cup Jalapeño Chiles-Canned; Sliced
2 Tablespoons Parsley Flakes
¼ Cup Chile powder
¾ Tablespoon Garlic; Chopped
¾ Tablespoon Oregano
1 Tablespoon Cumin; Ground
1 Teaspoon Salt
1 Teaspoon Red Pepper; Ground
1-½ Teaspoon Black Pepper
1 Teaspoon White Pepper

1. Combine red beans, kidney beans, diced tomato, crushed tomato, green chiles, in large pot (do not drain cans).
2. Add jalapeños, chile powder, chopped garlic, parsley flakes, oregano, and cumin. Brown the beef and add to the beans.
3. Brown onions and celery in grease from the meat, add them to the rest.

4. Add the salt, black pepper, white pepper, and red pepper.
5. This is a thick chili. Simmer for 2 - 4 hours.
Serve or refrigerate. This chili will age.

Backdraft Chili
The Geezer Cookbook, Dwayne Pritchett
1 Lb. Bacon; Cut into Pieces
3 Lb. Chuck Roast; Cubed
1-½ Lb. Pork Roast; Cubed
4 Cloves Garlic; Minced
3 Large Onions; Chopped
1 Can Green Chile Peppers; Chopped
2 Teaspoons Habañero Pepper; Dried, Chopped
2 Teaspoons Red Pepper; Dried
2 Tablespoons Chile powder
1-½ Tablespoons Paprika
4 Tablespoons Cumin
1 Tablespoon Black Pepper
1 Tablespoon Tabasco Sauce
2 Tablespoons Worcestershire Sauce
1 Can Beef Broth
1 Can Ro-tel Diced Tomato and Green Chile
2 Cans Chili Beans with Gravy; Hot

1. Fry bacon in #14 Dutch oven until just crisp. Remove and reserve bacon.
2. Pour off most of drippings into a large skillet. Leave a small amount in Dutch oven.
3. Brown meat and garlic in skillet in batches.
4. While meat is browning, sauté onions in Dutch oven.
5. Add meat as browned and stir well.
6. Add bacon, green chiles and dried peppers, spices, sauces, stock, and Ro-tel tomatoes. Simmer for 2 hours.
7. Add hot chili beans and simmer another 15 minutes. Serve.

Chili Ala Captain James McDonnell-Engine 81
Thomas Brown
1 Lb. Italian Sausage; Bulk, Mild
1 Lb. Ground Chuck
1 Large Yellow Onion; Diced
2 Cloves Garlic; Minced

1-½ Tablespoons Chile powder
6 Ounces Tomato Paste
1-½ Cups Water
1 Tablespoon Instant Coffee
1 Tablespoon Sugar
1 Tablespoon Paprika
1 Tablespoon Oregano
1 Teaspoon Salt
1 Teaspoon Pepper
1 Teaspoon Cumin

1. Brown sausage, ground meat, onion, and garlic in a pot.
2. Add remaining ingredients; bring to a boil, cover, and simmer 1-¼ hours.
3. Top with grated Monterey Jack cheese and finely chopped scallions.
Serve over spaghetti or noodles or just eat with crackers.

Chili Beans From San Francisco Fire Department
1 Lb. Pinto Beans; Dry
1 Can (10 Ounce) Red Chili Sauce
As Needed Water
¼ Cup Vinegar
1 Lb. Chuck; Ground
1 Tablespoon Chile powder
1 Large Onion; Chopped
1 Dash Hot Sauce
1 Can (16 Ounce) Tomatoes (Stewed)
To Taste Salt and Pepper

1. Cover beans with cold water, cover pot and bring to boil. Reduce heat and simmer for 3 hours, adding water as needed.
2. In a skillet, slowly brown ground beef. When crumbly, add onion and sauté until limp.
3. Add to beans along with rest of ingredients except the salt and pepper. Cover and simmer for three hours or until beans are tender and liquid is somewhat thickened.
4. Add salt and pepper and serve.
From: San Francisco Fire Department, Engine Company 32.

Fire Alarm Chili From College Park
Georgia's Station 2
2 Tablespoons Margarine
2 Lb. Ground Beef
4 Dashes Worcestershire Sauce
4 Tablespoons Chile powder
1 Teaspoon Sugar
2 Medium Onions; Chopped
2 Cans No. 2 Tomatoes
1 Can (No. 300) Chili Beans
To Taste Salt and Pepper

1. Melt the margarine in a large skillet. Crumble and brown the beef, adding salt and pepper to taste. Skim off excess fat.
2. Add the Worcestershire sauce, chile powder, sugar, and onions and continue cooking until onions are almost done.
3. Chop the tomatoes and add them along with the beans. Bring the mixture to a boil then lower heat to simmer for about 1 hour before serving.
6 servings.

Fire Camp Chili
100 Lb. Pinto Beans
4 Cups Jalapeño Chile Peppers; With Juice
40 Lb. Meat-Ham, Sausage, Pork, Bacon; Ground Beef, Etc.
12 Large Onions; Chopped
To Taste Salt

1. Soak Beans overnight, and then rise to a boil on high heat.
2. Add all ingredients and simmer until tender (about 6 hours).
3. Add Water as necessary. Stir occasionally.
Makes 60 gallons-120 servings.

Fire Eater's Chile-Chile Ardient
½ Lb. Pork Steak; Cubed
1 Tablespoon Flour
½ Teaspoon Garlic Salt
6 Tablespoons Red Chile powder
½ Teaspoon Salt
2 Cups Water; Cold, or 3 Cups

1. Brown pork in a medium-sized skillet over medium heat. Drain and add garlic salt and salt.
2. Stir in flour and cook for 1 minute.
3. Stir in chile and cook for an additional minute.
4. Gradually add water and stir until mixture is slightly thickened. Cook for 10-15 minutes.

Fire Extinguisher Chili
2 Cans (30 Ounce) Tomatoes, Whole
2 Cans (30 Ounce) Kidney Beans
2 Lb. Ground Beef; Extra Lean
1 Large White Onion; Whole
1 Large Green Pepper
2 Handfuls Chile Peppers; Whole
¼ Cup Lea & Perrins BBQ Sauce
¼ Cup Worcestershire Sauce
1 Teaspoon Red Pepper; To Taste, Crushed
1 Teaspoon Black Pepper; To Taste
1 Teaspoon Celery Salt; To Taste
1 Teaspoon Lemon Pepper; To Taste
1 Teaspoon Cayenne Pepper; To Taste
1 Teaspoon Garlic Powder; To Taste
1 Large Cooking Pot
1 Large Cast Iron Frying Pan
1 Large Electric Crockpot; W/Thermostat

My friend Donna won the 1994 San Diego regional Chili Cookoff with this recipe. She does it from memory, but I wrote it down for her once when she made it for me. Note the simmering time before you try this!

1. Empty beans and tomatoes into large pot, crushing tomatoes by hand.
2. Add chile peppers and red pepper. Allow to soak.
3. Dice green pepper to fingernail size.
4. Chop onion finely.
5. Sauté peppers and onions in ungreased frying pan until onions are lightly browned.
6. Empty into pot. In same pan, sauté ground beef slowly in onion/pepper residue.
7. Slowly add Worcestershire sauce.
8. Add remaining spices and L&P sauce.

9. When meat is half-cooked, begin heating pot with low heat.
10. As meat reduces, pile meat in center of pan.
11. Use slotted spoon to scoop dry meat off the top and into pot, do not stir.
12. Make sure to minimize fat transferred to pot.
13. Continue until all meat is a layer on top of other ingredients in pot. Stir.
14. Cover pot; raise heat to medium high until boiling. Stir often. Reduce heat. Simmer 2 hours, stirring occasionally.
15. Set Crockpot to low, transfer contents of cooking pot to Crockpot. Simmer 12-15 hours.
16. As serving time approaches, if chili is still too watery, stir in 1 tablespoon white flour once per hour.

Serve forth, supply fire extinguishers. Serves 10.

Fire Fighter's Chili #2682
½ Lb. Italian Hot Sausage
½ Lb. Ground Beef; Lean
1 Tablespoon Drippings
1/3 Cup Onion; Chopped
2 Cloves Garlic; Minced
1 Can (32 Ounce) Tomatoes; Undrained, Chopped
1 Can (16 Ounce) Kidney or Pinto Beans; Drained and Rinsed
½ Cup Dry Red Wine
½ Cup Water
½ Teaspoon Beef Flavor Instant Bouillon
1/3 Cup Worcestershire Sauce
3 Tablespoons Chile powder
1 Tablespoon Honey
¼ Teaspoon Red Pepper; Dried
¼ Teaspoon Celery Salt
¼ Teaspoon Tabasco Sauce
To Taste Salt

1. Remove the sausage from its casing. Brown the sausage and ground beef in a large skillet over medium heat.
2. Remove and drain, reserving the measured amount of drippings specified in the ingredients list.
3. Return the drippings to the skillet. Add the onion and garlic. Cook for 3 minutes.
4. Return the meats to the skillet.
5. Stir in all the remaining ingredients except the salt and pepper. Bring to

a boil over medium-high heat.

6. Reduce heat to a simmer. Cover. Simmer for 30 minutes, stirring occasionally.
7. Season to taste with salt and pepper.

Serve hot.

Firehouse Chili
1 Lb. Ground Beef
1 Cup Onion; Coarse Chopped
2 Cloves Garlic; Minced
1 Can (16 Ounce) Tomatoes; Crushed
2 Tablespoons Green Chile Peppers; Chopped
1 Tablespoon Chile powder
1-½ Teaspoon Salt
¼ Teaspoon Pepper

1. Sauté beef, onion and garlic until beef is brown.
2. Add remaining ingredients and simmer for 30 minutes.

Firehouse Special Chili
Ann Loftin
1-½ Lb. Ground Round
1 Medium Onion; Diced
1 Tablespoon Oil
2 Cans Cream of Chicken Soup
1 Can Milk
4 Ounces Green Chiles; Diced
24 Corn Tortillas
1 Lb. Cheddar Cheese; Shredded

1. Brown beef and onion in oil, stirring to crumble meat.
2. Combine soup and milk in saucepan and cook, stirring, over medium heat until smooth.
3. Then add chiles.
4. Cut tortillas in 1-inch squares and make 1 layer in baking dish using half of squares.
5. Spread with layer of half of cooked meat, then with half of soup mixture and half of cheese.
6. Repeat layers. Bake at 325F 20 to 30 minutes.

Fireman's Chili
3 Lb. Chili Meat
1 Can (15 Ounce) Tomato Sauce
1 Cup Water
1 Teaspoon Tabasco Sauce
3 Tablespoons Chile powder
1 Tablespoon Oregano
2 Medium Onions; Coarse Chopped
1 Teaspoon Cumin
To Taste Garlic; Finely Chopped
1 Teaspoon Salt
1 Teaspoon Cayenne Pepper
1 Teaspoon Paprika
12 Pods Red Peppers
4 Pods Chiles
2 Teaspoons Flour; Heaping

1. Sauté meat till gray.
2. Combine all ingredients except flour in a heavy pot. Simmer 1 hour and 15 minutes.
3. Thicken chili with mixture of flour and a little water. Simmer another 30 minutes.
4. Call the fire department to hose out your mouth.

Harrods Creek Fire Dept Vegetarian Chili
From AOL, Firehouse Chili Collection
3 Cups Tomato Juice
1 Tablespoon Pepper
¾ Cup Bulgur Wheat
5 Tablespoons Chile powder
2 Tablespoons Safflower Oil
½ Teaspoon Oregano
1 Medium Onion; Diced
1 Teaspoon Cumin
3 Stalks Celery; Chopped
1 Teaspoon Sweet Basil; Leaf
3 Medium Carrots; Chopped
4 Cloves Garlic; Pressed
1 Can (28 Ounce) Whole Tomatoes; Mashed
1-½ Medium Green Bell Peppers

1 Can (30 Ounce) Dark Red Kidney Beans
1 Tablespoon Lemon Juice
1 Tablespoon Salt
1-½ Cup Garbanzo Beans; Canned

1. Place 1 cup tomato juice in a saucepan and bring to a boil over medium heat.
2. Remove from heat immediately and add bulgur wheat. Cover and let stand for 15 minutes.
3. Heat safflower oil in a heavy pot over medium heat.
4. Add onion and cook until translucent.
5. Add celery, carrots, tomatoes, lemon juice, and spices. Cook until vegetables are tender, about 10-15 minutes.
6. Add diced green pepper and cook another ten minutes.
7. Add kidney beans, garbanzo beans, bulgur wheat mixture and rest of tomato juice to pot. Stir thoroughly and simmer for 30 minutes over low heat.
8. If too thick, add water as needed and stir occasionally so the bulgur doesn't stick.

Inch And A Half Hose Chili
The Geezer Cookbook, Dwayne Pritchett
1 Tablespoon Oregano
2 Teaspoons Paprika
11 Tablespoons Gebhardt's Chili Powder
4 Tablespoons Cumin
4 Tablespoons Beef Bouillon; Instant
3 Cans Beer; Non-Alcoholic
2 Lb. Pork Steak; Cubed
2 Lb. Chuck Roast; Cubed
6 Lb. Ground Chuck
4 Large Onions; Chopped
10 Cloves Garlic; Minced
½ Tablespoon Olive Oil
1 Tablespoon Red Pepper; Dried
¼ Cup Jalapeño Chile Peppers; Sliced
2 Teaspoons Coriander
1 Tablespoon Sugar
1 Teaspoon Tabasco Sauce
2 Teaspoons Louisiana Brand Hot Sauce

1 Cup Tomato Sauce
1 Tablespoon Corn Starch

This recipe will feed a whole troop.

1. In a #14 Dutch oven, add paprika, oregano, chili powder, beef bouillon, non-alcoholic beer, and 2c water. Let simmer. In a large skillet, brown meat in batches with olive oil.
2. Use slotted spoon to add each batch to Dutch oven. Stir after each batch. Continue until all meat is done.
3. Sauté, onion, garlic, and Jalapeños in remaining drippings. Add to Dutch oven.
4. Add water as needed.
5. Add dried red pepper, sugar, coriander, Tabasco, red-hot sauce, and tomato sauce. Simmer 45 minutes.
6. Dissolve cornstarch in ¼ cup warm water and add to mixture. Stir well and simmer another 30 minutes.
Serve.

Kathy Hirder's Fire Camp Chili
Kathy Hirder
100 Lb. Pinto Beans
48 Large Onions; Chopped
4 Cups Jalapeño Chile Peppers; With Juice
40 Lb. Meat-Ham, Sausage, Pork, Bacon Ends; Ground Beef, Etc.
4 Cups Chile powder
To Taste Salt

Serves 120 approximately.

1. Soak beans overnight, then rise to a boil on high heat.
2. Add all ingredients and simmer until tender (about 6 hours).
3. Add water as necessary. Stir occasionally.
Makes 60 gallons.

Tulsa Fire Department Chili
2 Lb. Ground Beef
1 Medium Onion; Chopped
2 Tablespoons Chile powder
1 Teaspoon Ground Cumin

1 Teaspoon Salt
2 Cloves Garlic; Crushed
2 Cans (10 ½ Ounce) Beef Broth
2 Cups Pinto Beans; Canned
1 Can (8 Ounce) Tomato Sauce
1 Tablespoon Flour; Or More
¼ Cup Water

1. Brown the meat and onion and pour off grease.
2. Add chile powder, cumin, salt, crushed garlic, broth, and tomato sauce. Cover and simmer for 45 minutes.
3. Add pinto beans and simmer 15 minutes more.
4. Thicken with a small amount of flour paste (dissolving 1 tablespoon flour in ¼ cup water).

Serve over cooked spaghetti or plain with crackers.

Tyler Texas Fire Department Chili
2 Lb. Ground Round
3 Large Onions
7 Cloves Garlic
3 Teaspoons Cumin; Ground
3 Teaspoons Cayenne Pepper
1 Tablespoon Red Pepper Flakes
5 Tablespoons Chile powder
2 Leaves Bay
2 Cans (28 Ounce) Tomatoes
1 Medium Bell Pepper; Diced
2 Cans (12 Ounce) Tomato Paste
1 Can (28 Ounce) Chili Beans
1 Can (3 Ounce) Jalapeño Peppers; Sliced

1. Brown beef, onions, and bell pepper.
2. Add garlic.
3. When browned add rest of the ingredients except beans and Jalapeños. Simmer for 2 hours.
4. Add beans and Jalapeño peppers and simmer for one hour longer.

Jails and Prisons

Chili Texas Prison System
Dr. George Beto, Director of Texas Prisons
25 Lb. Ground Beef; Coarse Ground
½ Lb. Comino
¼ Lb. Chile powder
1/8 Lb. Paprika
2 Handfuls Red Chile Peppers; Dried, Crushed
½ Lb. Garlic; Finely Chopped

Place in a cooking container, with enough water to cover, closed tight, and cook 15 minutes at high heat before stirring. After this, stir and simmer for 30 to 40 minutes.

The prison cooks never add water, although they "correct the seasoning to desired strength" in the final 30 minutes of simmering and put in two handfuls of MSG "for the desired balance."

Dallas Jailhouse Chili
½ Cup Olive Oil
2 Lb. Beef; Coarse Ground
2 Cloves Garlic; Minced
1-½ Tablespoons Paprika
1 Tablespoon Comino Seeds
3 Tablespoons Chile powder
1 Tablespoon Salt
1 Teaspoon White Pepper
3 Cups Water

Legend holds that this chili was so good that the good guys turned bad just to get thrown in jail for a taste of it!

1. Heat oil. Add meat, garlic and seasonings. Cover and cook slowly for 4 hours, stirring occasionally.
2. Add water; continue cooking until slightly thickened, about 1 more hour.

El Paso Jail Chili
Fred Gall, ICS-Member and Chili-Cook
½ Tablespoon Oregano
2/3 Tablespoon Paprika
3 Tablespoons Chile powder; Light

3 Tablespoons Cumin
2 Tablespoons Beef Bouillon; Instant, Crushed
12 Ounces Old Milwaukee Beer
2/3 Cup Water
2 Lb. Chuck; Chili Grind, Extra Lean
1 Lb. Pork; Chili Grind, Extra Lean
½ Lb. Chuck; Extra Lean, ¼ Cubes
2 Large Onions; Finely Chopped
4 Cloves Garlic; Finely Chopped
¼ Cup Wesson Oil; Or Kidney Suet
1 Teaspoon Mole (Powdered); Also Called Mole Poblano
1 Tablespoon Sugar
½ Teaspoon Coriander Seeds; From Chinese Parsley
1 Teaspoon Louisiana Brand Hot Sauce; (Durkee's)
16 Ounces Tomato Sauce
1 Tablespoon Masa Harina Flour
To Taste Salt

1. In a large pot, add paprika, oregano, MSG, chile powder, cumin, beef bouillon, beer and 2 cups water. Let simmer.
2. In a separate skillet, brown meat in 1 lb. or 1-½ lb. batches with Wesson oil or suet. Drain and add to simmering spices. Continue until all meat is done.
3. Sauté chopped onion and garlic in 1 tablespoon of suet.
4. Add to spices and meat mixture.
5. Add water as needed. Simmer 2 hours.
6. Add mole, sugar, coriander seed, hot sauce and tomato sauce. Simmer 45 minutes.
7. Dissolve masa harina flour in warm water to form a paste.
8. Add to chili.
9. Add salt to taste. Simmer for 30 minutes.
10. Add additional Louisiana Hot Sauce for hotter taste.

Hy Abernathy's Georgia Chain-Gang Chili
1 Cup Burgundy; Dry
½ Teaspoon Thyme; Dried
2 Leaves Bay
4 Cloves Garlic; Finely Chopped
½ Teaspoon Black Pepper; Freshly Ground
6 Lb. Beef; Coarse Ground

2 Large Chicken Breasts
1 Cup Water
2 Teaspoons Salt
2 Tablespoons Vegetable Oil
2 Medium Onions
3 Pork Chops; Coarse Ground
10 Tablespoons Red Chile, Mild; Ground
1 Teaspoon Cayenne Pepper
1 Teaspoon Oregano; Dried (Preferably Mexican)
½ Teaspoon Cumin
1 Sprig Rosemary
1-½ Cup Tomatoes; Italian Style
16 Ounces Tomato Sauce
8 Ounces Tomato Sauce; Mexican, Hot
1 Can Green Chiles, Mild; Whole
1 Can Jalapeño Chiles; Pickled
2 Tablespoons Hot Pepper Sauce, Liquid
1 Tablespoon Butter
3 Pods Green Chiles; Whole, Fresh
½ Cup Mushrooms
½ Cup Sauterne
12 Ounces Beer

1. In a large non-aluminum (preferably glass or glazed cast iron) bowl make a marinade by combining the burgundy, thyme, bay leaves, garlic, and black pepper.
2. Place all the beef in the bowl and mix lightly to coat the meat well.
3. Cover and refrigerate overnight. (If time is short marinate for 2 hours at room temperature.)
4. Place the chicken breasts in a saucepan with enough water to cover.
5. Add 1-teaspoon salt and simmer over low heat for ½ hour.
6. Remove the chicken reserving the liquid. Chop the chicken breasts fine and reserve.
7. Heat the oil in a large heavy pot.
8. Add the onions and cook until they are translucent.
9. Meanwhile, drain the beef, straining and reserving the marinade.
10. Mix the beef and pork together, and then combine the meats with the ground chile, cayenne pepper, oregano, cumin, rosemary, and the rest of the salt. Add this meat-and-spice mixture to the pot with the onions.
11. Break up any lumps with a fork and cook, stirring occasionally, until the

meat is evenly browned.

12. Add half the marinade, the reserved chicken, tomatoes, both tomato sauces, Jalapeños, and 1 tablespoon of liquid hot pepper sauce to the pot.
13. Melt the butter in a heavy skillet over medium heat.
14. Add the fresh chiles, mushrooms, and a small amount of the Sauterne and cook for 3 minutes. Add this to the pot.
15. Bring to a boil and simmer, uncovered, for at least 3 hours.
16. When the chili is cooking, from time to time stir in the remaining marinade, the remaining Sauterne, and beer.
17. If more liquid is needed, stir in the water the chicken was cooked in.
18. Taste and adjust seasonings.

Jailhouse Chili
M. Odom
3 Lb. Chili Meat; Coarse Ground Beef and Pork
1 Quart Water; Or More if Needed
8 Pods Chile; Dried Or
6 Tablespoons Chile powder
3 Teaspoons Salt
1 Teaspoon Cominos; Whole Cumin
1 Teaspoon Red Pepper; (Ground Cayenne)
1 Tablespoon Sugar
¼ Cup Olive Oil
10 Cloves Garlic; Chopped
1/2 Teaspoon Black Pepper
3 Tablespoons Paprika
6 Tablespoons Corn Meal
4 Tablespoons Flour

I'd like to offer my family's recipe for chili. It's based on Dallas County Sheriff Bill Deck's recipe that was allegedly so good the winos over in Fort Worth would come to Dallas and get themselves arrested in the wintertime just to have a bowl of it.

1. Sear meat in a deep pot in hot oil until gray, not browned.
2. Add water and cook covered a bubbling simmer for 1-½ to 2 hours.
3. Then add all other ingredients except the flour and corn meal. Cook 30 minutes more.
4. Mix corn meal and flour in enough cold water to make a thick batter-like consistency and add to chili, stirring constantly to avoid lumping.

701

5. Cook five minutes more to determine if more water is needed.

Serve hot with tortillas, chopped raw onion, and a little grated yellow cheese. This is the original version of rather an old recipe that we have messed around with for the past 22 years. For example many chile powders have lots of salt in them, so we adjust the salt as needed. Also, usually, we simply use corn meal to thicken the chili, not flour, too. The chile pods mentioned in the recipe would likely be a mix of ancho and dried red New Mexico and other large, not too hot red chiles

Mike's Modified Tucson Jailhouse Chili
1 Lb. Sweet Italian Sausage
1 Lb. Cheap Beef Roast; Cubed
1 Large Onion; Diced
6 Cloves Garlic; Diced
1 Can (4 Ounce) Green Chiles; Diced
½ Can (4 Ounce) Jalapeño Chiles; Diced
1 Can (16 Ounce) Tomato Sauce
1 Can (16 Ounce) Tomatoes; Diced
1 Can (6 Ounce) Tomato Paste
1 Can Beer
2 Tablespoons Chile powder
1 Tablespoon Cumin; Ground
1 Tablespoon Cider Vinegar
2 Tablespoons Brown Sugar
2 Cans (16 Ounce) Kidney or Pinto Beans; Drained
To Taste Salt and Pepper

1. Dice onions and garlic.
2. Sauté beef and sausage.
3. When starting to turn color, add the onion and garlic and sauté till meat is brown.
4. Add the rest of the ingredients; simmer for a couple of hours.
5. If the beef is real cheap and tough, longer simmer for tender.
6. If you used good stuff a couple of hours to let the flavors blend will do it.
Adjust seasoning to taste.

Police Headquarters Chili
Marlboro Country Cookin' Brochure 1992
3 Lb. Ground Beef; Lean, Coarse Ground
2 Small Green Peppers; Chopped

2 Medium Onions; Thinly Sliced
2 Cloves Garlic; Minced
¼ Cup Cooking Oil
3 Cans (16 Ounce) Tomatoes
3 Tablespoons Chile powder
2 Teaspoons Cumin Seeds; Crushed
1 Teaspoon Cumin; Ground
¼ Teaspoon Tabasco Sauce
1 Cup Water
3 Cans (15 Ounce) Pinto Beans; Or
3 Cans (15 Ounce) Kidney Beans

1. Cook beef, green peppers, onions, and garlic in oil in cast-iron kettle until beef is lightly browned.
2. Add all ingredients except beans. Cover and simmer 45 minutes.
3. Stir in undrained beans; cover and simmer 25 minutes.

Sheriff "Smoot" Schmidt's Of Dallas Chili
3 Lb. Chili Meat; Coarse Ground
½ Lb. Suet; Finely Chopped or Ground
3 Buds Garlic; Finely Diced
1-½ Tablespoons Paprika
3 Tablespoons Chile powder
1 Tablespoon Cumin Seed
1 Tablespoon Salt
1 Teaspoon White Pepper
1-½ Teaspoons Ground Dried Chile Pod
1 Teaspoon Oregano
3 Cups Water

1. Heat beef suet.
2. Add chili meat, garlic and seasonings. Cover and cook slowly 4 hours, stirring occasionally.
3. Add water; continue cooking until slightly thickened (about 1 more hour).
Serves 6. I've found that if using Teflon, cooking time is cut by ½.

Tucson Jailhouse Chili
1 Medium Onion
6 Cloves Garlic; Peeled
2 Lb. Ground Beef

1 Can (4 Ounce) Green Chiles; Diced
1 Can (12 Ounce) Jalapeño Chile Peppers
1 Can (12 Ounce) Tomatoes; Diced
1 Can (6 Ounce) Tomato Paste
6 Tablespoons Chile powder; Or More
3 Teaspoons Ground Cumin
1 Tablespoon Vinegar
2 Tablespoons Brown Sugar
1 Tablespoon Salad Oil
1 Lb. Pinto or Kidney Beans; Cooked and Drained
To Taste Salt
To Taste Pepper
As Needed Sharp Cheddar Cheese; Grated (Garnish)
As Needed Green Onions; Sliced (Garnish)

1. Dice onion; sauté in heavy Dutch oven.
2. Dice garlic and add when onions are clear. Stir for 30 seconds; add ground beef, green chiles, Jalapeño peppers, tomatoes, tomato paste, chile powder, cumin, vinegar, brown sugar, oil and drained beans. Simmer for 1-½ to 2 hours (do not boil).
3. Adjust seasoning with salt and pepper to taste.
Garnish with cheese and green onion. Serve with corn chips.
 Makes 6 servings.

Taverns and Drug Stores
Bunting's Drug Store Chili
4 Lb. Hamburger
1 Quart Water
3 Teaspoons Chile powder
½ Cup Bacon Grease
¼ Teaspoon Salt
As Needed Flour

1. Mix all ingredients, except flour, together and boil 10 minutes.
2. Thicken with flour to desired consistency, stirring constantly.
Chili will keep in refrigerator for up to a week.

Cold Spring Tavern
24 Ounces Black Beans; Dry
40 Ounces Meat (Venison, Buffalo or Rabbit)

24 Ounces Pasilla Chile Peppers; Fresh
24 Ounces Onions
12 Ounces Tomatoes; Diced
3 Ounces Chile powder
2 Ounces Cumin Seeds
To Taste Salt and Pepper
As Needed Water

Wild Game Black Bean Chili. The Cold Springs Tavern was originally a stagecoach stop on San Marcos Pass between the Santa Ynez Valley and Santa Barbara, California. While the stagecoaches are long gone, the tavern is still here serving great and hearty meals in the same rustic building that has stood for over 100 years. The Armchair folks have tried this chili at the Tavern and really like it. It is reminiscent of the black bean soups served in Haiti and the Dominican Republic, however, with a twist, it's chili. The Cold Springs Tavern has reduced the recipe to a manageable size for home use. While wild game is recommended, you can substitute a variety of meats (chicken, turkey, beef) and cuts to your taste. As with all chili recipes, experiment and modify the recipe to your liking.

1. Cook the beans in water according to package directions. This will dictate the basic amount of water to use. Feel free to add water to yield your preferred chili consistency.
2. In a frying pan, sauté, the meat until browned; reserve; sauté, the onions and chiles until the onions are transparent (use a little canola oil if fat from meat is insufficient).
3. Combine the beans, meat, onions and chile; add tomatoes.
4. Add seasonings and salt and pepper to taste. Simmer for one hour.

Suggested Serving: Ladle into a large bowl and top with a dollop of sour cream and a sprinkling of chopped Jalapeño. It's great with a crusty French or sour dough bread. Enjoy!

Old Ebbit Grill White Bean Chili

1 Lb. White Navy Beans
1 Small Red Bell Pepper; Diced
1 Small Green Bell Pepper; Diced
1 Medium Spanish Onion; Diced
2 Tablespoons Olive Oil
7 Cups Chicken Stock
2 Cloves Garlic; Diced

2 Teaspoons Cumin; To Taste
2 Teaspoons Chile powder; To Taste
3 Medium Plum Tomatoes; Chopped
To Taste Salt and Pepper
3 Breasts Chicken, Whole, Bone-in
2 Tablespoons Olive Oil
1 Teaspoon Chile powder
1 Teaspoon Cumin
1 Tablespoon Garlic; Diced
2 Tablespoons Cilantro (Fresh); Chopped
As Needed Salsa
As Needed Quesadillas; Or Corn Bread
Chopped Fresh Cilantro for Garnish

For the beans:
1. Soak beans overnight in water to cover. Drain.
2. Over low heat, stir peppers and onion in olive oil for one minute.
3. Add beans and sauté over medium heat for 5 minutes, stirring constantly.
4. Add stock, garlic, cumin and chile powder. Simmer, uncovered, until beans are soft, about 1-½ hours, adding more broth as necessary.
5. Stir in tomatoes about 20 minutes before beans are done and season to taste with salt and pepper.

To roast the chicken:
1. Crack the breastbones to flatten.
2. Rub breasts with oil and season with remaining ingredients.
3. Then roast in a preheated 350-degree oven about 30 minutes, being sure not to overcook.
4. Cool slightly and remove meat from bones. (If boneless breasts are used, grilling is preferable since they would dry out quickly if roasted.)

To serve:
1. Place a generous portion of beans in large, flat soup bowl.
2. Slice chicken thinly, keeping skin on (skin may be removed, but some of the seasoning will be lost) and place on top of the beans.
3. Garnish with salsa, sour cream, cilantro, and a warm quesadilla. (Make quesadillas by topping a soft flour tortilla with about 1.4 cup grated cheddar cheese, 2 tablespoons sour cream, and hot peppers to taste. Fold each into quarters and warm through in a 350-degree oven.)
Serving count: Makes 6 servings.

Old Tavern Chili
1 Lb. Ground Beef
2 Tablespoons Chile powder
1 Clove Garlic; Minced
1 Pouch Campbell's Onion/Mushroom Soup Mix
¾ Cup Beer or Water
1 Can (14-½ Ounce) Tomatoes; Undrained, Cut Up
1 Can (15 Ounce) Kidney Beans; Drained
As Desired Cheddar Cheese; Shredded
As Desired Sour Cream

1. Crumble beef into 2-quart microwave-safe casserole; stir in chile powder and garlic.
2. Cover with lid; microwave on high 5 minutes or until beef is no longer pink, stirring once during cooking to break up meat. Spoon off fat.
3. Stir in soup mix beer or water, tomatoes with their liquid and beans. Cover; microwave on high 3 minutes or until hot and bubbling. Stir again.
4. Reduce power to 50%. Cover; microwave 10 minutes or until flavors are well blended, stirring once during cooking.
5. Let stand, covered, 5 minutes.

Garnish with cheese and sour cream.

Chapter 13
Chili Recipes - Colors Other Than Red

Background
While red is my personal favorite color for chili, I will have to admit that some of the following recipes sound pretty good. Green and White are the only alternative colors that I have come across, but if you can think of others, I would love to hear from you. Enjoy!

Green
Adobo Verde De Lomo Cerdo Chili Verde
This dish has Latin American roots and has been made heart healthy by trimming all fat from the pork loin. To get two pounds of pork, buy 2-½ pounds of untrimmed meat. Serve with ½ cup rice.

2 Pounds Pork Loin, Trimmed and Cut into 1" Cubes
1 Cup Onion, Chopped
2 Cups Chicken Stock or Water
½ Teaspoon Black Pepper
¼ Cup Fresh Orange Juice

Sauce:
½ Pound Tomatillos (or 1 can Whole Tomatillos)
¾ Cup Onion, Diced
1 Teaspoon Garlic, Minced
6 Green Onions Cut in 1" Pieces
2 Cans Green Chiles, Diced
¼ Cup Cilantro, Chopped
2 Serrano Peppers
5 Leaves Romaine lettuce, Outer Leaves

1. Place pork, chopped onion and black pepper in a heavy kettle or cast-iron skillet.
2. Add water or chicken stock and bring to a boil.
3. Reduce heat, cover, and simmer for about 45 minutes, until the meat is almost tender.
4. While this is cooking, prepare sauce by pureeing the ingredients (Tomatillos, onion, garlic, green onions, green chiles, cilantro, peppers, and lettuce leaves) in a food processor or blender.
5. When pork is tender, uncover and reduce liquid, stirring to prevent burning.

6. Add sauce and cook 10 to 15 minutes more until very thick, stirring frequently to prevent scorching.
7. Add orange juice just before serving.

Austin Grill's Chili Verde
5 Pods Anaheim Chile Peppers; Seeded and Peeled
5 Pods Poblano Chiles; Seeded and Peeled
2 Tablespoons Olive Oil
1 Cup Yellow Onion; Diced
1-½ Teaspoons Garlic; Minced
1-½ Pods Jalapeño Chile Peppers; Minced
¾ Teaspoon Oregano
¾ Teaspoon Cumin
4 Cups Chicken Stock
1 Medium Idaho Potato; Cut in ½ Inch Cubes
1 Cup Cilantro (Fresh); Loosely Packed
To Taste Salt

1. Cut Anaheim, and Poblano chiles in half, remove the seeds, char and peel.
2. In a large skillet, heat the olive oil and sauté the onion until translucent.
3. Add the garlic, Jalapeño chiles, cumin and oregano, and sauté for several minutes.
4. Add the chicken stock and bring to a simmer.
5. Then add the potatoes and cook until just tender.
6. With a slotted spoon, remove 1 cup of potatoes and reserve.
7. Add the diced chicken and poach gently in the onion-chili-potato mixture until chicken is cooked through.
8. Remove from the heat immediately, transfer to a bowl, reserving ½ cup of the liquid in a small bowl.
9. Refrigerate the remainder to keep the chicken from overcooking. In a blender, puree the reserved potatoes, half the Anaheim and half the Poblano chiles, and the cilantro with the reserved half-cup of liquid.
10. When the chicken mixture is no longer warm, add the puree.
11. Dice the remaining half of the Anaheim and Poblano chiles in half-inch cubes and add to the mixture.
12. Season with salt.
13. Reheat just before serving to retain the fresh green color and flavor of the soup.

Authentic New Mexico Green Chile Stew
1-½ Lb. Pork Roast; Up to 3
1 Cup Flour
3 Cups Green Chile Peppers; Roasted, Peeled, Chopped
1 Medium Onion
3 Cloves Garlic; Finely Minced
To Taste Salt
To Taste Pepper
As Needed Chicken Broth; Or Chicken Base
1 Teaspoon Cumin
2 Medium Potatoes; Optional, Cubed, Up to 4

1. Cube pork roast, dredge in flour and brown until will caramelized.
2. Sauté onions until translucent.
3. Put ingredients in large pot, add water to cover. Simmer until meat and potatoes are tender.
4. Add salt to taste.

Onion and garlic may be added just before simmering is finished in order to keep separate flavor. Excellent served with flour tortillas or hard rolls. And remember, no self-respecting New Mexican ever spells chile with an "i."

Blake's Green Chile Chili
Blake Brown
¾ Lb. Ground Beef; Lean
1 Can (14-½ Ounce) Hunt's Whole Tomatoes; With Juice
2 Lb. Frozen Mild Green Chiles; Chopped (See Note 1)
½ Ounce Garlic Powder; Less if Desired
¼ Ounce Oregano; Ground
4 Cubes Wyler's Beef Bouillon; (See Note 2)

1. Cook meat and drain well.
2. Add tomatoes w/juice, tear or break up whole tomatoes.
3. Add garlic powder and oregano.
4. Add chiles letting it make its own juice or liquid as it cooks.
5. Cook slowly for about 3 hours, stirring often.
6. Add beef bouillon liquid and cook about ½ hour longer.

Green Chili Chili can be used as a sauce. It adds flavor to bland foods such as eggs.
　　Note 1: Use canned chopped green chiles if frozen is not available.
　　Note 2: Dissolve in a cup of hot water.

Caldillo-New Mexican Green Chili Stew
2 Lb. Beef Round or Pork; Lean
2 Tablespoons Oil
3 Medium Potatoes; Diced
½ Cup Onion; Sliced
1 Clove Garlic; Minced
2 Teaspoons Salt
6 Pods Green Chiles

1. Cube meat, sprinkle with salt and fry until brown in oil.
2. Add potatoes to browned meat together with onion, garlic, salt, chile and enough water to cover.
3. Continue to add water if necessary. It will have a soupy consistency.

Carne de Puerco con Chile Verde
3 Lb. Pork Roast; Boneless
4 Cans (12 Ounce) Tomatillos; Drained and Crushed
3 Cans (4 Ounce) Ortega Mild Green Chile Peppers; Chopped, Up to 6
5 Cloves Garlic; Crushed
1 Large Onion; Chopped
¾ Cup Water
To Taste Salt and Pepper
Optional: Your favorite fresh green chiles, chopped or sliced. Cilantro if you like it.

1. Slice up the pork and trim away most of the fat.
2. Dice both the lean meat and the fat into ½ inch cubes; set the diced fat aside.
3. In a heavy pot over a hot flame, cook the lean pork with the water, stirring until the water is gone and the meat begins to brown.
4. Add the onion and garlic and stir constantly until the onion becomes transparent.
5. Reduce heat to a simmer and add the tomatillos and canned chiles (be sure to drain the tomatillos before crushing; the water they are packed in is too salty). Cover the pot and simmer slowly for about an hour, stirring occasionally to prevent from sticking.
6. Meanwhile, render the diced pork fat into cracklings by sautéing in a skillet over medium heat until the pieces are brown and crispy.
7. Drain and salt the cracklings and set aside; save the lard for any other dish where you want some high-quality cholesterol stuff.

8. After an hour the chile verde should be pretty juicy but not watery.
9. Add a little water if it is too dry.
10. Add salt and pepper to taste, and if you want it hotter, add your fresh chiles now. Cover and simmer again for at least half an hour. The longer, the better.

To serve, sprinkle with chopped cilantro (if used) and the cracklings. Serve with Spanish rice, tortillas, black beans and ice-cold beer. Serves 6 or 8.

Carol's Mom's Green Chili
Larry Ottersbach
1 Medium Beef Roast
10 Large Green Chiles
1 Large Onion
1 Medium Stewed Tomatoes; Whole
To Taste Garlic Salt
1 Pinch Cumin
2 Cans Beef Gravy

1. Roast green chiles over grill until all skin is almost black. (You are not burning it, don't worry.)
2. Soak roasted green chiles (submerged) in bowl of cold water (ten minutes).
3. Peel skin off.
4. Dice chile into small, small pieces or mashed.
5. Cut up meat into bite size pieces.
6. Sauté meat with white onion about 10 minutes or just barely brown.
7. Add tomatoes, garlic salt, comino and gravy and simmer about ½ hour.

Chile Verde Ala Fay
2 Lb. Pork Butt; Boneless
2 Tablespoons Vegetable Oil
1 Medium Onion; Chopped
1 Clove Garlic; Minced
2 Teaspoons All Purpose Flour
1 Can (8-¼ Ounce) Tomatoes (Stewed)
1 Can (7 Ounce) Green Chiles
1 Can (10 Ounce) Tomatoes; With Hot Green Chiles
To Taste Salt and Pepper; Freshly Ground

1. Trim off fat and cut pork into 1-inch cubes.
2. Heat oil in a large heavy pot or Dutch oven.
3. Add pork and cook until brown.
4. Add onion and garlic.
5. Cook until tender.
6. Stir in flour. Cook and stir 1 to 2 minutes.
7. Add stewed tomatoes, chopped chiles and tomatoes with hot chiles, breaking up tomatoes with a spoon.
8. Season with salt and pepper to taste. Cover and simmer gently 1-½ hours or until meat is tender.

Makes 4 servings.

Chile Verde Stew
75 Lb. Pork; Boneless, 1-½ Inch Cube
2-1/3 Cups Vegetable Oil
1350 Ounces Corn Kernels; Canned, Drained
75 Stalks Celery; w/o Leaves, Diced
75 Medium Potatoes; Diced
75 Medium Tomatoes; Chopped Coarsely
112 Cans (4 Ounce) Green Chile Peppers; Diced
150 Cups Chicken Broth
1-½ Cups Cumin; Ground
¾ Cup Oregano; Dried
1 Tablespoon Salt

1. Lightly brown the pork cubes in a Dutch oven or deep skillet over medium high heat.
2. Add the rest of the ingredients. Cover. Simmer for 1 hour.

Serve hot with fresh corn or flour tortillas.

Yields 300 servings.

Chili Caldillo
1 Lb. Leftover Beef or Pork Roast; About
½ Cup Onion; Diced
2 Cups Green Chiles; Fresh, Frozen or Canned
2 Medium Potatoes; Cubed
½ Teaspoon Garlic Powder; Or
1 Clove Garlic; Minced
To Taste Salt
1 Tablespoon Flour

2 Cups Water
2 Cups Tomatoes; Canned

1. Place all ingredients, except flour and water, into a deep skillet.
2. Mix the flour with a little water until smooth; then add flour mixture and the rest of the water to the ingredients in skillet. Simmer for about 30 minutes, until potatoes are tender.
3. Add additional chile to taste, if desired.

Chili Verde
4 Pork Steaks
1 Medium Onion; Chopped
5 Tablespoons Flour
4 Cups Water
¼ Teaspoon Garlic
½ Teaspoon Red Pepper
½ Teaspoon Oregano
2/3 Teaspoon Cumin; Ground
2 Cans (7 Ounce) Whole Green Chiles

1. Cut fat off steaks. Cut steaks into bite size pieces. Fry until well done.
2. Remove meat and cook onion until tender.
3. Remove onion. Make gravy with drippings and flour and water.
4. Chop green chiles.
5. Return meat and onion to gravy with all other ingredients, simmer.
6. Add 2-3 hot Fresno chiles if desired.

Chili Verde Mexican
2 Lb. Pork; Cubed
½ Cup Water
1 Tablespoon Garlic; Minced
½ Cup onion; Dry
1 Can (14 Ounce) Tomatoes (Stewed)
1 Teaspoon Coriander; Ground
½ Cup Green Chile Peppers; Chopped
2 Tablespoons Cilantro (Fresh); Chopped
1 Cup Salsa Fresca

1. Cook pork and garlic in ½ cup water until all the water is absorbed.
2. Let the pork brown in it's fat for a few minutes.

3. Add onion and sauté till translucent.
4. Add tomatoes and chiles, cover and simmer for 30 to 40 minutes.
5. Just before serving, add the chopped cilantro, salt and pepper to taste, stirring well.

Serve with Salsa Fresca.

Crockpot Chili Verde

1. First, sauté one onion and one green pepper, coarsely chopped, with three or four cloves of garlic, minced, in olive oil.
2. Throw into the crockpot.
3. Also throw in a small can of diced green chiles.
4. Depending on your propensity for spicy food, you may add from one to three Jalapeños, sliced.
5. Then, throw some tomatillos in the pot. How many? Well, when I got fresh ones in San Diego, I'd get seven or eight. Peel off the husk and coarsely chop. Now that I've moved to Pittsburgh (don't ask me why), I've had to use canned ones on occasion. How many? Well, I don't really remember, it was one medium sized can, I think. Pay attention: I mean tomatillos, not green tomatoes. The Frugal Gourmet substituted celery and tomatoes. I haven't forgiven him yet.
6. Take about 2 pounds of lean pork (I trim off all the excess fat I can), cubed, and brown in the pan that you sautéed the onion, etc. in.
7. Into the pot.

Now, the seasoning mixture.

1. I prefer to grind up in my mortar oregano, some dried red chile peppers, sage, and cumin seed. Perhaps also some black pepper. I almost never put salt in anything, so I probably wouldn't here either, but you may want to. How much? Well, about 2 tsp. each of the oregano and the sage, 1 tsp. each of the cumin seed and dried red peppers. Salt and pepper to taste.
2. I probably will add a dash of beer (about ½ cup) for obscure reasons.
3. This crockpots all day, or could be simmered for probably about 2 hours. Traditionally, this is served in bowls, with hot flour tortillas, salsa, and cilantro. You can also have sour cream, grated cheese, olives, and pickled carrots and Jalapeños around. Of course, you wrap all this up in the tortillas, making killer burritos. I throw one twist into this, a technique that comes from carnitas. After cooking, I separate the meat from the broth, crisp the meat under the broiler, and reduce the sauce in the pan. This adds a great texture to the meat, and keeps the burritos from being too soggy.

Doc Martin's Green Chili
½ Lb. Ground Beef
½ Lb. Roast Beef; Cubed
½ Lb. Ground Pork
1 Medium Onion; Finely Chopped
1/3 Bunch Cilantro (Fresh); Chopped
1 Teaspoon Oregano; Leaf
1 Teaspoon Powdered Onion
1 Teaspoon Parsley; Dried
2 Tablespoons Flour
1 Can Mexican Beer
1 Medium Tomato; Diced
3 Tablespoons Butter
1 Clove Garlic; Minced
2 Teaspoons Tabasco Sauce
2 Teaspoons Garlic; Granulated
2 Teaspoons Cumin; Ground
½ Teaspoons Black Pepper
3 Cups Chicken Stock; Or Beef Stock
1 Pod Green Chiles; Diced, Peeled and Seeded
4 Tablespoons Butter
4 Tablespoons Flour

1. Sauté beef, pork and roast beef in butter, chopped onion and minced garlic until brown.
2. Mix in cilantro, Tabasco, oregano, granulated garlic, powdered onion, cumin, parsley, pepper and flour. Cook over low heat for a few minutes.
3. Add the chicken or beef stock, beer, green chiles and tomato. Bring to a simmer.
4. Thicken with the roux. The chili should be the consistency of a stew. Let simmer for at least 45 minutes to one hour.
5. Best when reheated.

Roux:
1. Four (4) tablespoons butter; four (4) tablespoons flour.
2. Melt the butter in a saucepan over medium heat.
3. Whisk in the flour one tablespoon at a time and cook for about 4 to 5 minutes, whisking constantly until the roux is thick and forms a ball.
4. Remove from heat and incorporate immediately into the chile.

Glen's Chili A La Bambi
Ladies Home Journal-August 1991
1-½ Lb. Venison Burger; 80% Venison, 20% Beef
3 Lb. Venison Sirloin; Cut into Large Chunks
2 Tablespoons Oil; Up to 4
2 Centiliters Garlic; Minced Fine
1 Large Onion; Chopped
2 Cans (29 Ounce) Tomatoes; Chopped
6 Tablespoons Chile powder
1 Tablespoon Cumin
1 Tablespoon Kosher Salt
½ Tablespoon Black Pepper
1 Teaspoon Smoked Habañero Powder
To Taste Chipotle Peppers; Smoked Jalapeños
To Taste Smoked Habañero Chiles

1. To make smoked Habañero powder:
   Smoke ripe red Jalapeños and ripe Habañeros for up to 24 hours until they are all shriveled and fairly dry.
   Completely dry in a dehydrator.
   Grind to a fine powder in a coffee grinder. Beware of the fumes while grinding!
2. In a large pot, sauté venison in oil until no pink remains.
3. Add onion and garlic and sauce until onion is wilted.
4. Add tomatoes, undrained.
5. Add remaining spices except Habañero powder. Simmer on low for about 3 hours, stirring occasionally.
6. Just prior to serving, sprinkle Habañero powder over chili and stir until mixed.

This is the 1998 First Place winner in the annual Chili Cook-Off.

Green Chile Stew
24 Pods Green Chiles; Fresh
2 Lb. Roast Pork (Shoulder or Butt); Cubed
¼ Cup Flour
2 Tablespoons Bacon Drippings
2 Large Onions; Finely Chopped
6 Large Tomatoes; Chopped
1 Can (6 Ounce) Tomato Sauce
2 Cups Water

2 Cloves Garlic; Crushed
2 Teaspoons Salt

1. Flour the pork and brown it in the drippings in a skillet.
2. Remove pork to a large stewing (or crock) pot, 3- to 5-quart size.
3. Add onions to the fat remaining in the skillet and cook until onion is translucent.
4. Add onions to the pork.
5. Cut the chiles into 1-inch slices; add to the meat and onions in the pot.
6. Add remaining ingredients and cook over medium heat for about 1 hour, until the stew is slightly thickened.
7. If you prefer the all day method, follow the same directions except put the ingredients in a crock-pot.
8. Cook on low for 10-12 hours or high for 5 hours.

I like using fresh Jalapeños. Depending on where the chiles are from, you can have a rather fiery brew! Make sure you have plenty of flour tortillas handy; you will not want to miss one tasty drop!

Green Chili-Triple HHH (Howard's Hotter'n Hell)
1 Tablespoon Oil
2 Lb. Chicken Breast; Boneless, Or Pork
2 Medium Onions
2 Teaspoons Garlic; Minced
1 Teaspoon Oregano
1 Teaspoon Cumin
2 Teaspoons Red Chile; Ground
1 Tablespoon Red Chile Flakes
1 Medium Tomato
1 Can Tomatillos
4 Lb. Green Chiles
4 Cups Wyler's Chicken Bouillon
3 Tablespoons Cornstarch

1. Chop chiles, tomato and tomatillos.
2. Add oil to heavy, preferably cast iron, skillet and brown chicken over high heat.
3. It is best to do it in two or three small batches.
4. Remove to large saucepan.
5. Add onions and garlic to leftover oil and brown until onions are soft.
6. Add oregano, cumin, and red chile, and cook for two or three minutes.

7. Transfer from skillet to saucepan with chicken.
8. Add tomato, tomatillos, chiles, and chicken broth. Bring to a boil and simmer for 3 - 4 hours.
9. Add water as necessary to maintain the desired consistency.
10. Add 3 - 4 tablespoons cornstarch mixed with water prior to serving to thicken as desired.

Eat from a bowl accompanied with a warm flour tortilla or use it as a sauce over chile rellenos, eggs, enchiladas, or just about anything. One of my favorite meals is to grill a steak until nice and juicy, smother with green chili, sprinkle some grated cheese on top and serve with Mexican rice.

Green Chili # 1
2 Lb. Pork; Chops or Roast
½ Teaspoon Garlic; Minced
1 Can (16 Ounce) Tomatoes
2 Tablespoons Flour
2 Cans (14 Ounce) Green Chiles
1 Teaspoon Mrs. Dash

1. Cover pork with water and cook until done.
2. Cool and shred pork, saving broth.
3. When cool, degrease.
4. In blender mix flour, garlic, tomatoes and Mrs. Dash.
5. Blend and add 2 cups broth in which pork was cooked.
6. If not enough broth, add water to make 2 cups.
7. Add shredded pork and simmer at least one hour.
Serve with warm tortillas.

Green Chili # 2
3 Lb. Roast Beef; Lean, Chuck or Sirloin
7 Cans (4 Ounce) Green Chiles
20 Ounces Tomatillos; Canned
1 Handful Hot Red Chile Peppers; Dried, See Note
1 Large White Onion
3 Large Tomatoes
2 Cloves Garlic; Or More
1 Teaspoon Cumin; Ground
1 Tablespoon Oregano; Mexican
Note: Arbol, finger-hots, Pequins, or Thai peppers.

1. Brown the roast as if making pot roast-coat meat with flour and brown every surface in olive oil. (Add beer and/or water up to one inch deep and cover.) Simmer meat by itself for one hour over low heat.
2. Lightly blend the tomatillos and three green chiles in blender.
3. Dice the remaining green chiles, garlic, onion, and tomatoes.
4. Add the sauces, vegetables, and spices to the pot with enough water to cover.
5. When the meat is falling-apart-tender (several more hours, typically), use two forks to shred it into small chunks.

Serve topped with slices of avocado and white cheese, along with sides of beans and Jalapeño cornbread. You might check out the interesting things you can make this with at Whole Foods Grocery, instead of beef, any kind of meat or game will work.

Green Chili Chili
1 Lb. Pork Shoulder; ¼ Inch Cubes
2 Tablespoons Flour
2 Tablespoons Lard, Butter, or Bacon Drippings
½ Cup Onion; Chopped
1 Clove Garlic; Minced
16 Ounces Tomatoes; Coarse Chopped
28 Ounces Green Chiles; Diced
¼ Teaspoon Oregano
2-½ Teaspoons Salt
2 Cups Water

1. Dredge meat in flour.
2. In a deep skillet or heavy pot, brown meat in lard.
3. Add onion and garlic. Cook 5 minutes more or until onions are tender but not browned.
4. Add remaining ingredients. Simmer, uncovered, 5 to 10 minutes more or until desired consistency.

Serves 4-6.

Green Chili With Pork
The Geezer Cookbook, Dwayne Pritchett
½ Cup Olive Oil
2 Large Yellow Onions; Chopped, About 4 Cups
8 Cloves Garlic; Peeled/Chopped
8 Pods Jalapeño Chile Peppers; Stemmed and Minced

3 Carrots; Peeled and Sliced, 1/2 Inch
1-½ Tablespoons Oregano; Preferably Mexican
3 Lb. Pork Shoulder; Cut in ½ Inch Cubes
5 Cups Chicken Stock; Or Canned Broth
1 To Taste Salt
28 Ounces Italian Plum Tomatoes; Drained and Diced
1 Ounce (8 Ounce) Potato Puree; Peeled and Grated
12 Large Poblano Chiles; Roasted and Peeled Or
1 Can (28 Ounce) Whole Green Chiles; Mild, Roasted, Drained

1. In a large heavy-duty casserole or Dutch oven (about 5 qt.) warm the oil over medium heat.
2. Add onions, garlic, Jalapeños, and carrots.
3. Cook, stirring once or twice, for 10 minutes.
4. Stir in oregano and pork cubes and cook until pork has lost its pink color, about 20 minutes. Stir occasionally.
5. Stir in the chicken stock, 1 teaspoon of salt, crushed tomatoes and the grated potato. Bring to a boil, then lower the heat and cook partially covered, for 1-½ hours, stirring occasionally.
6. Cut the Poblano into ½ inch strips. Add them to the chili and cook, stirring often, for another 30 to 45 minutes or until the pork is tender and the chili is thickened to your liking.
7. Taste for correct seasonings and let cook another 5 minutes.
Serve hot.
   Note: To roast Poblanos, stick them on a serving fork and turn over a gas burner until thoroughly charred. Wrap chiles in a paper bag after you roast them. When cool, rinse under cold running water, rubbing off the burned skin. Pat dry and de-stem chiles.

Green Chili With Pork
½ Cup Olive Oil
2 Large Onions; Chopped
8 Cloves Garlic; Minced
8 Pods Jalapeño Chile Peppers; Minced
3 Carrots; Cut in ½ Inch Pieces
1-½ Tablespoon Oregano
3 Lb. Pork Shoulder, Boneless; Cut in ½ Inch Pieces
2 Cans Chicken Broth
1 Can Italian Plum Tomatoes; Large, Drained
1 Potato; Peeled, Grated

4 Cans Green Chile Peppers; Mild, Chopped
1 Can Chili Beans with Gravy; Large, Hot

1. In a Dutch oven, heat olive oil and add onions, garlic, Jalapeños, and carrots. Sauté for 10 minutes.
2. Stir in oregano and pork cubes. Cook or 20 minutes, stirring occasionally.
3. Stir in chicken stock, 1-teaspoon salt, tomatoes, and potatoes.
4. Bring to boil, then lower and simmer 1-½ hours. Stir occasionally.
5. Add green chiles and beans to mixture and simmer another 30-45 minutes.
Serve.

Green Chili With White Beans
2 Large Bell Peppers; Seeded
3 Tablespoons Salad Oil
2 Cups Green Onions; and Tops, Sliced
8 Cloves Garlic; Minced/Pressed
4 Teaspoons Cumin; Ground
6 Cans (16 Ounce) Tomatillos
4 Cans (7 Ounce) Green Chile Peppers; Diced
6 Cans Italian White Beans; Drained
3 Lb. Pork Shoulder; Trimmed of Fat
4 Teaspoons Oregano
½ Teaspoon Cayenne Pepper
½ Cup Cilantro (Fresh); Lightly Packed

1. Thinly slice bell pepper crosswise.
2. Heat oil in a 10 qt. pot over med-hi heat; add bell pepper, onions, garlic, and cumin. Cook, stirring, until onions are soft.
3. Mix in tomatillos (break up with spoon) and their liquid, chiles, beans, pork oregano, and red pepper. Bring to boil; reduce heat and simmer until pork is tender when pierced (about 2 hrs.).
4. For a thin chili, cook covered; for thicker chili, cook uncovered to desired consistency. Stir occasionally.
5. Cover.
6. Refrigerate for 3 days.
7. Reheat before continuing.
8. Reserve a few cilantro leaves; chop remaining leaves.
9. Stir chopped cilantro into chili; garnish with reserved leaves.
Serve.

Guisado de Chile Verde (Green Chile Stew)
2 Lb. Pork or Beef
3 Cups Tomatoes
¼ Cup Flour
2 Cups Water
2 Tablespoons Shortening
½ Teaspoon Garlic Powder
2 Large Onions; Chopped
2 Teaspoons Salt
3 Cups Green Chiles; Chopped

1. Dredge the meat in flour.
2. Place the shortening in a heavy skillet and brown meat at medium heat.
3. Place meat in a large stewing pot.
4. Sauté the onions in the remaining shortening and add to stewing pot.
5. Add all remaining ingredients to stewing pot, simmer at low heat 1 hour.

Jill Albert's Green Hornet Chile
4 Lb. Pork (Shoulder is a Good Start); Cut in Cubes
As Needed Flour
To Taste Salt
To Taste Garlic
2 Cans Roasted, Peeled Green Chiles
2 Lb. Fresh Roasted, Peeled Green Chiles
1 Large Onion
1 Can Tomatoes; Ground
4 Cloves Garlic; Or More To Taste
½ Cup Lime Juice
½ Cup Cilantro; Chopped
As Needed Tomatillos

1. Dredge pork in flour and garlic salt and brown in heavy pot (add oil or pork fat as necessary to keep from burning).
2. Add chiles, onion, tomato, and garlic. Cook for hours.
3. Before serving add limejuice, cilantro and tomatillos.

Johnny's Chile Verde
John Fraga "Recipes To Kill For"
6 Tablespoons Chile powder
1 Can Tomatillos; Or

8 Medium Tomatillos, Fresh; Thinly Sliced (8-10)
1 Medium Onion; Chopped
1 Medium Tomato; Chopped
3 Pods Serrano Chile Peppers; Chopped
½ Teaspoon Cumin
½ Teaspoon Oregano
½ Teaspoon Salt
½ Teaspoon Black Pepper; Freshly Ground
¼ Cup Chicken Broth
4 Cloves Garlic; Split
2 Lb. Pork Shoulder; Lean, Cubed
1 Tablespoon Cooking Oil
1 Teaspoon Cornstarch; Optional
2 Teaspoons Water; Optional

1. Place ingredients 1 thru 11 (using only 3 cloves of garlic) in a food processor and process until well mixed.
2. Add oil to a large hot fry pan and brown pork a few minutes.
3. Sprinkle chile powder over pork in pan and continue to cook for 5 more minutes.
4. Place pork in a medium sized pot.
5. Add tomatillo mixture to pot.
6. Stir to combine with pork. Simmer for 1-2 hours until pork is very tender.
7. Crush and mince last clove of garlic, and add to pot during last 5 minute of cooking.
8. If mixture needs thickening, combine cornstarch and water, mix well and slowly stir into pot a little at a time until desired consistency.

Jonathan's Vegetarian Bowl of Southwestern Green (Chile)
Jonathan Kandell, Tucson, Arizona
This is an authentic tasting (i.e. addictive) recipe for New Mexico style green chile.

1. Start with roasted green chiles. I get mine from Las Cruces, New Mexico, but you can use anything you damn well please. The chile is the heart of this dish, and the better the quality of your chile, the better the results.
2. Roast the chile by placing them whole under a broiler until they blacken, then turn over till they blacken on the other side.
3. Remove stems, veins and seeds. (The skin should come off easily if they're fully blackened.)

725

4. There is no need to steam the peppers in a paper bag as is sometimes suggested.
5. Try to keep as much of the juice as possible. I buy my chile once a year and freeze them in small Baggies. You can also freeze them in their blackened skins.
6. Slice off enough of a frozen chile chunk to flavor the dish. You'll learn how much from experience; I use about six chiles worth.
7. Put it in a bowl and add in some salt, lots of oregano, a bit of marjoram.
8. Add five to ten 1-inch cubes of extra-firm tofu. (Press tofu before by hand if you have to; it should be "meaty" to the teeth.)
9. You can, optionally, add a small amount of red chile flakes, such as Chile Arbol.
10. In a medium pan, sauté 1 chopped large onion in olive oil until it turns translucent.
11. Add 2-3 chopped garlic cloves for a minute, stirring so it doesn't burn.
12. Add the chile/tofu/spice and sauté some for a couple minutes.
13. Add a small can of black beans plus its juice, and some of a large can of whole peeled tomatoes, to taste, about half the can. There should be enough juice from the beans and tomatoes and chiles to create a stew.
14. If necessary, you can cook this down.
15. Heat on warm for an hour, and then reheat when ready to serve.
It tastes even better if you can let it sit overnight.

Jon's Green Chile Stew
Cookin' With the Fat Boys!
Here's what you will need for this staple Mexican fare.

1. One big Round Steak a pork roast is traditional, but I find the round steak leaner and it tastes good.
2. Green Chile-we roast our own and pack it into Ziploc bags. I usually use one bag full per batch. This is comparable to about 3 small cans of prepared chile.
3. Cornstarch-Enough to dredge the meat.
4. Chicken Broth-This is a hint from our old friend Gene Gene the Dancing Machine. Use about 1 can, or one tablespoon of chicken base.
5. Onion-One small to medium onion, diced.
6. Garlic-Two cloves, smashed.
7. Potato-This is optional, and frankly I rarely use them. If I do, I only use one small potato cut into ½ inch cubes.
8. Water to cover.

Here's how to make it:
1. Cut the meat into ½ inch cubes.
2. Dredge the meat in the cornstarch.
3. Place the meat in a preheated soup kettle to brown.
4. While the meat is browning, clean your chile and cut into a large dice. If you're using canned chile, open the cans.
5. Dice the onion.
6. When the meat has browned, add the chile, onion, garlic, potato, chicken broth or base and water to cover.
7. Simmer covered at least until the meat is tender. The longer you simmer it, the thicker and tastier your stew will be!
8. Add more water if necessary.

Serve with flour tortillas and wait for the complements to roll in.

Karen's Classic Old-Fashioned New Mexico Green Chili
2 Teaspoons Olive Oil
½ Lb. Pork Loin (Remove Fat); Cut in ½ Inch Cubes
2 Tablespoons Jalapeño Chile Peppers; Chopped (Optional)
3 Cloves Garlic; Finely Minced
1 Teaspoon Cumin
1 Medium Red Onion; Finely Chopped
1/8 Teaspoon Salt
1 Tablespoon Flour
1/8 Teaspoon White Pepper
1 Tablespoon Cornstarch
2-¾ Cups Chicken Broth
2 Tablespoons Water
2 Large Tomatoes; Fresh, Pureed
1 Can (28 Ounce) New Mexican Chiles; Roasted, Peeled, Seeded,
1 Pod New Mexican Chiles; And Finely Chopped

1. In skillet, heat olive oil over medium-high heat. Sauté pork until all pink is gone (about 5 minutes).
2. Move meat aside and add garlic (and onion).
3. As soon as garlic sizzles, stir together with pork. Put into crockpot on high.
4. In a small bowl, make thickener by adding water to flour and cornstarch. (Add another tablespoon of cornstarch and a tablespoon of water if you prefer a thicker sauce.)
5. Add mixture to crockpot.

6. Add chiles, spices, and chicken broth to crockpot.
7. Bring to a boil, then reduce heat and add tomatoes.
8. Simmer on very low heat, covered, for at least 1 hour (preferably all day). Serve over plain or Mexican rice, burritos, chili rellenos, chimichangas, etc.

Note 1: Mexican food is a big part of my diet, so I finally spent an entire weekend preparing 10 different green chili recipes from several of my Mexican/Southwestern cookbooks and newspaper clippings, and had the family and neighbors pick their favorite version. This recipe is the result of merging and very slightly modifying the three favorites. (I'll keep fiddling with it, though!).

Note 2: The flavor of green chili is influenced most by the kind of green chiles you decide to use. Traditional New Mexican green chiles are a special type; although you might find them in your grocery store, you may well have to order them. When I can't get fresh New Mexican "Big Jim" chiles straight from New Mexico, then I buy a more common New Mexican chile (Josie's brand) in 14-Ounce white plastic containers (already roasted and chopped) from the frozen foods section. However, canned green chiles or Anaheim chiles may be an acceptable (though much milder) substitute for the timid, with a rather different flavor. If anybody is particularly interested, I order mine (frozen) from a place in Hatch, New Mexico.

Navajo Green Chili # 1
Mary R. Neh, Home Economist, Navajo Cultural Center
3 Lb. Pork Shoulder; Trimmed of all fat
2 Cups Tomatoes (Stewed)
3 Tablespoons Bacon Drippings
1 Can (6 Ounce) Tomato Paste
1/3 Cup Flour
3 Cups Water
3 Medium Onions; Chopped
2-½ Teaspoon Salt
6 Cloves Garlic; Minced
½ Teaspoon Oregano; Preferably Mexican
2 Cans (16 Ounce) Green Chiles; Whole

1. Melt bacon grease in a skillet over med-high heat.
2. Put flour into a paper bag and shake the meat with the flour to coat meat.
3. Add the meat to the bacon grease a little at a time and brown well and evenly.
4. Remove the meat to a 5-quart Dutch oven.

5. Add the onions and garlic to the skillet and sauté until translucent.
6. Add these to the pork in the pot.
7. Stir in the remaining ingredients, bring pot to a boil, and keep stirring every 2-3 minutes.
8. When boiling lower heat to low and simmer for 45 minutes.
9. Taste, adjust seasonings as per personal taste, and cook for 30 minutes more.

This recipe comes to us from the Native Americans we call the Navajo. They call themselves the Di-neh. It is a great chili and deserves your attention!
Enjoy!

Navajo Green Pork Chili
The Geezer Cookbook, Dwayne Pritchett
3 Lb. Pork Shoulder; Diced
2 Cups Tomatoes (Stewed)
1 Cup Tomato Paste
3 Cups Water
2-½ Teaspoons Salt
2 Cans (16 Ounce) Green Chiles; Whole
½ Teaspoon Oregano
3 Tablespoons Bacon Grease
1/3 Cup Flour
3 Medium Onions; Chopped
6 Cloves Garlic; Minced

1. Melt bacon grease in large skillet.
2. Put flour in gallon zip-lock bag and add ½ of pork.
3. Shake well to coat and brown in skillet.
4. Coat other ½ pork and add to skillet to brown.
5. Remove meat and place in Dutch oven.
6. Add onions and garlic to skillet and cook until clear.
7. Add to Dutch oven.
8. Stir in remaining ingredients and bring to boil. Lower heat and simmer 45 minutes.

New Mexican Green Chili Stew
2 Lb. Beef Round or Pork; Lean
3 Medium Potatoes; Diced
1 Clove Garlic; Large, Minced
6 Pods Green Chile Peppers

2 Tablespoons Oil
½ Cup Onion; Sliced
2 Teaspoons Salt

1. Cube meat, sprinkle with salt and fry until brown in oil.
2. Add potatoes to browned meat together with onion, garlic, salt, chile and enough water to cover.
3. Continue to add water if necessary.
4. It will have a soupy consistency.

New Mexico Green Chili
4 Medium Tomatoes; Canned, OK
1 Can (6 Ounce) Green Chile Peppers
4 Cloves Garlic
1 Large Onion; Chopped
1 Lb. Ground Round
To Taste Chile powder
To Taste Salt and Pepper

Chili made in New Mexico is often without beans as green chile peppers provide the basis of the cuisine in that state among the Hispanics. Indeed real chili in that state would not even have red chile powder and both the green chiles and the tomatoes would be fresh.

1. Brown the ground round, chopped garlic and onion.
2. Remove as much fat or grease as possible.
3. Mix the meat, chopped green chiles, chopped tomatoes, chopped garlic with water.
4. Salt and pepper to taste. Simmer for 1 hour.
This recipe is excellent with corn bread or soft tortillas.
   Note: Often the green chiles are enough to give all the spicy taste one desires, but you can add red chile pepper if you desire, I must warn you that I enjoy very spicy, hot food and this recipe is hot to the taste.

Not For The Tenderfoot Green Chili
2 Lb. Turkey Tenders; No Skin, No Bones
1 Tablespoon Salt
6 Pods Green Chiles; Fresh Roasted (up to 8)
1 Medium Onion; Chopped
3 Cloves Garlic; Chopped (up to 5)

1 Teaspoon Cumin; Ground
1 Cube Chicken Bouillon; (up to 2)
1 Teaspoon Salt

This is a spicy dish so beware.

1. Cook turkey in salted water till tender, cool and shred.
2. Add all the rest of ingredients. Simmer 1 hour

Optional: Thicken broth with 2 tablespoons of cornstarch in ¼ cup water. Wrap mixture in flour tortillas.

Note: Buy fresh green chiles. Roast till blackened under broiler, under running cold water, remove skins, stems and seeds. It is best to wear rubber gloves when doing this. You can use canned chiles but it makes for a much milder dish. You can adjust salt and spices to your own liking. Garlic adds great flavor.

Pork Chili Verde
6 Lb. Lean Pork
¼ Cup Vegetable Oil; Or Lard
2 Large Yellow Onions; Chopped
6 Cloves Garlic; Minced
1 Tablespoon Sea Salt
To Taste Black Pepper; Fresh Ground
1 Tablespoon Cumin
8 Medium Poblano Chiles; Seeded and Chopped
4 Large Jalapeño Chile Peppers; Seeded and Minced
2 Large Yellow Bell Peppers; Seeded and Chopped
4-½ Quarts Chicken Stock
3 Lb. Tomatillos, Fresh; Husks Removed
1 Bunch Cilantro Leaves; Chopped

1. Trim off any excess fat from the pork and cut into 2-inch squares.
2. In a large (6 to 8 quart) stockpot, over a high heat, sear the pork in the vegetable oil until golden brown.
3. Remove the pork from the pot and pour off any oil or fat drippings, but leave 2 tablespoons of oil. In the same pot, over a medium heat, add the chopped onion, garlic, salt, and pepper and sauté until transparent.
4. Add the cumin, pork, and chicken stock, and cook for ½ hour.

731

5. Add the Poblanos, Jalapeños, and bell peppers.
6. Puree the tomatillos and cilantro in a blender.
7. Add them to the pot and cook an additional 30 to 45 minutes.

Serve with white beans and rice. Garnish with grated sharp white cheddar cheese. Yield: 16 to 20 servings.

San Luis Green Chile Soup
Jim Vorheis
6 Medium Anaheim Chile Peppers; Fresh
1 Large Red Bell Pepper
1 Pod Jalapeño Chile Peppers; Fresh
2 Ounces Salt Pork; Diced
½ Lb. Chicken Breast; Boned, Thinly Sliced
½ Lb. Pork Butt Steak; Thinly Sliced
6 Tablespoons Butter
1 Medium Onion; Diced
½ Cup All Purpose Flour
1-½ Teaspoons Chile powder
1 Teaspoon Cumin; Ground
1 Clove Garlic; Minced, Small
¾ Cup Tomato Sauce
2 Quarts Chicken Broth
½ Cup Tomatoes; Peeled, Seeded and Diced
1 Tablespoon Cilantro (Fresh); Minced
As Needed Avocado; Sliced
As Needed Sour Cream

1. Roast Anaheim chiles, red pepper and Jalapeño under hot broiler close to heat until skins blister, turning to char on all sides.
2. Place in plastic bag for 10 minutes.
3. Peel, dice and set aside.
4. In large skillet, cook salt pork until fat is rendered.
5. Remove salt pork with slotted spoon; drain on paper towel.
6. Increase heat and sauté chicken and pork quickly until browned. Drain and set aside.
7. Melt butter in large saucepan. Add onion and cook until transparent.
8. Add flour and cook stirring until roux is golden brown.
9. Remove roux from heat and stir in chile powder, cumin, garlic and tomato sauce.
10. Whisk in warm chicken broth and heat to simmering.

11. Add chiles, red pepper, Jalapeño, salt pork, chicken and pork to soup.
12. Heat thoroughly and stir in tomatoes and cilantro. Heat to simmering.
Crème de Colorado Cookbook (1987) From the collection of Jim Vorheis.

Speedy Green Chili

2 Teaspoons Canola Oil
12 Ounces Ground Turkey; Or Ground Chicken
1 Medium Onion; Sliced
2 Cloves Garlic; Minced
2 Cans (15 Ounce) Pinto Beans
1-½ Cups Salsa Verde; Made with Tomatillos
2 Teaspoons Mexican Seasoning Blend

1. Heat oil in a non-stick skillet.
2. Add meat and onion and sauté, 8-10 minutes until thoroughly cooked and onion is soft.
3. Break up the meat with a wooden spoon. Pour off excess fat when done.
4. Add garlic, beans, Salsa Verde and seasoning. Cook until thoroughly heated.

Serve with rice.

Notes: Oh, yeah, "Mexican seasonings blend." Add a teaspoon of cumin to enhance authenticity. We used one jar of Mrs. Renfro's Hot Green Salsa with half a jar of Mollie Stone's Salsa Verde, about 2 cups total. We used 4 cloves of garlic and 1-¼ pound of meat. Start the rice, and then start this chili. They'll be ready at about the same time.

Spicy Green Pork Chili
Edwin Webb

1-½ Lb. Pork Chops; Boneless
16 Ounces Stewed Tomatoes
45 Ounces Black Beans
32 Ounces Light Red Kidney Beans
1 Large Yellow Onion
2 Cloves Garlic; Crushed
2 Pods Jalapeño Chile Peppers; Chopped
1 Teaspoon Cumin; Ground
1 Teaspoon Butter
To Taste Salt and Pepper
To Taste Tabasco Sauce
As Needed Water

1. Trim excess fat from chops; dice into bite-size chunks. Lightly sauté.
2. Drain on paper towel; sauté onion, garlic, and Jalapeño in butter.
3. Add pork, onion, garlic, and Jalapeño together in pot.
4. Add black beans, kidney beans, and stewed tomatoes.
5. Do not drain beans.
6. Add 7-ounce can of diced canned Jalapeño.
7. I usually use a crock-pot because the longer the chili simmers, the better it is.
8. When done, the pork should be really tender.
9. The pork will also darken due to the black beans.

Can serve in bowls as usual or over white rice.

Successful Green Chili Stew
4 Cans (Small) Green Chile Peppers; Diced, See Note.
1 Lb. Turkey; Finely Ground
1 Small Zucchini; Thinly Sliced
1 Cup Frozen Corn; Off the Cob.
14 Ounces Tomatoes; Peeled, With Juice
24 Ounces Water
4 Cloves Garlic; Minced, Up to 6, See Note
1 Teaspoon Cumin; Ground
1 Teaspoon Italian Seasonings
1 Teaspoon Salt

Note: I recommend 2 hot and 2 mild to get a good nose run while eating. Four (4) mild to be slightly hot all hot to be volcanic, of course. (You can of course also use the same amount, but frozen or fresh roasted.)
Note: Depends on your taste, and the clove size.
Note: I make no bones about this being full of fat and salt.

1. Brown the ground turkey. Just before it is done, add the garlic and sauté it with the meat.
2. Then put this into a large saucepan or Dutch oven. I did not drain the fat off; I think this is part of what made it taste so good. Besides, if it weren't a bit greasy, it wouldn't be authentic.
3. Turn on heat to medium high and add tomatoes and juice.
4. Use a spatula or something to cut up the tomatoes in the pan.
5. Then add the rest of the vegetables, the chiles, the water, and the seasoning.
6. Bring to a boil, then turn heat down and cook until zucchini becomes soft.

Spoon into bowls and eat. As with many things, this is also better the next day. I've been working on creating a good green chili stew for a while now. I finally did it! It turned out great! This was inspired by some that I had last Christmas at Jemez Pueblo. It is a traditional New Mexican dish.

Serves 4-6 (depends on appetite). Cooking time: 1 - 1-½ hours.

Serve with rice, and/or bread, and/or (fresh!) tortillas and butter, and/or sopapillas and honey, and/or chips and salsa with guacamole.

Texan Chili Verde
2 Lb. Pork, Boneless; Extra Lean, 1-Inch Cubes
1 Lb. Beef Chuck (Boned); Cut in 1-Inch Cubes
1 Large Green Bell Pepper; Cored, Seeded and Chopped
2 Centiliters Garlic; Minced
1 Can (28 Ounce) Tomatoes; Whole, Mashed
1 Can (4 Ounce) Green Chile Peppers; Drained
2 Tablespoons Parsley Flakes; Dried
1 Tablespoon Sugar
1 Tablespoon Cumin; Ground
2 Whole Cloves
½ Cup Beef Broth

1. Combine all the ingredients in the slow cooker.
2. Stir thoroughly. Cover. Cook on Low for 8 to 10 hours.
3. Adjust seasonings before serving.

White Chili

Chile Blanc
1 Lb. White Beans; Dried
1 Tablespoon Olive Oil
4 Cloves Garlic; Chopped
2 Teaspoons Cumin; Ground
¼ Teaspoon Cloves; Ground
6 Cups Chicken Stock
2 Lb. Chicken Breast; Boneless
2 Medium Onions; Chopped
2 Cans (4 Ounce) Green Chiles; Chopped
1-½ Teaspoons Oregano; Dried and Crumbled
¼ Teaspoon Cayenne Pepper
3 Cups Monterey Jack Cheese; Grated

1. Place beans in a heavy large pot.
2. Add enough cold water to cover by at least 3 inches and soak over night.
3. Place chicken in heavy large saucepan.
4. Add cold water to cover and bring to simmer. Cook until just tender, about 15 minutes. Drain and cool.
5. Remove skin. Cut chicken into cubes.
6. Drain beans.
7. Heat oil in same pot over medium high heat. Add onions and sauté until translucent, about 10 minutes.
8. Stir in garlic, then chiles, cumin, oregano, cloves and cayenne and sauté 2 minutes.
9. Add beans and stock and bring to boil.
10. Reduce heat and simmer until beans are very tender, stirring occasionally, about 2 hours.
11. Add chicken and one cup cheese to chile and stir until cheese melts.
12. Season to taste with salt and pepper.

Serve with remaining cheese, sour cream, salsa and cilantro.

Chili Con-Caucasian" (White Chili)

1 Can Cooking Oil Spray; (Pam)
1 Tablespoon Olive Oil
1 Lb. Chicken Breasts; Skinned, Boned and Diced
½ Cup Shallots; Chopped
3 Cloves Garlic; Minced
1 Can (18 Ounce) Tomatillos; Drained and Course Chopped
1 Can Ro-tel Diced Tomato and Green Chile; Chopped But Not Drained
1 Can (13 Ounce) Chicken Broth
1 Can Green Chile Peppers; Chopped and Undrained
½ Teaspoon Oregano Flakes
½ Teaspoon Coriander Seeds; Crushed
¼ Teaspoon Cumin; Ground
2 Cans Cannelloni Beans; Drained
3 Tablespoons Lime Juice; Fresh Squeezed
¼ Teaspoon Black Pepper
¼ Cup Sharp Cheddar Cheese; Grated

1. Spray a large skillet with Pam; add Olive Oil and heat on medium high until hot.
2. Add diced Chicken and sauté for 3 minutes or until done.
3. Remove Chicken from pan and set aside.

4. Add Shallots and Garlic to the pan and sauté until tender.
5. Stir in Tomatillos, Ro-tel Tomatoes, Chicken Broth, Chile Peppers, and Spices. Bring to a boil, reduce and simmer 20 minutes.
6. Add Chicken and Beans, cook for 5 minutes, stir in Lime Juice and Pepper, heat and serve up into Chili Bowls topped with Cheese.
7. Or place all ingredients, except Cheese, in a Crockpot and cook for 8 hours.

Don't forget the Tortilla Chips, Sour Cream, Avocado Dip and Mexican Beer. Good Eating.

Chili Blanco
1 Lb. Chicken Breast; Boneless, Skinless and Dice
1 Tablespoon Vegetable Oil
1-½ Cups Onion; Chopped
2 Tablespoons Garlic; Chopped
1 Can (7 Ounce) Ortega Green Chile Peppers; Diced
1 Tablespoon Ortega Jalapeño Peppers; Diced
2 Tablespoons Cumin; Ground
½ Teaspoon Oregano Leaves; Dried
2 Cans (15 Ounce) White Beans; Drained and Rinsed
½ Cup Chicken Broth
1-½ Cups Monterey Jack Cheese; Shredded
½ Cup Sour Cream
As Needed Sour Cream; Additional
As Needed Green Onions; Sliced
As Needed Cilantro (Fresh); Chopped
As Needed Tomatoes; Chopped, Optional

1. In a 4-quart pot, over medium heat, sauté chicken in 2 teaspoons oil for 5 to 6 minutes or until chicken is done.
2. Remove chicken from pot.
3. In same pot, over medium-high heat, sauté onions and garlic in remaining oil for 3 minutes.
4. Add chiles, Jalapeños, cumin and oregano; cook for 3 minutes more.
5. Add white beans, chicken broth and reserved chicken. Heat to a boil; reduce heat. Simmer for 10 minutes.
6. Add cheese and sour cream; cook and stir until cheese melts.

Serve topped with additional sour cream, green onions, cilantro and tomatoes, if desired.

Chili Blanco Especial-Jim Vorheis
Creme de Colorado Cookbook (1987)
1 Lb. White Northern Beans; Dry
5-¼ Cups Chicken Broth
2 Cloves Garlic; Minced
1 Large White Onion; Chopped
1 Tablespoon White Pepper; Ground
1 Teaspoon Salt
1 Tablespoon Oregano, Dried
1 Tablespoon Cumin; Ground
½ Teaspoon Cloves; Ground
1 Can (7 Ounce) Green Chiles; Diced
5 Cups Chicken Breast; Cooked and Diced
1-¾ Cup Chicken Broth
1 Tablespoon Jalapeño Peppers; Diced (Optional)
8 Flour Tortillas
As Needed Monterey Jack Cheese; Shredded
As Needed Black Olives; Sliced
As Needed Salsa (Chunky)
As Needed Sour Cream
As Needed Avocado; Diced

1. Soak beans in water to cover for 24 hours; drain.
2. In crock-pot or large kettle, combine beans, 5-¼ cups chicken broth, garlic, onion, white pepper, salt, oregano, cumin and cloves. Simmer covered for at least 5 hours until beans are tender, stirring occasionally.
3. Stir in green chiles, diced chicken, and 1-¾ cups chicken broth.
4. For hotter taste, add Jalapeño. Cover and simmer for 1 hour.
To serve, line each bowl with 1 flour tortilla. Spoon in chili and serve with all condiments for a very special chili.

Eneiman's Texas White Chili
Chuck Ozburn
1 Lb. White Beans; Dried
1-½ Quarts Chicken Stock
1-½ Medium Onions; Chopped
2 Cloves Garlic; Chopped
1 Teaspoon Salt
1 Tablespoon Vegetable Oil
4 Ounces Green Chiles; Diced

2 Teaspoons Ground Cumin
2 Teaspoons Oregano; Dried, Crushed
2 Teaspoons Coriander; Ground
1 Pinch Cloves; Ground
1 Pinch Cayenne Pepper
4 Chicken Breasts; Boneless and Skinless
½ Cup Monterey Jack Cheese; Grated
4 Small Green Onions; Thinly Sliced

1. In a large kettle, combine beans, stock, ½ the onions, garlic and salt; bring to a boil.
2. Reduce heat; cover and simmer 1-½ hours or until beans are very tender, adding more chicken stock as needed.
3. Heat oil in skillet. Add remaining chopped onions and cook about 5 minutes, until tender and clear.
4. Add chiles, cumin, oregano, coriander, cloves and cayenne; mix thoroughly. Cook 2 minutes more.
5. Add skillet mixture to bean mixture.
6. Portion chicken into 4 servings.
7. For each serving, put chicken in bottom of bowl, spoon chili over top and sprinkle with grated cheese and sliced green onion.

Makes 4 servings.

Fat-Free White Chili
1 Lb. White Beans; Washed and Sorted
2 Breasts Chicken; Skinned
7 Cups Water
2 Cloves Garlic
4 Cubes Chicken Bouillon
2 Medium Onions; Chopped
2 Teaspoons Cumin
¼ Teaspoon Cloves; Ground
¼ Teaspoon Cayenne Pepper
To Taste Salt and Pepper

1. Put beans and chicken in large soup pot with water and bouillon cubes and bring to boil. Reduce heat and simmer until chicken is done.
2. Take out chicken and cut up, then put back in pot.
3. Add remaining ingredients. Simmer 3 hours, until beans are tender.
4. Add more water if necessary.

Fresh Tomato White Chili

3 Large Tomatoes; Fresh, (1-½ Lb.)
1 Tablespoon Vegetable Oil
½ Cup Onion; Chopped
1 Can (4 Ounce) Mild Green Chiles
1 Teaspoon Garlic; Minced
1 Teaspoon Cumin; Ground
1 Teaspoon Oregano Leaves; Crushed
1 Teaspoon Sugar
1/8 Teaspoon Cloves; Ground
1/8 Teaspoon Red Pepper; Ground
1 Can (14-½ Ounce) Chicken Broth
1 Can (15 Ounce) White (Cannelloni) Kidney Beans; Rinsed and Drained
2 Cups Chicken; Cooked and Cubed

1. Core and coarsely chop tomatoes (makes about 4 cups); set aside.
2. In a large saucepan, heat oil until hot.
3. Add onion. Cook, stirring occasionally, until tender, about 5 minutes.
4. Stir in chiles, garlic, cumin, oregano, sugar, cloves, red pepper and the 4 cups reserved tomatoes. Reduce heat and simmer, stirring occasionally, until the tomatoes are softened, about 5 minutes.
5. Add chicken broth; bring to a boil, reduce heat, simmer, covered, to blend flavors, about 15 minutes.
6. Add beans and chicken; cook until hot, about 5 minutes.

Garnish with sour cream, shredded Cheddar cheese, diced tomatoes, and chopped cilantro, if desired.

Enjoy!

Jane's White Chili
Jane Sherr

2 Tablespoons Butter
2 Lb. Chicken; Boneless, Chopped
2 Medium Onions; Chopped
1 Cup Chicken Broth
8 Ounces Green Chiles
2 Centiliters Garlic; Chopped
2 Teaspoons Cumin
1 Teaspoon Oregano; Dried
¼ Teaspoon Cloves; Ground
¼ Teaspoon Cayenne Pepper; Or More

1 Jar (48 Ounce) Great Northern Beans
3 Cups Monterey Jack Cheese; Shredded

1. Sauté chicken, onions and garlic in butter until chicken is done.
2. Mix in seasonings and chiles and sauté for a few more minutes.
3. Add this mixture with chicken broth and beans to crock-pot. Cook on low for 4-8 hours.
4. Add cheese just before serving.

Jim's White Chili
O'Malia's Cooking School-"Soup's On" by Joanne Harked
1 Lb. Great Northern Beans; Dried
1-½ Quarts Chicken Stock
½ Teaspoon Garlic; Minced
2 Medium Onions; Chopped
1 Tablespoon Vegetable Oil
8 Ounces Mild Green Chiles; Chopped
2 Teaspoons Cumin; Ground
1-½ Teaspoons Oregano; Dried
¼ Teaspoon Cloves; Ground
¼ Teaspoon Cayenne Pepper
4 Cups Chicken; Cooked and Diced
3 Cups Monterey Jack Cheese; Shredded
As Desired Salsa
As Desired Sour Cream

1. Pick through beans, removing bad beans and stones. Soak overnight for faster cooking. Drain and rinse; rinse again.
2. Add chicken broth, garlic and only one half of the onions to the beans and cook until tender. Add more water if needed.
3. When beans are about done, sauté remaining onions, chiles and spices.
4. Add this and diced chicken to the pot. Simmer 1 hour longer.
Serve in individual bowls topped with jack cheese, salsa and sour cream.

Tip: For moist chicken, flatten chicken, put in skillet, cover with water and bring to a boil. When the water reaches boiling point, turn off heat and cover. Allow to sit 20 - 25 minutes. The chicken is poached and remains very moist. You can also use chicken broth instead of water to intensify the chicken flavor.

Michael Mark's White Chicken Chili Recipe
½ Lb. Navy Beans; Dried and Picked Over
1 Stick Butter; Unsalted (½ Cup)
¼ Cup All Purpose Flour
¾ Cup Chicken Broth
2 Cups Half & Half
1 Teaspoon Tabasco Sauce; Or To Taste
1-½ Teaspoons Chile powder
1 Teaspoon Ground Cumin
½ Teaspoon Salt; Or To Taste
½ Teaspoon White Pepper; Or To Taste
2 Cans (4 Ounce) Whole Mild Green Chiles; Drained and Chopped
5 Boneless Skinless Chicken Breasts; Cooked (About 2 Pounds)
1-½ Cups Monterey Jack Cheese; Grated (About 6 Ounces)
½ Cup Sour Cream
As Needed Coriander Sprigs; Fresh for Garnish
As Desired Tomato Salsa

1. Soak the beans overnight then drain them and cover with 2 inches of cold water.
2. Cook at a bare simmer until tender, about 1 hour, and drain.
3. In a skillet, cook onion in 2 tablespoons butter over moderate heat until softened.
4. In a heavy kettle, melt remaining butter over low heat and whisk in flour.
5. Cook roux, whisking continuously, 3 minutes.
6. Stir in onion and gradually add broth and half and half, whisking constantly.
7. Bring mixture to a boil and simmer, stirring occasionally, 5 minutes, or until thickened.
8. Stir in Tabasco, chile powder, cumin, salt, and white pepper.
9. Add beans, chiles, chicken, and Monterey Jack and cook mixture over moderately low heat, stirring, 20 minutes.
10. Stir sour cream into the chili.
Garnish chili with coriander and serve with salsa. Serves 4-6.

Southwest White Chili
1 Tablespoon Olive Oil
1 Lb. Chicken; Boneless, Chopped
¼ Cup Onion; Chopped
1 Cup Chicken Broth

1 Can (4 Ounce) Green Chiles
1 Teaspoon Garlic Powder
1 Teaspoon Cumin
½ Teaspoon Oregano; Dried
½ Teaspoon Cilantro; Chopped
1/8 Teaspoon Cayenne Pepper; Up to ¼ Teaspoon
1 Can (19 Ounce) Cannelloni Beans
As Desired Monterey Jack Cheese; Garnish

Fans of Southwestern cuisine will enjoy this version of white chili, flavored with chopped green chiles and onion, and simmered in a broth blended with garlic, oregano, cilantro and ground red pepper.

1. Heat olive oil in a 3-quart saucepan over medium-high heat.
2. Add chicken; cook 4 to 5 minutes, stirring often.
3. Remove chicken with slotted spoon, cover and keep warm.
4. Add chopped onion to saucepan; cook 2 minutes.
5. Stir in chicken broth, green chiles, garlic powder, ground cumin, oregano leaves, cilantro and ground red pepper; simmer for 30 minutes.
6. Stir in cooked chicken and kidney beans; simmer for 10 minutes.
Garnish with cheese and sliced green onions.

Southwestern White Chili
1 Tablespoon Olive Oil
1 Lb. Boneless Skinless Chicken Breast
½ Cup Onion
1 Cup Chicken Broth
4 Ounces Green Chiles; Chopped
19 Ounces White (Cannelloni) Kidney Beans; Undrained
1 Tablespoon Garlic Powder
1 Tablespoon Cumin
½ Teaspoon Oregano
½ Teaspoon Cilantro
1/8 Teaspoon Red Chile Pepper; Ground

1. Heat oil, cook chicken 4-5 minutes. Remove chicken, cover to keep warm.
2. Add onion to pan and cook 2 minutes.
3. Stir in chiles and spices with broth for 30 minutes.
4. Stir in cooked chicken and beans. Simmer.
Garnish with Monterey Jack cheese.

Spicy White Chili
2 Medium Onions; Chopped
1 Tablespoon Cooking Oil
4 Cloves Garlic; Minced
2 Cans Green Chile Peppers; Chopped
2 Teaspoons Cumin; Ground
1 Teaspoon Oregano; Dried
¼ Teaspoon Cayenne Pepper
¼ Teaspoon Cloves; Ground
2 Cans (14-½ Ounce) Chicken Broth
4 Cups Cooked Chicken; Cubed
3 Cans (15-½ Ounce) Great Northern Beans; Rinsed and Drained
2 Cups Monterey Jack Cheese; Shredded
As Needed Sour Cream; Optional
As Needed Jalapeño Chile Peppers; Rings, Optional

1. In a 3-qt. saucepan, sauté, onions in oil until tender.
2. Stir in garlic, chiles, cumin, oregano, cayenne and cloves; cook and stir 2-3 minutes more.
3. Add broth, chicken and beans; simmer, uncovered, for 15 minutes. Remove from the heat.
4. Stir in cheese until melted.
Garnish with sour cream and Jalapeño peppers if desired.
    Yield: 6-8 servings (2-¼ quarts).

Terry's Backflash White Chili
Terry Light
For The Beans:
1 Lb. White Navy Beans
1 Small Red Bell Pepper; Diced
1 Small Green Bell Pepper; Diced
1 Medium Spanish Onion; Diced
2 Tablespoons Olive Oil
7 Cups Chicken Stock
2 Centiliters Garlic
3 Teaspoons Cumin
3 Teaspoons Chile Powder
3 Medium Plum Tomatoes; Chopped
To Taste Salt and Pepper

For The Chicken:
3 Each Chicken Breasts; Bone-in
2 Tablespoons Olive Oil
1 Teaspoon Chile powder
1 Teaspoon Cumin
1 Tablespoon Garlic; Diced
2 Tablespoons Cilantro; Fresh, Chopped

Beans:
1. Soak overnight in water to cover. Drain.
2. Over low heat, stir peppers and onion in olive oil for one minute.
3. Add beans and sauté over medium heat for 5 minutes, stirring constantly.
4. Add stock, garlic, cumin and chile powder. Simmer, uncovered until beans are soft, about 1-½ hours adding more broth as necessary.
5. Stir in tomatoes about 20 minutes before beans are done and season to taste with salt and pepper.

Chicken:
1. Crack the breastbones to flatten.
2. Rub breasts with oil and season with remaining ingredients.
3. Then roast in a preheated 350 oven about 30 minutes being sure not to overcook.
4. Cool slightly and remove meat from bones. (If boneless breasts are used, grilling is preferable since they would dry out quickly if roasted.)

Serving:
1. Place a generous portion of beans in large flat soup bowl.
2. Slice chicken thinly, keeping skin on and place on top of the beans.
3. Garnish with salsa, sour cream, cilantro, and a warm quesadilla.
4. Make quesadillas by topping a soft flour tortilla with about ¼ cup grated cheddar cheese, 2 tablespoons sour cream, and hot peppers to taste.
5. Fold each into quarters and warm through in a 350 oven.

Texas White Lightning Chili
1 Lb. Navy Beans; Dried
4 Cans Chicken Broth; Ready-Serve
1 Large Onion; Chopped
2 Cloves Garlic; Minced
1 Tablespoon White Pepper
1 Tablespoon Oregano

1 Tablespoon Cumin
½ Teaspoon Cloves
5 Cups Chicken; Cooked, Chopped
1 Can (8 Ounce) Chiles; Chopped
1 Pod Jalapeño Chile Peppers; Seeded and Chopped
8 Flour Tortillas
As Needed Monterey Jack Cheese; Shredded
As Needed Salsa
As Needed Sour Cream

1. Sort and wash beans; place in large Dutch oven. Cover with water 2 inches above beans. Soak 8 hours; drain beans, and return to Dutch oven. Discard liquid.
2. Add 3 cans of broth and next 7 ingredients; bring to boil.
3. Reduce heat and simmer, covered, 2 hours or until beans are tender, stirring occasionally.
4. Add remaining can of broth, chicken, and next 3 ingredients. Cover and simmer 1 hour, stirring occasionally.
5. With kitchen shears, make 4 cuts in each tortilla toward, but not through, the center.
6. Line serving bowls with tortillas, overlapping cut edges of tortillas.
7. Spoon in chili, and top with cheese, salsa, and sour cream.
Serve immediately.

Timothy's White Chili
1 Lb. White Beans; Dried
6 Cups Chicken Broth
2 Cloves Garlic
2 Medium Onions; Chopped
1 Tablespoon Oil
1 Can (9 Ounce) Green Chiles
2 Teaspoons Cumin; Ground
1-½ Teaspoons Oregano
¼ Teaspoon Cloves; Ground
¼ Teaspoon Cayenne Pepper
4 Cups Chicken Breast; Cooked, Diced
3 Cups Monterey Jack Cheese; Grated
As Needed Salsa
As Needed Sour Cream

1. Combine beans, broth, garlic and ½ the onions in a large pot. Bring to a boil, reduce and simmer till beans are soft (2 hrs. or more) adding broth if necessary.
2. Sauté remaining onions in oil till tender.
3. Add chiles and seasonings and mix thoroughly.
4. Add to bean mixture.
5. Add chicken and simmer 1 hour.

Serve topped with grated cheese, salsa and sour cream.

Tweezer's White Chili
1 Lb. White Beans; Large
6 Cups Vegetable Broth
2 Cloves Garlic; Minced
2 Medium Onions; Chopped
1 Tablespoon Olive Oil
2 Cans (4 Ounce) Green Chiles; Chopped
2 Teaspoons Cumin; Ground
1-½ Teaspoons Oregano
¼ Teaspoon Cloves; Ground
¼ Teaspoon Cayenne Pepper
¼ Teaspoon Chile powder
3 Cups Monterey Jack Cheese; Grated
As Desired Salsa
As Desired Sour Cream

1. Combine beans, broth, garlic and half of the onions in a large soup pot. Bring to a boil.
2. Reduce heat, simmer until beans are soft (3 hours or more) adding more broth if it's necessary.
3. In a skillet, sauté remaining onions in oil until tender.
4. Add chiles and seasonings and mix thoroughly.
5. Add to bean mixture. Simmer 1 hour or until it's just the way to like it.
6. Serve topped with grated cheese, salsa and sour cream.

Salsa:
You can use store-brought chunky Mexico tomato or make your own with peeled tomatoes, green chiles, onion, garlic, green onion and fresh cilantro

White Bean Chicken Chili
Seattle Times
1 Tablespoon Olive Oil
1 Small Onion; Peel and Chop Fine
2 Cloves Garlic; Peeled and Chopped
1 Medium Red Bell Pepper; Chopped Finely
2 Cans (15 Ounce) White Beans; Undrained
1 Can (4 Ounce) Green Chiles; Diced
½ Teaspoon Cumin; Ground
1 Teaspoon Chile powder
1 Can (14 Ounce) Chicken Broth; Low Sodium
½ Lb. Chicken Breast Meat; Roasted
2 Tablespoons Lime Juice
2 Tablespoons Cilantro (Fresh); Minced
6 Tablespoons Salsa; Optional

1. In a large pot heat the olive oil over medium heat.
2. Add the onion, garlic and red bell pepper.
3. Stir white beans, chiles, cumin, chile powder and broth. Bring to a boil.
4. Stir in the limejuice and cilantro.
A tablespoon of salsa can be used to garnish.

White Chick Chili By Rhett Reyn
2 Large Onions; Chopped
4 Pods Red Peppers; Seeded, Cored and Diced
5 Pods Jalapeño Peppers; Seeded and Minced
6 Tablespoons Chile Powder; Best Quality
3 Teaspoons Cumin Seed
2 Teaspoons Coriander; Ground
1 Pinch Cinnamon
10 Whole Chicken Breasts; Skinned, Boned and Cut in Cubes
2 Cans (28 Ounce) Tomatoes; In Puree, Chopped
2 Cans (6 Ounce) Black Olives; Pitted, Slices
2 Cups Beer
To Taste Salt
As Needed Sour Cream
As Needed CoJack Cheese; Grated
As Needed Scallions; Sliced
As Needed Avocados; Diced
As Needed Flour Tortillas; To Line Bowl

My friend makes this, and it's the best!

1. Heat oil in large stockpot.
2. Add the onion and sauté 5 minutes.
3. Add red peppers and Jalapeño peppers and sauté additional 10 minutes.
4. Add the tomatoes and puree, olives and beer to pot.
5. Bring to a low boil and add chicken cubes. Simmer 45 minutes to 1 hour. Serve chili in tortilla lined bowls.

For mole, add 1 teaspoon unsweetened chocolate per 10 Ounces of chili (or ½ cup for the whole pot).

Pass sour cream, onions, cheese, and avocado.

White Chili # 1
2 Tablespoons Butter
1 Bunch Scallions; Chopped
1 Medium Sweet Yellow Pepper; Chopped
1 Centiliter Garlic; Minced
4 Pods Jalapeño Chiles; Fresh, Seeded and Stemmed
½ Teaspoon Ginger; Fresh, Grated
½ Teaspoon Salt
½ Teaspoon Sage
½ Teaspoon Cumin
1-½ Chicken Breast, Boneless; Skinned, Cut into Pieces
3 Tablespoons Butter
¼ Cup Flour
½ Cup Cream
2 Cups Chicken Broth
1 Can (17 Ounce) Corn
1 Jar (32 Ounce) Great Northern Beans
To Taste Cayenne Pepper
To Taste White Pepper
1 Jar (11 Ounce) Jalapeño Chiles; Pickled
To Taste Monterey Jack Cheese; Grated

Chicken Mixture:
1. Melt butter in a 5-quart pan. Sauté scallions, yellow pepper, garlic, fresh Jalapeños, ginger, salt, sage and cumin.
2. Add chicken and cook until just done. Do not overcook.
3. Remove chicken from pan and set aside.

Sauce:
1. Melt the 3 tablespoons butter in the same pan.
2. When bubbling, add flour, and whisk briskly while adding cream.
3. When smooth and thick, add chicken broth.
4. Stir until blended.
5. Stir in corn, beans, and chicken mixture and simmer 30 minutes.
6. If desired, add 2 shakes cayenne pepper, 1 shake white pepper, and 4 ounces of pickled Jalapeños with a little juice.

Serve chili hot, topped with grated cheese and accompanied by corn bread.

White Chili # 2
1 Medium Onion; Finely Chopped
½ Large Green Pepper; Finely Chopped
1 Clove Garlic; Large, Minced
1 Carrot; Shredded
2 Stalks Celery; Finely Chopped
1 Tablespoon Olive Oil
1 Tablespoon Butter
1-¼ Lb. Chicken; Cooked, Boneless
1 Can (15 Ounce) Chicken Broth
1 Can Pinto Beans; Drained and Rinsed
1 Can Pinto Beans; Not Drained and Rinsed
¾ Cup Vermouth, Dry, White
1 Can Chick Peas; Optional
1 Teaspoon Cumin; Ground
½ Teaspoon Tabasco Sauce
2 Teaspoons Chile powder
1 Tablespoon Honey
2 Teaspoons Hot Pepper Sauce, Liquid; Medium
As Needed Mozzarella Cheese; Shredded

1. In a medium saucepan, sauté in oil and butter over medium high temperature the onion, green pepper, garlic, carrot and celery 6-8 minutes.
2. Gently add the cooked chicken, broth and beans.
3. Add vermouth, chick peas, cumin, Tabasco sauce, chile powder, honey and hot sauce and simmer and stir on low for a half hour.

For a nice touch and added flavor, melt shredded mozzarella cheese on top of each serving.

White Chili # 3
2 Lb. Navy Beans; Dried
6 Cups Heavy Cream
6 Cups Chicken Stock
2 Ounces Peanut Oil
2 Cups Celery; Diced
2 Cups Onion; Diced
2 Cups Bell Peppers; Diced
1 Cup Jalapeño Chiles; Diced
2 Teaspoons Garlic Puree
3 Tablespoons Cumin
3 Tablespoons Chile powder
2-½ Tablespoons Salt
2-½ Tablespoons Pepper
2 Tablespoons Chicken; Diced
4 Tablespoons Tabasco Sauce

1. Cover beans with water and cook until soft. Drain well.
2. In small stockpot, bring cream, chicken and navy beans to a simmer.
3. In sauté pan, heat peanut oil, and then add celery, onion and peppers. Cook until onions are clear.
4. Add garlic puree, cumin, chile powder, salt and pepper to vegetables, toss well, and add to stockpot.
5. Add chicken and Tabasco. Simmer until thick, about 30 minutes.
6. Re-season to taste and cooking with cumin, salt and pepper.
7. Pour into individual ovenproof serving bowls, top with mozzarella cheese, melt under broiler.

Makes about 2-½ gallons but recipe can be cut.

White Chili # 4
Bob Springer in Fidonet Cooking
3 Lb. Ground Turkey
4 Cloves Garlic; Minced
2 Medium Red Onions; Diced
3 Ounces Green Chile Peppers; Diced
1 Bunch Celery; Sliced
2 Medium Red Bell Peppers; Diced
4 Leeks; Cleaned and Diced
2 Teaspoons Oregano
1 Cup Flour

3 Quarts Chicken Broth
2 Tablespoons Coriander; Ground
3 Tablespoons Chile powder
3 Tablespoons Cumin; Ground
2 Teaspoons Sugar
2 Cans Cannelloni Beans; Canned

1. In a skillet, brown ground turkey with garlic and onions. Drain off the fat.
2. Place the turkey mixture in a stockpot over medium heat.
3. Add the next 6 ingredients and stir until the flour is smooth-cooked.
4. Add the stock and stir until the mixture is thickened.
5. Add the remaining ingredients and simmer for 1 hour.

White Chili # 5
1 Medium Onion; Chopped
1 Clove Garlic; Minced
1 Teaspoon Cumin; Ground
2 Chicken Breasts; Skinned, Boned and Diced
1 Can (16 Ounce) White (Cannelloni) Kidney Beans; Drained
1 Can (19 Ounce) Garbanzo Beans; Drained
1 Can (12 Ounce) White Corn; Drained
2 Cans (4 Ounce) Mild Green Chiles; Diced
2 Cubes Chicken Bouillon
1-½ Cups Water
3 Drops Hot Pepper Sauce, Liquid
1 Cup Monterey Jack Cheese; Shredded

1. Preheat oven to 350 degrees. In a small saucepan over medium heat, cook onion, garlic, and cumin until onion is tender.
2. In 2-½ quart casserole, combine onion mixture with chicken, white kidney beans, garbanzo beans, corn, green chiles, bouillon, and 1-½ cups water (I use less liquid).
3. Cover casserole and bake 50-60 minutes until chicken is tender.
To serve, stir hot pepper sauce into chili to taste. Serve with shredded cheese on top.

White Chili # 6
4 Cups Chicken Broth
1 Can (19 Ounce) Cannelloni Beans; Drained and Rinsed
1 Can (16 Ounce) Navy Beans: Drained and Divided

4 Breasts Chicken Halves; Skinned
1 Cup Onion; Chopped
16 Ounces White Corn; Frozen
4 Ounces Green Chiles; Chopped
1 Teaspoon Cumin; Ground
¾ Teaspoon Oregano; Dried
¼ Teaspoon Red Pepper; Ground
1 Clove Garlic; Minced

1. Chicken breast should be skinned before cooking and cooked without salt.
2. Place 1 cup broth, ½ cup cannelloni beans, and ½ cup navy beans in container of a blender or food processor; cover and process until smooth.
3. Place bean mixture, remaining broth and remaining ingredients in Dutch oven.
4. Bring to a boil; cover, reduce heat and simmer 30 minutes (up to an hour if you like it thick). Stir occasionally.

May be topped with cheese to serve. The bowl looks nice edged with tortilla chips too.

White Chili # 7
Llywelyn's Restaurant St. Louis, Missouri
6 Cloves Garlic; Mashed
1-½ Medium Onions; Chopped
¼ Cup Vegetable Oil
2-¼ Teaspoons Cumin; Ground
½ Cup White Wine
4 Cups Chicken Broth
2-½ Lb. Turkey Breast; Cooked, ½ Inch Pieces
¾ Cup Barley; Uncooked
6-½ Cups Garbanzo Beans (Canned); Rinsed and Drained
1 Tablespoon Jalapeño; Minced
¾ Teaspoon Marjoram; Dried
3/8 Teaspoon Savory; Dried
1/8 teaspoon Cloves; Ground
¼ Teaspoon Cayenne Pepper; To Taste
½ Teaspoon Black Pepper; Fresh Ground
Arrowroot Plus ¾ Tsp.; Dissolve in 3 Ounces Water
As Desired Cheese; Grated
As Desired Sour Cream; For Garnish
As Desired Salsa; For Garnish

1. Sauté garlic and chopped onions in oil until limp. Do not brown.
2. Add cumin; mix well.
3. Add wine, broth, turkey breast, barley, beans, Jalapeño, marjoram, savory, cloves, red pepper, oregano and black pepper. Bring to boil; cover and let simmer 1 hour, being careful not to let scorch. Stir often.
4. Stir in arrowroot mixture; mix well and simmer 15 minutes more, stirring often.

Garnish with shredded cheese, sour cream and salsa. Yield: About 18 cups.

Note: Arrowroot is a fine powder used for thickening. If you can't locate it, you may thicken with 2 teaspoons cornstarch or 4 tablespoons all-purpose flour. However, the flavor and texture will be slightly different.

White Chili With Salsa
3 Cans (10 ½ Ounce) Chicken Broth (Low Salt); Divided
1 Can (19 Ounce) Cannelloni Beans; Drained
1 Can (16 Ounce) Navy Beans; Drained
4 Cups Chicken Breast; Cooked, Chopped
1 Cup Onion; Chopped
1 Package (16 Ounce) White Corn (Frozen); Thawed
1 Can (4 Ounce) Green Chiles; Chopped
1 Teaspoon Cumin; Ground
¾ Teaspoon Oregano; Dried
¼ Teaspoon Red Pepper; Ground
2 Cups Tomatillo Salsa or Tomato Salsa

1. Place 1 cup broth, ½ cup cannelloni beans, and ½ cup navy beans in container of an electric blender; cover and process until smooth.
2. Place bean mixture, remaining chicken broth, remaining beans, chicken, onion, corn, chile, cumin, oregano, and red pepper in a large Dutch oven.
3. Bring to a boil; cover, reduce heat, and simmer 30 minutes.

Ladle chili into individual bowls. Top with salsa.

White Chili With Salsa Verde
1 Teaspoon Lemon Pepper
1 Teaspoon Cumin Seed
4 Halves Chicken Breast
1 Teaspoon Olive Oil
1 Clove Garlic; Minced
1 Cup Onion; Chopped
18 Ounces Shoepeg White Corn; Frozen

1 Can (8 Ounce) Green Chile Peppers; Undrained, Diced
1 Teaspoon Ground Cumin; Ground
3 Tablespoons Lime Juice
30 Ounces Great Northern Beans; Undrained
2/3 Cup Tortilla Chips; Crushed
As Needed Monterey Jack Cheese; Shredded

Salsa
22 Ounces Tomatillos; Chopped and Drained
½ Cup Onion; Chopped
½ Cup Cilantro (Fresh); Chopped Or Parsley
1 Pod Jalapeño Pepper; Chopped
1 Clove Garlic; Minced
½ Teaspoon Lemon Pepper
½ Teaspoon Oregano Leaves; Dried
½ Teaspoon Adobo Seasoning; Or Garlic Pods
3 Tablespoons Lime Juice
2-½ Cups Water

1. If tomatillos are not available, substitute green tomatoes.
2. Adobo is a seasoning available at Hispanic food stores.
3. In a large saucepan, combine water, lemon pepper, and cumin seed; bring to a boil.
4. Add chicken breast halves. Reduce heat to low, cover and simmer 20-28 minutes or until chicken is fork tender and juices run clear.
5. Remove chicken from bones; cut into 1-inch pieces.
6. Return chicken to saucepan.
7. Spray medium skillet with cooking spray; heat over medium heat.
8. Add minced garlic; cook, stirring, for 1 minute.
9. Remove from pan; add to chicken mixture.
10. Add onions to skillet; cook, stirring, until tender.
11. Add cooked onions, corn, and chiles, ground cumin and lime juice to chicken mixture. Bring to a boil.
12. Add beans; cook until thoroughly heated.

Salsa:
1. Combine all salsa ingredients in medium bowl; mix well.
2. Refrigerate 30 minutes to blend flavors.
To serve, place some tortilla chips and cheese in 8 individual soup bowls; ladle hot chili over cheese. Serve with the salsa.

Chapter 14
Chili Recipes - Meats Other Than Beef

Background
While beef is the most often used meat in chili, lots of alternatives have been used. The following are a sample of how people have adapted to whatever was in the refrigerator. I have to admit that some of them sound pretty good. I frequently add sausage to my chili for a change of pace. Enjoy!

Game Meats

Aardvark Chili Recipe
1 Aardvark; Ground
1 Quart Jalapeño Juice
3 Cups Tomatoes; Chopped
6 Tablets Thorazine
1 Liter Bacardi 151 Rum
½ Cup Cheap Mexican Gas; See Note
5 Ounces Campbell's Cream of Weasel Soup
Note: Fina may be substituted.

Cooking It Up:
1. Fry Aardvark meat.
2. Throw away tomatoes.
3. Add other ingredients.
4. Simmer over low flame 4 to 5 hours (or until bad smell goes away).

Serving It Up:
1. Do we have to tell you people everything?
2. Hell, we just gave you our secret chili recipe!
3. Eat it out of a D-Cup bra for all we care!
4. It May Kill What Cures You!
5. Chili Head Go Home.

Alligator Chili Piquante
2 Lb. Alligator Meat; Diced
4 Tablespoons Chile powder
2 Large Onions; Chopped
1 Stalk Celery; Chopped
2 Medium Green Peppers; Chopped
1/3 Cup Oil
1 Teaspoon Garlic; Fresh Minced

1 Teaspoon Salt
1 Teaspoon Italian Seasonings; Thyme, Oregano, Basil
2 Leaves Bay
1 Teaspoon Red Pepper; Cayenne
½ Teaspoon Black Pepper
1 Can (8 Ounce) Tomato Sauce
1 Can (8 Ounce) Chili Sauce

1. Combine alligator meat, chile powder, onions, celery, and green peppers. Sauté in the oil until vegetables are translucent.
2. Add remaining ingredients and simmer for 1-½ hours.

American Deer Chili

2 Lb. Ground Deer
2 Tablespoons Oil
2 Cups Onion; Chopped
2 Cloves Garlic; Crushed
2 Cups Tomatoes; Canned
1 Cube Beef Bouillon
2 Tablespoons Chile powder
2 Teaspoons Salt
1 Teaspoon Oregano
2 Cans (15 Ounce) Kidney Beans

1. Brown deer meat.
2. Add onion, garlic, tomatoes, bouillon cube, chile powder, salt and oregano. Cover and simmer for 2 hours.
3. Add undrained beans and simmer 20 minutes.

Bear Chili

5 Lb. Bear Meat; Coarse Ground
1 Lb. Suet
2 Large Onions
1 Cup Chile powder
¼ Teaspoon Thyme
¼ Teaspoon Oregano
5 Cloves Garlic
1 Teaspoon Comino Seeds
¼ Teaspoon Comino Powder
¼ Teaspoon Marjoram Powder

To Taste Salt
1 Quart Water; More if Needed

1. Melt suet.
2. Add meat; braze before adding seasoning.
3. Cook slow about 6 to 8 hours.
4. Adding water if needed to keep from sticking to bottom of kettle.

Beaver Chili
½ Lb. Bacon
2 Lb. Beaver Meat; Cut in ½ Inch Chunks
1 Cup Onion; Chopped
1 Clove Garlic; Minced
1 Can (6 Ounce) Tomato Paste
4 Teaspoons Chile powder
1 Teaspoon Cumin
½ Teaspoon Pepper
3 Cans Red Beans
2-½ Cups Water

1. Cut bacon into small pieces and brown in a deep skillet.
2. Add the beaver and stir often to brown.
3. Add the water and simmer covered until meat is tender, about 1 hour.
4. Add more water if necessary.
5. Next, add your tomato paste and beans with your spices to the beaver.
6. Add water to proper consistency and simmer one more hour or put into a crock-pot and simmer several hours.
Make 6 to 8 servings.

Buckskin Chili
5 Lb. Venison; Boneless
½ Lb. Bacon
2 Cups Beaujolais Red Wine
1 Teaspoon Angostura Bitters
4 Tablespoons Cumin; Fresh Ground
3 Tablespoons Tabasco Sauce
3 Cloves Garlic; Minced
2-½ Cups Tomato Sauce
½ Cup Tomato Paste
2-½ Cups Tomatoes (Stewed)

3 Pods Jalapeño Chile Peppers; Minced
2 Medium Onions; Chopped
½ Cup Mushrooms; Chopped
3 Tablespoons Red Chile Flakes
½ Teaspoon Allspice
1 Teaspoon Mexican Oregano; Optional
2 Tablespoons Ancho Chile Peppers; Dried and Crushed
1-½ Teaspoons Salt

1. Fry bacon in a large, heavy pot. Remove bacon when done and set aside.
2. Add the venison that has been rough ground, the chopped onions, the minced garlic, and salt to bacon grease.
3. Fry the venison until done and remove from the pot. Drain off the grease; add the wine, tomato sauce, and the bacon that has been crumbled.
4. Bring wine to a boil, add the Jalapeños, venison mixture, Tabasco sauce, 3 Tablespoons of the cumin, the Allspice, bitters, salt, Anchos, red pepper flakes, and mushrooms.
5. Reduce heat after cooking for 3 minutes, add tomato paste, and cook for 1-½ hours. Stir often or as needed.
6. Add the remaining cumin, cook for 15 minutes more and serve.

Buffalo Chili
¼ Cup Sunflower Oil
½ Cup Beef Broth
6 Lb. Buffalo Meat; Ground
½ Cup Paprika
½ Cup Flour
½ Cup Chile powder
3 Cups Water
6 Tablespoons Cumin; Ground
¼ Cup Garlic; Minced
1 Teaspoon Cayenne Pepper
¾ Cup Green Bell Pepper
½ Teaspoon Black Pepper
½ Teaspoon White Pepper
¾ cup Red Bell Pepper
½ Cup Green Chile Peppers
4 Teaspoons Salt
¾ Cup Jalapeño Chile Peppers
2 Tablespoons Oregano

5 Cups Tomato Sauce
2 Teaspoons Chiles; Dried
3 Medium Onions; Diced

1. Sauté Buffalo meat, sunflower oil and flour together until meat is cooked.
2. Add remaining ingredients and simmer for 1 hour.

Buffalo Hump Chili
Wayne Preston Allen
3 Lb. Ground Bison
3 Pods Poblano Peppers; Fresh, Chopped
2 Medium Onions
30 Ounces Ro-tel Tomatoes; Diced
4-½ Tablespoons New Mexican Chile Powder
1-½ Teaspoons Cumin; Ground
1-½ Teaspoons Paprika
3 Cloves Garlic
1 Lime; Fresh

I found the bison at a health food store; that's a good bet for you, too. The New Mexico chile powder might be had from one of a number of mail-order resources if you don't have a local source. The Ro-tel tomatoes are hot, so you can substitute regular tomatoes to cool it a little (but it's gonna be hot anyway!).

1. Brown the bison meat. Bison is lean and clumpy, so add a little oil and break it up as you brown it.
2. Add finely chopped onions and garlic. When onions are clear, add tomatoes and spices.
3. Add water to barely cover, and simmer until meat is tender.
4. Add chopped Poblanos for last 20 minutes of simmer, and stir in limejuice before serving.
You're really gonna be surprised!

Caribou Chili
4 Lb. Caribou; Chunked Preferred or Ground
1 Large Onion; Chopped
2 Cloves Garlic; Minced
1 Teaspoon Oregano
2 Teaspoons Cumin

1 Cup Red Wine; Beef Broth or Beer
6 Teaspoons Chile powder
1-½ Cups Canned Tomatoes and Juice; or Small Can Tomato Paste
2 Teaspoons Liquid Hot Pepper Sauce; Or
½ Teaspoon Cayenne Pepper
To Taste Salt

1. Place meat, onion and garlic in a large heavy skillet or Dutch oven. Cook until light colored.
2. Add oregano, cumin, water, chile powder, tomatoes, hot pepper sauce (more or less to taste), and salt. Bring to a boil, lowering heat, and simmer for one hour.
3. Optionally, the sauce may be thickened with a little (1-2 Tablespoons) Masa or Corn meal.
4. If possible, allow chili to cool and sit for at least 6 hours before re-heating and serving. It always tastes better the second day.

Extra optional ingredients:
1 Cup Green Bell Pepper Chopped
1 Cup Red Bell pepper chopped Ancho, Pequin, Jalapeño or Other chile Peppers
½ Teaspoon All Spice
2 Tablespoons Cilantro; Freshly Chopped
1 Teaspoon Ground Coriander
A Little Red Wine Vinegar and an Equal Amount of Brown Sugar
Up to 2 Tablespoons Worcestershire Sauce,
As Desired Kidney or small red "chili" beans (This is "illegal" in Texas but quite common in the rest of the world!)
½ Cup Mushrooms; Chopped or More

Cold Spring Tavern-Wild Game Black Bean Chili
24 Ounces Black Beans
40 Ounces Meat (Venison, Buffalo or Rabbit; Coarse Ground)
24 Ounces Pasilla Chile Peppers; Fresh
24 Ounces Onion
12 Ounces Tomatoes; Diced
3 Ounces Chile powder
2 Ounces Cumin
To Taste Salt and Pepper

The Cold Springs Tavern was originally a stagecoach stop on San Marcos Pass between the Santa Ynez Valley and Santa Barbara, California. While the stagecoaches are long gone, the tavern is still here serving great and hearty meals in the same rustic building that has stood for over 100 years. The Armchair folks have tried this chili at the Tavern and really like it. It is reminiscent of the black bean soups served in Haiti and the Dominican Republic -- however with a twist -- it's chili. The Cold Springs Tavern has reduced the recipe to a manageable size for home use. While wild game is recommended, you can substitute a variety of meats (chicken, turkey, beef) and cuts to your taste. As with all chili recipes, experiment and modify the recipe to your liking.

1. Cook the beans in water according to package directions. This will dictate the basic amount of water to use. Feel free to add water to yield your preferred chili consistency.
2. In a frying pan, sauté the meat until browned; reserve; sauté the onions and chiles until the onions are transparent (use a little canola oil if fat from meat is insufficient).
3. Combine the beans, meat, onions and chile; add tomatoes.
4. Add seasonings and salt and pepper to taste. Simmer for one hour.

Suggested Serving: Ladle into a large bowl and top with a dollop of sour cream and a sprinkling of chopped Jalapeños. It's great with a crusty French or sour dough bread. Enjoy!

When you are in Santa Barbara County, check out the Cold Springs Tavern. It's a gateway to wine country in the Santa Ynez Valley where you can tour some notable California vineyards. Cold Spring Tavern, 5995 Stagecoach Road. Santa Barbara, CA 93105. Phone: 805-967-0066.

Count Gregor's Celtic Chili
3 Lb. Ground Chuck
1 Lb. Venison
1 Can (60 Ounce) Tomato Sauce
4 Cloves Garlic; Minced
8 Ounces Worcestershire Sauce
8 Ounces Mild Green Chiles; Chopped
20 Medium Jalapeño Chile Peppers; See Note
8 Ounces Datil Hellish Relish
8 Ounces Old El Paso Hot Relish
5 Large Vidalia Onions; Minced
2 Teaspoons Garlic Salt

1 Teaspoon Seasoned Salt
½ Teaspoon Oregano
4 Cans (15 Ounce) Kidney Beans
1 Can (15 Ounce) Pinto Beans

1. Brown meat in skillet with Worcestershire sauce, the oregano, garlic salt and seasoned salt.
2. Put tomato sauce, minced garlic green chiles, Jalapeños, hellish relish, kidney beans, pinto beans, onions, and Old El Paso hot relish and heat on medium high until near boiling.
3. When meat is browned add juice and all to the rest and cook for 1 and ½ hours over low heat.

This is pleasantly warm but not mouth burning hot! Enjoy!!!

Note: Chopped in rings then quartered.

Deer Camp Chili
1 Lb. Pinto Beans; Dried
1 Teaspoon Salt
2 Lb. Venison (About 4 Cups); Cut in ¾ Inch Cubes
1-½ Teaspoon Salt
2 Cloves Garlic; Chopped Fine
2 Teaspoons Cumin; Ground
4 Large Or 6 Medium Onions; Chopped
1 Tablespoon Hot Chile powder; Mexican Style, Or 2
1 Can (28 Ounce) Tomatoes (Concentrated); Crushed
1 Can (28 Ounce) Tomatoes; Peeled and Cut in Chunks

1. Wash beans and place in a pot with salt and enough water to cover. Bring to a boil; remove from heat and soak for 1 hour.
2. Add more water to cover and simmer while preparing rest of chili.
3. In large pot, brown salted venison cubes in 3 to 4 tablespoons oil.
4. Add garlic, onions and spices. Cook, covered until onions and garlic are soft.
5. Add both cans of tomatoes; heat until simmering.
6. Add beans, including bean juice (2 cans of pintos can be substituted). Bring to a slow boil, then lower heat and simmer for 3 to 4 hours.
7. It is better if served reheated the next day.

Serve topped with chopped raw onions or coarsely shredded cheese.

Deer Chili
2 Lb. Deer Meat
1 Cup Celery; Finely Chopped
¼ Cup Sugar
1 Teaspoon Salt
½ Cup Catsup
1 Can Tomato Soup
1 Large Onion; Chopped
1 Can (16 Ounce) Tomatoes; Peeled
1 Teaspoon Worcestershire Sauce
5 Tablespoons Chile powder
¼ Teaspoon Red Pepper
1 Can (15-¾ Ounce) Chili Hot Beans; In Chili Gravy

1. Cook and stir meat and onion in a 3-quart saucepan until meat is brown.
2. Add tomatoes, celery, chile powder, salt, sugar, Worcestershire sauce, red pepper, tomato soup and catsup. Bring to a boil. Stir, and then simmer for 1 hour with a lid on it.
3. Add chili beans and simmer for 15 minutes without a lid. Serves 6.

Diet Delight Deer Chili
4 Lb. Deerburger
2 Tablespoons Oil; If Beef Fat Has Not Been Added
1 Large Onion
1 Large Bell Pepper
1 Can Mushrooms; Sliced
1 Quart Tomatoes; Pureed
1-½ Quarts Water
1 Package Chili Mix

1. Cook meat in oil until done.
2. Pour meat into colander; rinse well to remove fat.
3. Cook onions, bell peppers and mushrooms in skillet until tender.
4. Then add cooked meat; combine in large pot.
5. Add tomatoes, water and chili mix; simmer for 30 minutes.
Can add beans, if desired.

Don's Venison Chili
4 Lb. Venison; Boneless, Cubed
2 Pods Jalapeño Chile Peppers; Seeded and Chopped

3 Tablespoons Bacon Grease
3 Tablespoons Soy Sauce
5 Tablespoons Cumin; Fresh Ground
½ Cup Green Bell Peppers; Chopped
5 Cloves Garlic; Minced
2 Medium Onions; Chopped
1-½ Cans Beer; Not Lite
1 Can (8 Ounce) Tomato Sauce
½ Teaspoon Cayenne Pepper
2 Cups Tomatoes (Stewed)
6 Pods Jalapeño Chile Peppers; Fresh, Whole
2 Tablespoons Masa Harina (Corn Flour)
½ Teaspoon Salt
1 Ounce Jack Daniels Whiskey

1. Brown meat in bacon grease.
2. Sauté the onions, the chopped Jalapeños, and the bell peppers in the bacon grease until the onions start to become transparent.
3. Meanwhile bring the beer and whiskey to a boil and add the meat, seasonings, except for 1 Tablespoon of cumin, and the onions/peppers to the pot.
4. Allow to boil for 5-7 minutes. Reduce the heat to medium then add the tomatoes and tomato sauce.
5. Stir occasionally while continuing to cook for 30 minutes. Reduce heat to simmer and cook for 1 hour.

This is an original venison chili recipe that I had sworn never to reveal ever to anyone. My daughter has asked that I give it to you so I will do so, with many 2nd thoughts.

Enjoy!

Earl's Venison Chili
3 Tablespoons Oil
1 Large Onion; Finely Chopped
1-¼ Lb. Venison; Cubed
¾ Lb. Venison; Ground
1 Can (28 Ounce) Tomatoes; Crushed
3 Tablespoons Red Wine Vinegar
3 Tablespoons Chile powder; Ground
2 Tablespoons Cumin; Ground
2 Tablespoons Worcestershire Sauce

½ Teaspoon Cayenne Pepper; Plus a Pinch
1 Medium Bell Pepper; Chopped
2 Teaspoons Salt; Or To Taste
To Taste Black Pepper; Fresh Ground
1 Can (10 Ounce) Red Kidney Beans; Drained
3 Tablespoons Corn Meal; Fine Mixed

1. Heat the oil in a very large skillet.
2. Stir in the onion, garlic, and chile pepper. Sauté over medium-high heat until the onion is just tender, about 5 minutes.
3. Add the cubed and the ground venison and continue cooking for about four to five minutes, stirring with a wooden spoon, until the ground meat is no longer red.
4. Add all the remaining ingredients except the beans and the masa harina (or cornmeal). Bring the mixture to a boil then reduce heat to medium and cook uncovered for 30 minutes, stirring occasionally.
5. The stew should be fairly thick.
6. Stir in the kidney beans and the masa harina and heat through.
7. Taste and adjust the seasonings.

Extra Thick Venison Chili
4 Lb. Venison; Ground
1 Medium Onion; Finely Chopped
2 Cans (16 Ounce) Tomatoes, Whole; Home Canned if Available
1 Can (Gallon) Chili Beans; In Sauce
2 Tablespoons Chile powder
1 Tablespoon Paprika
1 Teaspoon Cumin
4 Pods Red Chile Peppers; Chopped

1. Brown venison and onion in skillet.
2. Transfer to large stockpot (at least 8 quarts).
3. Add remaining ingredients. Simmer on low heat for 1 to 2 hours. Stir occasionally.

This chili is extra thick, but you can add water or ketchup to thin if you desire. Preparation time: 2 hours. Yield: 20 bowls.

Fast Venison Chili
1 Lb. Venison; Cooked, Ground
1 Lb. Bacon; Cooked, Diced

3 Medium Onions; Chopped
3 Cans (16 Ounce) Tomatoes; Diced
3 Cans (16 Ounce) Chili Beans; Hot
2 Cloves Garlic; Pressed or Finely Sliced
½ Cup Brown Sugar; Packed
3 Tablespoons Chile powder; Or More To Taste

1. Combine all ingredients in large pot and cook on medium heat for 2 to 3 hours or as long as possible.
2. The longer you cook chili the better the flavor it has.
Serve the chili over cooked minute rice in place of pasta or crackers.

Frank's Sure-Kill Venison Chili
3 Lb. Venison; Cubed or Coarse Ground
3 Cans Kidney Beans; As Extender
3 Cans Tomato Sauce
2 Cans Tomato Paste
1 Large Onion
¼ Lb. Butter
1 Lb. Mushroom; Fresh
6 Cloves Garlic
1 Can Tomatoes (Stewed); Optional
1 Cup Barbecue Sauce
½ Cup Sugar; More or Less to Taste
½ Cup Water
3 Tablespoons Red Pepper
6 Pods Jalapeño Chile Peppers; Diced
3 Tablespoons Louisiana Hot Sauce
4 Tablespoons Worcestershire Sauce
2 Tablespoons Oregano
½ Medium Bell Pepper; Finely Chopped
Other spices that look good that you have a mind to use.

1. Brown the venison (or other wild game) with some butter. Venison tends to be somewhat dry, so add butter as needed. Drain well.
2. Add to 6-8 quart slow cooker. (A large pot on the stove will work, but overnight cooking is preferred.)
3. Add other ingredients, mixing well.
4. Add only enough water to prevent burning. Cook covered for 2 hours at boil.

5. Reduce heat to 200 degrees and cook until you can't keep everyone away.
6. Consistency should be fairly thick. Cook uncovered if too thin.
Top with shredded cheese of choice and serve with fresh cornbread. Freezes well if any left over.

Mary Jane's Chili
3 Lb. Venison; Or Beef
3 Tablespoons Oil
1 Large Onion
1 Tablespoon Salt
1 Teaspoon Pepper
1 Can (46 Ounce) Tomato Juice
1 Can Beer
1 Bottle (3 Ounce) Gebhardt's Chili Powder
1 Package William's Chili Seasoning

1. Brown venison or beef chili meat and 1 large onion in oil.
2. Add salt, pepper, tomato juice, beer, Gebhardt's chili powder and William's chili seasoning. Bring to boil and simmer for 2 to 3 hours.

Ostrich Chili-Arkansas
1 Lb. Arkansas Valley Ground Ostrich
1 Pod Red Chile Pepper; Crushed
1 Large Onion; Chopped
2 Leaves Bay
2 Cloves Garlic; Minced
2 Tablespoons Chile powder
3 Tablespoons Olive Oil
1 Teaspoon Salt
1 Cup Tomato Sauce
1 Teaspoon Black Pepper
1 Can (Large) Tomato Paste
1 Can Green Chiles; Diced
1 Teaspoon Cumin
2 Cups Pinto Beans; Cooked
1 Teaspoon Oregano
2 Cups Water

1. Brown meat with onion and garlic in olive oil.
2. Add rest of ingredients except beans and cook until ostrich is tender

adding more water if necessary.
3. Add beans and adjust seasonings to taste. Return to boil and serve.

Red and Black Bean Buffalo Chili
Chicago Tribune, 10/07/93
1 Lb. Ground Buffalo Cut From Cobs; To 1-½ Lb.
3 Cups Red Beans; Cooked
1 Large Red Onion; Diced
3 Cups Black Beans; Cooked
3 Cloves Garlic; Minced
3 Tablespoons Chile powder
1 Medium Red Bell Pepper; Diced
2 Tablespoons Tamari Sauce
1 Medium Green Bell Pepper; Diced
1 Tablespoon Cumin; Ground
1 Medium Yellow Bell Pepper; Diced
1 Tablespoon Honey
½ Teaspoon Red Pepper; Crushed
2 Large Tomatoes; Diced
2 Ears Sweet Corn, Shucked; Kernels
As Desired Cilantro (Fresh); Chopped

1. Cook meat in large non-aluminum Dutch oven until no longer pink.
2. Stir in remaining ingredients except cilantro. Simmer gently, partially covered and stirring frequently, 40 to 45 minutes.
3. Taste and adjust seasonings.
4. Add cilantro at serving time.
This is adapted from a recipe used at the Heartland Cafe on Chicago's north side. It uses dried, cooked beans although canned beans are a fine short-order alternative. If desired, the chili can be served with grated cheese, sour cream, chopped green onions, tortillas or crackers.

Red Ink Chili
3 Lb. Beef or Venison; Lean, Cut in 1/2 Inch Cubes
16 Ounces Hunt's No-Salt Tomato Sauce
16 Ounces Water
10 Tablespoons Chile powder
4 Teaspoons Cayenne
2 Tablespoons Cumin
2 Teaspoons Oregano; Ground

1 Teaspoon Black Pepper
2 Pods Jalapeño Peppers; Finely Chopped
2 Medium Onions; Finely Chopped
4 Cloves Garlic; Pressed
2 Tablespoons Corn Meal

1. Measure and divide all dry spices into two small containers.
2. Lightly coat the Dutch oven or pot with corn oil. Heat the pot.
3. Spoonify the garlic around the pot for a minute or two, and then add the finely chopped onions and the finely chopped Jalapeños.
4. When the onions are as transparent as a politician's promises, add the meat.
5. Stir and sear the meat until the lively pink is converted to a light bureaucratic gray.
6. Add the tomato sauce, the water and half the spices.
7. Stir to mix well; bring to a boil. Cover and reduce the bubblistics to a joyful simmer.
8. Simmer for 2 hours, but give an occasional loving swirl of the spoon to let the developing chili know you really care.
9. After 2 hours, add the remaining spices.
10. Stir cautiously and affectionately until the spices are an integral part of the marriage.
11. After adding the final spices, bring the chili to an excited and mature heat by simmering for an additional hour.
12. Then, lightly sprinkle the cornmeal over the quivering surface of the chili, slowly massaging the cornmeal into the chili with tender, spoonful strokes.

Though many fine chili cooks establish a meaningful chilian relationship by simply dumping their spices into the pot, I add the final spices while mumbling a matrimonial incantation, a kind of ceremonial blessing:

Pepper, spices, chopped up meat Bubble, blend and share your heat.
May your flavor and your fire Give us zest and great desire.
Pepper, spices, chopped up meat Bubble, blend and share your heat.
Chili stir and chili stroke; May all cares go up in smoke.

Roast Boar And Black Bean Chili
¼ Cup Bacon Drippings
2 Cloves Garlic; Crushed
3 Tablespoons Chile powder

1/8 Teaspoon Cumin Seeds; Ground
¼ Teaspoon Black Pepper
4 Lb. Saddle of Wild Boar
1 Lb. Black Turtle Beans
2 Tablespoons Olive Oil
½ Cup Salt Pork; Diced
2 Medium Onions; Chopped
3 Cloves Garlic; Minced
1 Pod Jalapeño Chile Peppers; Minced
1 Cup Smoked Ham; Cooked
2 Cups Beef Broth
1 Leaf Bay
1 Teaspoon Oregano; Chopped
1 Teaspoon Red Wine Vinegar
2 Tablespoons Dark Rum
4 Scallions; Thinly Sliced
2 Eggs; Hard Cooked, Sieved

1. In a medium bowl, combine the bacon drippings with the crushed garlic, two tablespoons of chile powder, cumin, and freshly ground pepper.
2. Spread over the wild boar and let stand while preparing the beans.
3. In a large pot, cover the beans with cold water. Heat to boiling and boil for two minutes. Turn off the heat and let stand one hour. Drain.
4. Wipe out the pot and return beans, cover with cold water and heat to boiling.
5. Reduce heat and simmer for 30 minutes. Drain.
6. Preheat the oven to 325 degrees.
7. Cook the salt pork in boiling water for five minutes. Drain and pat dry.
8. Heat the oil in a heavy, deep casserole.
9. Stir in the salt pork and cook over medium heat until golden, about 3 minutes.
10. Stir in the onion, minced garlic, and Jalapeño pepper. Cook 1 minute.
11. Stir in the ham and cook two more minutes.
12. Stir the remaining chile powder into the onion mixture.
13. Add the beans, broth, bay leaf, oregano, vinegar and rum. Mix well.
14. Place the saddle of boar on top of the beans, cover and place in the middle of the oven. Cook for 1-½ to 2 hours or until internal meat thermometer reads 170 degrees.
15. Turn the meat twice and stir the beans.
16. Add more broth if dry.

17. Remove the meat and allow it to stand, covered, for 10 to 15 minutes.
18. Meanwhile, skim the fat from the chili.
19. Cut the meat from the bone and into thin slices.
20. Layer it over the beans.
21. If desired, stew, covered, to tenderize the meat.

Serve with hot rice and a sprinkling of scallions and sieved eggs.

Savory Venison Chili

¼ Lb. Slab Bacon; Cut in ¼ Inch Dice
1 Medium Onion; Coarse Chopped
6 Medium Carrots; Peeled and Halved Lengthwise
2 Teaspoons Chile powder
2 Teaspoons Cumin; Ground
1 Teaspoon Marjoram or Oregano; Dried
¼ Teaspoon Red Pepper Flakes
2 Lb. Venison Shoulder
1 Can (28 Ounce) Italian Plum Tomatoes; Crushed
1-½ Cups Defatted Chicken Broth; Or Beef Broth
½ Cup Red Wine
¼ Cup Tomato Paste
1 Can (16 Ounce) Dark Red Kidney Beans; Drained
1 Cup Baby Lima Beans
3 Cups Rice or Barley; Cooked, Optional

I like to start off this chili with bacon. Once it browns, use 2 tablespoons of the bacon fat to wilt the vegetables, and then one more tablespoon of the fat should be enough to brown the venison. Since the meat is lean, brown it quickly over high heat.

1. Brown the bacon in a skillet over medium heat for about 10 minutes or until golden brown. Remove bacon with a slotted spoon and set aside. Reserve 3 tablespoons of bacon fat; discard the rest.
2. Place 2 tablespoons of the bacon fat in a casserole; add the onion and carrots, sprinkle with chile powder, cumin, marjoram and red pepper flakes, then cook for 5 minutes.
3. Add the reserved bacon.
4. Pour the remaining tablespoon of bacon fat back into the skillet.
5. Brown the venison over medium-high heat in small batches and remove to the casserole with a slotted spoon. (The meat should brown quickly, so raise the heat to high if necessary.)

6. Add the tomatoes, broth, and wine and tomato paste. Bring to a simmer and cook, uncovered, for 40 minutes, stirring occasionally. Reduce the heat if the chili begins to boil.
7. Add the kidney beans and lima beans, and then adjust the seasonings. Simmer 10 minutes longer or until meat is tender.

Serve the chili hot in 6 bowls (over rice or barley, if desired).

Terry's Venison Chili

2 Lb. Venison; Coarse Ground
1 Cup Onion; Chopped
2 Cloves Garlic; Minced
1 Large Green Pepper; Cut in Strips
3 Tablespoons Chile powder
¼ Cup Vegetable Oil
3-½ Cups Tomatoes; Whole
1 Cup Tomato Sauce
½ Teaspoon Salt
2 Teaspoons Sugar
1 Cup Water
1 Lb. Pinto Beans

1. Brown venison in vegetable oil. (Ground beef can be substituted for venison and oil.)
2. Pour off excess oil; add onions, garlic and pepper, and cook 5 minutes stirring constantly.
3. Add chile powder, sugar, tomatoes, tomato sauce, water and salt. Simmer 1-½ hours.
4. If a thicker chili is desired, stir in 1-tablespoon flour mixed with 2 tablespoons water.
5. Just before serving, mix with 1 pound cooked pinto beans.

Makes 6 to 8 servings.

Texas Venison Chili

2 Lb. Venison; Or Ground Meat
¼ Cup Vegetable Oil
1 Cup Onion; Chopped
2 Cloves Garlic; Minced
1 Large Green Pepper; Cut in Strips
3 Tablespoons Chile powder
2 Teaspoons Sugar

3-½ Cups Tomatoes
1 Cup Tomato Sauce
1 Cup Water
½ Teaspoon Salt
1 Tablespoon Flour; Mixed With 2 Tbs. Water
2 Cups Kidney Beans; Cooked

1. Brown meat in heated oil in a heavy pan; add onion, garlic and green pepper. Cook about 15 minutes, stirring constantly.
2. Add chile powder, sugar, tomatoes, tomato sauce, water and salt; then let mixture simmer for about 1-½ hours.
3. If a thickened chili is desired, stir in the flour and water paste and cook for 5 minutes or until mixture thickens.
4. Just before serving, add the red beans and allow chili to heat for a few additional minutes.

Uncle Buck's Venison Chili
Uncle Buck's Venison, Littleton, NH
2 Tablespoons Olive Oil
1 Medium Bell pepper; Chopped
2 Medium Onions; Chopped Finely
2 Cloves Garlic; Crushed
1 Lb. Venison; Ground
1 Lb. Venison; Cut in Chunks
8 Ounces Tomatoes; Canned
4 Tablespoons Tomato Paste
1 Leaf Bay
1 Teaspoon Cumin; Ground
1 Teaspoon Oregano
¼ Teaspoon Cayenne Pepper
1 Tablespoon Chile powder; Mild
To Taste Salt and Pepper
1 Cup Beef Stock
2 Tablespoons Dark Brown Sugar; To Taste
2 Cans Chile Peppers; Small
1 Can (14 Ounce) Red Kidney Beans

1. Heat olive oil in large saucepan. Add onions, garlic and bell peppers. Fry until soft.
2. Brown all meat and add to above.

3. Stir in tomatoes, tomato paste, and seasonings and beef stock with a wooden spoon. Bring to a boil. Reduce heat to low and cover.
4. Add chile peppers. Simmer for two hours, stirring occasionally.
5. Add kidney beans and simmer for another 30 minutes.
6. Remove bay leaf and serve.

Venison Chili # 1
Cathy In Memphis
2 Lb. Venison; Ground
6 Tablespoons Oil
1 Cup Onion; Chopped
¼ Cup Green Pepper; Chopped
1 Dash Garlic Powder
2 Pints Tomatoes; Canned
2 Tablespoons Flour
½ Cup Chile powder
½ Teaspoon Cumin; Ground
1-½ Teaspoons Salt
16 Ounces Chili Beans; Hot

1. Cook venison, onion, pepper and garlic till onion is tender.
2. Add flour, then remaining ingredients and heat to boiling. Reduce heat and simmer 1 hour.

It's wonderful on a cold night, especially with a side of Mexican corn bread!

Venison Chili # 2
6 Tablespoons Olive Oil
2 Large Onions; Chopped
4 Cloves Garlic; Minced
1 Can Green Chiles; Hot
2-½ Lb. Venison; Cut in ½ Inch Cubes
2-½ Lb. Venison; Ground
2 Cans Tomatoes; Large, Crushed
6 Tablespoons Red Wine Vinegar
6 Tablespoons Chile powder
4 Tablespoons Cumin
4 Tablespoons Worcestershire Sauce
1 Teaspoon Cayenne Pepper
1 Medium Green Pepper; Chopped
4 Teaspoons Salt

2 Teaspoons Black Pepper
2 Cans Chili Beans with Gravy; Large
As Needed Corn Starch

1. Heat olive oil in Dutch oven and stir in onion, garlic, and chiles. Sauté about 5 minutes.
2. Add cubed and ground venison. Stir until round meat is browned.
3. Add all remaining ingredients except beans. Bring mixture to boil, and then simmer uncovered 30 minutes. Stir occasionally.
4. Stir in beans and simmer covered 15 minutes.

Serve.

Venison Chili # 3
¼ Cup Oil; More if Needed
4 Lb. Venison, Boneless; Chopped into Medium Dice
2 Lb. Pork, Boneless; Chopped into Medium Dice
12 Cloves Garlic; Minced
2 Cups Yellow Onions; Diced
¾ Cup Mixed Ancho and Pasilla; Chile Purees
8 Medium Tomatoes; Chopped
2 Tablespoons Cumin; And 1-Teaspoon Divided
1 Cup Red Bell Pepper; Diced
1 Cup Green Bell Pepper; Diced
½ Cup Paprika
2 Tablespoons Cayenne Pepper
2 Tablespoons Black Pepper
2 Tablespoons Kosher Salt
2 Tablespoons Chile powder
1 Cup Masa Harina (Corn Flour)
2 Quarts Beef Stock
4 Cups Cowboy Beans; Cooked
2 Cups Cilantro Leaves; Chopped

1. Heat oil in large stockpot over medium heat and add venison, pork, garlic, and onion. Cook 15 minutes.
2. Add chili purees, tomatoes and 1-teaspoon cumin; cook 15 minutes more.
3. Add peppers, paprika, cayenne, remaining cumin, black pepper, salt and chile powder; cook 5 minutes more.
4. Add Masa harina and beef stock. Bring to a boil over medium-high heat, then reduce heat and simmer 45 minutes.

5. Add cowboy beans and simmer 5 more minutes.
6. Taste and adjust seasonings.

Garnish each serving with chopped cilantro.

  Makes 10 to 12 servings.

Venison Chili # 4

2 Lb. Venison; Ground
As Needed Bacon Drippings
1 Medium Lemon; Juice of 1 Lemon
1 Large Onion; Chopped
2 Cloves Garlic; Minced
To Taste Salt and Pepper
½ Cup Flour
3 Tablespoons Chile powder
1 Teaspoon Comino Seeds
½ Teaspoon Oregano
1 Can (46 Ounce) Tomato Juice
2 Cans No. 2 Kidney Beans
3 Cups Water

1. Sprinkle meat with lemon juice.
2. Brown venison in bacon drippings; add onion, garlic, salt and pepper. Cook until well browned, then add flour and spices; mix well.
3. Add tomato juice, beans and water. Simmer about 2 hours, stirring occasionally.

Venison Chili Ala Fred
Bill Saiff's Rod and Reel Recipes for Hookin' and Cookin'

1 Lb. Venison; Ground
½ Cup Onion; Chopped
½ Teaspoon Salt
¼ Teaspoon Pepper
4 Cups Tomatoes; Canned, Chopped
¾ Cup Catsup
1 Can (15 Ounce) Kidney Beans

1. Combine the venison, onions, salt and pepper, and brown in a skillet, stirring 'til crumbly.
2. Add the remaining ingredients, and simmer for 45 min. or 'til it is of the desired consistency.

Wes and Kathy's Killer 4-Star Venison Chili

3 Lb. Venison, Chopped Fine; Neck or Shoulder Cuts
12 Ounces Beer; Not Lite
½ Cup Beef Broth
1 Medium Onion; Chopped
1 Tablespoon Oregano
4 Cloves Garlic; Crushed
2 Tablespoons Masa Harina (Corn Flour)
To Taste Salt
1 Teaspoon Coriander; Ground
¼ Cup Gebhardt's Chili Powder
¼ Cup Water; Warm
2 Tablespoons Olive Oil
1 Tablespoon Cumin; Ground

1. Sauté the meat in the oil until very lightly browned.
2. Add the onion and garlic.
3. Sauté until the onion is tender but not browned.
4. Add the chili powder, coriander and cumin. Cook over medium heat, stirring frequently, 4-5 minutes.
5. Add the beer and broth. Reduce heat to a medium simmer.
6. Cook, stirring frequently, until the meat is tender (45-60 minutes).
7. Dissolve the masa harina in the warm water.
8. Add to the chili.
9. Continue to simmer, stirring frequently, for 30 minutes. Remove from the heat. Cover.
10. Let sit for at least 6 hours.
11. Reheat.
Serve hot.

Wild Game Chili With Black Beans
Gloria Ciccarone-Nehls, the Big Four Restaurant

½ Cup Vegetable Oil
4 Medium Yellow Onions; Cut in Medium Dice
2 Pods Jalapeño or Serrano Chiles; Seeded, Finely Chopped
3 Tablespoons Chile powder
2 Tablespoons Cumin; Ground
3 Tablespoons Thyme; Dried
1 Teaspoon Oregano; Dried
1 Teaspoon Celery Seeds

1 Teaspoon Paprika
½ Teaspoon Black Pepper
½ Teaspoon Anise Seeds
½ Teaspoon Cayenne Pepper
¼ Teaspoon Cloves; Ground
4 Leaves Bay
3 Lb. Wild Game Meat; Cut in 1 Inch Pieces, See Note
30 Ounces Red Chile Sauce
1-½ Quarts Beef Stock or Broth; Up to 2
5 Cups Black Turtle Beans, Cooked; 2 Cups Uncooked
To Taste Salt and Pepper
Note: Venison, antelope, rabbit, elk, duck, game sausage.

1. Heat oil in an 8-quart casserole or Dutch oven; add onions and chiles, and sauté over medium heat until soft.
2. Add spices and bay leaves and sauté several minutes longer.
3. Add meat and cook until lightly browned.
4. Add chile sauce and bring to a boil.
5. Add stock to barely cover the ingredients and return to a boil. Reduce heat and simmer 30 minutes. Cover and bake in a 375 degree F. oven for 2 hours, stirring every 30 minutes.
6. Add beans and salt and pepper to taste.

If desired, garnish with grated sharp cheddar or Jack cheese and chopped red onions.

Note: This recipe also works well with lamb or beef.

Heidy Haughy Cusick writing in the San Francisco Chronicle, 12/18/91.

Lamb
Chili With Lamb And Black Beans
1-¾ Cups Black Beans; Sorted and Rinsed
2 Quarts Water; Or More as Needed
2 Lb. Lamb Bones
4 Sprigs Thyme
4 Sprigs Parsley
1 Leaf Bay
3 Cloves Garlic; Crushed
6 Tablespoons Olive Oil
2 Large Yellow Onions; Chopped
1-½ Lb. Lamb Shoulder; Ground
2 Tablespoons Chile powder

As Needed Salt
2 Tablespoons Ginger; Fresh, Minced
2 Tablespoons Thyme; Fresh, Minced or
2 Teaspoons Thyme; Dried, Crumbled
1 Tablespoon Jalapeño Chile Peppers; Seeded and Deveined
1-¼ Teaspoon Marjoram; Dried and Crumbled
¾ Teaspoon White Pepper; Freshly Ground
¾ Teaspoon Black Pepper; Freshly Ground
¾ Teaspoon Cayenne Pepper
¾ Teaspoon Allspice
2 Lb. Italian Tomatoes; Chopped
1-¼ Cups Light Zinfandel Wine

For Beans:
1. Soak Beans overnight in 2 quarts of water. In a large saucepan, bring beans to a boil.
2. Add lamb bones and bouquet garni and 1 crushed garlic clove.
3. Reduce heat and simmer till beans are tender but not mushy. Skim occasionally and add more water if necessary to keep beans submerged for 2 hours.

For Chili:
1. Heat 3 tablespoons of oil in large heavy saucepan over moderate heat.
2. Add onions and cook until soft, about 10 minutes.
3. Add 2 cloves garlic, minced, and stir about 3 minutes.
4. Transfer onion and garlic mixture to a plate, using a slotted spoon.
5. Add remaining oil to pan. Increase heat to medium high.
6. Add lamb and cook until no longer pink, breaking up with spoon, about 6 minutes.
7. Return onion mixture to pan; add chile powder, ginger, thyme, red chile, marjoram, peppers and allspice. Stir 5 minutes.
8. Add tomatoes (and half of their liquid, if canned). Bring to a boil then reduce heat and simmer for another 5 minutes.
9. Add ¾ cup of Zinfandel. Simmer, skimming occasionally, for 30 minutes.
10. Drain beans and reserve the cooking liquid.
11. Discard the bones and garni.
12. Add beans and remaining Zinfandel to chili mixture.
13. Salt and season as necessary. Simmer 30 minutes, adding bean-cooking liquid as needed to keep chili moist (or soupy, as you like it).
14. This chili is best made ahead and allowed to season in the refrigerator for

24 hours.
15. Reheat before serving.

Firestone Lamb and Black Bean Chili
4 Cups Chicken Broth
5 Ounces Ancho Chile Peppers; Dried, Stemmed and Seeded
3 Pods Chipotle Chile Peppers; Canned in Adobo Sauce
¼ Cup Olive Oil; Plus 2 Tablespoons
5 Lb. Leg of Lamb; Boned and Trimmed
2 Large Onions; Diced
4 Cloves Garlic; Finely Chopped
12 Ounces Firestone Double Barrel Ale
1 Can (28 Ounce) Tomatoes; Chopped and Drained
¼ Cup Pasilla Chile Powder; Ground
3 Tablespoons Cumin; Ground
5 Cans (15 Ounce) Black Beans; Rinsed and Drained
¼ Cup Lime Juice; Fresh
As Needed Avocado Salsa
3 Large Avocados; Ripe, Peeled, Pitted and Diced
7 Tablespoons Lime Juice; Fresh
¼ Cup Red Onion; Finely Chopped
6 Tablespoons Cilantro (Fresh); Chopped
3 Pods Jalapeño Chile Peppers; Seeded and Minced
To Taste Salt and Pepper

This recipe is a serious stew-like chili contributed by owner Adam Firestone's wife, Kate Firestone. You should consider serving it over a bed of white rice with the avocado salsa described, sour cream, cilantro, a crunchy green salad, French bread or soft rolled tortillas and a lemon tart for dessert! Do this and accompany it with a pint of Firestone Double Barrel Ale, my friend, and you will be a happier person ... and most likely quite full too.

1. Bring stock to a boil in heavy medium saucepan. Remove from heat.
2. Add ancho chiles. Cover and let stand until soft, about 30 minutes.
3. Transfer ancho chiles and 2 cups stock to processor or blender, add chipotle chiles and puree the lot of em!
4. Stir into remaining stock and set aside. Heat ¼ cup oil in large Dutch oven or covered pot over high heat and add lamb meat and reserved bones in batches. Cook until meat is brown about 3 minutes per batch.
5. Transfer to bowl using slotted spoon.

6. Add remaining 2 tablespoons of oil to Dutch oven and sauté onions and garlic for 3 minutes.
7. Return meat, bones and juices accumulated in bowl to Dutch oven.
8. Add your brew and simmer for 10 minutes.
9. Have a brew.
10. Add stock mixture, tomatoes, chile powder and cumin and simmer until lamb is tender, about 1 hour, 10 minutes.
11. Mix beans and limejuice into chili.
12. Season with salt and pepper.
13. Mix all of your avocado ingredients in a bowl just prior to serving.

Note: Lamb bones add flavor to the stock. Ask the butcher to bone a Leg of Lamb and cut the bones into 2 inch pieces and the meat into ¾ inch cubes, leaving off as much fat as possible (unless you're into that fat thing, which is okay). Serves 8.

Lamb and Black Bean Chili
Reprinted From Cooking Light Website
1-½ Lb. Ground Lamb; Lean
1 Cup Onion; Chopped
2 Cloves Garlic; Minced
2 Cans (14-½ Ounce) Whole Tomatoes; No-Salt Added
1 Cup Dry Red Wine
1 Tablespoon Chile powder
1-½ Teaspoons Cumin; Ground
1-½ Teaspoons Oregano; Dried
1 Teaspoon Sugar
¼ Teaspoon Salt
3 Cans (15 Ounce) Black Beans; Drained
¼ Teaspoon Hot Sauce
1 Sprig Cilantro; Optional

1. Combine first 3 ingredients in a Dutch oven; cook over medium heat until browned, stirring to crumble.
2. Drain in a colander; pat dry with paper towels.
3. Wipe drippings from pan with a paper towel; return mixture to pan.
4. Add tomatoes and next 6 ingredients (tomatoes through salt); bring to a boil. Cover, reduce heat, and simmer 2 hours; stir occasionally.
5. Stir in beans and hot sauce. Cover; simmer 30 minutes.

Garnish with cilantro sprigs, if desired.

Spicy Lamb Chili
1-¼ Lb. Lamb Shoulder; Boneless, ¾ Inch Cubes
As Needed All Purpose Flour
2 Tablespoons Olive Oil
½ Cup Shallots; Chopped
8 Cloves Garlic; Chopped
2 Tablespoons Sweet Hungarian Paprika
1 Teaspoon Hot Hungarian Paprika
1 Tablespoon Cumin; Ground
1-½ Cups Beef Broth; Canned
1 Teaspoon Instant Coffee Powder
1 Teaspoon Dark Brown Sugar
1 Can (15 Ounce) Pinquitos or Pinto Beans

1. Season lamb with salt and pepper.
2. Coat lamb with flour, shaking off excess.
3. Heat oil in heavy large saucepan over high heat. Add half of lamb and sauté until brown, about 8 minutes. Transfer lamb to bowl.
4. Repeat with remaining lamb, scraping up any browned bits. Reduce heat to medium-low.
5. Add shallots and garlic and sauté 5 minutes.
6. Return lamb and any juices to pan.
7. Mix in both paprikas and cumin, then broth, coffee and sugar. Bring chili to boil, scraping up browned bits. Reduce heat to low. Cover and simmer until lamb is tender, about 50 minutes.
8. Add beans; simmer uncovered until chili thickens, about 5 minutes.
Serve hot.

Pork

Chili (Spicy Pork)
David Knight
1 Lb. Pork; Ground
2 Large Onions; Chopped
4 Centiliters Garlic; Minced
1 Medium Pepper; Sweet Red, Chopped
1 Medium Pepper; Green, Chopped
1 Cup Celery; Chopped
2 Cans (13-¾ Ounce) Tomatoes; Diced, in Juice
1 Can Kidney Beans; Drained and Rinsed
1 Can (6 Ounce) Tomato Paste

¾ Cup Water
2 Teaspoons Brown Sugar
1 Teaspoon Oregano; Dried
1 Teaspoon Chile powder
¼ Teaspoon Red Pepper Flakes; Dried
¼ Teaspoon Cayenne Pepper
1 Dash Hot pepper sauce

1. In a Dutch oven, brown pork and onions until pork is no longer pink; drain.
2. Stir in the garlic, peppers and celery. Cook for 5 minutes.
3. Add remaining ingredients; bring to a boil. Reduce heat; cover and simmer for 45 minutes.

Makes about 2-½ quarts.

Navajo Pork Chili
3 Lb. Pork Shoulder; Cubed
2 Cans Stewed Tomatoes Lean Tomato Paste
3 Cups Water
2-½ Teaspoons Salt
2 Cans (16 Ounce) Whole Green Chiles
½ Teaspoon Oregano
3 Tablespoons Bacon Grease
1/3 Cup Flour
3 Medium Onions; Chopped
6 Cloves Garlic; Minced

1. Melt bacon grease in large skillet.
2. Put flour in gallon zip-lock bay and add ½ of pork.
3. Shake well to coat and brown in skillet.
4. Coat other ½ pork and add to skillet to brown. Remove meat and place in Dutch oven.
5. Add onions and garlic to skillet and cook until clear.
6. Add to Dutch oven.
7. Stir in remaining ingredients and bring to boil. Lower heat and simmer 45 minutes.

Pork And Black Bean Chile
2 Tablespoons Olive Oil
2 Medium Onions; Finely Chopped

2 Tablespoons Fresh Garlic; Finely Chopped
4 Lb. Pork Butt; Cubed to ½ Inch
6 Pods Jalapeño Peppers; Sliced Thin and Seeded-Opt
2 Pods Habañero Peppers; Finely Chopped
2 Tablespoons Cumin; Ground
1 Tablespoon Oregano
1 Tablespoon Thyme; Ground
1 Teaspoon Cayenne Pepper; Red
2 Tablespoons Sugar
1 Tablespoon Salt
4 Teaspoons Chicken Bouillon; Or 4 Cubes
6 Medium Tomatoes; Diced ½ Inch
5 Cans Beer
1 Lb. Black Beans; Cooked Package Instructions

1. Brown the pork in the oil and drain.
2. Place all ingredients except beans in a large pot (not aluminum) and simmer, covered, for two hours.
3. Add beans and simmer, uncovered, stirring occasionally, for another hour.
Serve with Tortillas and Monterey Jack or sharp cheddar cheese on the side.

Pork And Tomatillo Chili
1 Cup Orange Juice
1 Bottle (12 Ounce) Dark Beer
1 Lb. Tomatillos; Peeled and Quartered
1 Cup Peanut Oil; (We Use Less)
1 Head Garlic Peeled; (About 12 Large Cloves)
2 Lb. Pork, Boneless; Cut in ½ Inch Cubes
To Taste Salt and Pepper
2 Large Onions; Thinly Sliced
2 Lb. Roma Tomatoes; chopped
3 Pods Jalapeño Chiles; Diced
1 Teaspoon Hot Red Chile Peppers; Crushed (or to Taste)
1 Bunch Cilantro; Leaves Chopped
1 Can (16 Ounce) Black Beans; Rinsed and Drained
As Desired Cooked Rice
As Desired Avocado; Peeled and Sliced
As Desired Cilantro Leaves
As Desired Sour Cream

1. Combine orange juice, beer and tomatillos in large saucepan. Cook over medium heat about 20 minutes.
2. Heat peanut oil in large skillet.
3. Add garlic cloves and cook 2 minutes.
4. Stir in ½ of cubed pork and season to taste with salt and pepper.
5. Brown pork on all sides, remove pork with slotted spoon and add to tomatillos. Cook remaining pork in skillet.
6. Remove pork and garlic and add to tomatillos.
7. Pour off all but ¼ cup oil in skillet.
8. Add onions and lightly brown.
9. Add to tomatillo and pork mixture.
10. Mix in tomatoes, Jalapeños, crushed red pepper, and cilantro. Cover and cook over low heat 2 hours. (Chili can also be baked in 350-degree oven for 2 hours.)
11. Add beans. Cook covered, ½ hour more.
12. Adjust seasonings to taste.

Serve over rice, garnished with sliced avocado, sprigs of cilantro and Lime Sour Cream. Makes 6 servings.

Lime Sour Cream: ½ cup of sour cream mixed with grated zest and juice of 1 lime.

Pork Chile Con Carne With Sweet Potatoes
4 Lb. Pork Roast Rib End; Boned, Diced 2 Lb. 12 Ounces.
2 Tablespoons Paprika; Hot
¼ Teaspoon Cayenne Pepper
2 Teaspoons Oregano
1 Teaspoon Cumin Powder
1 Head Garlic; Peeled and Chopped
2 Pods Red Chile Peppers; Sliced
2 Tablespoons Soy Domenico; Tangerine Vinegar
1 Pods de Arbol Chiles
4 Medium Onions
2 Tablespoons Oil or Rendered Pork Fat
4 Ounces Smoked Bacon Rind; Or Ham Hock Skin
4 Medium Sweet Potatoes; Peeled and Diced
1 Cup Tomatoes; Crushed
To Cover Stock, Beer or Water; beer or water, to cover

1. Bone and dice the rib end of pork. You should get about 70% of the original weight. A 4 lb. roast gives about 2-¾ lb. of diced meat.

2. Put the dice of pork, the spices and chopped garlic into a bowl and pour the vinegar over them.
3. Mix well, and allow to marinate over night in the refrigerator.
4. Pour the oil or rendered fat over them and mix well.
5. Add the onions and chiles, and the diced potatoes. (I square off the potatoes to dice them and chop the trimmings fine, so they will over cook and thicken the sauce.) Put this in a 350 oven to brown.
6. When it is well browned, transfer to a heavy pot.
7. Deglaze the pan and add the chile de arbol and the bacon skin, and chopped tomatoes to the pot.
8. Cover the contents by half an inch or so with stock, beer or water, or any combination thereof.
9. Bring to the boil, and simmer slowly until the meat is spoon tender.
10. The sauce will thicken itself.
11. Re-season as required.
12. The spice heat of this recipe is mild to moderate.
13. Increase the chiles de arbol for more heat.

I brown the bones along with the meat, and add them to the pot, and remove them before serving. The gravy for this dish is thin. If you like it thicker, you can easily add more sweet potatoes.

Notes: Serve with Yellow Rice, or Yellow Rice and Beans. Plantanos maduros, ripe banana fritters, go very well.

Pork Chili
"Wild About Chili" by Dotty Griffith (1985)
1-½ Lb. Boneless Pork; Cut in 1-Inch Cubes
1 Tablespoon Vegetable Oil
1 Medium Onion; Chopped
1 Centiliter Garlic; Crushed
1 Tablespoon Flour
¼ Cup Chile powder
1 Tablespoon Cumin; Ground
1 Teaspoon Salt
½ Teaspoon Pepper
2 Cans (16 Ounce) Tomatoes, Whole-Peeled; Cut Up
1 Can (8 Ounce) Tomato Sauce

1. Cook pork in oil in medium pot until pork begins to brown.
2. Add onion and garlic and cook 5 minutes or until onion is transparent.
3. Stir in flour, chile powder, cumin, salt, and pepper.

4. Stir to coat meat.
5. Stir in tomatoes and tomato sauce. Simmer, uncovered, 1 hour or until pork is tender and stew is thickened.

Pork Chili With Artichoke

3 Lb. Pork Stew Meat; Trimmed of all Fat and Gristle
As Needed Flour; For Dredging
To Taste Salt
To Taste Pepper; Freshly Ground
1 Tablespoon Olive Oil
1 Large Onion; Chopped
30 Milliliters Garlic; Minced
1 Pod Chile Pepper; Fresh or Canned, Minced
2 Tablespoons Chile powder
1 Tablespoon Cumin; Ground
1 Leaf Bay Fresh or,
1 Teaspoon Bay Leaf; Dried
1 Teaspoon Thyme Leaves; Dried
1 Teaspoon Oregano Leaves; Dried
2 Tablespoons Flour
½ Cup White Wine
3 Cups Chicken Broth; Defatted
5 Medium Plum Tomatoes; Peeled and Chopped
1 Can (19 Ounce) Artichoke Hearts; Drained and Quartered
1 Can Cannelloni Beans; Or Small White Beans, Drained
1 Tablespoon Lemon Juice
¼ Cup Cilantro (Fresh); Minced

1. Dredge the pork in flour seasoned with salt and pepper and brown over high heat on all sides in the olive oil. Set aside.
2. Turn meat down to medium and add the onions. Cook until softened, about 1 minute.
3. Add 2 cloves of the garlic and the minced chile pepper and cook another 10 seconds.
4. Add the chile powder, cumin, bay leaf, basil, thyme, oregano, and flour, cooking another minute, stirring constantly.
5. Add the reserved meat and toss together.
6. Add the wine and heat to a boil, scraping any brown bits clinging to the bottom of the pan into the liquid with a wooden spoon.
7. Add the chicken broth and tomatoes, and simmer partly covered for 30 to

45 minutes, until the pork is tender.

8. Add the artichoke hearts, and white beans and simmer 10 minutes more.
9. Remove from the heat and stir in the lemon juice, cilantro and remaining clove of garlic.

Makes 6 servings.

Pork Mole Chile With Black Beans
Holiday Brochure Published for SuperFresh Supermarkets

2 Tablespoons Olive Oil
2 Medium Onions; Finely Chopped
1 Gram Garlic; Minced
4 Lb. Pork; Cut into Cubes
1/3 Cup Chile powder
1 Tablespoon Cumin; Ground + 1 Teaspoon
1 Tablespoon Oregano; + 1 Teaspoon
1 Teaspoon Cinnamon; Ground
1 Tablespoon Sugar
½ Teaspoon Cayenne Pepper
1 Can (14.5 Ounce) Tomatoes; Whole
4-½ Cups Chicken Broth
1-½ Squares Unsweetened Chocolate; Chopped
2 Cans (16.5 Ounce) Black Beans; Rinsed and Drained
2 Corn Tortillas; Torn into Bite-Size Piece

1. In a large, wide, non-aluminum saucepan, cook onions and garlic in a little oil, covered over low heat, until onions are soft. Remove to a bowl.
2. Add the pork to a little oil. Cook over moderate heat until no longer pink. Pour off drippings.
3. Stir in cooked onions, chile powder, cumin, oregano, cinnamon, sugar, and cayenne pepper. Cook, stirring for 5 minutes.
4. Break up tomatoes and add them with juice, broth, and chocolate.
5. Bring to a boil, lower heat and simmer, uncovering, stirring occasionally, for 1 hour 30 minutes.
6. Add beans and simmer 30 minutes longer or until chili has thickened. Stir in tortillas. Simmer until they have dissolved into sauce, about 10 minutes.

Notes: This chili has a very unique taste. My family of "Chili connoisseurs" loves it.

Roast Pork And Black Bean Chili
The Geezer Cookbook, Dwayne Pritchett
¼ Cup Bacon Drippings
2 Cloves Garlic; Minced
3 Tablespoons Chile powder
1/8 Teaspoon Cumin
4 Lb. Pork Loin; Bone-in
1 Lb. Black Beans; Dry
2 Tablespoons Olive Oil
½ Cup Salt Pork; Diced
2 Medium Onions; Chopped
3 Cloves Garlic; Minced
1 Pod Jalapeño Peppers; Minced
6 Ounces Packages Cooked Ham; Diced
2 Cans Beef Broth
1 Leaf Bay
1 Teaspoon Oregano
1 Teaspoon Red Wine Vinegar
2 Tablespoons Rum Flavoring
1 Can (4 Ounce) Mild Green Chiles; Chopped
1 Can (Large) Hot Chili Beans; With Gravy

1. In a Dutch oven, heat olive oil and add onions, garlic, Jalapeño, and carrots. Sauté, for 10 minutes.
2. Stir in oregano and pork cubes. Cook for 20 minutes, stirring occasionally.
3. Stir in chicken stock, 1 teaspoon of salt, tomatoes, and potatoes. Bring to boil, then lower and simmer 1-½ hours. Stir occasionally.
4. Add green chiles and beans to mixture and simmer another 30-45 minutes.

Spicy Garlic Chill
6 Lb. Pork Butt, Boneless; Cut in 1-Inch Cubes
2 Medium Yellow Onions; Peeled and Chopped
60 Centiliters Garlic; Chopped, Or Prepared
½ Cup Jalapeño Pepper; Finely Chopped
1 Tablespoon Dark Brown Sugar
1 Can (28 Ounce) Tomatoes; Crushed, Undrained
¼ Cup Molasses
2 Ounces Unsweetened Chocolate; Melted
¾ Cup Chile powder

¼ Cup Cumin
1 Tablespoon Basil Leaves; Dried
1 Tablespoon Oregano; Dried, Plus 2 Teaspoons.
2 Teaspoons Dry Mustard
1 Teaspoon Coriander; Ground
1 Teaspoon Black Pepper; Fresh Ground
½ Teaspoon Cloves; Ground
24 Ounces Dark Beer
3 Cups Boiling Water
¼ Cup Dry Red Wine; Or Cider Vinegar
3 Tablespoons Soy Sauce
1 Tablespoon Salt; Plus 2 Teaspoons.
¼ Cup Habañero Pepper Sauce; To Taste
As Desired Sour Cream
As Desired Cilantro; Chopped

1. The day before serving, in a Dutch oven over high heat, brown the pork until it is crispy and as much fat as possible has been rendered.
2. Remove the pork with a slotted spoon and drain it well in a colander linked with paper towels.
3. Leave ¼ cup of drippings in the Dutch oven; refrigerate the remainder.
4. Over medium-low heat, stir in onion, garlic and Jalapeño; sauté until vegetables are soft, about 10 minutes.
5. Stir in brown sugar; cook a few minutes more. Remove from heat.
6. Stir in tomatoes, molasses and melted chocolate; stir in spices and reserved pork.
7. Refrigerate overnight.
8. The next day, heat refrigerated chili mixture.
9. Remove solidified fat from reserved dripping; discard.
10. Stir remaining drippings into chili.
11. Stir in beer, boiling water, red wine or vinegar, soy sauce and salt. Bring to a boil, stirring occasionally, until meat is very tender and the flavors have blended thoroughly, about 1-½ hours.
12. Stir in Habañero sauce to taste, simmer, covered for ½ hour.

Garnish each serving with sour cream and chopped cilantro.

Spicy Pork And Black Bean Chili
The Gazette, 1/8/92
1 Lb. Black Beans
1-½ Lb. Pork, Boneless; Lean, Cubed

5 Cloves Garlic; minced
1 Tablespoon Paprika
2 Teaspoons Cumin; Ground
1 Can (28 Ounce) Tomatoes; Chopped
2 Tablespoons Red Wine Vinegar
1/3 Cup Parsley; Or Coriander, Chopped
To Taste Black Pepper; Freshly Ground
2 Tablespoons Olive Oil
2 Large Onions; Chopped
4 Teaspoons Chile powder; (Or More)
2 Teaspoons Oregano; Dried
½ Teaspoon Chile Pepper Flakes
2 Cups Chicken Stock
3 Medium Green Peppers; Diced
To Taste Salt

1. In a large pot, cover beans with water and bring to boil; cook for 2 minutes. Cover and remove from heat. Let stand 1 hour.
2. Drain liquid and cover with 8 cups of cold water. Bring to a boil, reduce heat and let simmer for about 1-½ hours or until beans are tender. Drain and reserve.
3. Meanwhile, heat oil in a large saucepan on high heat and brown meat cubes on all sides. Remove from pan and set aside.
4. Add onions and garlic to pan; cook on medium heat until tender about 5 minutes.
5. Add chile powder, paprika, oregano, cumin and chile pepper flakes; cook, stirring for 1 minute.
6. Return meat to pan along with tomatoes, including juice, stock and vinegar. Bring to boil, let simmer, partly covered, for 1-½ hours or until meat is tender.
7. Add beans and peppers; season with salt and pepper. Cover and cook 15 minutes more or until peppers are tender.

Add chopped parsley or chopped coriander.

Poultry

Chicken And Sausage Chili
Pat Dailey, Staff Writer, Chicago Tribune 11/11/93.
¼ Cup Chile powder
4 Teaspoons Cumin; Ground
2 Teaspoons Pure Ground Chile

1-½ Teaspoons Salt
¼ Cup Vegetable Oil
1 Lb. Smoked Sausage; Such as Andouille
2 Whole Chicken Breast, Boneless; Skinned, Cut into Pieces
2 Large White Onions; Diced
3 Cloves Garlic; Minced
6 Large Tomatillos; Husked and Diced
4 Pods Anaheim Chiles; Or Poblano Chiles
1 Or 2 Green Bell Peppers; Diced
2 Small Red Bell Peppers; Diced
2 Pods Jalapeño Chiles; Minced
2 Cans (28 Ounce) Tomatoes; Chopped
1 Cup Beef Broth; Or Chicken Broth (1 or 2)
1/3 Cup Tomato Paste
4 Cans (16 Ounce) Mix of Pinto, Black and Navy Beans; Rinsed

1. Combine chile powder, cumin, ground chile and salt in a small dish; set aside.
2. Heat oil in a large Dutch oven.
3. Add sausage and chicken; cook until chicken is no longer pink; remove with a slotted spoon and set aside.
4. Add onion, garlic and half of reserved seasoning mixture. Cook over medium heat until onions begin to soften, about 5 minutes.
5. Add tomatillos, peppers, Jalapeño, tomatoes and their liquid, 1 cup of broth and tomato paste; heat to a boil. Reduce heat and add chicken, sausage and beans. Cook gently, partially covered, for 30 minutes.
6. Add remaining spice mixture; cook 5 more minutes, adding additional broth as needed.

Chicken Chili
1 Lb. Cannelloni Beans; Or Other Large White Bean
3 Cloves Garlic; Crushed
1 Medium-Large Onion; Chopped (1 cup or more)
2 Teaspoons Basil; Dried
1 Tablespoon Red Chile Pepper; Dried
8 Cups Chicken Stock
1 Cup Butter
3 Cups Chicken; Skinless and Boneless, Cook
1 Cup Cilantro (Fresh); Chopped
1 Teaspoon Salt

1 Tablespoon Chile powder
1 Teaspoon Cloves; Ground
1 Can (4 Ounce) Green Chile Peppers; Diced

1. Rinse beans.
2. Put first six ingredients in the order listed into slow cooking pot. Adjust to lowest heat setting and leave for eight hours or until beans are very tender. (In a pot on the stovetop this will only take about four hours on lowest heat and would require two or three gentle stirrings during cooking.)
3. When beans are tender, melt butter in a large pan.
4. Add chicken and stir-fry for 3-4 minutes.
5. Add remaining ingredients to chicken and continue cooking until chicken is done.
6. Add chicken mixture to bean pot. Stir gently.

Serve in large bowls garnished with a dollop of sour cream or a sprig of fresh cilantro.

Accompany with tortilla chips or hot crusty French bread, and a small salad.

Your favorite ice cream will make the best dessert after this spicy chili. Chef says: 3-4 cups of raw chicken equals approximately 5-6 skinless, boneless, chicken breast portions. This chili is really good the day that you make it, but even better the next day. So make it a day ahead. It can sometimes be difficult to obtain specialty beans like the cannelloni beans asked for in this recipe. Great Northern or other large white beans actually would be a fine substitute. But it always makes me feel like I'm cooking up something special when I use special beans. If you can't find them at your store, here is one of my favorite sources, a great place to find dried beans, grains, flours, herbs and spices: Phipps Country (Pescadero, CA) -- 800-279-0889.

Chicken Pumpkin Chili
Framingham, MA Newcomers Club From: Date: 05/28
2 Tablespoons Olive Oil
2 Cups Onion; Chopped
2 Cups Red Bell Pepper; Chopped
3 Tablespoons Jalapeño Peppers; Minced
1 Clove Garlic; Minced
1 Cup Beer
1 Cup Chicken Broth

¼ Cup Ripe Olives; Sliced
3 Tablespoons Chile powder
1 Teaspoon Coriander; Ground
½ Teaspoon Salt
1 Can (29 Ounce) Tomatoes; With Juice, Chopped
1 Lb. Chicken Breast; Skinless and Boneless/Diced
2 Cups Pumpkin or Butternut Squash; Peeled, Cubed and Cooked
2 Tablespoons Cilantro (Fresh)
1 Tablespoon Cocoa Powder
1 Can (16 Ounce) Pinto Beans; Drained
6 Tablespoons Scallions; Sliced
1-½ Ounces Cheddar Cheese; Shredded
6 Tablespoons Sour Cream

1. Heat the oil in a Dutch oven over medium heat. Sauté the onions until lightly browned-about 8 minutes.
2. Add the bell pepper, Jalapeño and garlic. Sauté for 5 minutes more.
3. Add the beer, broth, olives, chile powder, coriander, salt, tomatoes and chicken. Bring the mixture to a boil, reduce the heat, cover partially and simmer for 15 minutes.
4. Stir in the pumpkin, cilantro, cocoa and beans. Cook for 5 minutes.
Serve in individual bowls, topped with the cheese, sour cream and scallions. Try this with the quantities of Jalapeño, garlic, coriander and cilantro doubled.

Chunky Chicken Chili
Connie Rizzo
1 Lb. Chicken Breast; Cut into Pieces
1 Cup Onion; Chopped
½ Cup Celery; Sliced
½ Cup Carrot; Sliced
2 Cloves Garlic; Minced
1 Cup Tomato Salsa; Fresh
1 Can (28 Ounce) Tomatoes
1 Can (28 Ounce) Water
3 Teaspoons Chile powder
½ Teaspoon Cumin
1/3 Bag Garbanzo Beans; Soaked
1 Medium Green Bell Pepper; Chopped
4 Each Chicken Bouillon Cubes Or

2 Cans Chicken Broth
To Taste Salt and Pepper

1. Brown chicken, onions and garlic.
2. Add all tomatoes, water, and beans and simmer 30 minutes.
3. Add other ingredients and simmer until beans and vegetables are tender.

Contest Chili
½ Package Holly Farms Chicken Breast Nuggets
1 Medium Onion; Chopped
1 Clove Garlic, Large; Minced Or
2 Cloves Garlic, Small; Minced
1 Lb. Ground Turkey; Uncooked
1 Can (16 Ounce) Tomatoes (Stewed)
1 Can (6 Ounce) Tomato Paste
1 Can (10 Ounce) Old El Paso Tomatoes and Green Chiles
1 Tablespoon Spice Islands Chili Con Carne Seasoning; Up to 2
1 Teaspoon Chile powder
1 Leaf Bay
½ Teaspoon Seasoned Salt; Low Salt
½ Teaspoon Oregano; Dried
½ Teaspoon Hot Paprika
½ Teaspoon Curry Powder; Home Mixed
½ Teaspoon Cayenne Pepper
½ Teaspoon Red Pepper; Crushed
½ Teaspoon Black Pepper
½ Teaspoon Mrs. Dash
¼ Teaspoon Cumin; Ground
2 Cups Water

1. Dice chicken into small pieces and spray Dutch oven with Pam. Brown chicken and set aside.
2. Re-spray if necessary and add onions, cooking until tender.
3. Stir in turkey and garlic; cook until turkey is brown, breaking up large pieces with fork.
4. Return chicken to Dutch oven and stir in all remaining ingredients. Bring to a boil on high; immediately reduce heat and simmer on low, uncovered, about 1 hour.

Serve topped with dollop of Mock Sour Cream and shredded low-fat Cheddar cheese, if desired. Makes ½ gallon.

Dark Chicken Chili
1 Tablespoon Peanut Oil
2 Pods Ancho Chile Peppers
1 Pod Chipotle Chile Pepper; Or Another Smoked Chili Pepper
1 Cup Beef Broth; Defatted
2 Medium Onions; Finely Chopped
2 Lb. Chicken Meat; Skinless and Boneless/Diced
40 Milliliters Garlic; Minced
2 Teaspoons Cumin Seeds; Ground
1 Teaspoon Oregano; Dried
1 Teaspoon Thyme; Dried
½ Teaspoon Cinnamon; Ground
1 Cup Beer; Dark
1 Tablespoon Tomato Paste
To Taste Salt
To Taste Black Pepper; Finely Ground

1. In a heavy skillet, heat the oil until barely hot. Roast the pepper in the hot oil for 1 minute or less, just until they brown lightly. Remove the peppers from the oil and cool.
2. Let oil remain in skillet.
3. Stem and seed the cooked peppers, break into small pieces and grind in blender or spice grinder.
4. Bring the broth to a boil and add the ground chiles.
5. Remove from the heat and allow to steep while you proceed with the recipe.
6. Add the onion to the oil remaining in skillet. Cook until lightly browned.
7. Add the chicken and stir until the meat loses its raw look.
8. Add the garlic, cumin, oregano, thyme, cinnamon, and stir for another 10 seconds.
9. Add the broth chili mixture, beer and tomato paste. Bring to a boil and simmer 15 minutes.
10. Season to taste with salt and pepper.
11. Adjust seasoning and serve immediately over warm rice and/or beans.
Makes 6 servings.

Dove's Nest White Chili
3 Tablespoons Olive Oil
1 Medium Onion; Chopped
3 Cloves Garlic; Minced

2-½ Cups Tomatoes; Ripe, Chopped
6 Whole Tomatillos; Diced
1 Pod Jalapeño Chile Peppers; Seeded and Minced
2 Cups Chicken Stock
1 Cup Green Chiles; Chopped (17 Ounces)
2 Cups Chicken; Cooked, Chopped
½ Teaspoon Oregano
½ Teaspoon Cumin
4 Tablespoons Cilantro (Fresh); Chopped
2 Cans (19 Ounce) Cannelloni Beans; With Liquid
1 Tablespoon Lime Juice; Fresh

1. In a large pot, heat olive oil over medium-high heat.
2. Add onion and cook until onion begins to soften, 3-5 minutes.
3. Add garlic and cook 1-2 minutes longer. Do not brown.
4. Add tomatoes, tomatillos and Jalapeño, cook until tomatillos are soft.
5. Add chicken stock, green chiles, cooked chicken, oregano, cumin, cilantro, beans and limejuice.
6. Heat through and season to taste with salt and pepper.

Farm Hands Fat-Free Chili
Andrew Meurer, Cincinnati, OH
2 Lb. Honeysuckle White Ground Turkey
4 Cloves Garlic; Minced
1 Tablespoon Fresh Ginger Root
1 Tablespoon Red Pepper; Crushed
¼ Cup Sesame Oil
2 Medium Green Bell Peppers
1 Can (14 Ounce) Kidney Beans
1 Can (12 Ounce) Tomato Paste
1 Can (16 Ounce) Tomatoes; Crushed
1 Large Sweet Onion
1 Tablespoon Basil
3 Tablespoons Cayenne Pepper
2 Tablespoons Pepper; Ground
¼ Cup Worcestershire Sauce
¼ Cup Hot Sauce; Frank's Louisiana
2 Tablespoons Paprika
2 Cups Water
1 Bottle Beer; For Cook Or Chili

1. Pan fry at high heat, garlic, red pepper, and ginger for 2 minutes.
2. Add turkey.
3. Stir into pan's ingredients, brown, and drain. Do not cover.
4. In a large pot (2-3 quart) add browned turkey, tomato paste, crushed tomatoes, all remaining spices, sliced green pepper, chopped onion, and beans.
5. Add two cups of water, bring to boil, stirring frequently. Simmer covered for 1 hour at low heat (add beer now or drink it).
6. Ready to serve with grated sharp cheddar cheese and oyster crackers.
Winner in the Ground Turkey Competition

Fast Chicken Chili
1 Tablespoon Vegetable Oil
1 Medium Onion; Thinly Sliced, About 1 Cup
1 Large Red Or Yellow Bell Pepper; Cored, Seeded and Coarse Chopped
3 Cloves Garlic; Crushed
1 Tablespoon Chile powder
1 Teaspoon Cumin; Ground
1 Can (28 Ounce) Tomatoes; Crushed
1 Can (19 Ounce) White (Cannelloni) Kidney Beans; Rinsed and Drained
1 Can (19 Ounce) Black Beans; Rinsed and Drained
1 Package (10 Ounce) Smoked Chicken; Cooked
1 Tablespoon Jalapeño Chile Peppers; Or 2; Chopped
½ Cup Chicken Broth; Reduced Sodium or
½ Cup Water; Optional
4 Large Corn Muffins; Store Bought, Warmed, Optional
2 Tablespoons Cilantro (Fresh); Chopped, Optional

1. In 5-quart Dutch oven over medium-high heat, heat oil; add onion, bell pepper, and garlic; cook 2 to 3 minutes, stirring frequently until vegetables are softened. Stir in chile powder and cumin; cook 1 to 2 minutes, stirring to coat thoroughly with spices.
2. Add tomatoes, white and black beans, chicken, pickled Jalapeños, and chicken broth if necessary for moistness.
3. Cook, covered, about 10 minutes until mixture is heated through and flavors are blended, uncovering occasionally to stir.
Split warmed corn muffins, if using, in half; spoon chili over to serve. Sprinkle with chopped cilantro, if desired. Makes 4 servings.

Gobbledy Good Chili
Gary and Tracey Dean, Pryor, OK.
1 Each Honeysuckle White Turkey; 8 to 14 Lb. Traditionally
3 Lb. Ground Honeysuckle White Turkey
1 Pod Anaheim Chile Peppers; And/or
1 Pod Red Chile Pepper; Whole (Floaters)
1 Large Onion; Finely Chopped
1 Tablespoon Olive Oil; Or Health Nuts
¼ Cup Turkey or Chicken Broth
1 Can (28 Ounce) Tomatoes; Cheap Ones are OK
1 Can (15 Ounce) Tomato Sauce
2 Cloves Garlic; Pressed or Fine Chopped
½ Fresh Lime Juice; Other Half for Tequila
1 Tablespoon Lea & Perrins Worcestershire Sauce; Or Cheap Substitute
½ Teaspoon Tabasco Sauce; Accept no Substitutes
½ Teaspoon White Pepper; Ground
¼ Teaspoon Cayenne Pepper
3 Tablespoons Williams Chili powder; Or Cheap Substitute To Taste
1 Teaspoon Celery Salt
1 Teaspoon Cumin; Ground
1-½ Teaspoons Cilantro (Fresh); Or Dried, Finely Chopped
2-½ Tablespoons Brown Sugar
3 Ounces Quality Tequila; (Worm Optional)

1. Using your Grandmother's Family Recipe, roast an 8 to 14 lb. Honeysuckle White Turkey, and serve no more than ½ of same in the traditional manner.
2. If guests are present, do not offer "leftovers" to take home.
3. Get all the good leftover turkey meat, hopefully 3 to 4 lbs, and put it in a Ziploc bag until tomorrow.
4. The next day, cut the turkey (less skin and bones) into ¼ inch cubes.
5. If you are a purist, hand cube-if you're lazy (or time disadvantaged), give it a couple of spins in the food processor until it kind of looks cubed, "OK" to you.
6. Since you decided to use the food processor, dump the turkey in a bowl, and finely chop the onion until it looks like mush. (The food processor saves tears.)
7. Sauté (that's French for cook) the onion mush with the garlic in a little olive oil for a few minutes while you do other stuff.
8. Since the food processor is already dirty, add the can of whole tomatoes

801

and turn it into tomato juice.

9. Dump all the other stuff (except Tequila which you should taste to see if OK) into the pan with the onions.

10. Simmer (that's French for cook real slow) for about an hour.

11. Add a little water, wine, or other appropriate liquid if too thick, and add spices to taste. Just before serving, add 1 ounce of tequila (if you have any left) and stir around in the pot.

12. Bring the whole peppers to the top as "floaters" to enhance the "presentation" of the pot of Gobbledygood.

13. If it doesn't taste quite right, add catsup (Ketchup), which will fix the taste of anything. Serve in the traditional manner.

Winners in the Chopped Turkey Competition.

Ground Turkey and Black-Bean Chili

1 Tablespoon Oil
2 Cups Red Pepper; Finely Chopped
1 Cup Onion; Chopped
1/2 Cup Carrot; Finely Chopped
2 Cloves Garlic; Minced, Large
4 Teaspoons Chile powder
2 Teaspoons Cumin; Ground
1 Lb. Turkey Breast; Ground
2 Cans (15 Ounce) Black Beans; Rinsed and Drained
3 Cups Chicken Broth; Canned

1. Heat oil in large saucepan or Dutch oven over medium heat.
2. Add pepper, onion, carrot and garlic; sauté until tender, about 12 minutes.
3. Add chile powder and cumin; stir to blend. Increase heat to med high and add turkey; break up with spoon and sauté until turkey is no longer pink, about 3 minutes.
4. Add beans, broth and tomato paste and bring to boil. Reduce heat and simmer chili until liquid thickens, stirring occasionally, about 1 hour.
5. Season with salt and pepper.

Heart Healthy Turkey Black Bean Chili

2 Lb. Turkey; Ground
2 Cloves Garlic; Chopped
2 Teaspoons Olive Oil
½ Cup Red Onion
¼ Cup Red Bell Pepper

¼ Cup Yellow Bell Pepper
¼ Cup Carrot; Chopped
2 Pods Jalapeño Chile Peppers; Seeded and Chopped
2 Cups Black Beans, Cooked; Drained and Rinsed if Cannelloni
2 Tablespoons Cilantro
2 Tablespoons Lime Juice; Fresh

1. Sauté ground turkey in skillet with olive oil until browned.
2. Add remaining vegetables. Cook mixture, stirring often until vegetables are softened.
3. Stir in cooked black beans, cilantro, lime juice. Cook until heated through.
4. Add salt and pepper to taste.

Garnish: Chopped tomatoes, non-fat sour cream and cilantro sprigs.

Hearty Turkey Chili
1 Small Onion; Finely Chopped
1 Clove Garlic; Finely Chopped
1 Tablespoon Vegetable Oil
½ Lb. Ground Turkey, Prepared; Uncooked
1 Can Plum Tomatoes
1 Tablespoon Chile powder; Ground
1 Teaspoon All-Purpose Flour
1 Teaspoon Cumin; Ground
¼ Teaspoon Ginger; Ground
1/8 Teaspoon Salt
1/8 Teaspoon Pepper
½ Can Red Kidney Beans; Undrained

1. Sauté onion and garlic in oil in medium size saucepan until softened, 3 minutes.
2. Stir in turkey; cook until no pink remains and meat begins to brown.
3. Stir in tomatoes with their juices, chile powder, flour, cumin, ginger, salt and pepper. Bring to boiling. Lower heat, cover, and simmer for 25 to 30 minutes.
4. Stir in beans and heat.

Hot Time in the Old House Tonight Chili
3 Tablespoons Sunflower or Corn Oil
2 Large Onions; Chopped
2 Cloves Garlic; Minced

1 Lb. Honeysuckle White Ground Turkey
2 Tablespoons Chile powder
½ Teaspoon Red Chile Peppers; Ground or Flakes
2 Cans (16 Ounce) Del Monte Mexican Stewed Tomatoes
2 Cans (16 Ounce) Del Monte Original Stewed Tomatoes
¼ Cup Pace Medium Picante Salsa
¼ Cup Cilantro; Fresh, Chopped

1. Heat oil medium high in large pot.
2. Add onions and garlic; cook till wilted.
3. Add turkey; cook, breaking up, until all is brown.
4. Add chile powder and chile pepper; stir.
5. Add stewed tomatoes, salsa, and cilantro. Heat to boil and then reduce heat to simmer. Cook about one hour until flavors are blended.
6. Taste during cooking to adjust seasoning-you may want to add more hot pepper!

Leftover Turkey: Pumpkin Bean Turkey Chili
Anita A. Matejka
2 Cloves Garlic; Minced
1 Cup Bell Peppers; Chopped
1-½ Teaspoons Oregano
1-½ Teaspoons Cumin
1-½ Teaspoons Chile powder
1 Teaspoon Salt
½ Teaspoon Black Pepper
14-½ Ounces Chicken Broth
15-½ Ounces Great Northern Beans; Drained and Washed
16 Ounces Dark Red Kidney Beans; Drained and Washed
14-½ Ounces Tomatoes; Crushed, Undrained
16 Ounces Pumpkin
2-½ Cups Turkey Light Meat; Skinless, Cooked and Cubed
½ Cup Water

1. Heat oil in a saucepan over medium heat. Add onions, garlic, bell peppers, oregano, cumin, chile powder, salt, and black pepper; cook until vegetables are tender.
2. Stir in chicken broth, beans, tomatoes, pumpkin, turkey, and water. Bring to a boil, stirring occasionally.
3. Simmer 45 minutes over low heat.

Linda Purl's Duck Chili With Winter Vegetables
Linda Purl
As Needed Vegetable Oil
4 Lb. Duckling
2 Tablespoons Olive Oil
1 Lb. Onion; Finely Chopped
1 Medium Turnip; Grated
6 Medium Carrots; Grated
1 Can (16 Ounce) Tomatoes; Crushed
12 Ounces Chicken Broth
1 Tablespoon Chile powder; To Taste
1 Teaspoon Cumin; To Taste
1 Can (16 Ounce) Kidney Beans
1 Lb. Peas; Frozen or Canned
2 Medium Green Peppers; Seeded and Diced
2 Medium Red Peppers; Seeded and Diced
As Desired Rice; Cooked

1. Preheat oven to 350 F.
2. Coat a small roasting pan with vegetable oil.
3. Place duckling in pan and cook for 3 hours.
4. Allow duck to cool.
5. Separate meat from bones and dice.
6. Place in large pot with olive oil, onions, turnip and carrots, sauté for 15 minutes.
7. Add remaining ingredients and let simmer for 15 minutes.
Serve over rice.
   Enjoy!

Martin's Turkey Chili
1 Cup Black Beans
3 Tablespoons Olive Oil
1 Single Turkey Breast; Skinned (Half Breast)
4 Medium Yellow Onions; Chopped
4 Cloves Garlic; Minced
3 Ribs Celery; Sliced
1 Small Green Pepper; Chopped
1 Can (28 Ounce) Tomatoes; Crushed
½ Cup Water
4 Tablespoons Chile powder

½ Teaspoon Cayenne Pepper
1 Teaspoon Cumin Seeds; Whole

1. Soak the beans overnight in water to cover generously. Drain and rinse briefly.
2. Heat the oil in a large, heavy bottom pot over medium high heat.
3. When hot, brown the turkey breast well on all sides. Remove and set aside.
4. Add the onions, garlic, celery, and green pepper. Sauté, stirring frequently, until the vegetables are soft, 5-7 minutes.
5. Add the beans, tomatoes, water, chile powder, cayenne, and the turkey breast.
6. Heat until the pot starts bubbling, then reduce heat to a slow simmer, partially cover, and simmer for 1-½ hour. Stir occasionally, watching carefully that the bottom does not start to stick.
7. Remove the turkey breast, remove the bone, and coarsely shred the meat with two forks (hold the meat with one fork, tear with the grain with the other).
8. Return the meat to the pot. Heat a heavy bottom skillet over low heat.
9. Add the whole cumin seed and toast 2-3 minutes, shaking the pan occasionally, until lightly brown and aromatic. Remove from heat.
10. Coarsely crush the cumin in a mortar and pestle or with a rolling pin. Add to the pot. Cook an additional one hour, or until the beans are tender.

For a traditional approach, top with the cheese and sour cream, for the modern/healthy approach, top with the avocado.

Overnight Turkey Chili (No Beans)
2 Turkey Thighs; Skinned
1 Medium Onion; Chopped and Cubed
1 Clove Garlic; Minced
8 Ounces Tomatoes; Sliced, Undrained
¼ Cup Cilantro (Fresh); Chopped
2 Medium Green Peppers; Seeded
1 Tablespoon Cocoa Powder; Plain
2 Teaspoons Cumin Seeds
3 Pods Jalapeño Chile Peppers; Chopped
½ Teaspoon Cumin; Ground Or
1 Teaspoon Chile powder

Combine ingredients in a crock-pot. Cover and cook for 14 to 16 hrs. at low heat.

Note: Double the recipe to make 8 servings, and freeze extras in single serving portions if desired.

Paul's Camper Chili
Diana Devereaux
2 Cans (16 Ounce) Red Kidney Beans
2 Cans (16 Ounce) Tomatoes (Stewed)
1 Lb. Turkey; Ground
1 Small Onion; Chopped
1 Small Green Pepper; Chopped
1 Tablespoon Cooking Oil
1 Teaspoon Chile powder; To Taste

1. Brown onion in oil. Add meat. Brown and cook until almost done. Drain, if necessary.
2. Add remaining ingredients. Cook on low until hot through.
3. Taste and adjust chile powder if needed.

Picante Chicken Chili
1 Medium Onion; Chopped
3 Cloves Garlic; Minced
1 Tablespoon Vegetable Oil
½ Lb. Chicken Breast, Boneless, Skinless
2 Teaspoons Sage; Or 3 Teaspoons as Desired
¼ Teaspoon Salt
¾ Cup Picante Sauce
1 Can (16 Ounce) Kidney or Pinto Beans
¼ Cup Dry Vermouth
1 Leaf Bay
1 Medium Green or Red Bell Pepper; Cut in ½ Inch Pieces
1 Large Tomato; Seeded and Coarsely Chopped
As Desired Cilantro; Chopped
As Desired Sour Cream
As Desired Cheddar Cheese; Shredded

1. Cook onion and garlic in oil in large saucepan or Dutch oven until tender, about 4 minutes.

2. Stir in chicken; cook until chicken is no longer pink, stirring constantly.
3. Sprinkle sage, cumin and salt over chicken; cook and stir 1 minute.
4. Stir in Picante sauce, beans, vermouth and bay leaf. Bring to a boil; reduce heat. Cover and simmer 10 minutes.
5. Stir in green pepper and tomato; continue to simmer uncovered 10 minutes.
6. Discard bay leaf.

Ladle into bowls; top as desired and serve with additional picante sauce.

Makes 4 servings, about 5 cups chili. Uniquely flavored with sage, vermouth and bay leaf, this prize-winning chili takes kindly to a wide range of favorite chili toppings. Great served over or under rice, too!

Quick Spicy Turkey Chili

½ Lb. Ground Turkey
1 Teaspoon Oil
1 Medium Onion; Diced
1 Teaspoon Cumin; Ground
2 Cloves Garlic; Minced
1-½ Tablespoons Chile powder
1 Leaf Bay
½ Teaspoon Cinnamon; Ground
½ Teaspoon Allspice; Ground
1 Pod Jalapeño; Minced, Seed and Remove Membrane
1 Tablespoon Unsweetened Cocoa Powder
½ Tablespoon Worcestershire Sauce
1 Tablespoon White Vinegar
1 Teaspoon Oregano, Dried
1 Can (14 Ounce) Tomatoes (Stewed); 14 oz
¾ Cup Water; Or Less, See Note
½ Teaspoon Salt
1 Can (16 Ounce) Favorite Chili Beans; Pink, Red, Pinto, Etc.

This is a quick recipe that produces a slightly hot, very aromatic chili. I liked it very much.

1. Brown the turkey in a skillet. Transfer to a 3-quart pot.
2. Brown the onion in the oil (yes, in the skillet). Transfer to the pot.
3. Add all other ingredients except the beans to the pot and simmer, covered, for 20 minutes, stirring occasionally, adding a little more water if things dry out too much.

4. Drain the beans (or not, as you choose) and add them to the pot. Simmer another 10 minutes.

Speedy Sausage Chili
½ Lb. Turkey Sausage; Spicy
1 Can Tomato Soup
2 Teaspoons Chile powder
¼ Teaspoon Oregano; Dried
1 Dash Worcestershire Sauce
1 Can Beans, Black; Drained

1. Grill the sausages under the broiler until browned. Drain and discard any melted fat.
2. Combine with remaining ingredients in a saucepan. Simmer 5 minutes, until heated through.

Spicy Chili
Art and Doris Guyer
2 Lb. Ground Turkey; (2 to 3)
4 Medium Onions; Or Large
2 Heads Garlic
1 Medium Green Pepper
2 Cans (Small) Mushroom; Unsalted
2 Jars Hot Salsa (Or Your Own)
5 Cans Tomatoes; Whole, Unsalted
5 Cans Kidney Beans
4 Can-Small Tomato Sauce
2 Cans (Medium) Tomato Paste
½ Cup Kahlua or Bourbon
2 Cups Cilantro; Fresh
Jalapeño Peppers (To Taste)
SPICES:
3 Tablespoons Parsley
5 Tablespoons Cumin; Ground
1 Teaspoon Cinnamon; Ground
1 Tablespoon Basil
2 Teaspoons Cayenne
3 Tablespoons Chile powder
1 Tablespoon Oregano
3 Tablespoons Garlic Powder

1 Tablespoon Black Pepper
2 Tablespoons Hot Sauce

1. Brown turkey, drain and place in a large cooking pot.
2. Roughly chop onions and green pepper in food processor.
3. Finely chop garlic, cilantro, and Jalapeño peppers.
4. Sauté chopped vegetables and add to pot.
5. Add remaining ingredients (excluding spices) to pot. Cook over medium heat for about ½ hour, stirring frequently.
6. Add spices, one at a time, stirring well between each addition. Simmer for another ½ hour, stirring frequently.
7. Adjust spices to taste. Simmer for another ½ hour, stirring frequently.
8. Again adjust spices to taste.

This recipe makes about 10 quarts of mildly spiced chili and serves about 20 people.

Serve plain or over spaghetti, baked potato or rice, with grated low-fat cheese and chopped onions on the side. Tortilla chips or browned chunks of Italian bread are also good on the side. The chili freezes well. Freeze in plastic quart containers for quick 2 or 3 person meals. You probably will want to increase the "heat." I do too, but the grandkids can't take it.

Spicy Turkey Chili
7 Ounces Turkey; Ground
½ Cup Onion; Chopped
1 Cup Italian Tomatoes; Canned/Drained and Chopped
½ Cup Tomato Sauce
2 Teaspoons Chile powder
1 Teaspoon Worcestershire Sauce
1 Teaspoon White Wine Vinegar
1 Leaf Bay
¼ Teaspoon Salt
¼ Teaspoon Garlic Powder
1/8 Teaspoon Cinnamon
1/8 Teaspoon Allspice
1/8 Teaspoon Red Pepper; Crushed

1. Spray 3-quart saucepan with nonstick spray and heat over medium-high heat; add turkey and onion, and using back of a wooden spoon to crumble meat, cook, stirring occasionally, until turkey is browned, about 5 minutes.

2. Add remaining ingredients and stir well to combine.
3. Reduce heat to low and let simmer, stirring occasionally, until chili is thick, about 25 to 30 minutes.
4. Remove bay leaf before serving.

May be frozen for future use--just thaw and reheat. Makes two servings, each of which provides: 2-½ Protein and 2-½ Vegetables.

Super Bowl Chili-Chicken Stew
3 Whole Chicken Breasts; Split, Boned and Skinned
1 Cup Onion; Chopped
1 Medium Green Pepper; Chopped
2 Cloves Garlic; Minced
2 Tablespoons Vegetable Oil
2 Cans (14-1/2 Ounce) Tomatoes (Stewed)
1 Can (15-1/2 Ounce) Pinto Beans; Drained
2/3 Cup Picante Sauce; As Desired, Up to 3/4
1 Teaspoon Chile powder
1 Teaspoon Cumin; Ground
½ Teaspoon Salt

1. Cut chicken into 1-inch pieces.
2. Cook with onion, green pepper and garlic in oil in Dutch oven until chicken loses its pink color.
3. Add tomatoes, beans, picante sauce, chile powder, cumin and salt; simmer 20 minutes.
4. Ladle into bowls; top with cheese, onion, avocado, sour cream and more Picante sauce as desired.

Makes 6 to 8 servings, about 9 cups.

Optional Toppings: Shredded Cheddar cheese, green onion slices, diced avocado and sour cream.

Tex-Mex Turkey Chili-Southern
The Tampa Tribune, February 1993
2 Turkey Thighs
2 Each Chile powder; Or More
1 Cup Boiling Water
1-½ Teaspoons Cumin
28 Ounces Tomatoes; With Liquid
½ Teaspoon Oregano; Dried
2 Large Onions; Chopped

1 Large Salt and Pepper; Fresh Ground
3 Medium Green Peppers; Seeded and Chopped
¼ Cup Extra Virgin Olive Oil
2 Cloves Garlic; Minced
As Desired Cheddar Cheese; Or Jack Cheese, Optional

1. Put turkey thighs on a chopping board; slice meat away from the bones.
2. Cut meat in 1-inch cubes and discard skin.
3. Spray a non-stick pot (or pressure cooker) with cooking spray for no-fat frying.
4. Add cubed meat. Brown over moderate heat in its own melted fat (no added oil needed). Remove from flame and stir boiling water into juices in pot.
5. Pour liquid into a cup, set aside until fat rises to surface.
6. With a bulb-type baster, skim off and discard surface fat.
7. Return fat-skimmed liquid to pot. (Bones may be added for flavor and removed before serving.)
8. Add all remaining ingredients except cheese. Cover; simmer over low heat until tender, about 1 hour in conventional pot, or 20 minutes in pressure cooker.
9. Uncover, continue to simmer until most of the liquid evaporates and chili is thick.

Spoon into serving dish. Top with cheese.

The Best Turkey Chili Ever
Karen Monahan
2 Lb. Turkey; Ground
1 Medium Onion; Chopped
1 Clove Garlic; Chopped
3 Tablespoons Chile powder
1 Can (Small) Tomatoes; Crushed, Or Fresh Equivalent
1 Can Beef Broth
1 Can Cannelloni or Kidney, Etc. Beans; Up to 2
To Taste Salt
To Taste Cayenne Pepper; Or
To Taste Red Pepper; Crushed

1. Brown meat.
2. Add onion and garlic.
3. When transparent, add chile powder. Cook about 5 minutes over medium

heat.
4. Add remaining ingredients. Simmer, uncovered approximately 2 hours, stirring occasionally.

Top with Cheddar or Jack Cheese and serve with fresh bread and butter.

Comments: You can substitute Ground beef for the turkey, but drain off grease. This is supposed to serve 4-6 but in our house it serves 2-3!

Turkey Chili

2 Cans (Medium) Tomatoes (Stewed); Or Large Cans
As Desired Ground Turkey (Chopped Thanksgiving)
1 Medium Green Bell Pepper; 1 or 2
2 Pods Jalapeño Chile Peppers
1 Medium White Onion
1 Bag Chile powder; Crown Colony Recommended

1. Pour the two cans of stewed tomatoes into a large pot. Let simmer on medium heat.
2. Chop half of the white onion.
3. In a skillet, cook the turkey meat with the chopped onions.
4. Dump turkey meat and chopped onions into the pot of stewed tomatoes, along with the bag of chile powder.
5. Chop green bell peppers, the other half of the white onion, and the Jalapeño peppers.
6. Put all these ingredients into the pot. Bring chili to a boil on high heat, and then simmer immediately for at least 30 minutes. I recommend an hour for maximum taste.
7. Stir and taste occasionally.
8. Add pepper or water to your taste.
9. For thicker chili, add a bit of cornstarch.

Coming from Texas, I never add beans so do not add beans! Hope y'all like it! Great for Thanksgiving turkey leftovers or just a nutritious and delicious meal. This chili can keep for a while and tastes better "the next day."

Turkey Chili (No Beans)
Weight Watchers Favorite Recipes Book

7 Ounces Ground Turkey
½ Cup Onion; Chopped
1 Cup Italian Plum Tomatoes; Drained, Seeded and Chopped
½ Cup Tomato Sauce
½ Cup Water

2 Teaspoons Chile powder
1 Teaspoon Worcestershire Sauce; white wine vinegar
1 Teaspoon White Wine Vinegar
1 Leaf Bay
¼ Teaspoon Salt
¼ Teaspoon Garlic Powder
1/8 teaspoon Red Pepper; Crushed
1/8 Teaspoon Cinnamon; Ground
1/8 Teaspoon Allspice; Ground

1. Spray 3-quart saucepan with nonstick cooking spray and heat over medium-high heat; add turkey and onion, and using back of a wooden spoon to crumble meat, cook, stirring occasionally, until turkey is browned, about 5 minutes.
2. Add remaining ingredients and stir well to combine. Reduce heat to low and let simmer, stirring occasionally, until chili is thick, 25 to 30 minutes.
3. Remove bay leaf before serving.

Note: Serves 2. Each serving provides 2-½ protein exchanges, 2-½ vegetable exchanges, Per serving: 231 calories, 11 g. fat.

Note: May be frozen for future use. Just thaw and reheat. Delma Caylor of Lebanon, Indiana submitted it.

Turkey Chili Adios
Pat Stockett
3 Cups Turkey; Cooked, Minced
1 Medium Onion; Chopped
1 Cup Kidney Beans; Canned, Drained
1 Can (4 Ounce) Green Chile Peppers
2 Teaspoons Chile powder
1 Teaspoon Cumin Powder
2 Ribs Celery; Chopped
3 Cups Turkey or Chicken Broth
1 Cup Rice; Raw
1 Can (6 Ounce) Tomato Paste
1 Teaspoon Prepared Mustard

1. Combine all ingredients in a saucepan and cover and simmer, stirring occasionally until rice is tender, about 35 minutes.
2. For thicker, richer chili, puree one small can of kidney beans in a blender or food processor and add to chili.

Turkey Chipotle Chili

2 Pods Chipotle Peppers Canned; In Adobo Sauce
2 Pods Chipotle Peppers; Dried
1 Cup Water; Boiling Hot
2 Lb. Tomatillos, Fresh; Available in Hispanic Market
3 Cans (18 Ounce) Tomatillos; Drained
2 Large Onions; Chopped
8 Cloves Garlic
3 Tablespoons Vegetable Oil
2 Tablespoons Ground Cumin
4 Lb. Ground Turkey
2 Cups Chicken Broth
1 Leaf Bay
1-½ Teaspoon Oregano; Dried and Crumbled
2 Teaspoons Salt; Or To Taste
1 Medium Green Bell Pepper; Chopped
2 Cans (4 Ounce) Green Chiles, Mild; Drained and Chopped
1 Tablespoon Corn Meal
1 Can (19 Ounce) White Beans
½ Cup Coriander Sprigs; Chopped
As Needed Sour Cream; Accompaniment

1. In a large heavy kettle cook the onions and 5 of the garlic cloves, minced, in the oil over moderate heat, stirring, until the onions are softened, add the cumin, and cook the mixture, stirring, for 30 seconds.
2. Add the turkey and cook the mixture, stirring and breaking up the lumps, until the turkey is no longer pink.
3. Add the reserved chipotle puree, the reserved tomatillo puree, the broth, the bay leaf, the oregano, and the salt and simmer the mixture, uncovered, adding more water if necessary to keep the turkey barely covered, for 1 hour.
4. Stir in the bell pepper, the canned green chiles, and the cornmeal and simmer the mixture, stirring occasionally, for 30 minutes.
5. Stir in the white beans, the coriander, the remaining 2 garlic cloves, minced, and salt to taste, simmer the chili for 3 to 5 minutes, or until the beans are heated through, and discard the bay leaf.

Note: Chipotle is available at Hispanic markets, some specialty foods shops, and some supermarkets. If using the canned chipotle chiles, in a blender puree them with the water and reserve the puree. If using dried chipotle chiles, stem and seed them wearing rubber gloves, in a small bowl let them soak in the boiling-hot water for 20 minutes, and in a blender puree the mixture, reserving the puree.

Although this recipe doesn't produce the familiar-looking red chili--it's more green than red--it does turn out a chili that has become one of our staff favorites. The chili may be frozen or made 3 days in advance, cooled, uncovered, and kept covered and chilled.

Serve the chili with the sour cream.

Turkey-Bean Chili
Family Circle 2/22/94
1 Large Onion; Chopped
2 Cloves Garlic; Minced
1 Tablespoon Vegetable Oil
1 Lb. Ground Turkey
2 Tablespoons Chile powder
½ Teaspoon Oregano; Crumbled
1/8 Teaspoon Black Pepper
1/8 Teaspoon Cayenne Pepper
16 Ounces Tomatoes
2 Cans (8 Ounce) Tomato Sauce; No Salt
1 Cup Water
1-¼ Cup Long Grain White Rice
16 Ounces Black Beans; Canned, Drained
16 Ounces Cannelloni Beans; Canned, Drained
2 Teaspoons Vinegar

1. Sauté onion and garlic in oil in large saucepan over medium heat until tender. Increase heat to medium-high.
2. Add turkey; cook until browned.
3. Add chile powder, oregano, black and cayenne peppers; cook 30 seconds.
4. Add tomatoes, tomato sauce and water. Simmer, covered, 30 minutes.
5. Meanwhile, cook rice following package directions.
6. Stir beans and vinegar into chili.
7. Remove 1-½ cups chili and ¾ cup cooked rice for Chili Vegetable Soup.

Turkey-Black Bean Chili
2 Tablespoons Olive Oil
1 Lb. Turkey; Ground
1 Cup Onion; Chopped
2 Centiliters Garlic; Minced

1-½ Tablespoons Chile powder
1 Teaspoon Cumin
1 Teaspoon Oregano
1-¼ Teaspoon Salt
15 Ounces Black Beans; Rinsed and Drained
½ Cup Beef Broth
1 Cup Picante Sauce
1 Tablespoon Cornstarch

1. Heat oil in large pan. Add turkey, onions, and garlic; cook and stir 3 minutes.
2. Add chile powder, cumin, oregano and salt; cook and stir until turkey is cooked through and onion is tender.
3. Stir in beans and broth.
4. Combine picante sauce and cornstarch; add to pan. Bring to a boil; reduce heat. Simmer uncovered 10 minutes stirring occasionally.

Makes about 4-½ cups chili.

Turkey-Macaroni Chili
The Turkey Store Cookbook
2 Tablespoons Cooking Oil
1 Package Fresh Ground Turkey
1 Medium Onion; Chopped
1 Medium Green Pepper; Chopped
2-½ Cups Chicken Broth
1 Package (7 Ounce) Elbow Macaroni; Uncooked
1 Can (15 Ounce) Tomato Sauce
1 Tablespoon Vinegar
1-½ Teaspoons Sugar
1 Teaspoon Chile powder
1 Teaspoon Garlic Salt
¼ Cup Parmesan Cheese; Grated
2 Tablespoons Parmesan Cheese; Grated
1 Tablespoon Parsley

1. Heat oil in 4 quart Dutch oven over medium-high heat until hot.
2. Crumble turkey into Dutch oven; stir in onion and green pepper. Cook until turkey is no longer pink; drain, reserving juices in Dutch oven.
3. Stir broth into juices. Heat to boiling.
4. Stir in macaroni; reduce heat. Simmer, stirring frequently, until broth is

almost absorbed, about 10 minutes.
5. Stir in turkey mixture and remaining ingredients except 2 tablespoons of cheese. Cook over low heat 10 minutes.
6. Salt and pepper to taste.
7. Sprinkle rest of cheese on and serve.

Vintner's Turkey Chili
The Great Turkey Cookbook
1 Cup Bell Peppers; Chopped
1-¼ Cups Onions; Chopped
2 Cloves Garlic; Minced
½ Teaspoon Olive Oil
30 Ounces Kidney Beans; Undrained
28 Ounces Tomatoes; Crushed
3 Cups Turkey Light Meat; Skinless, Cooked and Cubed
2 Tablespoons Chile powder
1 Teaspoon Cilantro
1 Teaspoon Red Pepper; Crushed
1 Teaspoon Salt
½ Teaspoon Black Pepper

1. In a 3-quart saucepan over medium heat cook bell peppers, onions, garlic in oil until tender.
2. Add beans, tomatoes, water, turkey, chile powder, cilantro, red pepper flakes, salt, and black pepper. Increase heat to high and bring mixture to a boil; reduce heat to low and simmer mixture, uncovered for 25 minutes.
Serving Size: 6

White Bean Chili With Turkey
Bon Appetit September 1992
1 Lb. White Beans; Dried
1 Tablespoon Vegetable Oil
2 Cups Onion; Chopped
2 Cans (4 Ounce) Green Chiles; Diced
6 Cloves Garlic; Minced
1-½ Tablespoons Oregano; Dried and Crushed
1 Tablespoon Cumin; Ground
1 Tablespoons Chile powder
7 Cups Chicken Broth (Low Salt)
18 Ounces Tomatillos, Fresh; Or Canned, Chopped

1 Cup Cilantro; Fresh, Chopped
1-½ Lb. Turkey Breast; Boneless and Skinless
1 Cup Green Onions; chopped
2 Tablespoons Lime Juice; Fresh
Cilantro Cream
2/3 Cup Yogurt; Plain, Low Fat
3 Tablespoons Parsley (Fresh); Chopped
3 Tablespoons Cilantro; Fresh, Chopped
Garnish
1 Sprig Cilantro (Fresh)
½ Cup Cheddar Cheese; Grated

1. The recipe recommends soaking the beans overnight. Personally, I don't like to do that. I find the quick soak method works better. That is, cover beans with cold water. Bring to a boil and boil for 1-2 minutes (in Boulder we need 2 minutes because of the altitude). Turn off heat and let soak for 1-½ hours. Drain beans.
2. Heat vegetable oil in a large heavy Dutch oven over medium heat.
3. Add chopped onion and sauté 5 minutes.
4. Add diced chiles, minced garlic, oregano, cumin, and chile powder. Sauté for 5 minutes.
5. Add beans, chicken broth, chopped tomatillos and cilantro. It's important that the chicken broth contain little or no salt. Salt inhibits the softening of the seed coat of beans. Therefore, if you add salt too early the beans with never soften up.
6. Add turkey breast and simmer until just cooked through, about 20 minutes.
7. Transfer turkey to plate. Cover with foil and refrigerate.
8. Simmer chili until beans are tender, about 2-½ hours.
9. Cut turkey into ½ inch pieces.
10. Add turkey, green onions and limejuice to chili. Stir. Heat through.
11. Season with salt and pepper.
For cilantro cream: Combine yogurt, parsley, chopped cilantro in a medium bowl.

Ladle chili into bowls. Top with spoonful of cilantro cream. Sprinkle with cilantro sprigs and cheese. Can be prepared 1 day ahead. Cover chili and cilantro cream separately and refrigerate. Before serving, reheat chili over low heat. Like most chili, it tastes better the second day.

White Chicken Chili
1 Teaspoon Lemon Pepper
1 Teaspoon Cumin Seed
4 Medium Chicken Breasts, Boneless, Skinless
1 Clove Garlic; Chopped Finely
1 Cup Onion
1 Can (16 Ounce) Green Chiles; Undrained
1 Teaspoon Cumin; Ground
3 Tablespoons Lime Juice
1 Can (28 Ounce) Great Northern Beans; Undrained
2/3 Cup Tortilla Chips; Crushed
2/3 Cup Monterey Jack Cheese; Fat-Free

1. In a large saucepan, combine 2 and ½ cups of water with the lemon pepper and cumin seed. Bring to a boil.
2. Add the chicken breast halves, and return to a boil. Reduce the heat to low, and simmer 20 to 30 minutes, or until chicken is fork tender and the juices run clear.
3. Remove the chicken from the pan and cut into tiny pieces.
4. Defat the broth (put in fridge, and skim off congealed fat), return to the saucepan, and place the chicken back in the stock.
5. Spray a medium skillet with vegetable oil cooking spray, add the garlic, and cook and stir over low heat 1 minute.
6. Add to the chicken, and then sauté the onions in the same skillet, cooking until tender.
7. Add the cooked onions, corn, chiles, cumin, and lime juice to the chicken mixture. Bring to a boil.
8. Add beans and simmer until thoroughly heated, about 45 minutes.

To serve, place about 1 Tablespoon each of tortilla chips and cheese in 8 individual soup bowls, ladle hot chili over, and serve with salsa.

Wild Rice Turkey Chili
Waldine Van Geffen
1 Tablespoon Oil
1 Medium Onion; Chopped
10 Milliters Garlic; Minced
2 Cups Turkey; Cooked and Cubed
2 Cups Wild Rice; Cooked
1 Can (15 Ounce) Great Northern Beans; Drained
1 Can (11 Ounce) White Corn

2 Cans (4 Ounce) Green Chiles; Diced
14-½ Ounces Chicken Broth
1 Teaspoon Cumin; Ground
To Taste Hot Pepper Sauce, Liquid
6 Ounces Monterey Jack Cheese; Shredded

1. Heat oil in large pan over medium heat; add onion and garlic. Cook until tender.
2. Add turkey, rice, beans corn, chiles, broth and cumin. Cover and simmer over low heat to serving temperature.
3. Stir in hot pepper sauce.

Serve with cheese.

Fish and Seafood

Catfish Chili
2 Lb. Catfish Fillets; Chunked
1 Cup Green Pepper; Chopped
2 Tablespoons Butter
2 Cloves Garlic; Minced
1-½ Teaspoons Salt
1 Lb. Red Kidney Beans
1 Can (16 Ounce) Tomatoes; Undrained
6 Ounces Tomato Paste

1. Sauté green pepper and garlic in butter until tender. Add seasonings. Mix well.
2. Add beans and tomatoes. Cover and simmer 15 minutes.
3. Add fish. Cover and simmer 15 more minutes until fish flakes easily.

Crawfish Chili
From Justin Wilson's "Gourmet and Gourmand Cookbook"
2 Lb. Ground beef; Lean
2 Lb. Crawfish Tails
1 Teaspoon Garlic; Chopped Fine
2 Teaspoons Salt
1 Tablespoon Soy Sauce
1 Teaspoon Cayenne Pepper
1 Teaspoon Mint; Dried
1 Tablespoon Parsley; Dried
3 Tablespoons Chile powder

1 Can (8 Ounce) Tomato Sauce
1 Cup Dry White Wine
As Needed Water
1 Teaspoon Lemon or Lime Juice
1 Cup Onions; Chopped
As Needed Bacon Drippings

1. Brown meat in bacon drippings.
2. Combine all other ingredients with meat and bring to a boil. Simmer for a few hours.

Lobster Chili
2 1 Lb. Lobsters; Cooked, Any Method
1 Lb. Chorizo or Andouille Sausage
1 Medium Onion; Chopped
1 Small Green Pepper; Chopped
½ Cup Celery; Chopped
3 Large Cloves Garlic; Minced
1 Can (15 Ounce) Tomato Sauce
Chipotle Chile in Adobo Sauce
½ Teaspoon Paprika
Scallions; Green Part Only, Sliced
¼ Cup Bean Broth or Vegetable Broth; Not Bullion
To Taste Celery Salt
To Taste Pepper
As Needed Rice; Cooked

1. Shell the lobsters and crack the claws. Dice the claw meat. Cut the body meat in half lengthwise, and then cut it into cubes. Slice the tail meat into thick, uniform medallions. Refrigerate until needed.
2. Slice the sausage into thick rounds. Put them into a large stockpot with the onion, green pepper, and celery. When it starts to hiss, begin stirring. Stir fairly constantly; making sure the sausage is evenly browned, but not falling apart.
3. When the sausage is browned, remove most of the fat with a bulb baster.
4. Add the lobster meat and garlic, turn the heat to low and sauté long enough to heat the lobster.
5. Add the remaining ingredients except for the rice. Simmer, uncovered for 10 minutes. Serve hot over the rice.
Variation: Use shrimp instead of lobster.

Monkfish Chili
3 Large Turkish Bay Leaves
¼ Teaspoon Ground Cumin; Ground
¼ Teaspoon Basil; Dried and Crumbled
¼ Teaspoon Marjoram; Dried and Crumbled
¼ Teaspoon Red Pepper Flakes; Dried
1 Large Onion; Coarsely Chopped
1/3 Cup Tomato Paste
1-¾ Lb. Tomatoes; Peeled and Diced
2 Lb. Monkfish; Cut in ¼ Inch Dice
¼ Cup Chile powder
1 Tablespoon Cajun Seafood Magic
1 Teaspoon Salt
¼ Teaspoon Thyme; Dried and Crumbled
¼ Teaspoon Oregano; Dried and Crumbled
¼ Teaspoon Cayenne Pepper
2 Tablespoons Vegetable Oil
2 Medium Green Bell Peppers; Sliced
2-½ Cups Rich Fish Stock
2 Cups Red Kidney Beans; Cooked

1. Combine the first nine ingredients in a small bowl.
2. Heat oil in a heavy large saucepan over medium heat.
3. Add onion and cook until translucent, stirring, for about 8 minutes.
4. Mix in the bell peppers and continue to cook for another 3 minutes.
5. Add herb and spice mixture and stir for 5 minutes more.
6. Add tomato paste and cook for another 2 minutes. Keep stirring!
7. Add fish stock and tomatoes, increase heat to boiling.
8. Add beans and return to boil. Reduce heat and simmer until beans are heated through.
9. Add fish and sprinkle with chile powder, cook and stir for about 2 minutes, until fish is almost opaque.
10. Add Seafood Magic and stir, remove from heat, adjust seasoning and serve.

Seafood Chili
¼ Cup Olive Oil
2 Cups Onion; Chopped
2 Leeks, White Part Only; Trimmed and Chopped
1 Stalks Celery; Chopped

8 Cloves Garlic; Minced
5 Teaspoons Oregano; Preferably Mexican
35 Ounces Italian Plum Tomatoes; Undrained if Canned
16 Ounces Clam Juice
2 Cups Dry Red Wine
½ Cup Santa Cruz Red Chile Paste
5 Teaspoons Cumin Seeds; Freshly Toasted
1 Tablespoon Salt
1 Teaspoon Cayenne Pepper
2 Medium Red Bell Peppers; Seeded, Deveined, 1/2 Inc
12 Littleneck Clams
12 Mussels; Scrubbed and Debearded
1-½ Lb. Scrod or Other Lean White Fish; Cut in 1 Inch Pieces
12 Large Shrimp; Peeled and Deveined
¾ Lb. Bay Scallops
½ Cup Cilantro (Fresh); Minced

1. Heat oil in heavy Dutch oven over low heat.
2. Add onion, leeks, celery. Cover and cook until tender, about 15 minutes.
3. Add garlic and oregano, cook another 10 minutes then add tomatoes, breaking up with a spoon.
4. Blend in the clam juice, wine, chile paste, cumin, salt and cayenne. Bring to a boil, skimming occasionally. Reduce heat and simmer, partially covered, for about 1 hour, skimming.
5. Mix in bell peppers. Simmer uncovered for 20 minutes. Cool.
6. Refrigerate overnight.
7. Bring chili to a boil. Adjust heat so that liquid simmers briskly.
8. Skim well and adjust seasonings.
9. Add clams and mussels. Cover and cook until shellfish open, 5 to 10 minutes.
10. Discard any that do not open.
11. Gently stir in scrod and shrimp. Cover and simmer for a minute.
12. Add scallops, cover and simmer until fish is just opaque, about 2 minutes. Ladle chili into bowls. Top with cilantro.

Note; "Santa Cruz Red Chile Paste" is available from The Santa Cruz Chile and Spice Co., P.O. Box 177, Tumacacori, AZ 65640.

Seafood Chili With Black Beans
¼ Cup Olive Oil
1 Leaf Bay

1 Medium Red Pepper; Seeded and Diced
1 Medium Poblano Peppers; Seeded and Diced
1 Medium Yellow Onion; Diced
2 Tablespoons Garlic; Diced
1 Tablespoon Basil Fresh; Chopped
1 Tablespoon Thyme
1 Tablespoon Oregano
2 Teaspoons Cumin
1 Teaspoon Cayenne Pepper
½ Cup Chile powder; Toasted
¼ Cup Tomato Paste
3 Cups Rich Fish Stock
2 Limes; Juice Of
2 Cups Black Beans; Cooked
4 Roma Tomatoes; Diced
2 Lb. Mixed Fresh Seafood; Diced, Scallops, Shrimp,
To Taste Salt and Pepper
Cilantro Pesto Sour Cream; Recipe Follows
As Needed Cornstarch; Optional

1. Heat oil in large saucepan over high heat. Add bay leaf, peppers, onion, garlic, basil, thyme, oregano, cumin, cayenne and chile powder, stirring constantly. Cook 3 minutes.
2. Stir in tomato paste and cook 3 more minutes.
3. Add stock, lime juice, beans, tomatoes, seafood, salt and pepper and bring to a boil. Simmer 10 minutes over low heat.
4. Be sure seafood is fully cooked.

Serve very hot garnished with Cilantro Pesto Sour Cream. Serves 8 to 10.

Note: If chili needs thickening, dissolve a little cornstarch in cold water and stir in or just puree some of the black beans and stir in.

Cilantro Pesto Sour Cream:
1 Cup. Chopped Cilantro
½ Cup Olive Oil
1 Cup Sour Cream
To Taste Salt and Pepper

1. Puree cilantro in olive oil in blender or food processor until smooth.
2. Mix in sour cream and adjust seasoning.

Surf and Turf Chili
Michael Roberts-Prodigy Guest Chefs Cookbook
½ Recipe for Chili Base; See Recipe in Chile powder
1 Teaspoon Vegetable Oil
½ Lb. Skirt or Flank Steak
3 Cloves Garlic; Finely Minced
1/8 Teaspoon Allspice; Ground
½ Cup Chicken Stock; Or
½ Cup Low-Sodium Chicken Broth
8 Jumbo Shrimp; Peeled and Deveined
To Taste Salt
½ Bunch Cilantro; Chopped
12 Corn Tortillas
1 Cup Sour Cream

1. Prepare or defrost chili base (See Recipe in Chile powder Chapter).
2. Heat the oil in a Dutch oven over high heat on top of the stove.
3. Add the steak and brown well on both sides.
4. Pour off the fat and add the chili base, garlic, allspice and stock. Bring to a boil and place, covered, in the oven. Turn oven to 325 F and cook for 1 to 1-½ hours or until the steak is falling apart.
5. Add the shrimp, return to the oven and cook, uncovered, another 10 to 12 minutes.
6. Taste for salt and add if desired.
7. Using a fork shred the steak with the other chili ingredients.
Arrange the chili on a serving platter or in individual bowls and sprinkle with chopped cilantro. Serve with warm tortillas instead of bread and pass sour cream on the side.

Tuna Chili Texas-Style
1 Cup Green Or Red Bell Pepper; Cubes
½ Cup Onion; Chopped
½ Cup Celery; Chopped
1 Clove Garlic; Minced
2 Tablespoons Water
1 Can (28 Ounce) Tomatoes; Cut Up
1 Can (8 Ounce) Kidney Beans; Drained
1 Can (6-½ Ounce) Tuna; Drained and Diced
2 Tablespoons Red Wine Vinegar
2 Tablespoons Chile powder

1 Teaspoon Basil; Dried and Crushed
1 Teaspoon Oregano; Dried and Crushed
½ Teaspoon Ground Cumin
To Taste Hot Pepper Sauce, Liquid

1. In a 3-quart microwaveable bowl or casserole, combine bell pepper, onion, celery, garlic and water.
2. Cover with waxed paper; micro-cook on High power for 4-5 minutes or until vegetables are nearly tender.
3. Stir in remaining ingredients except hot pepper sauce. Cover; micro-cook on High power for 15-17 minutes, to allow flavors to blend, stirring every 3 minutes.
4. Season to taste with hot pepper sauce.

Makes 4 servings. Preparation time: 10 minutes.

Note: If you don't like it too hot, cut to 1 tablespoon chile powder.

Chapter 15
Chili Recipes - Vegetarian Recipes

Background

While chili is thought to have been cooked originally perhaps to mask the taste of meat that may not have been properly stored, vegetarian chili somehow seems to take that concept too far in my mind. However, there are enough vegetarian recipes that exist that the great taste of chili must have some universal appeal.

That being the case, here is my contribution to the cause of vegetarianism. Enjoy!

Amy Yasbeck's Vegetarian Chili

1 Can (12 Ounce) Tomatoes; Whole
¾ Cup Bulgur Wheat
2 Tablespoons Vegetable Oil
1 Medium Onion; Coarse Chopped
3 Stalks Celery; Chopped
3 Medium Carrots; Chopped
1 Tablespoon Lemon Juice
5 Tablespoons Chile powder
4 Cloves Garlic; Minced
1-½ Teaspoons Pepper
1 Teaspoon Cumin; Ground
1 Teaspoon Basil; Dried and Crumbled
½ Teaspoon Oregano; Dried and Crumbled
1-½ Cups Green Bell Peppers; Chopped
1 Can (14 Ounce) Red Kidney Beans; Drained
1 Can (15 Ounce) Garbanzo Beans; Drained
2 Cups Tomato Juice

1. Drain tomatoes and reserve liquid. Chop tomatoes coarsely and set aside.
2. Bring 1 cup (250 ml) reserved liquid to a boil over medium heat. Remove pan from heat and stir in bulgur.
3. Heat oil in a heavy, deep skillet over medium-low heat.
4. Add onion and cook until translucent, about 10 minutes, stirring frequently.
5. Add tomatoes, celery, carrots, lemon juice and spices, and cook until vegetables are almost tender, about 15 minutes, stirring frequently.
6. Add bell peppers and cook until tender, about 10 minutes.
7. Mix in bulgur, garbanzo beans and 2 cups (500 ml) tomato juice. Reduce

heat and simmer 30 minutes, stirring occasionally (add remaining tomato liquid if necessary).
Serves 4.

Andromeda Vegetarian Chili
Ben and Shirley Johnson
¼ Cup Vegetable Oil
1 Medium Onion; Chopped
1 Pod Jalapeno Pepper; Finely Chopped, Seeded
2 Tablespoons Chile powder
1 Tablespoon Masa Harina (Corn Flour)
2 Teaspoons Paprika
1 Teaspoon Cumin Powder
1 Teaspoon Oregano
1/8 Teaspoon Cayenne Pepper
6 Dried Apricots; Chopped
2 Cloves Garlic; Minced
1 Tablespoon Brown Sugar
1 Teaspoon Yellow Salad Mustard
15 Ounces Hunt's Tomato Sauce; W/Bits
1-½ Cups Water
1 Cup Heartline Meatless Meat; (Ground Beef Style)
¼ Cup Heartline Meatless Meat; (Beef Fillet Style)
½ Cup Beer
1 Tablespoon Tomato Paste

1. Heat oil in large cast iron skillet.
2. Add onions and jalapeno pepper and cook until the onion is transparent.
3. Add chile powder, Masa Harina, paprika, cumin powder, oregano and cayenne pepper. Stir until seasonings are slightly toasted.
4. Stir in apricots, garlic, brown sugar, mustard, tomato sauce, water, Heartline Meatless Meat, beer and tomato paste. Cook over medium heat for 15 to 20 minutes, stirring often.
5. Then cover and simmer over medium-low heat for 30 minutes to help combine the flavors.
Makes about 1 qt.

Note: Heartline Meatless Meats can be found in some health food stores or ordered from: Lumen Food Corporation, 409 Scott St., Lake Charles, LA 70601.

This chili was the winner in the 4th Annual Lone Star Vegetarian Chili

Cookoff, held in Dallas in October. It was the first place winner and People's Choice Award winner. Ben and Shirley Johnson of the South Texas Vegetarian Society in West Columbia, Texas entered it.

Annette's Vegetarian Chili
Ladies Home Journal-August 1991
2 Tablespoons Oil
1-½ Cups Celery; Sliced
½ Cup Onion; Chopped
10 Cloves Garlic
1 Tablespoon Chile powder
¾ Teaspoon Cumin
2 Cups Water
½ Cup Lentils
1 Can (16 Ounce) Tomatoes; In Juice, Chopped
2 Tablespoons Tomato Paste
2 Tablespoons Green Chiles; Chopped
1 Can (10 Ounce) Red Kidney Beans; Drained
To Taste Salt and Pepper

1. In a large saucepan, cook celery, onion and garlic till soft (about 4 minutes).
2. Add chile powder and cumin. Cook, stirring one minute.
3. Add water and bring to boil.
4. Add lentils, reduce heat, cover and simmer 20 minutes.
5. Add tomatoes and their juice, tomato paste, chopped green chiles, salt and pepper. Cover and cook for 25 minutes.
6. Add kidney beans and cook and stir 5 more minutes.

Serve over hot rice and sprinkle with cheese.

Another Chili Recipe
Fat Free Recipe Collection
1 Cup TVP; Rehydrate
8 Ounces Tempeh; Chopped, (Up to 16 Ounces)
8 Ounces Tofu; Crumbled, (Up to 16 Ounce)
1 Can Pinto Beans; Rinsed, (Up to 2 Cans)
1 Can Kidney Beans; Rinsed, (Up to 2 Cans)
1 Can White Beans; Rinsed, (Up to 2 Cans)
To Taste Any Other Bean You Like
2 Large Onions; Chopped, (Up to 4)

10 Cloves Garlic; Or More Chopped
2 Medium Green peppers; Chopped, (Up to 4)
1 Pod Hot Peppers of Your Choice-Or More; Jalapeño, Serrano-Minced
2 Cans (15 Ounce) Tomatoes; Crushed (Up to 4 Cans)
6 Ounces Tomato Paste; (Up to 12 Ounces)
½ Lb. Mushrooms; Coarsely Chopped (Up to 1)
1 Teaspoon Cayenne Pepper; Ground
2 Tablespoons Chile powder
2 Tablespoons Worcestershire Sauce
2 Tablespoons Vinegar
1 Leaf Bay
1 Teaspoon Cinnamon
½ Teaspoon Allspice
1 Tablespoon Cumin

1. Sauté the onion, peppers, hot peppers, and garlic until the onions are translucent.
2. Add all other ingredients and simmer a minimum of 30 minutes (about how long corn bread takes to cook).
3. Add water if chili is too thick.
4. Adjust seasonings during cooking to taste.

That's it! Last night's batch had TVP, 1 can pinto beans, 2 cans kidney beans, 1 can black eye peas, so I used double the spices and the higher amounts of the rest of the ingredients. Very tasty last night and of course even better today for lunch.

Black Bean and Quinoa Chili
Vegetarian Times, January 1995
1 Cup Quinoa; Rinsed and Drained
2 Cups Water
1 Tablespoon Vegetable Oil
1 Large Onion; Diced
1 Medium Green Bell Pepper; Seeded and Chopped
1 Cup Celery; Chopped
1 Pod Jalapeno Peppers; Seeded and Chopped
2 Medium Tomatoes; Cored and Diced
1 Cup Carrots; Diced
1 Can (32 Ounce) Black Beans; Drained
1 Can (28 Ounce) Tomatoes; Crushed
1 Tablespoon Chile powder

1 Tablespoon Parsley; Dried
1 Tablespoon Oregano; Dried
2 Teaspoons Cumin; Ground
½ Teaspoon Black Pepper
½ Teaspoon Salt
4 Single Green Onions; Chopped

1. Combine quinoa and water in saucepan, cover and bring to a simmer over medium heat. Cook until liquid is absorbed, about 15 to 20 minutes. Remove from the heat and let stand about 10 minutes.
2. Meanwhile, heat oil in a saucepan; add onion, bell pepper, celery and jalapeno. Sauté 7 minutes over medium heat.
3. Stir in fresh tomatoes and carrots; sauté 3 to 4 minutes.
4. Stir in beans, crushed tomatoes, and seasonings; cook about 25 minutes over low heat.

Ladle chili into bowls and top with green onions if desired. Makes 8 servings.

Bowl Of Compassion Vegetarian Chili
1/3 Cup Olive Oil
2 Medium Onions; Chopped
4 Cloves Garlic; Minced
2 Pods Jalapeno Peppers; Chopped
1 Medium Mild Pepper; Chopped
1 Medium Red Pepper; Chopped
1 Medium Green Pepper; Chopped
2 Large Tomatoes; Diced
8 Ounces Tomato Sauce
2 Cans Ro-tel Diced Tomato and Green Chile
2 Cans (15 Ounce) Dark Red Kidney Beans
3 Cups Water
4 Tablespoons Chile powder
2 Tablespoons Cumin
1 Tablespoon Paprika
1 Tablespoon Oregano
1 Tablespoon Lemon Juice
To Taste Salt and Pepper
To Taste Tabasco Sauce
1 Cup Textured Vegetable Protein; TVP

1. Sauté onions, garlic, and peppers in oil until onions are translucent.
2. Add spices and simmer for two minutes. Stir in remaining ingredients, adding the TVP last.
3. You can adjust the amount of TVP to obtain the desired texture and consistency.
4. You can substitute beer for the water for a more unique flavor.
5. One jalapeno makes a mild chili (two were used for the cookoff). Simmer from four to six hours.

It's even better the next day.

Bulgur Chili
6 Cups Water
2 Large Onions
2 Cloves Garlic; Minced
1 Medium Green Pepper; Chopped
1 Cup Cut Corn
1 Can Tomato Paste
28 Ounces Tomatoes; Crushed
½ Cup Bulgur
2 Tablespoons Chile powder
1 Tablespoon Sorghum
1 Tablespoon Cumin
2 Tablespoons Parsley; Chopped
3 Cups Kidney Beans; Cooked
3 Stalks Celery

1. Sauté garlic, onion and green pepper in a small amount of oil until tender.
2. Add water and remaining ingredients except beans. Simmer covered for 1 hour; stirring occasionally.
3. Stir in beans and simmer for 15 minutes more.

Chili (No Meat)
2 Tablespoons Oil
2 Cloves Garlic; Chopped
2 Medium Onions; Chopped
¼ Teaspoon Cayenne Pepper
2 Tablespoons Chile powder
1 Teaspoon Cumin
1 Teaspoon Oregano
1 Medium Green Pepper; Chopped

2 Cups Tomatoes; Chopped (Can Use Canned)
4 Cups Kidney Beans; Cooked and Drained
1 Teaspoon Salt

1. Heat oil in large saucepan and sauté garlic until it begins to color.
2. Add onion and cook for 3 minutes.
3. Add seasonings and green pepper and cook for one minute longer.
4. Add remaining ingredients, adjusting salt if needed. (If you use canned beans, they are usually salted and you don't need to add more.) Bring to boil, cover and simmer over low heat for 20-30 minutes 'til thickened.

It's great with a little shredded cheese or sour cream on top.

Chili Beans
Sunday Mirror Magazine
½ Lb. Pinto Beans; Dried
½ Cup Smoked Ham; Chopped
1 Cup Onion; Chopped
1 Can (8 Ounce) Passata (Sieved Tinned Tomatoes)
1 Can (4 Ounce) Green Chiles; Diced
¼ Cup Brown Sugar; Packed
1 Teaspoon Chile powder
½ Teaspoon Salt
½ Teaspoon Dry Mustard

1. Rinse beans. In a large saucepan combine beans and 4 cups water. Bring to the boil; reduce heat, simmer for 2 minutes. Remove from heat.
2. Cover and let stand for 1 hour. (Or, skip boiling the water and soak beans overnight.) Drain and rinse beans.
3. In the same pan combine beans and 4 cups fresh water. Bring to the boil; reduce heat.
4. Cover and simmer for about 75 minutes or until beans are tender, stirring occasionally. Drain beans, reserving liquid.
5. In a 2-pint casserole, combine beans, ham and onion.
6. Stir together half a cup of the bean liquid, Passata, chile peppers, brown sugar, chile powder, salt and mustard.
7. Stir into bean mixture, bake, covered, in a 160C/325F/Gas Mark 3 oven for about an hour.
8. Uncover and bake for about 45 minutes or more to desired consistency.

Chili Cilantro With TVP
1-½ Cups Onion; Chopped
1-½ Tablespoons Olive Oil
1 Large Bell Pepper; Diced
1 Can (32 Ounce) Pinto or Black Beans; Drained
1 Can (4 Ounce) Green Chiles; Chopped
4 Medium Tomatoes; Ripe, Diced
1 Can (16 Ounce) Tomato Puree
2/3 Cup TVP Granules
1 Cup Water
1 Teaspoon Cumin; Ground
1 Teaspoon Chile powder
½ Cup Fresh Cilantro; Chopped
1 Tablespoon Oregano; Fresh, Chopped

1. In a large stockpot, sauté onion in oil until translucent.
2. Add bell pepper and sauté until onion is golden, about 5 minutes.
3. Add remaining ingredients, except cilantro and oregano. Cover and simmer for 30 minutes, stirring occasionally.
4. Stir in cilantro and oregano.
5. If necessary, add water to give mixture the consistency of a thick stew. Serve warm.

Chili Penultimate Grooviness
1 Lb. Black Beans; Dried
½ Lb. Pinto Beans; Dried
¼ Lb. Kidney Beans; Dried
2 Pods Poblano Chiles; Chopped
1 Medium Green Bell Pepper; Chopped
2 Medium Tomatoes; Coarse Chopped
2 Medium Red Onions; Minced
2 Large Carrots; Minced
6 Cloves Garlic; Minced
2 Cans (15 Ounce) Tomatoes; Crushed
2 Tablespoons Tomato Paste
4 Tablespoons Chile powder
3 Tablespoons Cumin; Ground
1 Tablespoon Salt
½ Tablespoon Black Pepper
2 Cups TVP

1. Soak beans overnight or bring to a boil, then turn off heat and soak for one hour.
2. Sauté vegetables until soft and add to beans along with rest of ingredients except TVP.
3. Cook for one and a half hours, adding TVP the last 20 minutes of cooking.

Chili Rico

1 Medium Onion; Chopped
2 Cloves Garlic; Minced
2 Tablespoons Vegetable Oil
1 Can (28 Ounce) Tomatoes; Whole, Undrained
2 Cans (16 Ounce) Kidney Beans; Rinsed and Drained
1 Can (12 Ounce) Whole Kernel Corn; Drained
½ Cup Picante Sauce
1-½ Teaspoon Cumin; Ground
1 Teaspoon Oregano Leaves; Crushed
1 Teaspoon Unsweetened Cocoa
¼ Teaspoon Cinnamon
1 Medium Red or Green Bell Pepper; Cut in 1 Inch Pieces
As Desired Sour Cream
As Desired Green Onions; Chopped

1. Cook onion and garlic in oil in large saucepan or Dutch oven until onion is tender but not brown.
2. Add remaining ingredients except red pepper and optional toppings; bring to a boil. Reduce heat, cover and simmer 20 minutes.
3. Stir in red pepper; continue to simmer uncovered 5 minutes or until desired consistency.
Ladle into bowls; top as desired and serve with additional picante sauce.
Makes 6 servings, about 7-½ cups chili.

Brightly colored and boldly flavored, this meat-free chili is lightly seasoned with cinnamon. Its far-from-the-ordinary flavor and low fat and calorie counts make it a favorite of the fitness set.

Chili With Lentils

1 Lb. Lentils; Dry
1 Teaspoon Salt
5 Cups Boiling Water
1 Can (16 Ounce) Tomatoes; Or

1 Can (16 Ounce) Tomato Sauce
1-½ Tablespoons Chile powder
1 Medium Onion; Chopped
½ Cup Celery; Chopped
1 Clove Garlic; Minced

1. Rinse; dry lentils. Pick out any stems or stones.
2. Add salt and dry lentils to boiling water. Cover and simmer 30 minutes. Do not drain.
3. Add tomatoes or tomato sauce, chile powder, onions, celery and garlic. Cover and simmer 30 minutes more.

Serve over rice, spaghetti or corn chips. 7 Servings.

Chili With Vegetables and Bulgur Wheat
From 500 Fat-Free Recipes
¼ Cup Water
½ Cup Onion; Chopped
2 Cloves Garlic
½ Cup Mushrooms; Sliced
1 Cup Green Bell Peppers; Chopped
1 Tablespoon Chile powder
1 Teaspoon Cumin; Ground
3-½ Cups Tomatoes; Chopped, Canned or Fresh
½ Cup Yellow Squash; Diced
2 Cups Beans (I Use Pinto), Cooked or Cannelloni; Drained and Rinsed
½ Cup Bulgur; I Usually Throw in ¾ to 1 cup

1. Heat water in large nonstick saucepan over medium heat.
2. Add onion and garlic. Cook and stir for 5 minutes, adding more water if necessary.
3. Add mushrooms, green pepper, chile powder, cumin, tomatoes and squash. Cover and simmer for 15 minutes.
4. Add beans and bulgur. Cover and cook until warmed through.

Country Chili With TVP
The TVP Cookbook by Dorothy Bates
2 Cups Boiling Water
2 Cups TVP Flakes or Chunks
2 Tablespoons Ketchup
1 Large Onion; Chopped

1 Large Green Pepper; Chopped
2 Cloves Garlic; Chopped
1 Pod Jalapeno Pepper; Chopped
2 Tablespoons Olive Oil
2 Tablespoons Chile powder
2 Teaspoons Cumin
2 Teaspoons Oregano
1/2 Teaspoon Cayenne
2 Cans (28 Ounce) Tomatoes; Chopped
2 Cans (16 Ounce) Kidney Beans
2 Cups Hot Water or Vegetable Broth
1 Package (16 Ounce) Frozen Corn Kernels

1. Pour 2 cups boiling water over TVP chunks and ketchup and let stand 10 minutes.
2. Heat a large Dutch oven. Add olive oil.
3. Over medium heat sauté the onions, pepper and garlic a few minutes.
4. Sprinkle the spices over the TVP and stir with a fork.
5. Add the TVP to the pan and cook a few minutes.
6. Stir in the beans, tomatoes and water or broth. Cover and simmer 30 minutes to one hour.
7. Taste and add salt if desired.
8. Add the frozen corn during last 15 minutes.

Critterless Chili

3 Cups Beans, Dried; Soaked and Cooked
3 Tablespoons Chile powder
2 Large Onions; Chopped
2 Tablespoons Cumin
2 Large Carrots; Grated or Finely Chopped
2 Teaspoons Cayenne
1 Medium Bell Pepper; Chopped
1 Tablespoon Basil
6 Cloves Garlic; Chopped
1 Teaspoon Thyme
1 Pod Serrano Chile Peppers; Seeded and Chopped
¼ Cup Tamari
2 Tablespoons Olive Oil
1 Teaspoon Salt; To Taste
26 Ounces Spaghetti Sauce; Commercial

1. On medium-high, stir fry veggies, garlic and Serrano in olive oil for 5 minutes.
2. Add spices; stir-fry 5 minutes more.
3. Add drained beans; stir into spices for a few minutes.
4. Add spaghetti sauce, stir, and lower heat to simmer, and cook 30 minutes.

Extra Quick Chili
1 Bag Onions and Peppers
2 Cloves Garlic; Minced
1 Can (28 Ounce) Plum Tomatoes; Cut in Pieces
1 Teaspoon Beef Bouillon; Granules
1 Tablespoon Chile powder
2 Teaspoons Cumin
1 Pinch Cayenne Pepper; To Taste
2 Cans Kidney Beans; Or Black Beans
As Needed Whole Grains; Cooked

1. Combine all ingredients in a large pot, bring to a boil and simmer for 5-10 minutes.
2. Serve over the whole grain of your choice, if desired. 4-6 Servings.

Fresh Tomato Chili Soup
Georgeanne Brennan and Charlotte Glenn
8 Medium Tomatoes
1 Clove Garlic; Minced
½ Teaspoon Hot Chile powder; Or Cayenne Pepper
1 Cup Chicken Broth
1 Medium Green Onion; Chopped
To Taste Cilantro (Fresh); Chopped
To Taste Cumin Seeds; Crushed
As Needed Lime Wedges
As Needed Tortilla Chips

1. Wash tomatoes and broil until skins are brown and shriveled and interior is soft.
2. Skin and puree in food processor with garlic, chile powder and broth.
3. Garnish with green onion, cilantro, cumin and lime.
Serve hot or at room temperature with tortilla chips. Serves 4.
   From Peppers Hot and Chili by Georgeanne Brennan and Charlotte Glenn, Calgary Sun, Monday, July 30, 1990; Cinda Chavich.

Garden Chili
2 Cups Red Beans; Dried
2 Tablespoons Olive Oil
2 Medium Onions; Chopped
4 Cloves Garlic; Minced
1 Medium Bell Pepper; Chopped
2 Pods Jalapeno Chile Peppers; Seeded and Rinsed
2-½ Tablespoons Chile powder
2 Teaspoons Cumin; Ground
2 Quarts Tomatoes; Chopped
1 Cup Yellow Summer Squash; Chopped
1 Cup Green Summer Squash; Chopped
1 Ear Corn; Cut off Cob or
1 Cup Corn; Frozen
2 Tablespoons Oregano; Fresh, Minced
To Taste Salt
1 Cup Scallions; Chopped-Garnish
1 Cup Cheddar or Jack Cheese; Shredded-Garnish

1. Place beans in a large pot and add enough water to generously cover. Bring to a boil. Cover pan, reduce heat and simmer until almost tender about 1 to 1-½ hours.
2. Stir occasionally and add more water if necessary to keep beans covered.
3. Drain beans, and then return to pot with 2 cups cooking liquid.
4. In a large pot or Dutch oven, heat oil, add onions and sauté on medium heat for 5 minutes.
5. Add garlic, bell pepper, chile pepper, and sauté minutes longer.
6. Stir in chile powder, cumin, and tomatoes, including juice.
7. Add the cooked beans and their liquid and simmer covered for about 30 minutes.
8. Add squash, corn, and oregano. Simmer 30 minutes longer, stirring occasionally.
9. Add salt to taste and more chiles if desired.

Serve with scallions and cheese to spoon over. Serves 8 to 10.

Garden Harvest Chili
2 Tablespoons Cooking Oil
2 Cloves Garlic; Minced
1 Medium Sweet Red Bell Peppers; Chopped
1 Medium Green Bell Pepper; Chopped

1-½ Cups Mushrooms; Fresh, Chopped
½ Cup Onion; Chopped
1 Can (28 Ounce) Tomatoes; Whole, Cut up, Undrained
1 Can (15 Ounce) Tomato Sauce
2 Tablespoons Chile powder
2 Teaspoons Sugar
1 Teaspoon Cumin; Ground
1 Can (16 Ounce) Kidney Beans; Drained and Rinsed
2 Cups Zucchini; Sliced
1 Package (10 Ounce) Sweet Corn; Defrosted
1-½ Cups Cheddar Cheese; Shredded (Optional)

1. In a skillet, heat oil over medium-high. Sauté garlic, peppers, mushrooms and onion until tender.
2. Add tomatoes with liquid, tomato sauce, chile powder, sugar and cumin; heat to boiling. Reduce heat to low; add beans, zucchini and corn. Simmer, uncovered, about 10 minutes or until zucchini is tender.

Spoon into bowls; sprinkle with cheese if desired. Yield: 6 Servings (2-½ Quarts).

Golden Butternut Squash Chili
2 Tablespoons Olive Oil
2 Medium Onions; Cut in 1/4 Inch Pieces
2 Tablespoons Garlic; Finely Chopped
2 Medium Red Bell Peppers; Cut in ½ Inch Pieces
3 Tablespoons Chile powder
2 Tablespoons Cumin; Ground
¼ Teaspoon Allspice; Ground
1-½ Tablespoons Oregano; Dried
1 Pinch Red Pepper Flakes
2 Cans (28 Ounce) Plum Tomatoes; Peeled and Chopped
½ Cup Dry Red Wine
2 Medium Butternut Squash; Peeled and Sliced, ½ Inch Pieces
To Taste Zest of Orange
To Taste Salt
To Taste Pepper; Fresh Ground
2 Cans (15-½ Ounce) Red Kidney Beans; Drain Liquid
2 Tablespoons Cilantro (Fresh); Chopped
2 Tablespoons Parsley (Flat Leaf); Chopped

1. Heat olive oil over medium heat in a large, heavy pot.
2. Add onions, garlic and red peppers. Cook for 10 minutes, stirring occasionally, until the vegetables have wilted.
3. Add the chile powder, cumin, allspice, oregano and red pepper flakes; cook for 1 minute longer, stirring to coat vegetables well with spices.
4. Add chopped tomatoes with their juices, red wine, diced butternut squash and orange zest. Bring all ingredients to a boil; reduce heat to medium-low and simmer, uncovered, for 20 minutes, or until squash is tender.
5. Add salt and pepper to taste, and adjust seasonings.
6. Add the kidney beans and fold in gently. Cook 10 minutes more.
7. Just before serving, stir in the chopped cilantro and parsley.

Note: Butternut squash can be difficult to cut, because the pulp is very firm and the outer skin is slightly tough, so work carefully. I find that the easiest way to work with it is to cut the squash in half crosswise at the base of large neck. Then carefully cut in half lengthwise. Scoop out any seeds in the cavity and slice the halves into ½ inch lengths crosswise. Peel the skin from each piece and then cut into dice.

Great Vegetarian Chili
1 Cup TVP; Reconstituted
1-½ Cups Onion; Finely Chopped
1-½ Teaspoons Garlic; Minced-Fresh
1/3 Cup Green Chile Peppers; Canned, Undrained
1 Cup Tomatoes; Diced
½ Teaspoon Vegit (Salt Substitute)
1 Teaspoon Oregano Leaves; Dried
1 Teaspoon Cumin
1-¼ Teaspoons Chile powder
3 Cups Red Kidney Beans; Canned/Drained and Rinsed
1-½ Cup Tomato Juice; Low Sodium

1. Combine the onion and garlic in large skillet or saucepan and cook, covered, over low heat until soft, stirring frequently to prevent scorching.
2. Add all other ingredients and mix thoroughly. Cook over medium heat until bubbling hot.

Iron Rich Tempeh Chili
Canadian Living magazine August 95
1 Tablespoon Vegetable Oil
¾ Lb. Tempeh; Thawed, Crumbled

843

1 Medium Onion; Chopped
½ Medium Sweet Green Pepper
2 Cloves Garlic; Minced
28 Ounces Tomatoes; Canned, Undrained
19 Ounces Kidney Beans; Canned, Drained
5-½ Ounces Tomato Paste
¼ Cup Cider Vinegar
¼ Cup Molasses
1 Tablespoon Soy Sauce
1 Tablespoon Dijon Mustard
2 Teaspoons Chile powder
1 Teaspoon Basil; Dried
1 Teaspoon Oregano; Dried
½ Teaspoon Salt
¼ Teaspoon Pepper

1. In large saucepan, heat oil over medium heat; cook Tempeh with ½ cup water, stirring, for 5 minutes or until browned.
2. Add onion, green pepper and garlic; cook, covered and stirring occasionally, for 5 minutes or until onions are softened.
3. Chop tomatoes; add to mixture along with beans, tomato paste, vinegar, molasses, soy sauce, mustard, chile powder, basil, oregano, salt and pepper. Bring to boil; reduce heat and simmer for 15 minutes.

Per serving: about 312 calories, 19 g Protein, 8 g fat, 47 g carbohydrate very high source fiber, excellent source iron.

Note: Tempeh is of Indonesian origin, is fermented soybean patty made from split, hulled and cooked soybeans. The soybeans are inoculated with a starter and fermented for 24 hours to produce an extra firm tofu with a chewy quality similar to meat. Tempeh is sold frozen in health food stores.

June's Vegetarian Chili
1 Large Onion; Chopped
1 Medium Green and Red Peppers; Chopped
2 Cloves Garlic; Minced
1 Small Zucchini; Cubed
1 Can (16 Ounce) Great Northern Beans; Rinsed and Drained
1 Can (14-½ Ounce) Tomatoes (Stewed)
1 Package Chili Seasoning Mix; Mild
1 Can (7 Ounce) Whole Kernel Corn

1. Spray a non-stick pot with cooking spray and sauté onion, pepper, and garlic until softened, about 5 minutes.
2. Add zucchini, beans, tomatoes, and chili seasoning. Cover and simmer until vegetables are done to your taste.
3. Add corn immediately before serving.

Lady April's Renaissance
April and James Hall of San Antonio
12 Cups Water
2 Cups Pinto Beans; Dried
2 Pods Jalapenos; Chopped, Or More
1-½ Cup Mexican Beef Style Heartline; Meatless Meat
1 Medium Onion; Chopped
2 Cups TVP
1 Can (15 Ounce) Tomato Sauce
2 Medium Tomatoes; Chopped
4 Teaspoons Salt
1 Teaspoon Pepper
2-½ Tablespoons Chile powder
1 Tablespoon Garlic Powder
2 Teaspoons Cocoa
4 Teaspoons Sugar
½ Teaspoon Red Pepper; Crushed
2 Tablespoons Tomato Paste; Heaping

1. Clean and rinse beans. Bring to a boil in 12 cups water, turnoff heat and soak for one hour.
2. Add jalapenos and Heartline Meatless Meat and cook until beans are tender.
3. Add rest of ingredients and simmer 30 minutes more.

Makes about 3 quarts.

This recipe was the first place winner in the 5th Annual Lone Star Vegetarian Chili Cook-Off, held in San Antonio, Oct. 3. It was created by April and James Hall of San Antonio.

Source: South Texas Vegetarian Society newsletter, November-December.

Lentil Chili
Tanya Heikkinen
2 Cups Lentils
5 Cups Water
1 Can (28 Ounce) Tomatoes
1 Medium Bell Pepper; Chopped
2 Pods Jalapenos; Chopped
1 Large Onion; Chopped
4 Cloves Garlic; Minced
1 Tablespoon Chile powder
2 Teaspoons Cumin
1 Teaspoon Oregano
To Taste Salt
To Taste Cayenne Pepper

1. Rinse the lentils and cook until soft. There will be extra water, but since this is soup, that's okay.
2. Add the tomatoes and veggies, and cook until the onion is soft.
3. Add the spices to taste.

Variations: As someone else pointed out, adding bulgur (or brown rice) is tasty and satisfying. Add ½ cup of grain to the lentils and add another 1 cup of water. Shredded carrots and corn are also good. In fact, I've found that you can make just about any gloopy mass into chili by adding chile powder. Kidney beans are also very good in this recipe.

Tanya Heikkinen, University of Idaho From Fatfree Digest April-May 1994.

Low Fat Vegetarian Chili
1 Teaspoon Olive Oil
2 Medium Onions
2 Cloves Garlic; Minced
56 Ounces Tomatoes; Or 3 Lb. Fresh
15-½ Ounces Red Kidney Beans
15 Ounces White Kidney Beans
15 Ounces Chickpeas
1-½ Cups Celery; Chopped
1 Medium Green Pepper; Chopped
3 Tablespoons Lime Juice; Or 2 Tbs. Lemon Juice
1 Tablespoon Chile powder
1-½ Teaspoons Oregano

1-½ Teaspoons Cumin
¼ Teaspoon Cinnamon
12 Ounces Light Beer
As Desired Dry Roasted Peanuts
As Desired Cheddar Cheese

1. In a large pot, heat oil and sauté onions and garlic until soft.
2. Add all ingredients except beer, peanuts and cheddar cheese. Cover and simmer 1-½ hours.
3. Add beer and simmer uncovered for 30 minutes.
4. Add handful of peanuts and sprinkle cheese on each serving.

Maple Leaf Chili
"Vegetarian Gourmet" Winter, 1995

2 Cloves Garlic; Minced
4 Medium Onions; Chopped
1 Tablespoon Oil
1 Tablespoon Chile powder
2 Teaspoons Cumin; Ground
¼ Teaspoon Cinnamon
3 Tablespoons Basil; Chopped
1 Tablespoon Oregano; Chopped
1 Tablespoon Marjoram; Chopped
¼ Teaspoon Cayenne
1 Cup Celery; Chopped
1-½ Cups Green Bell Pepper; Chopped
4 Cups Tomatoes; Crushed
½ Cup Unsalted Peanuts; Toasted
4 Cups Kidney Beans; Cooked
1 Tablespoon Molasses
To Taste Salt and Pepper

1. Sauté garlic and onions in oil in a large skillet.
2. Stir in the chile powder, herbs and spices. Let cook for a few minutes longer.
3. Stir in the celery, bell pepper and tomatoes. Simmer for 15 minutes.
4. Coarsely chop the peanuts and stir in with the remaining ingredients. Simmer gently for 20 to 30 minutes.
Serve hot.

Margaret Ann's Better Than Chili
Nathalie Dupree Cooks (1996)
2 Tablespoons Vegetable Oil
2 Medium Onions; Chopped
4 Large Carrots; Chopped
2 Medium Red Bell Peppers; Seeded and Chopped
2 Medium Green Bell Peppers; Seeded and Chopped
1 Can (32 Ounce) Black Beans; Drained and Rinsed
1 Cup Bulgur; Soaked, See Note
1 Can (32 Ounce) Tomatoes; Whole, Undrained
2 Cups Chicken Broth; Or Alternative
¼ Cup Chile powder
1 Tablespoons Cumin; Ground
1 Tablespoon Coriander; Ground
¼ Teaspoon Cayenne Pepper
To Taste Salt and Black Pepper
1 Cup Yogurt; Plain
6 Green Onions; Sliced, As Desired
¼ Lb. Cheddar Cheese; Grated

1. Soak bulgur for 20 to 30 minutes in 2 cups boiling water.
2. Broth: Use chicken or vegetable, homemade or canned. Heat the oil in a 6-quart Dutch oven.
3. Add the onions, carrots, and the red and green bell peppers and cook over medium heat for 5 to 8 minutes.
4. Add the black beans, bulgur, tomatoes, chicken stock, chile powder, cumin, coriander, and cayenne pepper.
5. Bring to a boil, reduce heat, simmer for 30 to 45 minutes, until thickened.
6. Season to taste with salt and pepper.
Serve in bowls with yogurt, green onions, and grated cheese as condiments for topping the chili.
   Yield: 8 to 10 servings.

Mean Lean Vegetable Chili
3 Large Carrots (About ¾ Lb. Total); Peel and Chop Fine
1 Large Onion; Coarsely Chopped
1 Can (28 Ounce) Tomatoes
1 Can (16 Ounce) Black Beans or Pinto Beans
3 Tablespoons Chile powder
½ Cup Sour Cream; Or Unflavored Yogurt

1. In a 4- to 5-quart pan over high heat, combine carrots, onion, and ½ cup water.
2. Stir often until liquid evaporates and vegetables begin to brown and stick in pan, about 10 minutes.
3. Add tomatoes (break up with a spoon) and their liquid, beans and their liquid, and chile powder.
4. Bring to a boil, and then reduce heat and simmer, uncovered, to blend flavors, about 15 minutes.
5. Ladle chili into wide bowls; add sour cream and crushed chiles to taste.

Makes 6 to 8 servings.

Per serving: 228 calories (17 % from fat); 4.3 grams fat, 863 mg sodium and 6.3 grams cholesterol.

Meatless Chili

2 Tablespoons Corn Oil
3 Cloves Garlic; Minced
½ Teaspoon Cumin; Ground
1 Medium Green Pepper
1 Can (16 Ounce) Chick Peas
1 Package (10 Ounce) Corn; Frozen
1-½ Cup Onions; Chopped
2 Tablespoons Chile powder
1 Cup Carrots; Diced
2 Cans (15 1/2 Ounce) Tomatoes; In Juice
1 Can (15 Ounce) Kidney Beans; Drained
2 Pods Jalapeno Chile Peppers; Pickled

1. Chop the Jalapeno peppers.
2. Do not discard the juice from the can tomatoes.
3. In 5 quart saucepot heat corn oil over medium heat.
4. Add onions, garlic, chile powder and cumin; sauté 5 minutes or until tender.
5. Add carrots and green peppers; sauté 2 minutes.
6. Add tomatoes with juice, crushing tomatoes with spoon.
7. Stir in chickpeas, kidney beans, corn, and jalapeno peppers. Bring to boil. Reduce heat; cover and simmer 30 to 35 minutes.

If desired, serve with rice.

Makes 8 servings, about 1-½ cups each.

Meatless Chili Terlingua Style
16 Ounces Tomato Sauce; Unsalted
4 Cups Water
1 Medium Onion; Chopped
5 Cloves Garlic; Minced
2 Ounces Chile powder
5 Dashes Cayenne Pepper; To Taste
¼ Teaspoon Oregano
1 Dash Paprika
2 Cups TVP Granules
¼ Teaspoon Cumin; Ground
As Needed Corn Meal

1. Place the tomato sauce and 4 cups of water in a deep 6 to 8 quart pot.
2. Add onion and garlic. Bring to a boil. Reduce heat and simmer for 30 minutes.
3. Add chile powder, cayenne, oregano, and paprika, stirring well.
4. Add texturized vegetable protein, stir well, and simmer for 30 minutes.
5. Stir in cumin, and water if needed for the desired consistency, and cook for 5 more minutes.
6. If additional thickness is desired, stir in 1 tablespoon or masa (corn flour) or corn meal. Cook for 8 to 10 minutes after adding the masa.

Serve this chili over cooked pinto or kidney beans if desired. It may also be used as a filling for tacos or enchiladas. Many people like chili with a small amount of grated low-fat cheese or toasted tortilla chips.

Meatless Mission Chili
2 Tablespoons Safflower Oil
1 Clove Garlic; Minced
1 Medium Green Bell Pepper; Chopped
1 Stalks Celery; Chopped
1 Small Onion; Chopped (¼ Cup)
1 Single Carrot; Shredded
1 Medium Zucchini; Shredded
1 Can (18 Ounce) Tomatoes; With Juice
1 Can (15 Ounce) Kidney Beans; Drained
8 Cans (8 Ounce) Tomato Sauce; 1 Cup
¼ Cup Water
1-½ Teaspoons Chile powder; To Taste
¼ Teaspoon Hot Pepper Sauce, Liquid; To Taste

1 Teaspoon Basil
1 Teaspoon Oregano
½ Teaspoon Black Pepper

1. In a Dutch oven or 4-5 qt. saucepan, heat oil.
2. Sauté garlic, green pepper, celery, onion, carrot, and zucchini until crisp/tender, about 3 minutes.
3. As mixture cooks, stir in remaining ingredients. Bring to a boil over high heat, and then reduce heat to medium.
4. Cover and cook until heated through, about 5 minutes.

Top each serving with a garnish, if desired. If you wish, set under broiler to melt cheese.

Variations: Add ½ cup whole raw cashews. If reheating, add additional liquid, such as water, tomato juice, or vegetable stock.

Garnish: Corn, chopped scallions, shredded Cheddar or Monterey jack cheese, or a combination, optional.

Moosewood Vegetarian Chili
2-½ Cups Kidney Beans; Raw
6 Cups Water
1 Teaspoon Salt
1 Cup Tomato Juice
1 Cup Bulgur Wheat; Raw
As Needed Olive Oil; For Sauté
4 Cloves Garlic; Crushed
1-½ Cups Onion; Chopped
1 Cup Carrot; Chopped
1 Cup Celery; Chopped
1 Teaspoon Basil
1 Tablespoon Chile powder; Or More, to Taste
1 Tablespoon Cumin; Ground
To Taste Salt and Pepper
1 Dash Cayenne; To Taste
1 Cup Green Pepper; Chopped
2 Cups Tomatoes; Fresh, Chopped
½ Juice Lemon
3 Teaspoons Tomato Paste
3 Teaspoons Dry Red Wine
As Desired Cheese
As Desired Parsley

1. Put kidney beans in a saucepan and cover them with 6 cups of water. Soak 3 4 hours. Add extra water and salt. Cook until tender (about 1 hour). Watch the water level, and add more if necessary.
2. Heat tomato juice to a boil.
3. Pour over raw burgher. Cover and let stand at least 15 minutes. (It will be crunchy, so it can absorb more later.)
4. Sauté onions and garlic in olive oil.
5. Add carrots, celery and spices.
6. When vegetables are almost done, add peppers. Cook until tender.
7. Combine beans, burgher, sautéed vegetables, tomatoes, lemon juice, tomato paste, and wine and heat together gently, either in kettle over double boiler, or covered in a moderate oven.

Serve topped with cheese and parsley.

Mulato Chili With Cocoa
2 Tablespoons Oil
1 Teaspoon Cinnamon
1 Medium Onion; Chopped
1 Teaspoon Garlic Salt
3 Cloves Garlic; Minced
2 Cans (Large) Tomatoes (Stewed)
4 Pods Mulato Chiles; Dried
1-½ Cups Black Beans; Cooked
1 Tablespoon Cumin
2 Teaspoons Cocoa Powder; Unsweetened
1 Tablespoon Oregano
As Needed Tomato Juice; For Thinning

1. Soak the chiles in hot water for 25 minutes or until they become soft.
2. Sauté the onion in oil until translucent.
3. Add the garlic, chile powder, spices and the stewed tomatoes (with their juice), simmer for 25 minutes.
4. Add the cocoa powder and black beans. Stir well.
5. If the chili is too thick add tomato juice till the desired consistency is achieved.

Pawtucket Chili
1 Can (40 Ounce) Kidney Beans; Or
2 Cans (16 Ounce) Kidney Beans
1 Can (15 Ounce) Chick Peas

2 Cloves Garlic; Minced
1 Medium Onion; Chopped
1 Tablespoon Olive Oil
8 Ounces Tomato Sauce
1 Can (14-½ Ounce) Tomatoes; Whole
1 Tablespoon Oregano
½ Teaspoon Thyme
1 Teaspoon Cumin
½ Teaspoon Basil
3 Tablespoons Chile powder

1. Rinse kidney beans and chickpeas to remove salt. Set aside.
2. Sauté garlic and onion in olive oil.
3. Add beans, chickpeas, and remaining ingredients and bring to a boil. Simmer for 20 minutes (or longer) until thick.

Quick and Easy Vegetarian Chili
Let's Live Magazine August 1990
1 Medium Onion; Chopped
1 Stalks Celery; Chopped
2 Tablespoons Vegetable Oil
4 Cups Kidney Beans; Cooked and Drained
9/16 Cup Tomato Sauce
3 Tablespoons Vinegar
2 Teaspoons Molasses
1 Teaspoon Basil
1 Teaspoon Oregano
2 Tablespoons Chile powder; To 3

1. Sauté onion and celery in oil until soft.
2. Add remaining ingredients and simmer over low heat for 20 minutes.
Serve or chill several hours and reheat to serve. Makes 4 servings.

Roasted Vegetable Chili
1 Medium Red Bell Pepper
2 Tablespoons Olive Oil
½ Teaspoon Garlic Salt
¼ Teaspoon Black Pepper; Ground
1 Large Zucchini; 1 Inch Thick Slices
2 Small Eggplants; Cut into ½ Inch Slices

2 Large Beefsteak Tomatoes; Cored and Thickly Sliced
6 Large Mushrooms; Stems Trimmed
1 Small Onion; Chopped
2 Teaspoons Cumin; Ground
1 Teaspoon Coriander; Ground
2 Teaspoons Chile powder
1 Pinch Oregano; Dried
1 Can (19 Ounce) Kidney Beans; Drained
1 Can Cannelloni Beans; Drained
½ Cup V8 Juice

1. Heat the broiler. Place the pepper on a rack 4" under the broiler and cook until the skin blackens, about 4 minutes.
2. Turn and continue to cook, turning every 2 or 3 minutes until the pepper is charred all the way round.
3. Place the pepper in a loosely closed paper bag and set aside for at least 10 minutes.
4. Meanwhile, mix the oil with garlic salt and pepper.
5. Rub the sliced zucchini, eggplant, tomatoes and mushrooms lightly with half the oil and put under the broiler until browned and tender. This will take about 5 minutes per side.
6. Remove the skin from the bell pepper with your fingers. Take out the stems and seeds.
7. Cut the pepper, zucchini, eggplant, tomatoes and mushrooms into ½ inch dice. Set aside. In a saucepan, heat the remaining oil.
8. Add the onion and cook over medium high heat until soft, about 1 minute.
9. Add the cumin, coriander, chile powder and oregano. Cook for another 10 seconds.
10. Add the beans, reserved roasted vegetables and vegetable cocktail juice and simmer for 10 minutes.

Makes 4 servings.

Rob's Veggie Chili
Robert Bjornson
As Needed Olive Oil
½ Large Yellow Onion; Diced
2 Cloves Garlic; Minced
1 Medium Red Bell Pepper; Diced
1 Medium Green Bell Pepper; Diced
2 Cans (Large) Tomatoes; Crushed

1 Tablespoon Cumin
1 Teaspoon Cayenne; To Taste
1 Package Corn; Frozen
2 Cans Black Beans
1 3/16 Cups Picante Sauce
To Taste Salt
As Desired Cashew Nuts

1. Sauté onions in the olive oil. (I used cooking wine instead to cut out the fat.)
2. Add garlic a bit later.
3. After onion and garlic have turned golden brown, add cumin, cayenne, and whatever other spices you might like. Fry for a couple of minutes.
4. Next, add the peppers, sauté them for a few minutes.
5. Put the crushed tomatoes, corn, beans and Picante sauce into the crock-pot, and add the onion mixture. Cook on low about 10 hours.

Serve with cashew nuts, if desired.

Note: I didn't have room in my crockpot for 2 cans of crushed tomatoes, and I had to cut back a little on the corn too, so you will have to vary the sizes above depending on the size of your crockpot.

Roomie's Low Fat Vegetarian Chili
1 Teaspoon Olive Oil
2 Medium Onions
2 Cloves Garlic; Minced
56 Ounces Tomatoes, Canned; Or 3 Lb. Fresh
15-½ Ounces Red Kidney Beans
15 Ounces White Kidney Beans
15 Ounces Chickpeas
1-½ Cups Celery; Chopped
1 Medium Green Pepper; Chopped
3 Tablespoons Lime; Or 2 Tsp. Lemon Juice
1 Tablespoon Chile powder
1-½ Teaspoons Oregano
1-½ Teaspoons Cumin
¼ Teaspoon Cinnamon
12 Ounces Light Beer
As Desired Dry Roasted Peanuts
As Desired Cheddar Cheese

1. In a large pot, heat oil and sauté onions and garlic until soft.
2. Add all ingredients except beer, peanuts and cheddar cheese. Cover and simmer 1-½ hours.
3. Add beer and simmer uncovered for 30 minutes.

Add handful of peanuts and sprinkle cheese on each serving.

Spicy Fatfree Chili

1 Cup Hard Wheat Berries; Uncooked
2 Medium Onions; Chopped
2 Cups Pinto Beans; Cooked
3 Tablespoons Cinnamon; Approximately
¼ Cup Chile powder; Approximately
1 Jar (16 Ounce) Picante Sauce
2 Cans (14-½ Ounce) Chili
1 Medium Tomatoes
1 Can (4.5 Ounce) Green Chile Peppers
1 Can (7 Ounce) Jalapeno Chile Relish

1. Cook the wheat berries in 2.5 cups of water (it will take about an hour).
2. Combine the remaining ingredients and simmer while the wheat berries are cooking.
3. Add the wheat berries when they are done and enjoy!
4. If the wheat berries do not absorb all the water, drain them before adding to the chili. They should be a little chewy.

I didn't measure the cinnamon or chile powder; the measurements should be close though. The pinto beans were fresh.

Spicy Lentil Chili
Hyatt Regency-San Antonio, TX

3 Tablespoons Olive Oil
2 Cups Carrots; Finely Chopped
2 Cups Zucchini; Finely Chopped
2 Cups Eggplant; Finely Chopped, Unpeeled
1-½ Cups Onion; Chopped
1-½ Tablespoons Jalapeno Chile Peppers; Chopped, Seeded
1 Tablespoon Garlic; Finely Chopped
5 Teaspoons Oregano; Dried
1-½ Tablespoons Cumin; Ground
½ Teaspoon Cayenne Pepper
1 Leaf Bay

2 Cans (28 Ounce) Tomatoes; Diced, in Juice
2-½ Cups Chicken Broth (Low Salt); Or Vegetable Broth (Canned)
1-½ Cups Red Or Brown Lentils

1. Heat oil in a heavy large pot over medium heat.
2. Add carrots, zucchini, eggplant, onion, jalapeno and garlic and sauté until almost tender, about 5 minutes. Add oregano, cumin, cayenne pepper and bay leaf and stir until fragrant, about 30 seconds.
3. Add tomatoes with juice, stock and lentils; bring to boil. Reduce heat; simmer uncovered until lentils and vegetables are tender, about 40 minutes.
4. Season to taste with salt and pepper.

From January 1998 Bon Appetit Magazine.

Spud Chili
1 Large Onion; Chopped
2 Tablespoons Oil
4 Cloves Garlic; Minced
1 Pod Jalapeno; Seeded and Minced
1 Tablespoon Chile powder
1 Teaspoon Cumin; Ground
1 Teaspoon Allspice; Ground
1 Teaspoon Basil; Dried
½ Teaspoon Oregano; Dried
2 Cans (14.5 Ounce) Stewed Tomatoes
3 Cups Vegetable Broth
3 Medium Potatoes; Scrubbed and Diced
1 Medium Bell Pepper; Finely Chopped
2 Cans (15 Ounce) Pinto Beans; Rinsed and Drained
To Taste Salt and Pepper

1. In a Dutch oven, sauté onion in oil over high heat until browned.
2. Add garlic, jalapeno, chile powder, cumin, allspice, basil, and oregano. Sauté, stirring often, about 2 minutes.
3. Add tomatoes with juice and vegetable broth, stirring to loosen bits of browned food on bottom of pan. Bring to a boil.
4. Add potatoes and bell pepper, bring to a boil. Cook, uncovered, over med. heat for 15 minutes, stirring occasionally.
5. Add beans and cook another 10-15 minutes.
6. Season with salt and pepper to taste.

Sultry No-Meat Chili
4 Cubes Chicken Bouillon; Or
The Equivalent Bouillon Powder
3 Cups Water
8 Ounces Tomato Sauce
½ Cup Onion; Chopped
1 Tablespoon Garlic; Minced
8 Tablespoons Hot Chile powder; I Use Tone's Brand, Up to 10
1 Tablespoon Cumin
¼ Cup Carrot; Chopped Or Grated
2 Medium Tomatoes; Diced
1 Can Pinto Beans
1 Can Black Beans
½ Cup Bacon Bits

1. First, make your bouillon with cubes or powder and the water.
2. Now add tomato sauce, onion, and garlic.
3. Next, add your chile powder.
4. Start with 8 tablespoons and go from there.
5. Add cumin. Bring it back to a boil.
6. Now add the carrot and tomatoes.
7. Turn your heat down to low and let it simmer for about 45 minutes.
8. Ten minutes before your chili is done, add the beans.
9. Now is also the time to thicken it if you wish. Mix about ¼ cup of masa flour with enough water to make a thick but flowable mixture, and stir it in. When your chili is done, you can add Monterey jack cheese and/or sour cream. You can also garnish your bowl with cilantro leaves.

Summer Chili
½ Cup Onions; Chopped
1-½ Cloves Garlic; Minced
½ Teaspoon Olive Oil
10 ½ Ounces Chicken Broth
1 Cup Dark Red Kidney Beans; Drained and Rinsed
¼ Cup Celery; Chopped
¼ Cup Carrots; Sliced
1 Cup Squash; Chopped
1 Cup Zucchini; Chopped
1 Cup Bell Peppers; Chopped
2 Cups Mushrooms; Sliced

½ Cup Tomatoes; Chopped
2 Teaspoons Chile powder
1 Teaspoon Cumin
¼ Teaspoon Black Pepper
1/8 Teaspoon Cayenne Pepper
8 Ounces Tomato Sauce; No-Salt Added
1 Teaspoon Honey

1. In a large saucepan, cook onion and garlic, in oil until tender.
2. Add water, kidney beans, celery, carrots, squash, zucchini, pepper, mushrooms, tomatoes, tomato sauce, and honey until soft.
3. Mix in chile powder, cumin, black pepper, and cayenne until blended. Simmer all ingredients about 1 to 2 hours or until bubbly.

Three Bean Chili
12 Ounces Heinz Home Style Brown Gravy
16 Ounces Tomatoes
1 Tablespoon Chile powder
15 Ounces Spicy Chili Beans
15 Ounces Garbanzo Beans; Drained
15 Ounces Pinto or Kidney Beans
4 Ounces Green Chiles; Chopped
Yogurt; Or Sour Cream
Green Onions; Sliced
Cheese; Shredded

1. Combine gravy, tomatoes and chile powder in 3-quart saucepan.
2. Bring to a boil, and then stir in beans and chiles.
3. Cover; simmer 15 minutes, stirring occasionally.
Serve with desired toppings.

Tofu Chili
The Best Little Tofu Cookbook from Marjon by Marcia Mil
1 Package Tofu
2 Tablespoons Soy Sauce
1 Tablespoon A-1 Sauce
2 Tablespoons Oil
1 Teaspoon Garlic; Minced
1 Medium Onion; Chopped
1-½ Teaspoons Chile powder

1-½ Teaspoons Cumin; Ground
1 Can (16 Ounce) Tomatoes
1 Can (15 Ounce) Tomato Sauce
2 Cans (16 Ounce) Kidney Beans

1. Thaw tofu quickly by placing bag in boiling water. Rinse with cool water. (This is because tofu that has been frozen and thawed can be easily crumbled.) Take tofu from bag and squeeze to remove excess water.
2. Shred tofu into small pieces with fork.
3. In a bowl combine tofu, soy sauce, and A-1 sauce.
4. Meanwhile, medium heat a large skillet or a heavy cook-pot.
5. Add oil sauté garlic and onion; add chile powder, add cumin.
6. Add tofu mixture to seasoned onions in the pot, and mix well.
7. Add chopped tomatoes with juice, tomato sauce, and two cans of beans. Cook 15-20 minutes.

Tomato Cafe's Vegetarian Chili
"Taste of Vancouver" from Tomato's Restaurant
1-½ Cup Red Kidney Beans; Dried
4 Cups Cold Water
3/4 Cup Bulgur Wheat
1-½ Cups Boiling Water
2 Tablespoons Vegetable Oil
3 Cloves Garlic; Minced
1 Large Onion; Chopped
1 Cup Celery; Sliced ½ Inch Thick
1 Cup Carrot; Sliced ½ Inch Thick
1 Cup Butternut Squash; Cut in ½ Inch Cubes
1 Cup Eggplant; Cut in 1-Inch Cubes
1 Cup Mushroom; Fresh, Halved
1 Medium Red, Yellow, Green Bell Pepper; Cut in 1 Inch Squares
1 Large Zucchini, Green; cut in ½ Inch Slices
½ Teaspoon Tabasco Sauce
3 Tablespoons Chile powder
2 Tablespoons Cumin; Ground
¼ Cup Basil; Fresh, 1 Tsp. Dried
¼ Cup Dill; Fresh, 1 Tsp. Dried
¼ Cup Oregano; Fresh, 1 Tsp. Dried
1 Pod Jalapeno; Or 2, Minced
To Taste Salt and Pepper

¼ Teaspoon Red Pepper Flakes; Dried
56 Ounces Italian Plum Tomatoes; Chopped and Undrained
3 Cups V-8 Juice
2 Ounces Tomato Paste
1 Cup Corn Kernels; Frozen, Thawed
½ Cup Sharp Cheddar Cheese; Shredded &
½ Cup Monterey Jack Cheese; Shredded, Mixed
1 Medium Red Onion; Sliced

1. Cover the beans with cold water. Bring to a boil and simmer 45 minutes until tender. Strain, saving the liquid. Set both aside.
2. Soak the bulgur in the boiling water 5 minutes, until the liquid is absorbed. Set aside.
3. In a large stockpot, heat the oil and sauté the garlic, onion, celery, carrots, butternut squash and eggplant until the vegetables are crisp-tender, about 15 minutes.
4. Add the remaining vegetables, Tabasco, spices, herbs and flavorings and sauté for 5 minutes.
5. Add the tomatoes with juice, V-8, beans and bean liquid and simmer uncovered over medium heat about 30 minutes, until the vegetables are still slightly crunchy.
6. Add the soaked bulgur and corn. Taste for seasonings. Cool and chill overnight until ready to serve.
7. Make at least a day ahead.

To serve, reheat uncovered until hot. Serve in bowls. Top each serving with grated cheeses and sliced red onions. Freezes well.

TVP Chili
1 Cup TVP; Boiling Water to Cover
2 Tablespoons Taco Seasoning Mix; More or Less
To Taste Chile powder
To Taste Salt
1 Medium Green Pepper
1 Medium Onion; Chopped
2 Cloves Garlic
As Desired Wine or Balsamic Vinegar
1 Can (16 Ounce) Tomatillos; Diced
2 Cans Kidney Beans
1 Can (8 Ounce) Tomato Sauce
To Taste Chile powder

½ Teaspoon Basil; Dried, Up to 1
As Needed Pace Medium Picante Salsa

1. Soak about 1 cup of TVP in boiling water, to cover, with several Tablespoons taco seasoning, extra chile powder, and salt to taste, let it sit until the TVP has soaked up much of the water and flavor from the spices.
2. Meanwhile, sauté 1 chopped green pepper, 1 chopped medium/large onion, and 1-2 cloves finely chopped garlic in wine or balsamic vinegar until the onion is translucent.
3. Stir in one can of diced tomatoes (16 Ounce), one or two cans of drained and rinsed kidney beans, one can of tomato sauce (8 Ounce), chile powder, and ½ 1 teaspoon dried basil (or several chopped leaves if fresh).
4. Drain excess liquid from the TVP (so there isn't a puddle of water, it can still be wet) and add to the rest. Bring to a boil, reduce heat, and simmer 20 minutes or more.

To each bowl I like a big blob of Pace medium pica, but my 6 year old likes it plain with baked Tostitos.

Two-Day Chili
1 Lb. Black Beans; Soaked Starting in The Early Morning
1 Cup Brown Rice; Medium Grain
1 Can (28 Ounce) Tomatoes; Diced With Sauce
2 Large Onions; Chopped (2 or 3)
3 Large Carrots; Diced
1 Clove Garlic; Chopped, To Taste
To Taste Chile powder
To Taste Cumin

1. Cook brown rice and soaked beans in water to cover in crockpot set to high (overnight).
2. In the morning, add sautéed veggies, canned tomatoes and spices.
3. Continue cooking on high (watch the water level) until dinner for flavors to blend.

Serve over rice/potatoes/tortillas, etc. I made some black bean chili last week (black beans, canned tomatoes, sautéed onions and carrots, spices)-from scratch-a crockpot full. And added a "secret ingredient"-brown rice, which I added when I started to cook the (presoaked) beans-overnight at high in the crockpot. All my SAD friends who ate it thought it was great, and thought it contained meat (actually, no added fat, no added meat-just what was in the rice, etc.). ;-)

Uncle Roy's Chili
3 Tablespoons Olive Oil
1 Can (28 Ounce) Stewed Tomatoes; Broken Up, W/Liquid
1 Can (15-16 Ounce) Mexican-Style Tomatoes; Broken Up, W/Liquid
3 Tablespoons Chile powder
1 Tablespoon Tabasco Sauce
2 Medium Onions; Chopped
2 Cans (15-16 Ounce) Kidney Beans; Rinsed and Drained
2 Cloves Garlic; Minced
½ Cup TVP Granules; Optional
To Taste Habañero Powder

1. Heat olive oil in a large skillet or Dutch oven.
2. Add onions and garlic and cook until soft.
3. Add stewed tomatoes and spices and simmer about 30 minutes.
4. Add beans and simmer another 20-30 minutes.

The cooking time is very flexible. The main reason for the longer cooking time is to allow the spices to blend with the other ingredients. Notes: Habañero powder is a specialty item available from Stonewall Chili Company and possibly some other similar companies.

Vegetable Chili
The Gazette, 2/27/1991
1 Teaspoon Olive Oil
1 Large Onion; Chopped
2 Cloves Garlic; Chopped
2 Medium Carrots; Sliced
1 Cup Celery; Sliced Diagonally
1 Medium Zucchini; Quartered
1 Medium Red Or Green Pepper
2 Pods Jalapeno Peppers
1 Can (28 Ounce) Tomatoes; Chopped
1 Can (19 Ounce) Kidney Beans
1 Tablespoon Chile powder
1 Teaspoon Cumin; Ground
1 Teaspoon Oregano; Dried
To Taste Salt
To Taste Black Pepper; Freshly Ground
1 Pinch Granulated Sugar
As Needed Mozzarella Cheese; Shredded

1. In a large 3-quart casserole dish, combine the oil, onion, garlic, carrots and celery.
2. Microwave covered at High for 7 to 8 minutes or until vegetables are almost tender.
3. Add zucchini, peppers, canned tomatoes including liquid, kidney beans including, chile powder, cumin and oregano.
4. Microwave covered at High for 16 to 18 minutes or until zucchini is tender. Let stand, covered for 5 minutes.
5. Season to taste with salt, pepper and pinch of sugar.

Ladle chili into warm soup bowls; sprinkle with shredded cheddar or mozzarella and serve. Serves 4.

Vegetable Chili With Millet
1 Lb. Kidney Beans; Dried, Picked Over and Rinse
2 Tablespoons Olive Oil
2 Medium Onions; Peeled and Diced
4 Cloves Garlic; Peeled and Minced
1 Large Green Bell Pepper; Cored, Seeded and 1/4 Inch
1 Pod Jalapeno Peppers; Trimmed and Minced
4 Cups Water
1 Can (35 Ounce) Plum Tomatoes
½ Cup Tomato Sauce
3 Tablespoons Chile powder
1 Tablespoon Cumin; Ground
1 Teaspoon Turmeric
1 Teaspoon Oregano; Dried
1 Cup Millet; Rinsed and Drained
To Taste Salt
2 Cups Yogurt; Plain (Garnish)
1 Bunch Scallions; Trimmed, Cut in Round
2 Medium Oranges; Peeled and Sectioned

1. Place the beans in a large saucepan. Add boiling water just to cover and let set 1 hour.
2. Drain the beans, cover with fresh water, and bring to boil over high heat.
3. Reduce heat to medium, cook; partially cover, until tender but not soft- about 50 minutes to an hour. Drain and set aside.
4. Heat oil in large saucepan over medium-high heat. When hot but not smoking, add onions, garlic, and bell pepper, Jalapeno.
5. Reduce heat to medium and cook, stirring frequently, until onions turn

translucent-about 9 minutes.

6. Add reserved beans, 2 cups water, tomatoes, tomato sauce, spices and oregano. Mix well and bring to boil.
7. Reduce heat to medium-low, cook, partially covered, 1-½ hours.
8. Add millet and remaining 2 cups water, stir, and continue cooking until millet and beans are cooked through but not mushy, the flavors have mellowed and chili is rich and aromatic-at least 2 hours. Stir occasionally, being sure mixture doesn't stick to bottom of pan.
9. Salt to taste.

To serve, ladle the chili into warmed bowls, and either top with yogurt, scallions and oranges or pass them separately.

Vegetable Laden Three Bean Chili
Vegetarian Times, April 1993
1 Medium Orange Bell Pepper
1 Medium Red Bell Pepper
1 Medium Yellow Bell Pepper
2 Medium Fennel Bulbs
1 Tablespoon Olive Oil; Extra Virgin
¼ Teaspoon Red Pepper; Crushed
1 Tablespoon Coriander Seeds
1 Tablespoon Cumin Seeds
1 Teaspoon Oregano
2 Tablespoons Chile powder
3 Medium Tomatoes; Peeled and Chopped
1-½ Cups Green Beans; Cut
1-¾ Cups Kidney Beans; Cooked
3-¼ Cups Black Beans; Cooked
1-¾ Cups White Beans; Cooked
As Needed Water; Or Tomato Juice
To Taste Salt and Black Pepper; Fresh Ground
½ Cup Cilantro; Or Parsley, Chopped

1. Seed bell peppers and cut into ½ inch squares.
2. Remove tops from the fennel bulbs, cut out the core with a small knife and finely chop. Set aside.
3. Warm oil, crushed red pepper, coriander and cumin in a heavy 4-quart saucepan over moderate heat. Fry until seasonings darken slightly.
4. Add peppers, fennel, oregano and chile powder, and sauté about 5 minutes. Stir in tomatoes and all beans and bring to a boil. Reduce heat

to low and simmer for about 30 minutes, adding water or tomato juice as needed if too much liquid evaporates.

5. Season with salt and pepper, and stir in cilantro or parsley.

Serve in shallow bowls.

Vegetables Chili

2 Cloves Garlic; Minced
1 Medium Green and Red Pepper; Chopped
½ Lb. Mushrooms; Sliced
½ Cup Onion; Chopped
1 Tablespoon Canola Oil
1 Can (28 Ounce) Tomatoes; Crushed
1 Can (15 Ounce) Tomato Sauce
2 Tablespoons Chile powder; Mexican
1 Teaspoon Cumin; Ground
2 Cans (15 Ounce) Kidney Beans; Drained and Rinsed
1-½ Cups Zucchini; Diced
1 Package (10 Ounce) Corn (Frozen); Thawed

1. Use crushed tomatoes with added puree. Cook and stir garlic, peppers, mushrooms and onions in oil 5 minutes or until vegetables are tender.
2. Add tomatoes, tomato sauce, chile powder and cumin. Heat to a boil. Reduce heat to low, add beans, zucchini, and corn. Simmer 15 minutes or until vegetables are tender.

Makes 8 servings.

Notes/Hints: For fat free, spray vegetables with Pam and omit oil, thus "wilting" them instead of cooking in oil. Wilt means using little heat and covering the pan. Also, because of use of canned vegetables, this recipe may not be suitable for those on a low-sodium diet. Suggested toppings for chili: non-fat sour cream, non-fat cheddar cheese substitute, and chopped scallions.

Vegetarian Cashew Chili

1 Medium Onion
2 Cloves Garlic
1 Medium Green Pepper
1 Medium Carrot
1 Stalk Celery
1 Can (28 Ounce) Tomatoes; Whole
½ Cup Cashews; chopped raisins
½ Cup Raisins; Chopped

1/3 Cup Bulgur; Optional
2/3 Cup Boiling Water
½ Teaspoon Chile powder
½ Teaspoon Cumin
½ Teaspoon Basil
½ Teaspoon Oregano
½ Teaspoon Salt and Pepper
½ Teaspoon Hot Peppers; Optional
2 Leaves Bay

1. Sauté onion and garlic in large pot until transparent; green pepper, carrot and celery, sauté until tender crunchy.
2. Add tomatoes (chopped in quarters or smaller), cashews, raisins and seasonings.
3. Put bulgur and boiling water together; let stand, covered, 20 minutes.
4. Add to chili pot above; simmer ½ hour or all day on a wood stove.
5. May want to add small can tomato sauce, corn or other vegetable or increase spices.

Vegetarian Chili
Mark Shlosberg
2 Medium Onions; Chopped
1 Jar (15 Ounce) Nopalitos (Cactus); Drained and Rinsed
2 Cups Textured Soy Protein; (Dry Measure)
½ Lb. Mushrooms; Sliced
4 Cloves Garlic; Peeled and Minced
4 Cans (14 Ounce) Pinto Beans; Drained
2 Cans (14 Ounce) Tomatoes; Crushed
2 Large Green Bell Peppers; Seeded and Diced
¼ Cup Chile powder; According to Taste
2 Cups Vegetable Broth
2 Single Bay Leaves
4 Tablespoons Corn Oil
As Needed Water

1. Place soy chunks in a large bowl and cover with boiling water; allow to stand until softened but still firm. Drain and reserve the water for thinning the chili to desired constancy.
2. In a heavy 6 qt. pot heat the oil to the smoking point. Add the onions, garlic, bell peppers and mushrooms, and stir-fry until vegetables are just

limp and starting to "sweat."

3. Add vegetable stock, bay leaves and chile powder; stir until all the chile powder is dissolved.
4. Add remaining ingredients, and enough water to reach desired thickness, bring to a quick boil, reduce heat to medium low and simmer. Stir occasionally for 1 hour.
5. If chili gets too watery thicken with a little cornstarch dissolved in vegetable stock.

Vegetarian Chili # 1

1 Can (16 Ounce) Pinto Beans; Drained
1 Can (16 Ounce) Kidney Beans; Drained
1 Can (16 Ounce) Tomatoes; Diced (Recipe Ready)
1 Can (16 Ounce) Tomato Sauce
1/3 Cup Ripe Olives; Sliced
1 Can (4 Ounce) Mushroom; Drained and Sliced
½ Cup Onion; Chopped
½ Cup Celery; Chopped
¼ Cup Green Pepper; Chopped
1/3 Cup Carrot; Shredded
2 Tablespoons Cooking Oil
1-½ Teaspoon Salt
2 Teaspoons Mexican Chile powder
¼ Teaspoon Ground Pepper
½ Teaspoon Dry Mustard
1 Clove Garlic; Minced
6 Dashes Tabasco Sauce; (Up to 8)

1. In medium saucepan, heat cooking oil. Sauté, onion, celery, green pepper and carrot until tender.
2. Add tomato sauce, tomatoes, beans, olives, mushrooms, salt, chile powder, pepper, mustard, garlic and Tabasco Sauce. Bring to boil. Reduce heat and simmer for 1 hour.

Serves 4-6.

Vegetarian Chili # 2

1 Tablespoon Olive Oil
2 Cups Onion; Chopped
¾ Teaspoon Ground Cumin
¼ Teaspoon Cinnamon; Ground

1 Tablespoon Garlic; Minced
1 Can (35 Ounce) Plum Tomatoes; Undrained
½ Cup Water
1 Teaspoon Hot Pepper Sauce, Liquid
1 Teaspoon Salt
¾ Cup Bulgur Wheat; Or 6 Ounces Wheat-Pilaf Mix
1 Can (19 Ounce) Kidney Beans
1 Box Frozen Corn; (10 Ounce)

1. Heat oil in 12-inch skillet over medium heat.
2. Add onions and cook 8 to 10 minutes, stirring occasionally, until tender.
3. Stir in cumin, cinnamon, and garlic. Cook 1 minute longer.
4. Pour liquid from tomatoes into skillet.
5. Add water, hot pepper sauce, and salt. Bring to a simmer, stir in bulgur and simmer 5 minutes.
6. Chop tomatoes (in the can with kitchen scissors works well) and rinse and drain the beans.
7. Add to skillet along with corn. Cook 12 minutes for flavors to blend.
Serve with a dollop of low-fat sour cream or plain yogurt and a sprinkling or chopped onions and fresh cilantro.

Vegetarian Chili # 3
1 Medium Onion; Chopped
1 Medium Carrot; Sliced
3 Cloves Garlic; Smashed (Up to 4)
1 Can (Large) Tomatoes, Whole; (Garden Tomatoes if You Have Them)
1 Pod Chayote; Rough Chopped
2 Pods Poblano Chile; Rough Chopped
½ Package Corn
1 Can (Large) Black Beans; Drained and Rinsed
1 Can (Large) Kidney Beans; Drained and Rinsed
3 Tablespoons Chile powder; Or More (Up to 4)
1 Tablespoon Cumin; Or More (Up to 2)

1. Sauté, the onions, carrot and garlic in a little oil.
2. Add the tomatoes, chayote, Poblanos and bring to a simmer.
3. Add corn, beans and spices. Simmer a few minutes.
4. Season if you want to.
We serve this in a bowl with cheese on top and then eat it with chips or corn tortillas.

Vegetarian Chili # 4
1 Tablespoon Olive Oil
1 Medium Onion; Chopped
1 Medium Red Pepper; Chopped
2 Cloves Garlic; Crushed
1 Can (14 Ounce) Tomatoes
1 cup Kidney Beans; Dry, Cooked or
2 Cans (15 Ounce) Kidney Beans
½ cup Green Lentils; Dried, Cooked
1 Teaspoon Paprika; Mild
2 Tablespoons Chile powder
To Taste Black Pepper
To Taste Sugar

1. Heat the oil in a large saucepan and sauté the onion and pepper for 10 minutes.
2. Add the garlic and cook for two minutes.
3. Then add the tomatoes.
4. Drain the beans and lentils, reserving the liquid; add both to the tomato mixture, along with the paprika and chile powder. Simmer for 15 minutes, adding the bean water as needed for consistency.
5. Season, add sugar and serve.

Vegetarian Chili Texas Style
2 Cups Granule Burger
2 Cups Boiling Water
¼ Cup Salad Oil
1 Cup Onion; Chopped
1-½ Medium Green Pepper; Diced
2 Centiliters Garlic; Crushed
1 Can (28 Ounce) Tomatoes; Whole
2 Cans (15 Ounce) Kidney Beans
3 Cans (8 Ounce) Tomato Paste
1 Cup Water
1 Tablespoon Chile powder
½ Teaspoon Cumin; Ground
4 Tablespoons Sugar
2 Teaspoons Salt
1 Teaspoon Oregano; Leaves

Good slow pot recipe. Longer cooking enhances the flavor.

1. Soak granule burger in boiling water for 10 minutes or more.
2. Place oil in heavy saucepan.
3. Combine onions, green pepper, garlic and sauté in oil.
4. Add the granule burger to the sautéed vegetables, cook for 5 minutes.
5. Add the rest of the ingredients. Simmer at least 1 hour.

Vegetarian Green Chile
1 Medium Onion; Chopped
3 Cloves Garlic; Smashed or Chopped
1 Tablespoon Olive Oil
6 Cups Vegetable Stock or Bouillon
12 Pods Green Chile Peppers (Roasted); Peeled and Chopped
2 Tablespoons Flour; Or Cornstarch
To Taste Salt and Pepper

I serve this sauce over enchiladas, burritos, eggs, beans, using fresh New Mexico green chiles. Do not use canned chiles for this recipe. (They just don't taste like green chiles to me.) Amounts are approximate. I usually just dump ingredients, especially chile and garlic, until it looks "right." This is a very forgiving recipe and very basic. I so much appreciate the taste of fresh, unadulterated green chile and garlic, that I rarely add any other seasonings.

1. Sauté, onion, garlic in olive oil.
2. Add chile, stock.
3. Add salt and pepper.
4. Dissolve flour or cornstarch in a cup of hot water and add, stirring to prevent lumps. Simmer for 45 minutes.

Optional ingredients:
1-2 Medium Potatoes; Diced (½" or so)
1-2 Medium Chopped Tomatoes
1-2 Whatever Else Cilantro, Cumin, Oregano
Add with the chile and stock. Potatoes help thicken the chile, especially after it has been frozen since they tend to disintegrate in the freezer. Add the cilantro after it has simmered to retain the fresh cilantro flavor.

Vegetarian Red Chile With Pepitas
6 Ounces Ancho Chile Peppers
3 Tablespoons Olive Oil
2 Cups Onions; Coarse Chopped
2 Cups Leeks; Coarse Chopped
2 Cups Carrots; Coarse Chopped
2 Cups Celery, With Leaves; Coarse Chopped
1 Cup Parsnips; Peeled and Chopped
2 Cups Waxy Potatoes; Chopped
2 Cups Mushrooms; Chopped
1 Tablespoon Fennel Seeds
1 Tablespoon Coriander Seeds
2 Teaspoons Cumin Seeds
¾ Cup Parsley (Fresh); Coarse Chopped
3 Leaves Bay
3 Tablespoons Sage (Fresh); Chopped
1 Teaspoon Oregano; Dried
2 Teaspoons Thyme; Dried
6 Cups Tomatoes Fresh or Canned; Coarse Chopped
2 Cups Dry Red Wine
4 Quarts Water
As Needed Salt and Black Pepper; Freshly Ground

1. Cover the Ancho chiles with warm water. Weight down with a plate to submerge. Let stand 1 hour to soften.
2. In a large stockpot, heat the olive oil.
3. Add the onions, leeks, carrots, celery, parsnips, potatoes, and mushrooms. Sauté, until they just begin to color.
4. Drain the Anchos and remove the seeds and stems; then add them to the stockpot along with the spice seeds, herbs, tomatoes, red wine, and water. Bring to a boil. Reduce the heat and simmer, partially covered, for 1 hour.
5. Season with salt and pepper.
6. Strain carefully, to remove all the solids.
7. Cool.

The stock can be covered and stored in the refrigerator for up to 3 days, or frozen indefinitely.

Note: If more "heat" is desired, leave half the seeds in the Ancho chiles. The seeds of chiles contain more of the heat than the flesh.

Yield: 4 quarts.

Veggie Chili
1 Medium Onion
1 Can Plum Tomatoes; Whole
1 Medium Green Bell Pepper
1 Can Tomato Paste
1 Medium Red Bell Pepper
2 Cups Vegetable Broth; (Bullion)
3 Pods Jalapeno Chile Peppers; Or 4
1 Can Red Kidney Beans
3 Cloves Garlic
1 Tablespoon Oil; (Up to 2)
3 Tablespoons Chile powder; Or More
1 Teaspoon Cumin
To Taste Salt and Pepper; Other Spices to Taste

1. Sauté, onions and garlic in oil until slightly soft.
2. Cut peppers into 1" cubes mince Jalapenos and add to onions. Cook until slightly soft.
3. Add veggie bullion, tomatoes (mashed up) with juice, ½ can tomato paste and chile powder. Let it boil down for about 30-45 minutes, adding additional tomato paste if needed.
4. When almost thick enough to eat add kidney beans and cook for another 10-15 minutes.

Serve with cornbread, tortilla chips and shredded Jack cheese.

White Chili With Tempeh
Vegetarian Times; July 94
8 Ounces Tempeh; Cut in 1-Inch Cubes
1-½ Cups Onion; Chopped
2 Cloves Garlic; Minced
1-¾ Cups Vegetable Broth; Or More if Needed
2 Teaspoons Fresh Ginger Root; Minced
3 Cups Mushrooms; Sliced
1 Teaspoon Cumin; Ground
1-½ Teaspoons Chile powder
¼ Teaspoon Cloves; Ground
2 Cups Navy Beans; Cooked
1 Cup Green Bell Pepper; Chopped
1 Cup Red Bell Pepper; Chopped

1. In large saucepan over medium heat, cook Tempeh, onion and garlic in ½ cup vegetable broth, stirring occasionally, until onion is soft and liquid has evaporated, about 10 minutes.
2. Mix in remaining 1-¼ cup broth and remaining ingredients; simmer 15 to 20 minutes.
3. Add additional broth as necessary.

Serves 4.

Yam Chili

1 Can (40 Ounce) Yams (Sweet Potatoes)
1 Can (29 Ounce) Tomato Puree
2 Cups Dry Beans
¼ Cup Barbecue Sauce
1 Tablespoon Onion; Dehydrated, Minced
1 Teaspoon Black Pepper
1 Tablespoon Chile powder
½ Teaspoon Cinnamon

1. Cook up the beans normally (soak, boil, simmer).
2. Pour yams into pot, including liquid. Smash lightly.
3. Add tomato puree and stir through.
4. Add spices and stir through.
5. Add cooked beans and stir through. Simmer for a few minutes to mellow out.

Beans: I keep a 'bean bucket' of mixed beans, usually including pea beans, black-eyed peas, pinto beans, split peas, lentils, navy beans, pinto beans; often including great northern beans, roman beans, pink beans, chili beans, barley, and others. Whenever there's room in the bucket I pour in a bag of something that seems under represented. This would probably be better with fresh yams and tomatoes, but the canned yams were on sale half price the day after Thanksgiving.

Zazie's Veggie Chili
Jose Kahan

1 Can Kidney Beans
1 Tin Chick Peas; See Note
1 Tin Tomatoes
1 Large Onion
3 Cloves Garlic
1 Pod Chile Pepper; Dried

1 Pod Chile Pepper (Fresh); Or Chile Powder
½ Teaspoon Coriander
¼ Teaspoon Ginger
1 Medium Green Pepper
2 Curettes
As Desired Carrots and Mushrooms
1 Tablespoon Oil; Or 2

1. Put oil in pan and add chopped onion. Cook on a low heat until the onion starts to go transparent.
2. Add the crushed garlic and the spices, and cook for a few more minutes, stirring from time to time.
3. Add the mushrooms, curettes and pepper, stir well, and cook for a few more minutes.
4. Finally, add the remaining ingredients and allow to simmer for about 15 -20 minutes.
5. Adjust seasoning if required before serving.

Serve with boiled rice, soured cream and guacamole. Hope you like it!! This may make too much for you but it can always be kept in the fridge and then re-heated the next day. I always prefer to put the onion in a few minutes before the garlic, as it takes longer to cook, so if you add garlic at the same time it may go brown.

Notes: Garbanzo Beans to an American, not sure what you will call them. Quantities depending on how much you want to make.

Zucchini Chili
6 Tablespoons Olive Oil
1-½ Cups Zucchini; Cut in ½ Inch Cubes
1 Cup Yellow Onion; Coarse Chopped
2 Cloves Garlic; Crushed
1 Cup Green Pepper; Cut in ½ Inch Cubes
2 Cups Tomatoes Canned; Crushed
1 Tablespoon Chile powder
1-½ Teaspoons Cumin
1-½ Teaspoons Oregano; Dried
¼ Cup Parsley (Fresh); Minced
To Taste Salt and Pepper
2 Cups Kidney &/or Garbanzo Beans; Canned

1. Heat olive in a large skillet. Add zucchini, onion, garlic and green pepper. Sauté 10 minutes until softened.
2. Transfer to a saucepan and add tomatoes, chile powder, cumin, oregano, parsley, salt and pepper. Cook over low heat, uncovered, for 10 minutes.
3. Stir in beans and cook 10 minutes more on low heat.
4. Adjust seasonings.

Serve chili rolled up in a warm flour tortilla or on a bed of brown rice.
Serves 4.

Variation: Substitute unpeeled medium eggplant, cut into ½ inch cubes, for the zucchini.

Manufactured By: RR Donnelley
                     Momence, IL USA
                     January, 2011